THE BOOK OF THE SOUL

RATIONAL SPIRITUALITY FOR THE TWENTY-FIRST CENTURY

IAN LAWTON

First published in 2004 by Lawton Publishing, Southampton, England.

All enquiries to be directed to *www.ianlawton.com.*

A CIP catalogue record for this title is available from the British Library.

ISBN 0 9549176 0 X

Design by Cor Ltd.
www.cor.eu.com

Author photograph by James Franklin.
www.jamesfranklin.com

Printed and bound by Hobbs The Printers, Southampton, England.

Permission to quote excerpts from other authors' work has been appropriately obtained. For more details see the source references section.

Ian Lawton was born in 1959. Formerly a chartered accountant and IT consultant, he turned his back on the commercial world in his mid-thirties to become a full-time writer-researcher on ancient civilizations, esoterica and spirituality. His first two books, *Giza: The Truth* and *Genesis Unveiled*, were published by Virgin and have gained widespread acclaim, selling over 30,000 copies worldwide. He has an established reputation for thorough scholarship, and for an innovative approach to his subject matter that creates a unique blend from the best of orthodox and alternative material. He has lectured about his work extensively in both the UK and US.

Julie

All Best Wishes

*This book is dedicated to the memory of my sister Sheila,
a true child of nature if ever there was one;
my mother Beryl, the most selfless woman I have ever known;
and my father Syd, a brilliant role model and true friend.*

FOOD FOR THOUGHT

…on the infinite (from Jung, *Memories, Dreams, Reflections*)
*Only if we know that the thing which truly matters is the infinite can we avoid
fixing our interest upon futilities.*

…on God (from Cannon, *Between Death and Life*)
*The concept of God is the sum of all, of everything. We are God. We are
collectively God. We are individual pieces of God. God is not one, but God is all.*

…on life after death (from Stevenson, *Where Reincarnation and Biology
Intersect*)
*I am well aware that the fear of death may encourage a belief in life after death.
It is true that many of us want to believe in this, but our wish that something may
be true does not make it false.*

…on reincarnation (from Whitton and Fisher, *Life Between Life*)
*Dr Whitton's subjects, whose religious backgrounds are as varied as their initial
prejudices for or against reincarnation, have testified consistently that rebirth
is fundamental to the evolutionary process in which we are enveloped. At death,
they say, the soul leaves the body to enter a timeless, spaceless state. There,
our most recent life on earth is evaluated and the next incarnation is planned
according to our karmic requirements.*

CONTENTS

7. THE DYNAMICS OF KARMA: *Are We Punished?*

Pioneers' views on karma; repetitive and progressive karma; different interlife experiences; the four stages of karmic evolution; repetitive karma as learning rather than paying off debts; any punishments are self-inflicted; untimely death and disability as progressive learning experiences; carrying forward talents and abilities; gender misidentity and nature versus nurture; the sleeping prophet on karma; reliability of channeled material; perceptions of hell; the concept of reversion to animal form; regression insights as alternatives to revealed wisdom.

The sleeping prophet on earth changes; individual progressions in current lives; group expectations of catastrophe; group progressions to the twenty-second and twenty-fourth centuries; individual progressions into future lives; detailed but changeable futures; preeminence of karmic choice and free will.

Soul energy division; sub-personalities; spirit possession; demonic possession; soul fragmentation; walk-ins; the soul as individuality; imprints and cross-talk; the binary soul doctrine.

Logistics of reincarnation; human soul birthing; alternative animal or elemental origins of souls; accelerating rates of reincarnation; soul advancement and levels; physical versus astral versus ethereal planes; body versus spirit versus soul, and the process of death; incarnations on other planets, evolution by intelligent design, and the meaning of 'human'; Atlantis and Lemuria, root races and life swarms; levels of amnesia, and humanity's fall from grace; returning to the Source; practical advice; an approach to meditation; stress, and the importance of personal control; the emerging synthesis of philosophy, religion and science.

PREFACE

This book wasn't even planned at the beginning of this year. After I completed my last one, *Genesis Unveiled*, I thought I might never do another, because my writing wasn't paying enough for me to earn even a basic living. And my refusal to 'sex things up' wasn't helping my commercial potential. I wanted to continue with my writing and research, of course, because I believe in what I do. But we all have to eat! And I don't believe it's possible to write on the subjects that I and many colleagues do without devoting one hundred per cent attention and focus to the job in hand. Trying to mix it with some other form of job just doesn't work.

I worked as a courier for a while, just to have some money coming in, waiting to see what would happen. It was worth it for the experience. How many of us do menial jobs, treated with varying levels of disdain, all the while thinking 'I'm worth more than this'? But after I was able to free up the last remnants of my capital, left over from what now feels almost like a past life in which I was a well-paid member of the commercial world, I had a real choice to make. Should I risk all on one last throw of the dice, and write again? Or give it up and do something 'sensible', as so many well-meaning friends advised? The answer would depend entirely on whether anything came up that I felt was worth the risk. It had to be something important enough that it would effectively leave me with no choice.

It won't come as a great surprise that I believe in karma, and that I knew that if I was meant to carry on something would present itself to me. At the beginning of this year I treated myself to the luxury of a two-week holiday in Cancun, partly justifying it on the basis that at last I would get to see some of the Mayan pyramids in the Yucatán about which I had heard and read so much. Needless to say I was impressed by them. But not as much as I was by the simple beauty of the pure white sand of the beaches, and its incredible effect on the colour of the water. And it was while I was contemplating this one day that I received my first intuitional prompt for this book.

As it turned out, this prompt was an initial 'blind'. I was following up some of the research I had done for *Genesis Unveiled*, and reading a book about hypnotic regression. It suddenly made sense that I should train as a regression therapist myself! That way I could help people but still earn a living! On my return I investigated the possibility, and wasn't necessarily put off by the lengthy training in basic psychology that would be required if I really meant to do the job properly. But, as you will see in the opening chapter, other factors started to come into play. Within a short space of time a wealth of corroborating research for the spiritual worldview I had written about in *Genesis Unveiled* came to my notice – research that hadn't received the attention I felt it deserved. And pretty soon I had my confirmation that there was at least one more book I had to write.

But don't think for one moment that I am just another of those spiritual writers for whom everything seems to fall into place because they are on their 'chosen path'. Indeed, one of the important lessons in this book is that a spiritual path is not necessarily an easy one. Sometimes we are given really difficult hurdles to overcome – indeed, as you will find out, I argue that we *ourselves* probably plan many of them. Because it is not always the unbroken tranquillity of our lives that measures our spiritual progress, but how we handle the problems we face – and what we learn from the process of striving to get over them.

For a long time I had asked for help during my meditations. Help to make the job of carrying on with my writing and research a little easier. So, having received that assistance in the form of locating important material for another book that I knew I had to write, I made the mistake of assuming that my existing publishers, Virgin, would be just as excited about it as I was. How wrong we can be! Although they were keen to work with me again if only I would write another history-cum-archaeology book, they felt completely unable to take a book that was so clearly focused on spiritual issues alone. My resolve was challenged even further when my proposal for what was then titled *Interlife* was rejected by several other publishers. So did I have the determination to continue and again, just as with *Genesis Unveiled*, complete a book without having a publishing deal already signed and sealed?

The answer was yes. But even then my efforts were not exactly assisted by my personal situation. In trying to keep my living expenses down, I was renting a room in a house shared with my nephew in a less than salubrious area of my home city in the south of England. My combined bedroom and office lay next to the dividing wall of the other half of our semidetached house, which was occupied by probably the most psychotic family on the planet. Have you ever tried to distil some of the finer points of the meaning of life while being bombarded with loud urban music at all hours of the day and night? Or by vicious arguments so punctuated by swear words that there is very little room left to say anything at all constructive?! Since previous attempts to complain about the noise had met with threats and scratched cars, it seemed that the only option was to grin and bear it. Which is what I did, even if at times I thought I might go mad.

So I was, I think justifiably, quite proud when finally the first draft was finished – after only six months of intense writing and research. But I didn't realise at the time that the hardest part was *still* yet to come! I began my final read-through with some anticipation that within days all would be complete. It started well. But by the time I got halfway through and arrived at the chapter that concerns the dynamics of karma, I got stuck. It is very unusual for me to have to make significant amendments to my work after the first draft, because a great deal of thought goes into that initial effort. But here I was rewriting the first half of that chapter again, and again, and again. Each time thinking I had solved the problem, only to go back again and realise I hadn't. This time I really did think I was going mad. I just didn't seem to be able to find any clarity about certain discrepancies in the modern research. So even when my 'eureka' moment finally arrived, I had no great confidence that I'd actually cracked it.

But a few days' break with a friend in the Isle of Man did the trick, and when I returned refreshed and ready for the fight to go on I realized that my fears were groundless. What I thought might read like the ramblings of a deluded idiot finally made some sense. And when I took my findings to their ultimate conclusion, I realised that I had something on my hands that was perhaps rather more important than even I had at first envisaged. It was at this point that I took the perhaps bold, perhaps foolish decision to change the title to *The Book of the Soul*. And to press ahead with the courage of my own convictions, and use what capital I had left to publish it myself.

If the arguments I present here are correct they provide a new spiritual framework for the twenty-first century, which is arguably the first in the history of humanity that can be truly described as 'rational'. Elements of this book will undoubtedly upset some people, albeit that I have tried hard not to be overly confrontational. But those who might want to question my claim would do well to make sure they approach the task with similar logic, rather than repeat simplistic rejections of evidence that I have already shown to be reductionist and wholly unsatisfactory.

Before we begin, there are a number of people whose contribution I would like to acknowledge. Sarah Axford, who did as much as anyone to put me on this path. My good friends Mia Kelly and Sean Lee, the former for giving me inspiration and encouragement when I needed it most, and the latter for his professional layout and distinctive cover design. David Southwell for his invaluable input and marketing assistance, and even more for his general support for my work. Ian Allen for his thoroughly professional editing. And Liz Swanson, not only for her feedback, but also for the faith she has shown in both me and my work.

Ian Lawton
November 2004

1

A PERSONAL JOURNEY
Who Was I, Who Am I Now?

March 30, 2004. I am lying on the couch of one of Britain's leading practitioners of hypnotic regression. His name is Andy Tomlinson, and he is going to attempt to take me back in time. Way back in time, into a past life. Neither of us knows where this will go. Never having done this before, I am not even sure if I will make a good subject. But here we go anyway…

Be aware of what you have on your feet.
Some sort of tights. With shoes.
Just be aware of those shoes, the color of them, what they look like.
Black with some sort of a buckle.
Do they look new or old, how do they appear?
New.
Be aware of what other clothes you are wearing. Describe them to me.
Sort of billowy trousers. With stripes.
Are you aware of what color these are?
Green, maybe with gold stripes. The jacket matches, with billowy arms on it.
Just be aware of the clothes you have on the top part of your body.
Some sort of a white shirt, and then the jacket.
This jacket, perhaps it has a color or a texture?
The same as the trousers. Shiny.
Do you get the sense that you are a man in this life?
Yes.
Do you get a sense of whether you are a younger or an older man?
Late twenties, early thirties.
Just be aware of those things that are around you, and describe them.
It's like the central market area of a town. It's daytime.
What sort of things are they selling in this market?
Food, clothes and cloth and things.
How are these other people dressed that are in the market?
Some the same as me, some not so well dressed.
Are you carrying anything, or with anybody?
Don't think so.

As you are aware of this market around you, and all these busy people, just be aware of what feelings or thoughts you have at this moment.
Quite proud. Perhaps even arrogant.
Do you have a different social standing than all these other people?
Not all of them, but most of them.
What is it that you've come to this market for? Is there something you've got to do?
I have some sort of official capacity.
Tell me a little bit about this official capacity that you have.
I've got to read some document out or something, I'm not sure. I think I might have to read something out to the people around the market.
Go to that point when you're reading the information out to the people, and tell me what's happening?
I don't think it's very good.
How are you feeling about that?
I'm hoping it's not something to do with religious persecution, but I think it might be.
What, some sort of execution? Go through the things you've got to read out, tell me what it's about… Is it about an execution?
No. I don't think so.
You're stood there in front of everybody, and they're all stood around you, looking at you, and you've got something to read. Just go through it slowly, bit by bit, the information you've got to read to them.
I think I'm laying down a list of rules or something.
Is there a penalty if people don't follow these rules?
Yes, big time. Torture or death.
What sort of rules have they got to follow?
It's all to do with religion and heresy. And I'm feeling very pompous about it.
Is there any specific aspect of these rules that you can tell me about? Is there a particular religion they've got to follow?
It's Catholicism.
And if people deviate from Catholicism, this is where the torture and death comes in is it?
Yes.
And you're reading this to everybody?
Yes. I think it's just the start of it.
Are you aware of what country you're in?
It's Spain.
There are some people around that have got other beliefs and religions, aren't there?
Yes. And we're not prepared to tolerate that.
The job that you have, is that connected with the Church in any way, or do you just have to read out things?
I think I'm only reading the stuff out. I'm not in the Church. I might be in

the civic administration or something, I'm not sure.

And what's the reaction of all the people after you read this out to them.

They're scared. A lot of them aren't very happy, but they're scared.

Yes, because they know about the torture and the death.

Yes.

Do you tell them how they're going to be tortured?

No, I think it's been happening in other parts of the country, and it's just come to wherever I am now. So I don't have to tell them about it… they know.

When you've finished reading this to them, what happens?

I've done my job.

Your job was just reading things out, wasn't it, you've done your job?

Yes. I can't see anything else at the moment.

How are you thinking about things. Do you agree with it all?

I don't think I do, but I don't think I'm allowing myself to be honest, because I'm too busy doing my job.

OK, when I count to three we're going to go to the next significant event in this life, and I'd like you to tell me what's happening. One… two… three… now. Just move into that significant event. And as you get awareness of it, just explain what it is that's happening.

I think I'm in the shit.

What's happening?

I think I've finally denounced what's been going on.

You've got involved in some way, have you?

Yes. I stood up and said that what's been going on is wrong.

And what's happened to you?

I'm suffering the same fate as all the other poor buggers.

OK, just describe whereabouts you are at the moment.

Not sure I want to go into this.

OK, but what does it look like all around you?

I think I'm in a prison.

Is it a light or dark place, what's it like in this prison?

Dark and not very nice.

Just be aware of whether there are other people in the place where you are. Or are you by yourself?

[Sighs] Well, I'm in a cell. And I can hear other people being tortured and stuff. I know that's going to happen to me as well.

What sort of sounds can you hear?

Not good.

Screams?

Yes.

You know it's something that's going to come your way, don't you?

Yes [sighs].

Just be aware of what clothes you're wearing right now.

7

Pretty much the same stuff as I had before, but very ragged. Posh clothes still, but ragged. I think I've been here for a little while. I've already been roughed up a bit.

Just be aware of whether you've been hurt in any way.

I haven't been tortured yet. I've just been roughed up.

That was when you were arrested, was it?

Yes.

How did that happen?

I think I must have stood up in public.

And someone grabbed hold of you and took you here, did they?

Yes... but it's worse for me because I was in authority before and helped to bring it all in... so for me to stand up now is... much worse for them.

So they were pretty quick about grabbing you, were they?

Yes... and they're going to be that much harder about trying to... get me to retract. It's going to be more important for them to get me to retract if they can... so I'm scared shitless at the moment... but I also know that I've got to do what's right.

Whereabouts in your body do you carry this scaredness?

In my chest.

Have they given you anything to eat in this cell?

[Wry laugh] I don't think I'm very hungry!

No. You're just waiting for something to happen, aren't you?

Yes. I don't think it will be very long.

OK. Go to that point when you become aware someone's coming for you. Just go through it very slowly, bit by bit. Is it a noise you hear? Do you see someone?

I can hear them coming down the corridor. The keys jangling.

Do you hear any voices?

Yes, there is a bunch of them, they are coming to get me.

And it's rather dark, isn't it?

Yes.

Are you able to see a vague outline of them... do they become clearer as they come closer?

Yes. They're all wearing uniforms.

What sort of uniforms are they wearing?

Some sort of blue tops and white trousers... dark blue, I think, the tops.

Do they have any metal on them anywhere?

Yes, gold buttons and stuff.

Do they say anything to you as they open the door?

Yes. Come on you, you're coming with us.

And do you offer any resistance, or do you just go with them?

I just go with them.

Describe where they take you. Do they take you down the corridors?

Yes.

And you're following them. Is there two of them in front, or one?

8

One on each side of me. One ahead, and a couple behind.
Are they holding your arms?
Yes. I mean, I'm handcuffed anyway. I think my feet might be shackled as well, they're dragging a bit... not sure.
And what happens next?
[Big sigh] To start with they take me to see the people who are in charge of the whole thing.
Tell me about that encounter.
Not good.
How many of them are there?
Three, I think. There might be a load of other hangers-on, but...
And how are they dressed?
There's one serious one. He's got all his Catholic regalia on. Purple, I think. Lots of big chains and crosses, some big high ruff collar, I think, something like that.
What about the other two?
Just subordinate. I suppose they've got the same, but not as ostentatious.
And what do they say to you?
[Big sigh] How long have I held those views?
And what do you say to them?
I've always held them, but I was too afraid to speak out before.
And what do they say back to you?
I think they're trying to argue with me intellectually, to make out that I'm being stupid... I know that I have to defend my position, and in fact it's a much easier one to defend than theirs is, from an intellectual point of view. So that's what I do, and it's not very difficult.
How do you manage to defend your position?
Because it's the right one, so it's easy.
And what do they say to you once you've defended your position?
They're very upset because... I'm making them look a little bit foolish so they don't like it.
And what happens then?
They get rid of me as quick as they can.
Do they say what's going to happen to you?
We all know what's going to happen to me.
And do they give you an option of changing your views?
Yes, they did say we'll see how you feel about this after a period of time... you know where.
So they're going to torture you to try and make you change your mind, are they?
Yes, if they can. And just for the hell of it anyway. It's a sport to them.
And what's the expression on their faces as you're about to be taken away?
Very mixed. They're scared by what I've just said to them, deep down, but they can't really show it. So they have... on the surface... to keep their

veneer of control and correctness.

Do the same guards that brought you take you away?

Yes.

And whereabouts are they taking you now? You know where you're going to go, don't you?

No. I think they're going to give me another night in the cell just to think about it, and get very scared about it, that's their way.

Another night of listening to the sounds of other people?

And knowing that I'll be next, yes.

That's part of the torture, isn't it?

Of course.

And as you go through that night, and listening to those sounds, does anything change inside you? Or are you still of the same mind?

Well, I'm still scared shitless but know that I've got to do the right thing. I'm praying for strength.

Let's go through to when they come for you next. And tell me what happens.

It's the next morning. I haven't slept. I think they've got me chained to the wall anyway, I'm not even sure if my feet are on the ground.

Are they going to do this thing inside your cell, or are they taking you to somewhere else?

No, they're taking me to where all the equipment is.

When you enter this place with all the equipment, just describe what it is you first become aware of.

I've seen it all before anyway.

What is there?

You don't want to know. The usual stuff [sighs].

Just describe it for me, what the usual stuff is.

[Sighing throughout] Racks... there's people hanging around the walls in here anyway, just been left there to hang... there's clamps for holding your hands so they can pull your fingernails out... and toenails.

Are there any of those things that you fear the most?

No. I know they're all bloody awful... what I don't know is how long they're going to try and do this for, how long I'm going to be conscious, and how many days I might have to put up with this for.

What's the first thing that they work with? Feet, hands, rack?

[Big sigh] I'm not sure I want to go through this.

Just go through it slowly, bit by bit. Just be aware of what you can smell, what you can hear. What sort of smells are there in this place?

I'm not sure that reliving this is going to help me.

OK, we're going to put an energy around you right now, golden energy. This golden energy means that you'll be able to recall one or two aspects of what it is that happens to you. And it will give you protection, there's no need for you to go through and relive the emotions and the body sensations that went with it. So just go through it slowly, bit by bit, the first things that they do to you.

[Sighs] The nails… the fingernails.

Do they start with one hand or the other?

Left hand.

Do they pull out the nails one by one?

[Sighing heavily throughout] Yes. They do the first one… they ask you if you've had enough after each one, obviously. Actually I think the first time they did the whole hand, without even stopping, one by one, because they know damn well you're not going to give in just after that first one… even though it hurts like hell. After the first hand is finished, they give you the chance to say something.

And then they started the second hand?

Yes. They do the same.

They stopped at every finger did they, and asked you the same? Or did they do the whole hand?

I think they do two or three, and ask, and then the last couple.

Did you change your mind?

No, no. I haven't changed my mind all the way through.

And when they finished with the nails, what did they do next?

[Big sigh] They're not in a hurry with me… it's more important for them to drag this out over a period of time, they think that's a better chance for them to get me to change my mind… they know if they do it too quick it will be much easier for me to just go with it and then die.

So how do they drag it out? Do they just leave you for a while, having done the nails?

Yes, I think that first time they just did the nails and then took me back…

Took you back to the cell?

Yes.

We'll just move things on to the next time you went back, what sort of things did they do then?

That was the rack.

Whereabouts was your body being held?

All four corners.

Is that the hands and legs, or…

Ankles and wrists. They're clamped.

What are they clamped with, is it metal or…

Metal clamps. The table's in two halves… and they rotate a wheel to pull the two halves apart.

And how did they know when to stop.

[Sighing heavily throughout] When you pass out… they throw a bucket of water over you, and do it again.

Do you recall how many buckets of water were thrown over you to revive you?

[Big sigh] At least two or three.

11

Your body was getting very weak at that point, was it?
Yes… yes.
Is there anything else that was done to you before you got to the point of taking your last breath?
No, this wasn't it. [Big sigh] They didn't stop there… I think they had two or three goes on the rack, and then I passed out… maybe they couldn't even bring me round again… I think I must have come round back in the cell again. Whatever else they did after that, I'm not sure I want to remember it… I just know it wasn't good.
There's lots of pain.
[Slightly incoherent] It didn't go on for weeks, thank god, but it must have been days, I guess.
Went on for days but it seemed like weeks?
Well, it seemed like an eternity. But it wasn't weeks, it was only days I think.
OK, go to that point just before you're taking your last breath in that life.
I hardly know who or what I am any more anyway… I've been knocked around so much… my body's just broken… completely a ruin.
Go to that point, just before you take your last breath. Are you conscious at the time, or are you unconscious of what's happening to you?
I'm just so grateful it's all going to be over… and that I've held firm.
You know you're about to die, don't you?
Yes! I want to die [wry laugh].
You want to die…
Of course I want to die! I don't want to carry on going through this any more.
Are you in the middle of being tortured, or are you in the cell?
No, I think they're doing something to me but they've just stopped, and I know I'm going to go now…
OK. Just go to that point where you stop breathing and your heart stops beating, and just be aware of whether you stay with your body, or you leave it.
I leave it… I'm in a hurry to get out [wry laugh].
And do you miss your body?
No, I've left it behind. It's an incredible release.
And are you able to reflect on that life. Are there any thoughts or feelings that you take away at the point of death?
Yes, I'm proud, enormously proud. Proud that I had the guts to stand up, even though I knew what was going to happen to me. Proud that I was given the strength to take what came to me without recanting.
Yes, your body went through so much in that life, didn't it?
Yes.
It took incredible courage not to give in to all that physical pain.
Yes, but… I was given help, wasn't I?
Do you have any regrets, thinking back on that life as you leave that body,

any regrets that some aspect of that life could have been different?
I don't know if there was something that I could have done much earlier... I
think I must have had a position of some influence... could have influenced
things in terms of not letting them get out of hand in the first place.
*OK, just be aware you've left your body behind you... perhaps you can look
down at the scene below you and describe it in some way?*
The people who do the torturing are... strange people, because obviously
the job they have to do they have to be pretty ruthless and unpleasant...
but they're saying, privately, they admire that I stuck to my principles... I
know all of them do, inside, even the cardinal or whatever he is.

That was an exact transcript of the session, which lasted for over an
hour. In fact we continued on into the afterlife, after I had died, to check
out any lasting karmic problems that may have arisen from what I had been
through. My hypnotized – or perhaps 'higher' – self insisted that there were
none, and that all of us in this drama knew what we were doing and what
roles we had to play. I did ask for forgiveness from the many other people
that were tortured at that time because I had failed to act any earlier, but it
was impressed upon me that to have done so would have been incredibly
difficult, and may not have made any difference anyway.

Does this *prove* that I have lived before? Not in the slightest. Could it
easily have been assembled in my subconscious, from my imagination and
from historical information I already possessed? Of course. There are no
real details in there that I would not have already known, and there may
even be some aspects that an expert on the Spanish Inquisition – which
I am not – would be able to spot as incorrect. Given that I come out of it
reasonably well, was it all just a big ego trip? Possibly. But if I tell you that
the most recent past life I was regressed into in a separate session was that
of a very poor, simple farmer, who did nothing of note other than love his
family, hopefully this possibility is reduced.

Was I genuinely in trance? Yes, because although I was sufficiently
conscious throughout that I remembered what had happened, it took
some hours for me to return to normal. Did Andy effectively make the
story up for me with his questioning? As you can tell from the transcript,
most of the session was led by his questions, although I suspect that was
mainly because I was not a particularly good subject, and needed plenty
of prompting to remember things. But, in any case, you can also see that
most of the information did come from me, and on a few occasions I even
contradicted him when he appeared to be leading me in the wrong direction.
Did it feel real? Yes, something you would understand better if you heard
the recordings of my deep sighs as I recalled some of the more unsavory
aspects of that life, despite my having been instructed not to feel them too

deeply because we were primarily engaged in research rather than therapy. Do I personally believe it was a genuine recall of a past life? On balance, yes, I do, even if some aspects may have been inserted or distorted by my imagination.

Although I felt this exercise was essential to the research for this book, it also marked a major milestone in my own spiritual journey. For years I had studied the work of others, and written about it. Admittedly, for some time I had been attempting to become more in touch with my intuition or, again, higher self, essentially via private meditation – although not always with the consistency and commitment I would have liked. But this was the first time I had really put my beliefs to the test, and opened myself up to a process that even until recently I regarded with some suspicion.

Why the suspicion? For me, it derives from making the distinction between genuine spirituality and 'new age' nonsense. And this is not easy because there is much of the latter about, which detracts from the real spiritual business at hand and can give it a bad name. As a consequence many people probably lump these two together. But inasmuch as I suspect my experiences are fairly typical, I hope they will show that you can hold a spiritual worldview *and* still have your feet planted firmly on the ground. This is important, because while interest in orthodox religion has been steadily waning in the western world, our increasingly affluent and materialistic lifestyles are still leaving many of us feeling deeply unfulfilled. So, for me, it is vital that ordinary people, who sense there must be something more to life but are alienated by the dogma of many orthodox religions, are not also put off from their own spiritual exploration from fear of turning themselves into a new age laughing stock. It does *not* have to be like that and, although the new age movement has been invaluable, I believe it is now time for us to move forward and bring proper, grounded spirituality into the mainstream of western culture.

For me to provide a proper perspective on all this I need to take you back a little into this lifetime. For a long time, I thought religion was just for losers. Like so many of us, at least of my generation and before, at home and at school I was brought up within a nominally Christian but hardly committed environment. I even underwent confirmation, but in truth a major motivation was that we got a weekend away from school and some girls from another school would be there. And I guess it was appropriate that I stood to receive the blessing rather than kneeling, my left knee having being immobilized in a rugby accident, because as my intellect developed in my later teens I increasingly refused to bow down to any notion of divinity.

Actually this was no great intellectual process; it was based much more on practical observations. Of the way in which most people only prayed when they were in deep trouble, or as part of a repetitive ritual that seemed to have no real meaning or relevance. And of the fact that most of the really devout pupils at my school, the ones in the voluntary Christian fellowship group, genuinely did come across as the most weak and insecure among us; and I should know because at one point – when lonely and in desperation after being on the receiving end of a bad period of bullying – I joined them, but found the atmosphere insufferable. Of course, I knew that throughout history there had been thousands of people who had shown immense courage and integrity in helping others or in defending their religious beliefs – whether Christian or otherwise – and nothing I say even now is intended to detract from their bravery and selflessness. But I also knew that there were plenty of others who had used religion as a cloak to attempt to control and subjugate their fellow man, and to garner power and prestige. So when I left school I proudly trumpeted my atheism to anyone who would listen. I even looked up the word 'agnostic' in the dictionary just to make sure, but no, I was definitely an 'atheist'. I was convinced that real power and strength comes from within oneself, not from some external deity.

What I did not know, in my youthful arrogance, was that there was far more to this than met the eye. You will be pleased to hear that I am not going to bore you with a detailed history of how I personally came to take a spiritual path. Suffice to say that mine was not a dramatic conversion, and the scales took many years to fall from my eyes. And, as with so many things, when asked to comment about why I now write books with a strong spiritual content I find the mists of time have clouded much of my recollection of the process. But I can at least provide a few pointers that will set the scene.

As far as I can remember, the first thing I realized was that the various phenomena categorized as paranormal, which had always fascinated me, seemed incapable of proper explanation within my materialist framework. What if ghostly apparitions and other paranormal phenomena were not *all* the products of delusion or fevered imagination? What if, despite the fact that some so-called mediums were clearly using nothing more than clever psychological manipulation to produce their readings and spirit communications, it was wrong to 'throw the baby out with the bathwater' and assume this was true of *all* of them? What if, as I increasingly suspected, some part of us really did survive physical death?

Then, by now in my mid-thirties, I gave up the commercial career that had hitherto seemed the only proper modus operandi for a sensible ex-accountant like me, with the vague aim of researching ancient mysteries and the like. Of course, many people thought I must have lost several marbles from my already small collection, but my inner voices were pretty insistent – even though at that time I had little proper appreciation of the vital importance of intuition and communications from the higher self. And in case you are already thinking that someone who talks of inner voices as if they have some sort of special calling is just the sort of new age dreamer they claim to want to avoid, I should emphasize that I do not regard myself as at all special in having taken this path. I am sure many other people hear similar inner voices and would love to have the time to research the mysteries of life, but are prevented from so doing by family and other commitments that I do not have. If it helps, all I can say is that the grass is not always greener, and if I had properly appreciated the financial hardships and other frustrations in advance I might have tried harder to shut the voices out.

In any case, as my research progressed it gradually filtered into a desire to concentrate on examining all the most ancient written texts and native traditions from around the world concerning the flood catastrophe – and especially the suggestion that a sophisticated race of 'forgotten ancestors' had lived before this and been almost totally wiped out. This research went on for many years, although interrupted for some time by my collaboration with my good friend Chris Ogilvie-Herald on our first book, *Giza: The Truth*. Published in 1999, as the name suggests it was a comprehensive review of the various theories of the construction, purpose and so on of the pyramids and other monuments at Giza in Egypt. After diligent research of both the mainstream and alternative views of these issues, we found that in most cases we sided with the former. And although our motives – as independent researchers who dared to question the leading lights of the alternative Egypt scene – were subsequently put under close scrutiny, in hindsight this first book has had two important outcomes. From a general perspective, I think it is fair to say that it has become accepted by many as a reliable source of reference, and may even in time contribute to a considerable tightening up of the scholarship employed within the alternative history genre; of this result alone Chris and I would be enormously proud. But on a more personal and at the time unforeseen level, given the path my research has taken subsequently, I hope that it may have helped to establish my credentials as someone who does have his feet planted on terra firma.

When that project was completed I returned to my study of the ancient texts and traditions, and that was when some key elements of a new spiritual jigsaw really started to fit into place. I was becoming increasingly convinced that, despite the inevitable distortions that make them seem to be in conflict, all the world's religions and earlier, less dogmatic spiritual approaches derived from a common source of universal wisdom that has been available to humankind since time immemorial. And that the fundamental principles of this wisdom are threefold.

First, the soul is separate from the physical body and survives its death. For the moment I use the word soul as synonymous with spirit, mind, or consciousness to refer to that part of us that is essentially nonphysical, ethereal or pure energy. Only in the final chapter will I complicate matters by considering ways in which these terms may need to be distinguished from each other.

Second, the soul reincarnates repeatedly in different bodies to gain karmic experience. Most people think of karma as a principle of cause and effect, or action and reaction, whereby positive actions and attitudes are rewarded, while negative actions and attitudes are punished. But, as we will see, this is a massive misunderstanding. Karmic dynamics are complex, but I deliberately use the terms *progressive* and *repetitive* rather than *positive* and *negative* to reflect the fact that, while some of us do tend to attract the same experiences again and again in a repetitive cycle both within and across lives, fundamentally karma does involve personal choices and learning – and attaining ultimate balance by experiencing both sides of every coin. Viewed in this light, even apparently disadvantageous circumstances or events should be seen as opportunities for growth, rather than punishments for past mistakes.

Third, the aim of repeated incarnation is to advance sufficiently from a karmic perspective that, ultimately, we escape the 'earthly karmic round' and reunite permanently with the 'Source'. We all come from this source, and we all return to it. It is variously termed the Ultimate, the Absolute, or the All in some esoteric teachings, while others might use more descriptive terms such as the ultimate 'creative power' or even 'divine energy or unity'. The important thing is that it does not represent an *externalized* deity or 'god' of any sort. From an ethereal, nonphysical or energy perspective it is an *internalized*, integral part – indeed the very basis – of everything throughout the universe. And, looking at it the other way, everything throughout the universe is also by definition a tiny, but integral, part of it. So I was right when as a teenager I decided that real power and strength comes from within oneself. I just failed to appreciate that this power is, indeed, a divine one.

Needless to say these are all ideas that we will explore fully in the course of this book, just as we will consider why the major, relatively modern religions of Judaism, Christianity and Islam have discarded the principles of reincarnation and karma. But for now it is worth pointing out that I deliberately use the general phrase *spiritual worldview* when describing what I regard as a universal wisdom in order to distinguish it from the more dogmatic and formalized religions – especially those of the West, and Near and Middle East. Unfortunately these tend, at least when applied in practice, to be far more about politics and power than about philosophy. But philosophy is where our attention should be concentrated if humankind is to move forwards.

To return to my research of the ancient texts, it also became clear to me that the story of our forgotten ancestors needed to be interpreted far more from a spiritual than a technological perspective. In particular that their destruction in the worldwide catastrophe of 11,500 years ago might well be regarded as something of a universal karmic reaction to what the texts consistently describe as their increasing materiality and loss of spiritual roots. If my interpretations are correct, of course they have major implications for our manic and seemingly insatiable desire for material rather than spiritual progress at the start of the twenty-first century. But, on top of that, new interpretations of ancient views of the origins of the world and the creation of man also emerged as part of this great spiritual jigsaw, and the result was the publication in 2003 of my second book, *Genesis Unveiled.*

The materialists that have dominated intellectual culture in the West since the late nineteenth century have the same attitude of total skepticism towards any sort of spiritual worldview that I had when I was younger. Any such worldview is based entirely upon belief and faith, insist the movers and shakers of the intellectual elite – often with the barely veiled insinuation that any holders thereof are possessed of the intellectual capacity of an amoeba.

I happen to believe this is demonstrably wrong, and that it is high time the materialist establishment was shaken out of this smug complacency and given a bloody nose. In fact, I would argue that a broad spiritual worldview provides a far more logical and philosophical framework for understanding the universe than a materialist one – indeed that it is the far more rational position to adopt, which is at least partly why I have coined the term *rational spirituality* to describe it. And anyone who shares my desire to place a spiritual worldview within a practical and well-grounded context has a huge weapon up their sleeve. Because the starting point for proving the case for rational spirituality lies in the realms of pure science itself – more specifically in the arena of theoretical physics, which provides indisputable evidence that there is far more to the universe than the apparently physical and material world that dominates our normal perceptions.

In highly simplified terms, the old Newtonian view that all matter is made up of elementary particles like protons and electrons has been proved to be fatally flawed. The paradox that all subatomic particles behave sometimes like particles, and sometimes like waves, was solved by the postulation that they are actually energy waves emitted in packets, or quanta. So atoms and their nuclei do not contain any fundamental building blocks of matter, and solid physical form is merely a sensory perception of humans and presumably other sentient animals. This perception is underpinned partly by the various quanta showing a marked stability under normal unchanged conditions, not only in the atomic but also in the molecular sense, and partly by the incredible speed with which they revolve in their orbital confinement, thus giving all matter its apparent solidity.

But this is merely a more technical restatement of ancient esoteric wisdom, which universally regards the physical world – I will continue to use this word out of familiarity, even though we now realize it means something rather different – as a mere illusion. Such wisdom even suggests that the more advanced adept or initiate can not only transcend the physical but also, if they choose, manipulate it at will. This would include not only highly advanced capabilities, such as the levitation of objects and other such apparently magical feats, but also the more prosaic ability to manipulate one's own karmic path. This latter is highly similar to the modern concept of 'positive thinking', even if most of its contemporary proponents are unaware of this correspondence.

And recent scientific findings take us even further. In the search for a 'theory of everything' that will unite the macroscopic world of gravity and relativity with the microscopic quantum world, a number of models have been suggested, one of the most developed and publicized being string theory. A number of versions of this exist, but they all work on the principle that there exist vibrating strings of pure energy whose varying states of excitation produce the quanta that we are able to measure in the physical world. Above all, almost all versions propose that there are at least ten space–time dimensions in total, most of them obviously not physical in terms of being perceptible to current scientific equipment. String theory has many opponents, not least because it has yet to be experimentally verified, but even if it is ultimately replaced by some other theory the idea of nonphysical dimensions will almost certainly remain.

A more esoteric description of this revelation would be that what we perceive as the physical world is merely the 'plane' in which various energy forms vibrate in their densest mode. So is there anything we can say about the nature of these other nonphysical dimensions, which science knows exist but has so far been unable to analyze? It is surely not too far-fetched to suggest that they must be at least related to the 'ethereal realms' that all esoteric teachings discuss, and which are the true home of the discarnate soul.

So it seems to me that, by grounding our spiritual beliefs in good, firm science, we ensure that a broad spiritual worldview cannot be dismissed as based on pure faith and a need to believe. Moreover, it is the materialist rather than the spiritual position that should be ridiculed as illogical, based on all the evidence we now have. Indeed it is a supreme irony – often, unfortunately, lost on my colleagues in the alternative genre – that modern science, rather than holding back humanity's spiritual progress, is at the very forefront of it; and that the materialist intelligentsia will ultimately be brought down by the real movers and shakers of science in their very midst. These leading lights have for some time recognized that science and theology must once again be merged into a philosophical whole – just as they were in the Classical Greek era – if we are to make any genuine progress in shedding further light on the nature of the universe in which we live.

Of course, all of this begs the question as to what sort of spiritual worldview is the most rational to adopt. And to me the only fundamental issue is whether or not it should be based around the dual principles of reincarnation and karma. I have already indicated that I came to the conclusion that it should from my research into the ancient texts and traditions. But there is also a basic logical argument that underlies this position.

As so many enlightened commentators have suggested for millennia, how do we account for the different circumstances we all encounter in life? How do we, for example, compare someone born into a loving environment that lasts throughout their life, with someone orphaned, rejected or abused from an early age, and for whom the whole of life is a constant struggle just to survive? If this were our only life, what kind of god would present the latter with almost unendurable tests, and the former with such an easy ride? If we accept a spiritual approach, where is the logic, let alone justice? By contrast, such differing circumstances are perfectly logical elements of a worldview under which we have many lives in which to experience both sides of every coin.

Further backup for this position is provided by modern research that points virtually conclusively to the idea of reincarnation. When I presented the manuscript of *Genesis Unveiled* to my publishers they insisted that, because I was basing my entire set of arguments around my spiritual worldview, I had better provide some hard evidence for it and insert it in a new chapter right at the beginning. And because I had already come across the pioneering and widely respected research of psychologist Ian Stevenson into children with astonishing recall of past lives, which we will consider later, I set to work.

But it was only when I was browsing through a list of books on the internet that I thought might have some additional bearing on the matter that one of those important coincidences happened – coincidences to which a spiritual worldview teaches us to pay serious attention. Because it was my discovery of the work of Californian psychologist Michael Newton that set me on the path to writing this book, even though I was then unaware of this potential outcome. Although at the time I was somewhat skeptical about hypnotic regression into past lives in general, I was genuinely dumbfounded by the consistency of his subjects' reports of their experiences in the ethereal realms between earthly incarnations, for which I use the term *interlife*. These included not only the idea that we engage in extensive reviews of our past lives, which was one I had encountered before, but also that we are closely involved in the planning of our next one. Quite apart from the additional support this consistent testimony gave to the evidence for reincarnation, to me this represented a massive step forward in our potential understanding of a spiritual worldview. Above all, it has huge implications for our appreciation of the degree of personal control that we as individual souls exercise on our many lives. Accordingly, I included a fairly comprehensive review of his findings in *Genesis Unveiled*.

Since that book was published, this has proved to be one of the major topics people wanted to discuss – unfortunately at the expense of many of my own ideas about humankind's spiritual history, but that is another story. What is more, I have found myself talking about Newton's work more and more openly to people from all sorts of backgrounds, and it seems to engage them completely. Another piece of this jigsaw slotted into place when further research revealed that a number of other pioneering psychologists have engaged specifically in interlife research, and that in most aspects their findings are entirely consistent with Newton's. Unfortunately much of this research has had little exposure, especially outside of America, and many of the books that arose out of it are now out of print. Nor has it previously been properly collated and compared to highlight the many consistencies, but also critically examine the few discrepancies.

When I first set out to write this book it was this interlife material that I wanted to concentrate on exclusively. But to set the scene I also spent more time examining the phenomenon of near-death experiences, and came to realize that my initial skepticism about these was entirely misplaced. Perhaps far more important, though, was that as I continued with my regression research great confusion entered my mind in one area in particular – that of the workings of karma. The findings of those pioneers who were concentrating more on regression therapy, with patients who were suffering from varying degrees of psychological and psychosomatic problems, were somewhat different to those who were concentrating more on the interlife experience. But their insistence that the more repetitive type of karma they were encountering was a form of paying off karmic debts simply did not sit well with the actual evidence of many of their case studies.

I already knew that it was important to make the distinction between repetitive and progressive karma, and had developed a framework that shows how we all encounter these different stages as our soul evolves. But I was still struggling to understand the underlying dynamics. That was until, eventually, and after much searching and deliberation, it dawned on me that the answer had been staring us in the face all along. We had simply been blind to the truth because of our age-old reliance on the revealed wisdom that karma involves action and reaction. It does not. Even in the repetitive stage, it is primarily about *learning* – to have the appropriate emotional reactions and to make the right choices. This then forced me to recognize that, for all that I am reluctant and entirely unqualified to act as any sort of guru myself, there were a number of practical guidelines we can all follow in life to progress our karma and to escape from repetitive traps.

This book can effectively be divided into two parts. By way of introduction, in chapters 2 and 3, and the first half of chapter 4, I attempt to bring together all the modern research into near-death experiences, children who spontaneously remember past lives, and past-life regression. Some readers will have at least some familiarity with this material, although I should stress that these chapters include what is arguably a more thorough analysis of these phenomena than is often provided. Nevertheless, anyone who finds themselves reading material they are already familiar with may prefer to scan this part section by section, and to pick out only those elements that are new to them. After this we will enter far less well-charted territory – which includes the background to interlife regression, the past-life review and next-life planning elements of the interlife, the dynamics of karma, hypnotic progression, and spirit and even demonic possession – before finally considering the ultimate questions: '*Why are we here, and what should we do?*'

2

NEAR-DEATH EXPERIENCES
Does Our Soul Survive After Death?

The next thing I recall was the sound: it was a natural 'd'. As I listened to the sound, I felt it was pulling me out of the top of my head. The further out of my body I got, the more clear the tone became. I had the impression it was like a road, a frequency that you go on. I remember seeing several things in the operating room when I was looking down. It was the most aware that I think that I have ever been in my entire life. I was metaphorically sitting on Dr Spetzler's shoulder. It was not like normal vision. It was brighter and more focused and clearer than normal vision. There was so much in the operating room that I didn't recognize, and so many people.

I thought the way they had my head shaved was very peculiar. I expected them to take all of the hair, but they did not.

The saw thing that I hated the sound of looked like an electric toothbrush and it had a dent in it, a groove at the top where the saw appeared to go into the handle, but it didn't. And the saw had interchangeable blades, too, but these blades were in what looked like a socket wrench case. I heard the saw crank up. I didn't see them use it on my head, but I think I heard it being used on something. It was humming at a relatively high pitch and then all of a sudden it went *Brrrrrrrr!* like that.

Someone said something about my veins and arteries being very small. I believe it was a female voice and that it was Dr Murray, but I'm not sure. She was the cardiologist. I remember thinking that I should have told her about that. I remember the heart-lung machine. I didn't like the respirator.

Thirty-five-year-old Pam Reynolds was in a good deal of trouble. It was 1991, and her doctors in Atlanta, Georgia had diagnosed a massive aneurism – a weakness in the wall of an artery that causes it to balloon out – at the base of her brain. Its size and awkward location meant that it was not just life threatening, but also virtually inoperable. But she had one last chance. She had been referred to Robert Spetzler, a leading neurosurgeon in the Barrow Neurological Institute in Phoenix, Arizona, who had pioneered a new form of surgery known as hypothermic cardiac arrest. Nicknamed 'standstill' by his team, the procedure involved the blood in her body being cooled from its normal ninety-eight degrees Fahrenheit down to a mere sixty degrees, during which time her heart went into deliberate cardiac arrest and stopped beating. Once cooling was complete, her body was inclined on the operating table and her blood allowed to drain out so that the incredibly delicate and complex procedure of excising the aneurism could take place. At this lower temperature her brain could survive the lack of blood supply for longer than normal without sustaining permanent damage, but Spetzler still had only a maximum of thirty minutes to work his magic. Nevertheless, not only did Pam survive to tell the tale, but the tale itself has had huge reverberations in both medical and wider circles.

Although they offer no obvious support for the idea of reincarnation per se, near-death experiences have received increasing attention since psychiatrists Elizabeth Kubler-Ross and Raymond Moody presented their pioneering investigations into the subject in the seventies, with Moody's classic 1975 book *Life After Life* capturing the public's imagination with its groundbreaking findings. Research methods were improved and standardized in the following decade, with psychologist Kenneth Ring and cardiologist Michael Sabom making leading contributions to our understanding of the phenomenon. However, by their very nature these experiences tend to occur in a somewhat haphazard fashion, to people suffering a sudden trauma such as a heart attack or a serious accident that brings them close to death.

In recent years attention has become increasingly focused on whether these experiences can be used as evidence that the soul, or perhaps more accurately in this case consciousness, survives physical death. Needless to say, because such research goes to the very heart of the debate between materialists and those who hold a spiritual worldview of whatever variety, it has engendered serious discussion. And one of the main sticking points has been the issue of the *timing* of the recollections that have arisen from near-death experiences, and in particular of recollections of hospital procedures or other circumstances that can be independently verified from surgical reports or by other corroboration.

Pam Reynolds' case, collected by Sabom as part of his Atlanta Study, is regarded as crucial because her near-death experience occurred under the most stringently controlled, planned and monitored conditions that it is possible to achieve. When it was featured in one of the BBC's highly respected *Horizon* documentaries in 2003, entitled 'The Day I Died', viewers were given the clear impression that Pam was clinically dead when her experience took place. And when I studied the details of the case provided by Sabom in his 1998 book *Light and Death*, which were compiled from a mixture of Pam's subsequent recollections and the notes of the surgical team, it was clear that for a period of time during surgery she was clinically dead under all three of the criteria that are normally used. First, the electroencephalogram or EEG was registering no activity in her cerebrum or higher-brain functions. Second, the electrogram that was monitoring the reaction of her brainstem to automatic sound stimuli was similarly inactive, despite the continued pulses being transmitted into Pam's ears via small molded speakers. And third, all blood had been drained from her brain.

Although we will consider the rest of Pam's experience shortly, for now the key issue is whether she was clinically dead when she 'witnessed' the verifiable clinical procedures she recounts in the passage quoted above. And verifiable they are. Sabom has proved beyond any reasonable doubt that Pam's visual recollections of the saw used to open up her skull, and its accompanying case with alternative blades, were both accurate and – because of its unusual similarity to an electric toothbrush – totally beyond any general knowledge she might have picked up during her lifetime. Nor were they explainable by pure guesswork. Nor could she have seen them when being wheeled into theater, because all such instruments are surgically sealed and hidden from view at that point.

As for the conversation concerning the size of her arteries, this too was confirmed by the surgical team, who were readying the femoral arteries in her groin for attachment via tubes to the cardiopulmonary bypass machine that would cool her blood. When the right artery was found to be too small to do the job alone, the left one was also prepared. A skeptic might suggest that Pam could have guessed at this occurrence, given that from her account above she already seems to have known she had small arteries, and suggesting she should have told the doctors about it also seems to infer that at some point before surgery she might have been briefed by the team about the nature of the bypass procedure. But in another description of her experience provided for the Horizon documentary, this possibility is eliminated: 'I do remember wondering what are they doing – because this is brain surgery! And what had happened was that they had accessed the femoral arteries in order to drain the blood, and I did not understand that.'

So we have two descriptions provided by Pam – one of an instrument and one of a procedure – which she could not have known about beforehand, and which were subsequently confirmed by the surgical team. She recalled them having happened more or less simultaneously, a fact that has again been confirmed. *But what was the state of her brain at this point in the operation?* Sabom's account indicates that Spetzler was opening her skull in order to perform a preliminary investigation of the aneurism using a flexible tubular microscope, which was then threaded between the various lobes of her brain down to the location of the aneurism. It was only when he established some two hours later that it was 'extremely large and extended up into the brain' that the need for standstill was proved beyond doubt, and the blood cooling procedure initiated.

So it is clear that it was only *after* this lengthy initial investigation that clinical death was induced. Fifteen minutes into the cooling process, just after her heart went into complete cardiac arrest, the EEG stopped recording any activity in the cerebrum. She was now 'flatlining'. It took a further twenty minutes before the electrogram showed that her brainstem too had stopped functioning, at which point the pump in the bypass machine was switched off and the operating table inclined so her blood would drain. At the time of her *verified* recollections some two and a half hours beforehand, she was heavily anesthetized and had already been totally unconscious for nearly an hour and a half while her body was prepared for surgery... but she was *not* clinically dead.

Nevertheless, this case still raises some important issues that cannot easily be explained. She had verifiably *seen* the saw that was used to open her skull – and yet not only was she deeply unconscious at the time, but her eyes had been lubricated and then taped shut right at the outset. She had verifiably *heard* the conversation between the bypass team – and yet, as we have already noted, her ears were plugged by small speakers that the surgeons confirm would have prevented any other external noise from getting through. As her own account suggests, she was quite clearly seeing and hearing these events via a process that did not involve the conventional use of her physical eyes and ears – and all at a time when she was deeply unconscious. When we come to the more typical subsequent aspects of her near-death experience, it is quite acceptable – even if not persuasive – for skeptics to argue that they *could* have derived purely from her imagination. But we have already ruled out the use of imagination for these verifiable events, so that explanation simply does not hold up here.

Can there be any sensible explanation other than that she was having an out-of-body experience, during which whatever nonphysical part of her that was out of her body was able to see and hear these verifiable events by an entirely nonphysical process – *and* then bring a recollection of them back to be stored in her brain's physical memory once the experience was over? In my opinion, no, there is not. So this alone forces us to accept there is something very out of the ordinary going on here, something that involves an entirely nonphysical process. And that in turn should force us to take not only the rest of Pam's near-death experience seriously – as rather more than just a set of conditioned brain responses, or a pure flight of imagination – but also those of the multitude of others who have had similar experiences.

On that basis, let us allow Pam to continue the story in her own words:

There was a sensation like being pulled, but not against your will. I was going of my own accord because I wanted to go. I have different metaphors to try to explain this. It was like the Wizard of Oz – being taken up in a tornado vortex, only you're not spinning around like you've got vertigo. You're very focused and you have a place to go. The feeling was like going up in an elevator real fast. And there was a sensation, but it wasn't a bodily, physical sensation. It was like a tunnel but it wasn't a tunnel.

At some point very early in the tunnel vortex I became aware of my grandmother calling me. But I didn't hear her calling me with my ears. It was a clearer hearing than with my ears. I trust that sense more than I trust my own ears. The feeling was that she wanted me to come to her, so I continued with no fear down the shaft. It's a dark shaft that I went through, and at the very end there was this very little tiny pinpoint of light that kept getting bigger and bigger and bigger.

The light was incredibly bright, like sitting in the middle of a light bulb. It was so bright I put my hands in front of my face fully expecting to see them and I could not. But I knew they were there. Not from a sense of touch. Again, it's terribly hard to explain, but I knew they were there.

I noticed that as I began to discern different figures in the light – and they were all covered with light, they *were* light, and had light permeating all around them – they began to form shapes I could recognize and understand. I could see that one of them was my grandmother. I don't know if it was reality or projection, but I would know my grandmother, the sound of her, anytime, anywhere.

Everyone I saw, looking back on it, fits perfectly into my understanding of what that person looked like at their best during their lives.

I recognized a lot of people. My uncle Gene was there. So was my great-great-Aunt Maggie, who was really a cousin. On Papa's side of the family, my grandfather was there. They were specifically taking care of me, looking after me.

They would not permit me to go further. It was communicated to me – that's the best way I know how to say it, because they didn't speak like I'm speaking – that if I went all the way into the light something would happen to me physically. They would be unable to put this me back into the body me, like I had gone too far and they couldn't reconnect. So they wouldn't let me go anywhere or do anything.

I wanted to go into the light, but I also wanted to come back. I had children to be reared. It was like watching a movie on fast-forward on your VCR: you get the general idea, but the individual freeze-frames are not slow enough to get detail.

Then they were feeding me. They were not doing this through my mouth, like with food, but they were nourishing me with something. The only way I know how to put it is something sparkly. Sparkles is the image that I get. I definitely recall the feeling of being nurtured and being fed and being made strong. I know it sounds funny, because obviously it wasn't a physical thing, but inside the experience I felt physically strong, ready for whatever.

My grandmother didn't take me back through the tunnel, or even send me back or ask me to go. She just looked up at me. I expected to go with her, but it was communicated to me that she just didn't think she would do that. My uncle said he would do it. He's the one who took me back through the end of the tunnel. Everything was fine. I did want to go.

But then I got to the end of it and saw the thing, my body. I didn't want to get into it. It looked terrible, like a train wreck. It looked like what it was: dead. I believe it was covered. It scared me and I didn't want to look at it.

It was communicated to me that it was like jumping into a swimming pool. No problem, just jump right into the swimming pool. I didn't want to, but I guess I was late or something because he pushed me. I felt a definite repelling and at the same time a pulling from the body. The body was pulling and the tunnel was pushing. It was like diving into a pool of ice water. It hurt!

This account has all the hallmarks of the typical near-death experience. First, the out-of-body experience, where the subject sees their immediate physical surroundings from a remote location, can float around at will, and experiences extremely heightened senses. Second, the journey through the dark tunnel and out into the brilliant light, accompanied by a sense of tranquility and euphoria. Third, the meeting with at least one or more etheric or energy beings who emanate unconditional love and compassion, usually identified as family members or other close acquaintances, or as spirit guides or guardian angels. Fourth, the telepathic communication and instant rapport with these beings. Fifth, the sense of a point of no return or barrier that must not be crossed. And sixth, the usually somewhat reluctant but nevertheless accepted decision to come back through the tunnel and return to the physical body, more often than not because of unfinished business, particularly to do with immediate family and, especially, young children.

But again, Pam's case is unusual in that there are other aspects of her report that allow us to speculate about the timings of her experience far more than is normally the case. This is how she somewhat comically describes the moment she returned to her body:

When I came back, they were playing 'Hotel California' and the line was 'You can check out any time you like, but you can never leave'. I mentioned [later] to Dr Brown that that was incredibly insensitive.

Sabom was able to confirm that the junior members of the surgical team involved in the closing procedures *were* playing this music once the operation was complete and her brain, heart and lungs were returning to full function. The bypass machine that had by now reheated her blood to just under ninety degrees was switched off approximately one hour after the surgery proper had commenced – although of course at this point Pam was still heavily unconscious, so that this verifiable auditory recall provides another important piece of nonimaginary evidence. This means that we have an interval of approximately three and a half hours between the time of her first verifiable recollection and her last. And we do know that for the thirty minutes of the second half of the third hour, when Spetzler was actually excising the aneurism, she was clinically dead.

All reports of the ethereal realms suggest that time has no real meaning there, or at least it is experienced in a very different way from in the physical. Nevertheless, would it make any logical sense to suggest, as skeptics undoubtedly might, that her experiences were bunched purely into the two and a half hours before she was clinically dead, and then carried over and resumed for the half-hour that followed? It is important to remember that she had a verifiable experience at the beginning and another at the end, and she herself makes no suggestion that there was any sense of a break in her total experience. And although it is clearly a debatable point, with the backing of the fact that her verifiable experiences while deeply unconscious cannot be explained by any normal physical process anyway, I would argue that her total experience was most likely to have been an unbroken one that continued *right through* the time she was clinically dead.

I repeat that I would suggest this case alone has everything we need to take the near-death experience seriously as something that *does* relate to the nonphysical world of the ethereal realms, and of the separate consciousness or soul. But in order that I am not accused of being unduly selective, we should turn our attention to the broader spectrum of cases and the various materialistic explanations put forward to account for them.

While the pioneering investigators such as Kubler-Ross, Moody, Ring and Sabom tended to concentrate on evidence from their home setting of America, more recently research has been conducted in Britain by psychiatrist Peter Fenwick and medical doctor Sam Parnia. Broadly speaking their findings corroborate those from across the Atlantic, and we now have literally thousands of documented near-death experiences on file from various studies.

The most remarkable aspect of these studies is the consistency of the core experience. It is fair to say that subjects' descriptions of the realms they enter do vary. Whereas Pam Reynolds describes a place of pure light and love without apparent physical detail, many accounts describe beautiful green fields or gardens and vivid blue skies. But while Pam is aware that the people she meets are light or energy beings, she also gradually perceives them taking a simulation of physical form that corresponds to her best and most comfortable memories of them. In other words, I think it is safe to surmise that everyone forms their own constructs of what these realms look like, at least during such initial encounters; and whereas some seem comfortable to impose minimal physical detail on their surroundings and accept the ethereal, energy nature of the environment, others show a greater need to ground their experience in the familiar. However, the basic elements of the experience that I listed earlier stand as highly consistent and universal features.

The first objection put forward by skeptics is that, now that reports of near-death experiences have gained widespread exposure, people are culturally conditioned to have them. They argue that this severely undermines their credibility as objective evidence for consciousness existing independently of the physical body. And although this modern exposure cannot be denied, there is strong evidence that it does not play a significant role in at least some of the cases collected to date.

Fenwick was instrumental in setting up the British branch of the International Association of Near Death Studies in 1987. After appearing on various radio and television shows, he received a huge number of replies to his request for first-hand accounts of near-death experiences. From these he selected five hundred people to whom he sent a detailed and standardized questionnaire, to which three hundred and fifty responded. One of the key questions was whether they had been aware of the phenomenon before they had their own experience: and, despite the exposure it has gained, a mere two per cent answered in the affirmative. In reading through the multitude of cases reported in Fenwick's 1995 book *The Truth in the Light*, one of the major reasons for this appears to be the advanced age of many of the respondents, and the fact that their experience occurred many decades before. They universally express their delight that at last they could share their experience with someone who would understand it, whereas they had always been too afraid of ridicule beforehand, even in many cases from their nearest and dearest. Fenwick also points out that a significant number of very young children have reported near-death experiences that are essentially the same as that of adults, and that the chances of these arising from cultural preconditioning are particularly remote.

While we are considering the issue of potential subjective distortions, one of the other materialistic explanations for near-death experiences is that subjects are merely imposing their existing religious or spiritual beliefs on whatever experience they are having; and that they are effectively conjuring up a psychological safety net from a combination of these beliefs and their imagination when faced with the daunting prospect of death. There can be little doubt that, despite the basic consistency of the experience, broad cultural factors do have a part to play. Fenwick compares research in America, Britain, India and China in which there are clear differences of emphasis. But his own British study shows some surprising results. A massive eighty-two per cent of his respondents indicated they were of a Christian denomination of one form or another, and when asked about their commitment to their religion a still significant thirty-nine per cent reported that it was important to them. And yet an incredibly small number suggest that they met with an identifiable religious figure such as Jesus during their near-death experience. And although a larger number use the broad terminology of meeting with 'God' or 'their Maker', even these subjects describe the experience as involving a broad spirituality that had little or nothing to do with their exposure to orthodox religion and its associated dogma. Indeed, many found their spiritual horizons considerably widened by their experience.

That is not to say that subjective beliefs are never imposed on the near-death experiences of others. For example, although Sabom deserves high praise for the generalized early research that led to his 1981 book *Recollections of Death*, and for documenting the Reynolds case in his second book, a significant portion of the latter is unashamedly devoted to interpreting the phenomenon from a Christian perspective. Given my introductory comments, it will come as no surprise that this is not especially to my personal taste. Needless to say, I too am guilty of placing it within the context of my own broader spiritual worldview, which will similarly offend those of a strictly scientific and materialist persuasion. But at least this is more in keeping with the spiritual direction that the majority of near-death experiencers themselves appear to have subsequently taken. Plus, of course, I am prepared to present a considerable quantity of other evidence to support this view.

Having dealt with the issue of subjectivity, what other potential psychological explanations for the near-death experience have been put forward? A leading advocate of the materialist school is British psychologist Susan Blackmore, whose 1993 book *Dying to Live* incorporates all their major arguments. This takes us right into the heart of the brain-versus-mind debate, and the million-dollar question is this: is the brain the originator of the mind, or merely the vehicle through which the essentially nonphysical mind – or consciousness, or soul – expresses itself in the physical world? Materialists continue to maintain the former, on the basis of the huge advances in our understanding of brain processes achieved in recent decades.

Brain scanning experiments have increasingly shown that certain sets of cells in various areas become chemically active in response to the stimuli of different thoughts or feelings. But in no sense does this prove that these cells are responsible for *producing* the thoughts or feelings in the first place. In my opinion they are far more likely to have originated quite separately from the brain in the nonphysical mind, so that the brain is merely *responding* to them. These scientific studies have also proved that when we dream or imagine images or sounds we stimulate the same cognitive areas of the brain, that is the visual and auditory cortices, that are stimulated when we see or hear with our eyes and ears. But again this proves nothing about the *source* of the stimuli.

Moreover, what happens when these areas of the brain are simply not functioning, as is the case during many near-death experiences? Even if the brain is not completely shut down during the experience, in many cases the subject is at least unconscious, whether deliberately through anesthesia or not. Conventional medical wisdom universally acknowledges that the unconscious brain cannot build coherent cognitive models, whether real or imagined. Unconsciousness is global; it works on the entire brain, not just parts of it. So an unconscious person might reflexively pick up snippets of external sound, for example, but should not be able to put them into a coherent overall context; and they certainly should *not* be able to put them into memory for future recall. All the above is even more true if the brain is more severely impaired, or has shut down completely. And yet we repeatedly encounter near-death experiences in which these conditions prevail, but the subject is subsequently able to recall their experience from *memory* in *lucid* detail. Pam Reynolds is a perfect case in point.

Nevertheless, skeptics are still prone to suggest that near-death experiences are nothing more than dreams or imagination. But not only have we already seen that the verifiable elements cannot be explained away so glibly, there are also clear differences. Although they sometimes feel extremely real at the time, we normally recognize dreams for what they are as soon as we awake – and they rarely, if ever, show the sort of lucidity and consistency that is so characteristic of the near-death experience, let alone have the same lasting and profound impact.

Drugs too have often been cited as a likely cause of near-death experiences, and it is true that certain drug-induced hallucinations display many similarities. But studies show that no drugs of any kind are involved in the majority of cases. Indeed Ring quotes studies that suggest the presence of medical drugs may impair, or even reduce the likelihood of, a near-death experience. So while the phenomenon may be *similar* to certain drug-induced hallucinations, in no way can they be offered as a universal *cause* of it. Of course hallucinogens have been deliberately used throughout the ages to induce an altered state of consciousness in which enlightenment may be attained – the same being true of meditation or deliberate isolation for lengthy periods – and these are issues that we will consider in more detail in the final chapter. So surely the near-death experience is best regarded as a kind of automatic enlightenment experienced by some people when close to death.

What about the idea that people facing death attempt a 'psychological shutdown'? Psychiatry recognizes conditions known as 'dissociated states' that are triggered to protect the person from extremely painful emotions. On the one hand, 'derealization' involves shutting out the outside world so that it becomes unreal, as if a dream; by contrast, 'depersonalization' allows people to become detached from themselves, as if looking at themselves from outside. But this latter in particular involves a shutting down of emotions that is completely at odds with the typical near-death experience. Moreover, there is an overwhelming sense of *genuine reality* in the vast majority of cases. We have already seen that Pam Reynolds emphasizes the clarity of her vision, and we repeatedly encounter the suggestion that whatever is released from the physical body is the 'real me', while the ethereal realms are described as 'far more real' than the physical world. Indeed in many cases we find subjects reporting an experience of 'total knowledge or wisdom', both about themselves and the universe as a whole, even if they cannot recall any of the details when they return.

Another intriguing aspect of near-death experiences that has yet to be explained by conventional science is the existence of relatively rare cases that involve people who have been blind from birth. In their 1999 book *Mindsight*, Ring and fellow psychologist Sharon Cooper present their findings from a two-year study of over thirty such cases, over eighty per cent of which involve some sort of visual perception. One example also quoted by Fenwick is that of American Vicki Umipeg, who was blinded by excess oxygen in her incubator at the age of only three months. She was then involved in a road accident when she was twenty-two years old:

> The first thing I clearly remember was being on the ceiling, looking down and seeing this body. I was really terrified by this ability to see. At first, I couldn't relate to that body, and then I realized it was me. I could hear

the doctor telling the others: 'There's blood on her eardrum. Now she's probably going to be deaf as well as blind.' I was screaming at him, 'But I can hear! I can hear!' and I felt this terrible desolation because I couldn't get through to him. Then the nurse said that I'd be in a vegetative state. I tried to talk to her, but she couldn't hear me either.

Then I was pulled up through the roof and I had this glorious sense of freedom. I could move wherever I wanted to. I was above the street, above the hospital, and I was ecstatic about being able to move wherever I wanted to.

Among many other things in a lengthy account, Vicki goes on to describe in great detail how she was sucked into a tunnel with regular openings – through which she saw other people moving through other tunnels – after which she came into the light and saw what she describes as Christ with bare feet, a bright garment, long hair and light around his head. Whether or not her physical description of this figure was influenced by her membership of the Pentecostal Church, she was still reporting that she was 'seeing' all these things. She also 'saw' various family members and acquaintances – even though she was not allowed to touch them as would have been her wont in the physical world – as well as birds, trees and flowers.

It is well-known that attempts to use surgery to restore such people's sight can prove problematic, because it takes them many years to get used to a faculty they have never had before, and their whole model of the world is turned upside down. In some cases the apparent beneficiaries have even wished they could return to their former unsighted state, so traumatic was the experience. And yet the blind subjects of near-death experiences report visual sensations as if they were perfectly normal, and appear quite able to cope with the supposedly new cognitive models involved – albeit perhaps after some initial confusion and trauma. In its own right this evidence has massive potential implications. Because, even if 'seeing' in the ethereal realms is not the same as in the physical, it strongly suggests that at least some of our basic cognitive models do not originate from the physical brain at all.

If we now turn to materialist attempts to provide physiological or neurological explanations, the first argument is that oxygen starvation of the brain, or anoxia, might cause near-death experiences because the temporal lobe of the brain responds by generating strong feelings of emotion and often euphoria. But huge numbers of deliberate studies of anoxia conducted with, for example, pilots and medical students, reveal that the experience is also one of increasing confusion and loss of perception before the subject lapses into unconsciousness. This is the complete antithesis of the lucid near-death experience, and none of the thousands of subjects in these experiments has ever reported anything even remotely similar in the detail.

Blackmore also argues that anoxia can produce the 'tunnel and light vision' so typical of near-death experiences. She suggests that, because a larger number of eye cells are devoted to the centre of the visual field than to the periphery, then, as oxygen levels reduce, random cell activity causes lots of bright lights to flash at the centre, making the outside seem dark; and, as the condition worsens, this central light becomes larger and larger. This is intriguing, but it can hardly account for the huge number of near-death experiences that do not involve anoxia at all, let alone for the numerous other aspects of the typical experience.

Related to anoxia is what at first sight appears to be the most promising materialist explanation, that of hypercarbia. This involves a build-up of carbon dioxide in the blood, which is normally a by-product of reduced oxygen levels. As he describes in his 1950 book *Carbon Dioxide Therapy*, Hungarian-born psychiatrist Ladislas Meduna experimented by deliberately making patients inhale controlled amounts of carbon dioxide mixed with oxygen as part of their therapy. What he found was that many reported dreamlike experiences that they felt were real, and that sometimes involved an out-of-body experience, a tunnel effect, feelings of euphoria and total wisdom, and communication with higher spiritual beings. There is clearly a significant similarity between this range of experiences and the typical near-death experience. But again there are problems with this explanation. Meduna was closely regulating the 'carbogen' mixture so that the amount of carbon dioxide inhaled was fixed at thirty per cent, and his patients were not as a rule lapsing into unconsciousness. In a normal near-death-experience setting, significant increases in carbon dioxide in the blood would automatically be associated with a reduction in levels of oxygen, as in anoxia. If there was close medical supervision this situation would automatically be rectified if possible, and if not the patient would swiftly lapse into unconsciousness. So, even if subjects of hypercarbia appear to have intriguingly similar experiences to those who are near death, all the old problems arise again in terms of attempting to offer hypercarbia as a comprehensive *cause* of the near-death phenomenon.

Finally, what about endorphins or endogenous morphine? Materialists argue that the brain automatically produces these in response to severe pain or emotional stress, and as with all opiates they have a calming and euphoric effect, similar in some ways to aspects of the typical near-death experience. But many cases result from circumstances so swift that the body has no time to produce endorphins, while euphoria is just one small aspect of the phenomenon. So, yet again, we have a putative scientific cause that does not stand up to close scrutiny as a complete explanation for the broad spectrum of circumstances that accompany near-death experiences, and of their typical components, that we have on record.

In his 1982 book *Life at Death* Ring makes the following observation:

> It is not difficult – in fact it is easy – to propose naturalistic interpretations that could conceivably explain some aspect of the core experience. Such explanations, however, sometimes seem merely glib and are usually of the 'this-is-nothing-but-an-instance-of' variety; rarely do they seem to be seriously considered attempts to come to grips with a very puzzling phenomenon. A neurological interpretation, to be acceptable, should be able to provide a *comprehensive* explanation of *all* the various aspects of the core experience. Indeed, I am tempted to argue that the burden of proof has now shifted to those who wish to explain near-death experiences in this way.
>
> In the meantime, I think it is fair to conclude that physiological or neurological interpretations of near-death experiences are so far inadequate and unacceptable.

Over two decades later, and after plenty of new research effort on both sides of the debate, I would argue that his conclusion still holds true.

Whether or not one accepts that Ring's words are still valid, one thing remains clear above all else. And that is that conventional science remains completely unable to explain how the *verifiable* aspects of near-death experiences can be *memorized* by subjects who are unconscious or even brain-dead. So it seems appropriate that we should close by examining a few more of these intriguing cases.

Cardiologist Pim van Lommel has performed an extensive thirteen-year study of the near-death experiences of patients in ten Dutch hospitals, publishing his results in the prestigious medical journal *The Lancet* in 2001. During the pilot phase, a patient in one of the hospitals had the following out-of-body experience, as later reported and verified by a nurse:

> During a night shift an ambulance brings in a 44-year-old cyanotic, comatose man into the coronary care unit. He had been found about an hour before in a meadow by passers-by. After admission, he receives artificial respiration without intubation, while heart massage and defibrillation are

also applied. When we want to intubate the patient, he turns out to have dentures in his mouth. I remove these upper dentures and put them onto the 'crash cart'. Meanwhile, we continue extensive CPR. After about an hour and a half the patient has sufficient heart rhythm and blood pressure, but he is still ventilated and intubated, and he is still comatose. He is transferred to the intensive care unit to continue the necessary artificial respiration.

Only after more than a week do I meet again with the patient, who is by now back on the cardiac ward. I distribute his medication. The moment he sees me he says: 'Oh, that nurse knows where my dentures are.' I am very surprised. Then he elucidates: 'Yes, you were there when I was brought into hospital and you took my dentures out of my mouth and put them onto that cart, it had all these bottles on it and there was this sliding drawer underneath and there you put my teeth.' I was especially amazed because I remembered this happening while the man was in deep coma and in the process of CPR. When I asked further, it appeared the man had seen himself lying in bed, that he had perceived from above how nurses and doctors had been busy with CPR. He was also able to describe correctly and in detail the small room in which he had been resuscitated as well as the appearance of those present like myself. At the time that he observed the situation he had been very much afraid that we would stop CPR and that he would die. And it is true that we had been very negative about the patient's prognosis due to his very poor medical condition when admitted. The patient tells me that he desperately and unsuccessfully tried to make it clear to us that he was still alive and that we should continue CPR. He is deeply impressed by his experience and says he is no longer afraid of death. Four weeks later he left hospital as a healthy man.

Did this comatose patient just play a joke on the staff, and strike lucky with his guess about where they had put his teeth when he was comatose? Perhaps, but such an explanation smacks of desperation.

I have already suggested that the vast majority of near-death experiences tend to have a profound and permanent impact on their subjects, an impact that dreams rarely if ever match. As in the case above, almost all report they no longer have any fear of death; and, as I suggested earlier, a significant number have also developed a broad spiritual outlook on life – even if they had none beforehand. Nowhere is this more true than in the most unusual case of George Rodonaia, a Russian neuropathologist and avowed atheist whose near-death experience occurred after he was involved in a car accident in 1976. He was immediately pronounced dead, and his body lay in a morgue for *three days*. Again his was a lengthy and detailed experience, but this is how the verifiable element is described in pediatrician Melvin Morse's 1993 book *Transformed by the Light*:

[During his near-death experience] George could go visit his family. He saw his grieving wife and their two sons, both too small to understand that their father had been killed. Then he visited his next-door neighbor. They had a new child, born a couple of days before George's 'death'. George could tell that they were upset by what happened to him. But they were especially distressed by the fact that their child would not stop crying. No matter what they did he continued to cry. When he slept it was short and fitful and then he would awaken, crying again. They had taken him back to the doctors but they were stumped. All the usual things such as colic were ruled out and they sent them home hoping the baby would eventually settle down. While there in this disembodied state, George discovered something:

'I could talk to the baby. It was amazing. I could not talk to the parents – my friends – but I could talk to the little boy who had just been born. I asked him what was wrong. No words were exchanged, but I asked him maybe through telepathy what was wrong. He told me that his arm hurt. And when he told me that, I was able to see that the bone was twisted and broken.'

Eventually the doctor from Moscow came to perform the autopsy on George. When they moved his body from the cabinet to a gurney, his eyes flickered. The doctor became suspicious and examined his eyes. When they responded to light, he was immediately wheeled to emergency surgery and saved. George told his family about being 'dead'. No one believed him until he began to provide details about what he saw during his travels out of body. Then they became less skeptical. His diagnosis on the baby next door did the trick. He told of visiting them that night and of their concern over their new child. He then told them that he had talked to the baby and discovered that he had a greenstick fracture of his arm [meaning it was only partly broken]. The parents took the child to a doctor and he x-rayed the arm only to discover that George's very long-distance diagnosis was right.

This experience had such a profound effect on George that he went on to study for a doctorate in the psychology of religion, and then became an ordained priest. Of course, skeptics would suggest that this must be an anecdotal story full of embellishments, but George is a highly respected former research scientist who has retained documented proof of his experience in terms of hospital and autopsy records. Materialists would clearly struggle to explain how George was able to diagnose a broken arm in his neighbors' child that had baffled their doctor, using some sort of x-ray vision – even if he had been allowed to examine the child in person. So to ask them to attempt to explain it when he had been pronounced clinically dead and was lying in a morgue is probably being unduly cruel. But, if we accept that George was operating outside of normal physical constraints and with somewhat enhanced perception, this case causes us no great problems.

Nevertheless, it also raises some new and even more intriguing questions. Why could George communicate with the baby but, as usual, none of the adults? Was the baby still so young that it somehow remained more in touch with both its own and George's ethereal essence? In the next chapter we will see that young children do indeed seem to be more in touch with their ethereal nature, in a variety of ways. But, perhaps even more baffling, how could the baby sensibly communicate what was wrong with it when so young, even if by telepathy? I would suggest that this aspect of this case, when coupled with the mounting evidence that young babies are far more intelligent than we normally suspect, may be best explained by the concept of reincarnation – and we will expand on this in chapter 6.

At the time of writing Fenwick and Parnia are embarking upon a novel experiment with twenty-five hospitals under the auspices of their new Horizon Research Foundation, based in Southampton General Hospital in the UK. This will involve placing boards with various messages on them in locations in hospital rooms that can only be seen from the ceiling, and in this way they hope to obtain easily verifiable evidence from anyone who goes out-of-body during a near-death experience. If they obtain consistent, verifiable results from these experiments, under proper scientific conditions, it will be harder still for materialists to claim that the mind is merely a product of the physical brain.

I have some personal experience of death. My mother suffered a major stroke just before her seventieth birthday and, although she was conscious and alert when I first got to see her in hospital, she slipped into a coma that night from which she never emerged. Throughout that last week my family took it in turns to sit by her bedside, reading to her or just talking, and we all sensed that she could still hear us. When I sat with her the night before she died, as I read something particularly poignant to her a teardrop appeared in the corner of her eye and ran down her cheek, and I felt her gently squeeze my hand. Although the hospital staff were very supportive, with their constant exposure to death they were somewhat blasé, and dismissed our pleas that they should not say anything too clinical or harsh when in her room – such as when they were taking the decision to remove her drip. They would argue that her teardrop and squeeze of my hand were automatic physical reactions that had no origin in her conscious brain. But our strong intuition that she could hear what we were saying is borne out by the near-death-experience research we have considered in this chapter.

And there is another source that tends to confirm this view. We will meet

American psychiatrist Brian Weiss properly in chapter 4, but one of his patients who had suffered from chronic fear of choking after an operation on her throat relived the experience under hypnosis:

> When they give you anesthesia, can you hear? You *can* still hear! Your mind is very much aware of what's going on. They were talking about my choking, about the possibility of me choking when they did the surgery on my throat.... That's why I had all the problems.... They should be very careful of what they say.

Weiss himself was shocked by this, especially when he recalled the flippant conversations he had had during surgery when he was initially training at medical school. A shake-up in how the medical profession views anesthetized or comatose patients is long overdue. It seems doctors and nurses should be far more sensitive in their attitude towards them – indeed, if they treated them exactly as they would if they were fully conscious, they would not go far wrong.

My father's death provides a contrasting but no less relevant experience. He had been an extremely active and vibrant man throughout his long life, but suffered a series of minor strokes in his early eighties, which were also accompanied by the gradual onset of dementia. We were fortunate enough that he retained his sense of humor throughout, and did not suffer the terrors of complete disorientation that so often accompany this condition – instead merely reverting to a somewhat childlike existence. I did not see him for the last few days before he died peacefully in his sleep, but my eldest brother did. And he said that when you looked into his eyes they had changed. They were empty, and lifeless. His own interpretation was that my father's soul had already departed, and all that was left was for his physical body to shut down completely. This experience is not dissimilar to one reported by Fenwick, in which a young boy having a spontaneous out-of-body experience was reported to look like an 'empty shell' by his terrified sister, who walked in on him.

Is this yet more proof that our real *essence*, be it our soul, our consciousness or whatever, exists completely independent of the physical body? Do we now have enough evidence to agree with the conclusions of a growing number of professional medics and psychologists that near-death experiences are genuine spiritual experiences, which cannot be explained by rational, reductionist science alone? And, as a nonscientist who is not constrained to limit his conjecture, dare I suggest that the tunnel so frequently described in the typical near-death experience might best be thought of as an interdimensional gateway through which, sooner or later, all of us will pass into the ethereal realms – where our normal understanding of space and time will be turned upside down, and we will experience a oneness, understanding and love way beyond anything we could possibly conceive in the physical realm?

3

CHILDREN WHO REMEMBER PAST LIVES
Are They Making It Up?

The following story appeared on the ABC news website on 15 April 2004:

> Nearly six decades ago, a twenty-year-old Navy fighter pilot on a mission over the Pacific was shot down by Japanese artillery. His name might have been forgotten, were it not for six-year-old James Leininger.
>
> Quite a few people – including those who knew the fighter pilot – think James is the pilot, reincarnated. James' parents, Andrea and Bruce, a highly educated, modern couple, say they are 'probably the people least likely to have a scenario like this pop up in their lives'. But over time, they have become convinced their little son has had a former life.
>
> From an early age, James would play with nothing else but planes, his parents say. But when he was two, they said the planes their son loved began to give him regular nightmares. 'I'd wake him up and he'd be screaming,' Andrea told ABC News' Chris Cuomo. She said when she asked her son what he was dreaming about, he would say, 'Airplane crash on fire, little man can't get out.'
>
> Andrea says her mom was the first to suggest James was remembering a past life. At first, Andrea says she was doubtful. James was only watching kids' shows, his parents say, and they weren't watching World War II documentaries or conversing about military history. But as time went by, Andrea began to wonder what to believe. In one video of James at age three, he goes over a plane as if he's doing a preflight check. Another time, Andrea said, she bought him a toy plane, and pointed out what appeared to be a bomb on its underside. She says James corrected her, and told her it was a drop tank. 'I'd never heard of a drop tank,' she said. 'I didn't know what a drop tank was.'
>
> Then James' violent nightmares got worse, occurring three and four times a week. Andrea's mother suggested she look into the work of counselor and therapist Carol Bowman, who believes that the dead sometimes can be reborn. With guidance from Bowman, they began to encourage James to share his memories – and immediately, Andrea says, the nightmares started to become less frequent. James was also becoming more articulate about

his apparent past, she said.

Bowman said James was at the age when former lives are most easily recalled. 'They haven't had the cultural conditioning, the layering over the experience in this life, so the memories can percolate up more easily,' she said.

Over time, James' parents say he revealed extraordinary details about the life of a former fighter pilot – mostly at bedtime, when he was drowsy. They say James told them his plane had been hit by the Japanese and crashed. Andrea says James told his father he flew a Corsair, and then told her, 'They used to get flat tires all the time.' In fact, historians and pilots agree that the plane's tires took a lot of punishment on landing. But that's a fact that could easily be found in books or on television.

Andrea says James also told his father the name of the boat he took off from – *Natoma* – and the name of someone he flew with – 'Jack Larson'. After some research, Bruce discovered both the *Natoma* and Jack Larson were real. The *Natoma Bay* was a small aircraft carrier in the Pacific. And Larson is living in Arkansas.

'It was like, holy mackerel,' Bruce said. 'You could have poured my brains out of my ears. I just couldn't believe it.'

Bruce became obsessed, searching the internet, combing through military records and interviewing men who served aboard the *Natoma Bay*. He said James told him he had been shot down at Iwo Jima. James had also begun signing his crayon drawings 'James 3'. Bruce soon learned that the only pilot from the squadron killed at Iwo Jima was James M Huston Jr.

Bruce says James also told him his plane had sustained a direct hit on the engine. Ralph Clarbour, a rear gunner on a US airplane that flew off the *Natoma Bay*, says his plane was right next to one flown by James M Huston Jr during a raid near Iwo Jima on March 3, 1945. Clarbour said he saw Huston's plane struck by anti-aircraft fire. 'I would say he was hit head on, right in the middle of the engine,' he said.

Bruce says he now believes his son had a past life in which he was James M Huston Jr. 'He came back because he wasn't finished with something.' The Leiningers wrote a letter to Huston's sister, Anne Barron, about their little boy. And now she believes it as well. 'The child was so convincing in coming up with all the things that there is no way in the world he could know,' she said.

But Professor Paul Kurtz of the State University of New York at Buffalo, who heads an organization that investigates claims of the paranormal, says he thinks the parents are 'self-deceived'. 'They're fascinated by the mysterious and they built up a fairy tale,' he said.

James' vivid, alleged recollections are starting to fade as he gets older – but among his prized possessions remain two haunting presents sent to him by Barron: a bust of George Washington and a model of a Corsair aircraft. They were among the personal effects of James Huston sent home after the war.

It is not often that the story of a child remembering a past life receives widespread media coverage. As we can see, when it does it causes immediate polarization of opinion between those who regard such cases as proof not only of an afterlife but also of reincarnation, and those who think that the children and families involved make such stories up because they love the mystery – and perhaps even the limelight. It is apparently easy for skeptics to write off such cases by claiming they are purely anecdotal and the family have got carried away – without, usually, having properly interviewed them – in just the same way that they offer simplistic and reductionist explanations for near-death experiences. But are there other cases like this that have received less media attention? And have they been more rigorously investigated?

Enter Ian Stevenson, former head of the Department of Psychiatry at the University of Virginia, and the undisputed pioneer of research in this area. He and his team have investigated over 2600 similar cases since 1960, and he has published many books and academic papers as a result. The best introductory overview is his 1987 book *Children Who Remember Previous Lives*, which contains summaries of twelve cases, although he provided full details of other cases in his earlier 1974 book *Twenty Cases Suggestive of Reincarnation*.

One thing that shines through in Stevenson's work is that he approaches it with about as much scientific professionalism as it is possible to muster in such an area of study. He and his team have developed a formal methodology for investigating cases that makes every possible effort to account for the child subject's memories by normal mechanisms, and they only ever regard a case as 'solved' if the child's recollection indubitably points to the life of a clearly identifiable and now deceased individual. It is also notable that, as a professional researcher attempting to maintain a high degree of scientific rigor, he avoids overtly placing his work in the context of any declared religion or philosophy.

Although there are other factors at work here, as we will shortly see, we can in general conjecture that the reason only young children tend to remember their most recent past life spontaneously – that is, without hypnosis or other deliberate induction – is because they are closer to it in time. To that extent these memories seem to work like any other, in that they fade over time. It is also likely that their innate and intuitive recollection facilities have been less culturally suppressed than those of an adult – which is why most people experience déjà vu and lucid repetitive dreams far more in childhood than in later life. Nor is it irrelevant that, as we saw in the last chapter, George Rodonaia was able to communicate telepathically with the baby during his near-death experience, but not the adults. To repeat my assertion from that chapter, young children appear not only to be more in touch with their ethereal essence, but also to retain far more hidden intelligence – from their experiences in past lives and in the ethereal realms – than we normally suppose. But, more importantly for attempts to convince skeptics, these cases have the built-in advantage that young children have had less time to assimilate historical details by normal means, so the process of crosschecking possible normal sources can be far more comprehensive and reliable than with an adult.

One of the most impressive of Stevenson's cases is that of Swarnlata Mishra, who was born in 1948 in the Madhya Pradesh district of India. When she was only a little over three years old her father took her on a lengthy journey from their home in Panna, and on their return through a town called Katni she suggested they should go to 'her house'. From then on she began to recall the details of the life of a girl called Biya Pathak, who she said had lived there in a white house with four stuccoed rooms, black doors fitted with iron bars, and a stone slab floor. She also said they had owned a motor car, which was a rare occurrence for that place and time; she recalled that the house was adjacent to a girls' school, a railway line and a lime furnace; and she identified the district in which it was located. It appears that her father did not discourage these memories, but nor did he make any attempt to verify them until some considerable time later when, at the age of ten, Swarnlata was introduced to a woman who she was told originally came from Katni, and identified her as a friend from her former life. From this point a local investigator became involved and was able to identify the correct Pathak family home – out of the many families of that name in Katni – from the detailed statements she had already made. They confirmed they had had a daughter called Biya who had died in 1939.

Stevenson tabulates forty-nine statements made by Swarnlata about her previous life, only a few of which could be regarded as in any sense inaccurate, and eighteen of which were made before there had been any contact whatsoever between the two families. Not only were her memories more abundant and detailed than in many cases, but it is also clear that there was no attempt to consistently feed information to her, or to lead her on subjectively, in the subsequent meetings and investigations. In fact, on a number of occasions she was deliberately *misled* by Biya's family. For example, it was arranged that Biya's husband and one of their sons would arrive to see her anonymously, mixed in with a number of other people from her own town, some of whom she knew, some not. From this group she correctly identified Biya's husband with little difficulty. But she also insisted that Biya's son was indeed her son even when he insisted on pretending for twenty-four hours that he was not. At the same time he lied to her that a friend he had brought with him was Biya's other son, but Swarnlata stuck to her guns that he was not. On another occasion when finally in the presence of this other son, the first son turned the tables and told her this other son was someone else, but again she insisted that he too was Biya's son. And on yet another occasion, Biya's youngest brother lied to her that a man she had identified correctly as their family's former cowherd could not be him as he was dead, but again she stuck to her guns; while he also lied to her that Biya had lost her front teeth, with her again objecting correctly that Biya had retained them, albeit with gold fillings.

Even if we accept as Stevenson does that Biya's family were reasonably well-known business people in the area, Swarnlata's more intimate knowledge appears to rule out any possibility that it could have been obtained by conventional means. For example, she identified that Biya had had a throat infection and more or less correctly identified the name of the doctor who had treated her – albeit that she claimed this was what had killed her, when in fact she had died several months later of heart disease. She recalled having attended a wedding with the woman she first recognized as Biya's friend from Katni, and how they had difficulty in finding a latrine. On separate occasions she recognized another of Biya's younger brothers, and the son of yet another brother, and addressed them using the nicknames 'Babu' and 'Baboo' respectively that Biya had always used for them. She reminded Biya's husband that he had taken twelve hundred rupees from her moneybox, something only he and Biya knew about. She commented that a friend of the Pathak family was now wearing spectacles, which they had not when Biya was alive. And she enquired about a neem tree in the compound of the family house, and a parapet at the back, both of which were no longer there but had been in Biya's day.

Another highly unusual factor in Swarnlata's case is that she had more fragmentary memories of another life in the nine years between these two, which appears to have resulted in some early confusion and accounts for some of the inaccurate answers she gave about Biya's life. She gave her name in this other life as Kamlesh, and said she had lived in Sylhet in Assam, now in Bangladesh, where she had died at the age of nine. Even more remarkable was that from about the age of five she spontaneously performed songs and dances in what was subsequently recognized by an expert as Bengali, whereas she and her family had only ever been exposed to Hindi in Madhya Pradesh. Two of the three songs were identified by the expert, who then compared them to performances given at a professional Bengali dance institute, finding them substantially the same in terms of words and music. However, Swarnlata was completely unable to converse in Bengali with the expert, and nor could she translate the songs into

Hindi for her family. Moreover, she would never sing the songs without performing the appropriate dance at the same time, as if the two were inextricably linked in the recall process.

As we will shortly see, Swarnlata's case is unusual not only in terms of the depth and breadth of her memories, and of her 'intermediate' life recall and resulting skills, but also because she retained her memories for longer than most children. Nor does it appear that there were any undue psychological stresses from her previous lives, or for that matter deaths, that resulted in her astonishing recall; and apart from her Bengali songs she displayed no obvious behavioral traits, or indeed phobias, arising from them. Nor does she seem to have suffered from any conflict of interest between her current family and that of her previous incarnation, and it is heartening to hear that – despite the testing time she was given by some of Biya's family in the early stages – she was soon accepted by them as her reincarnation.

I have only outlined one of Stevenson's cases here, because I would necessarily have to summarize any others even more, and it is in the detail that his research gains its credibility – indeed, he is at pains to point out that any serious researcher should consult his more detailed papers on each case. He also deliberately includes a few weaker and unsolved cases in his books to demonstrate his methods and his laudable attempts at scientific impartiality.

His cases come from all parts of the world, but especially India, Sri Lanka, Myanmar or formerly Burma, Thailand, Lebanon, Syria, Turkey, West Africa and the northwestern tribal regions of North America. He has also investigated cases in other parts of North America and in Europe, although these appear to occur less frequently, and he surmises that one of the reasons for this geographical disparity, although by no means the only one, is that many of the former regions have a widespread and ingrained belief in reincarnation, unlike the latter. Consequently, as a general rule the children in potential western cases are more likely to be misunderstood, ignored or deliberately silenced – although there are signs that this attitude may be changing.

That having been said, Stevenson makes it clear that his cases can hardly be regarded as fully representative of a world population of billions of people. Many factors affect a bias, including the relatively haphazard way in which reports of cases come to him, and the decisions he has made in selecting the regions he has taken the time and trouble to visit. He also admits that clear variations arise in different cultural settings. However, just as with near-death experiences, he has identified a number of common characteristics of typical cases.

First, most children start to talk about their previous life at some time between the ages of two and four, which is hardly surprising given that this is more or less when we expect a child to start talking with any degree of lucidity. This seems to indicate the memories are with them more or less from birth, and arguably confirms my previous suggestion that they are born with far more hidden intelligence than we normally suppose. The vast majority stop talking about their previous life between the ages of five and eight, although here there is more variety based on the extent to which they are encouraged or discouraged to do so by their families, and on the degree of forcefulness with which their memories impinge on them. But this still shows that cases need to be investigated early in the child's life if they are to have real merit.

Second, the children's memories almost always relate to the later years of the deceased person's life, and particularly to their mode of death, especially if this was violent, sudden and unexpected, or occurred at an early age. This in itself is interesting, because it appears there is a far greater incidence of these types of death in Stevenson's cases than exists in the general population, suggesting this factor itself plays a significant part in making memories of a past life more prevalent. The other common trait at work is if the deceased in some way felt they had unfinished or ongoing business. The interval between lives in the cases studied is normally less than three years, with in some cases hardly any interval at all. This is significantly less than the intervals reported from other research into the adult population, as we will see in the final chapter, and seems to indicate that the children who most easily remember a past life are also those who were in the most hurry to come back. Again, this all suggests that memories of past lives work in exactly the same way as normal incarnate memories, inasmuch as they fade over time, and is backed up by the fact that hardly any of the children remember more than one previous life.

Third, these children often express an intense desire to visit the location and family of their previous life, which if identifiable are usually not far away. In these more forceful cases, they often use the present tense when referring to the past life, as in 'my name is…' or 'I live in…', and may also refer to their previous parents, for example, as their 'real parents'. This is where the plot becomes more complex, because as soon as such communication takes place there is a far greater chance of supposed memories being influenced or obtained by perfectly normal means. For this reason Stevenson places relatively small reliance on statements made after such contact has been made, although in some instances it does provide further compelling evidence. This is particularly the case when recognitions of people or places are made completely spontaneously, without prompting, and without the accompanying adults having any knowledge of the place or person recognized, so that these are only subsequently verified. Recall of private nicknames of people known by the deceased, or of private events in their lives known only by themselves and perhaps one other person, all add to the authenticity of many cases. And, in a substantial number, the idea that the previous 'personality' has survived with a clear sense of ongoing purpose gains further support from the attitudes the children adopt to acquaintances from the past life, showing friendship or animosity in exactly the measure that would have been expected of the deceased.

Fourth, these children often display behavioral traits that are completely out of character for their present life, but entirely in keeping with their previous one. These include phobias, such as of guns, knives or water, which are usually related to the manner of their previous death, and are displayed even before they start to speak about their past-life memories. Sometimes they display a fondness for certain types of food, or for tobacco or alcohol, or interests in and aptitudes for a particular profession to which they have had no exposure in their current life. In a smaller but still significant number of cases, they may totally reject their current gender on the basis that they still identify with the opposite gender of their previous life. And, in rarer still but extremely intriguing cases, they display what Stevenson refers to as 'subliminal cognitive' skills, such as unusual aptitudes for learning or speaking a foreign language, or playing a musical instrument to which, again, they have had no exposure in the current life. Swarnlata Mishra's Bengali songs and dances are a limited example of this, and we will return to these unlearned skills in the next chapter.

Stevenson examines a number of materialistic alternative explanations for the cases he has studied. First, he accepts that in a very few cases fraud has been proved, and that in just a few more it may have occurred but not been discovered. Second, he acknowledges that gross self-deception is another valid explanation in a few cases, especially those tending to involve suggestions of the reincarnation of a famous or prominent person. Third, he assents that there may be a few cases in which the information in the child's memory was obtained in an entirely normal way by transmission from someone who was acquainted with the deceased, but this transmission has been entirely overlooked and forgotten. Fourth, he gives some weight to the possibility of significant parental exaggeration of sparse early comments made by the child, so while this is neither deliberate fraud nor self-deception as such, it could lead to a case appearing to be far stronger than it really is.

Stevenson's arguments against these materialistic explanations are detailed, but we can make a few general observations that to some extent apply to them all. First, his research methods have been deliberately designed to reveal any of the above alternatives, and while some dubious cases might have slipped through the net, they are unlikely to be more than a handful. Second, none of them can properly account for the genuine and unusual behavioral traits and phobias displayed by a great many child subjects. Third, there is far less motive for fraud, self-deception or exaggeration than might normally be assumed. While there is no doubt that in some cases the children or their family gain a degree of attention and notoriety from their experience, in many others the children place themselves in an extremely awkward position in relation to the rest of their family, for example because of their unusual behavioral traits. Moreover, the family of the child often faces rejection in favor of the family of the deceased, or at least rivalry for the child's affection; while conversely the family of the deceased sometimes suspects the motives of the child and its family, especially if they are wealthier, or are fearful of revelations about them that they would prefer remained private.

Stevenson also considers the possibility that somehow past-life memories are passed on genetically through the offspring of the deceased. But it is clear that in most cases the interval between the death of the previous personality and the birth of the child subject is far too short for this to be possible, quite apart from the fact that in many cases the possibility of their being even in any distant blood relationship is virtually zero.

Accordingly, he finally turns to the paranormal alternatives to reincarnation. The first of these is extrasensory perception, whereby the memories might be assumed to come from telepathic communication either with living acquaintances of the deceased, or with the discarnate soul of the deceased themself, or with a more universal etheric memory or consciousness. But Stevenson's child subjects are hardly ever reported to have any particular gifts in this regard, and again telepathy does not appear to offer a sensible explanation for the unusual behavioral traits so often encountered. The second is actual possession of the subject by the soul of the deceased, which on the face of it might better explain the behavioral traits. But it still cannot explain why these traits, and the memories of the other life, almost always fade away at a relatively consistent early age.

Above all, none of the aforementioned alternatives to reincarnation can account for the most unusual of all phenomena associated with children who remember previous lives, which I have so far not revealed. And that is the astonishing fact that sometimes child subjects have birthmarks or other physical birth defects that have been found to correspond to the fatal wounds of the deceased person whose life they remember. Stevenson has now collated over two hundred such cases, which are covered in detail in his lengthy medical monograph *Reincarnation and Biology*. This is an expensive two-volume work, but over one hundred cases are summarized, with some photographs and drawings, in his shorter 1997 book *Where Reincarnation and Biology Intersect*. By their very nature these are predominantly 'solved' cases where the deceased has been identified, and in most he has been able to obtain their medical records – usually in the form of a postmortem report – in order to make the comparison. As part of his protocol, and to ensure there is no confusion with subsequent injuries to the child, he also insists that at least one informed adult, usually a parent, must testify that the marks or defects were present at birth.

If we start by considering cases involving birthmarks, although almost all of us have them, they usually only take the form of small areas of increased skin pigmentation or moles. By contrast, in most of Stevenson's cases the marks are 'hairless areas of puckered, scarlike tissue, often raised above surrounding tissues or depressed below them'. A few are areas of decreased pigmentation, some are reported to be bleeding or oozing when the baby is born, and even those that only resemble normal moles tend to be larger and often in unusual places. Of course, when we are only dealing with ordinary moles that appear to correspond to wounds on the deceased, there is an increased possibility of pure chance coming into play if there is only a single correspondence, but in fact in most of these 'ordinary' cases there are two or even more matching marks.

Chanai Choomalaiwong was born in 1967 in Thailand. He had one small, round birthmark at the back of his head, about half a centimeter in diameter, and another larger and more irregular one behind the hairline above his left eye, this one about two centimeters long and half a centimeter wide. Photographs clearly show that neither resembles a normal mole. From the age of two he lived with his grandmother at a place called Nong La Korn. Not long after, she noticed that when he played with other children he would pretend to be a schoolteacher, and he soon began to talk about a previous life when he had held just such a position and his name had been Bua Kai. He said he had lived in a place not far off called Khao Phra, where he had had a wife and children, and begged to be taken there. More chillingly, he also said he had been shot and murdered on his way to work.

When he was still less than four years old his grandmother acceded to his request, and on entering the village he immediately took her to a house and identified the people who came to the door as his former parents.

They *had* had a son called Bua Kai Lawnak who exactly matched Chanai's description of him. It appears that he was not only a schoolteacher, but also something of a gangster who had multiple affairs. He had already survived one shooting attempt when, one morning in 1962, he set off for his school on his bicycle. He never got there. He was ambushed from behind on his way, and shot through the back of the head, dying instantly. The police removed the body, and his wife and younger brother were both called to examine it, along with a doctor. Although by the time Stevenson investigated the case no one could remember the name of the doctor – and nor were any postmortem records available because there had never been a trial – both his wife and brother confirmed that from Bua Kai's injuries it appeared the gunshot had entered the back of his head and exited at the front above his left eye. Of course, bullet wounds always tend to be larger at the point of exit than at the point of entry.

Chanai also made a number of statements that were verified, for example concerning Bua Kai's possessions, and identified other members of the family on subsequent visits to his former parents' house, including correctly naming a friend of Bua Kai's that he had never seen before. He further displayed attitudes to members of Bua Kai's family that were entirely inappropriate for a three-year-old child, but entirely appropriate for his former personality. For example, he insisted that unless Bua Kai's twin daughters addressed him as 'father' he would not speak to them; despite the fact they were by this time seventeen years old, they acceded, because by now all of Bua Kai's family had accepted that Chanai was Bua Kai reincarnated. So, despite the lack of a postmortem report, Chanai's case appears to be a strong one.

The birth of Cemil Fahrici in Antakya, Turkey in 1935 was preceded by an 'announcing dream', a reasonably common occurrence among several of the cultures that Stevenson has investigated. The night before, his father dreamed that a distant relative, Cemil Hayik, would be reborn as his son. This is how Stevenson describes the colorful life, and death, of the older Cemil:

> Cemil Hayik had been a picturesque bandit whose troubles began when he killed two men who had raped two of his sisters. Although arrested for the murders, he contrived to escape, and for about two years he maintained a precarious freedom in the sparsely inhabited mountainous area between the cities of Antakya and Samandag. It was not difficult for him to stop travelers in that isolated region and rob them of whatever he needed. In those days (the early 1930s) France occupied the province of Hatay, which Turkey was trying to recover; and the mountain people probably only gave limited assistance to the French police hunting Cemil Hayik.

Eventually, he and his brother (who had joined him) were betrayed, and the French police surrounded the house in which the brothers had taken refuge. A conventional shoot-out occurred, until finally the police were able to approach closely enough to pour gasoline on the house and set it on fire. As the fire consumed the house, the shots from inside ceased. Then the silence was broken by two more shots, and a further silence ensued. Cautiously, the police approached the house and kicked the door open. Inside, they found the bodies of Cemil Hayik and his brother. It appeared that Cemil Hayik had first killed his brother and then, putting the muzzle of his gun to chin, he had set off the trigger with his toe and killed himself. The bullet entered his head beneath the right side of his chin. The bodies of the bandit brothers were taken into Antakya and displayed in the courthouse square, perhaps as a demonstration of French police competence, perhaps as a deterrent to other persons feeling inclined to take up banditry. Cemil Fahrici was born a few days after Cemil Hayik died.

At birth, the younger Cemil was found to have a prominent scarlike birthmark under the right side of his chin, which bled sufficiently and for long enough that it had to be stitched in a hospital. Of course, this confirmed the belief of his parents from the announcing dream that he was the reincarnation of his older relative, which was strengthened when from the age of two to about six or seven he had a number of accurate memories, as well as nightmarish dreams about the French police. They had in fact christened him Dahham, but his insistence on being called Cemil was so strong that they gave in and changed his name. Nevertheless, and despite the birthmark, a skeptic might suggest that this case is not a strong one. But that is before we come to the final twist.

When Stevenson was interviewing one of the older Cemil's sisters she revealed that the bullet that killed him had exited through the top of his skull, lifting a portion of it up with its force, and this fact was confirmed by one of the French gendarmes who had been present at the final shoot-out. Stevenson returned to the younger Cemil and asked him whether he had another birthmark – and, without hesitating, he pointed to a linear hairless area about two centimeters long and two millimeters wide at the top of his head. Again, photographs show that neither of his birthmarks resembled a normal mole.

Although not all cases are as detailed or as strong as these two, there are numerous others that are highly persuasive, and it is the combined depth and breadth of Stevenson's investigations that give them such credibility. In India, Sunita Singh was born with an enormous port-wine stain-type birthmark on her right upper chest and arm, and others on her neck. They were subsequently found to correspond well with the sword wounds detailed in the postmortem report of a woman named Ram Dulari, who Sunita had already insisted was her previous personality. She had also spontaneously recognized her former daughter-in-law – who she claims was responsible for Ram's death, and of whom she showed great fear – as well as her former son. In Turkey, Necip Ünlütaskiran was born with six birthmarks, some more prominent than others, which were subsequently found to correspond almost exactly with those noted in the postmortem report of a man named Necip Budak, who had been repeatedly stabbed in a quarrel. Not only had the young Necip previously recalled the older one's death, but he had also described how he had once stabbed his former wife in the leg, something her own scars later confirmed. And in Thailand, Tong In Songcham was born with three thin, linear birthmarks along the line of her spine, each about six to eight centimeters long, and one of which was bleeding when she was born. These were subsequently found to correspond well to the injuries sustained by a woman called See who she had already claimed was her previous personality, reporting that she had been killed by axe blows to her back in a quarrel with her brother-in-law – which information was later confirmed.

Birth defects are of a somewhat different nature, not least because one must consider the extent to which a given defect occurs normally in the population when assessing the likelihood of chance being a factor in any given case. But Stevenson is also right to assert that even when a single genetic and possibly hereditary factor is regarded by science as the most likely cause for a particular birth defect, even this is rarely sufficient on its own to explain why, for example, only one twin in an identical pair suffers from the defect. So are other, more obscure factors sometimes at work?

The birth of Ma Khin Mar Htoo in Tatkon, Upper Burma in 1967 was preceded by her mother having an announcing dream in which an acquaintance called Ma Thein Nwe claimed she would be reborn as her daughter. This girl, nicknamed Kalamagyi, had earned her living selling flowers at Tatkon station. Unfortunately, one day in 1966 she had been using the central track to distribute her wares to the passengers of a stationary train, unaware that a sudden fault on the rails meant that a fast-approaching express train could not be switched to the other outside track. Although the driver braked at the last minute, she was hit and killed. Her body was horribly mutilated as one might expect, but in particular her right lower leg was severed and found at a considerable distance from the rest of her body.

When Ma Khin Mar Htoo learned to speak she recalled many details of Kalamagyi's life, although none that, as far as we can tell, she might not have learned from her mother. But she was also born with a rare malformation called hemimelia – her right leg was completely absent from just a few inches below the knee.

Similarly, just before Semih Tutusmus' birth in Sarkonak, Turkey in 1958, his mother dreamed that a man called Selim Fesli would be 'coming to stay' with her and her husband. In the dream his face was covered in blood, and he said he had been shot in the ear. This was accurate in that Selim was well-known to Semih's father, and he had been shot and killed while dozing in a field. The postmortem report described 'penetrating shotgun wounds of the right parietal and frontal areas of the skull'. A neighbor had been accused of his murder, but pleaded that it had been a hunting accident and only received a two-year jail sentence.

Even before he was two years old Semih started recalling events in the life of Selim, giving first the name of the man who shot him, and then of his wife and all six of his children. He made a number of other verifiable statements but, again, none that he could not have obtained by normal means from his father. On the other hand, from a behavioral point of view his intense hostility towards the man accused of his murder continued right through until his late teens. And there is more. Semih was born with only a linear stump where his right ear should have been, and the right side of his face was markedly underdeveloped.

These two are typical of Stevenson's birth defect cases in that in both the former personality in the announcing dream is an acquaintance of at least one of the parents, so that the child subject's subsequent statements could all have been obtained by normal processes. Therefore a skeptic would probably dismiss them en masse as the work of parents imposing these known former personalities on the children after they had been born with defects that just happened to correspond with the former's fatal injuries. But in many cases, and certainly these two, the defects are extremely rare in the general population, so to put them down to pure chance is hardly convincing. In addition, the announcing dreams themselves arguably add to rather than distract from the credibility of the cases, unless we are to assume that in all cases the parents made them up subsequently.

Whether or not these birth defect cases stand up, Stevenson does document a number of other such cases in which the former personality was indeed unknown to both parents. For example, Ma Htwe Win was born in Kyar-Kan in Upper Burma in 1973. Her mother had previously dreamed that an unknown man walking on his knees – or perhaps on stumps – was following her, and she could not shake him off. She did not understand this until Ma Htwe Win started to talk, when she said she had had a previous life as a man called Nga Than, who had been killed by three men. This is how Stevenson takes up her story:

> He had tried to fight back, but when he made a thrust with his sword it got stuck in the wall, and he was left defenseless. They stabbed him in the left breast, cut his fingers, and hit him on the head. His assailants evidently thought they had killed him. In fact, Nga Than seems to have remained conscious for a time, so that Ma Htwe Win later remembered hearing the murderers drinking while they discussed how best to dispose of the body. They finally decided to compress it into as small a space as possible by tying the legs back on the thighs, which would appreciably shorten the body and make it easier to put in a gunny sack and drop in a nearby dried-up well.

It would appear that Nga Than's wife had engineered this crime so she could marry one of his murderers, but some time later they quarreled and a neighbor overheard them discussing the murder and the location of the body. The police duly found it in the well, trussed up exactly as Ma Htwe Win would subsequently describe.

Ma Htwe Win not only made correct statements about her death, but also spontaneously recognized one of Nga Than's assailants, showing great fear, and his son. She maintained a number of masculine traits for some time, as well as an intense determination to take revenge on the murderers. But what of her birth defects? She was born with prominent birthmarks on her lower left chest and head, the fifth finger of her left hand missing, constriction rings just above both ankles and a severe constriction ring around the middle of her left thigh. Apart from the absence of a similar constriction of her right thigh, these rings are exactly what we might expect if the lower legs had been bent up behind the thighs and tied tight. Was this the last mental image that Nga Than retained, and then carried not only into an announcing dream but also into his next incarnation?

Stevenson begins his own analysis of birthmark and defect cases by discussing various psychosomatic phenomena: for example, those of stigmata, and of physical changes brought about by hypnosis in particularly impressionable subjects. He concludes that intense concentration on a physical change might be able to bring that change about. One solution that he therefore takes seriously is the possibility of 'maternal impression', a separate phenomenon not normally associated with children's past-life memories. In such cases, birth defects appear to have been brought about by a mother's obsession with a particular defect they had encountered in themselves or a relative, or an injury to which they had seen someone exposed. In most of the cases Stevenson studied this stimulus had caused considerable shock or fear, and had occurred either before, or during the first three months of, pregnancy. He concludes that these could have a part to play in some cases, in particular those in which the mother was acquainted with the former personality and with the wounds from which they died.

This is an interesting potential explanation that deserves closer scrutiny. If we start with the birthmark cases I describe above, Chanai Choomalaiwong's birth was not preceded by an announcing dream, and his family had no connection with Bua Kai's. Cemil Fahrici's father dreamed about Cemil Hayik, but only on the night before the younger Cemil's birth; and, as a distant relative, his mother was probably aware of the circumstances of the older Cemil's death, but it hardly seems something with which she was obsessed. Sunita Singh's birth involved no dreams, and her family had no connection with Ram Dulari's family. Necip Ünlütaskiran's mother dreamed at some unidentified time before he was born of a man with bleeding wounds, which might have caused her some distress, but he was unknown to her. And Tong In Songcham's aunt had a dream before her mother became pregnant, but only about an unknown woman who followed her mother home, and no injuries were included. In all the cases in which the previous personality was unknown to the subject's family, there is no reason to suppose they knew any details about their death from exceptional media coverage, and still less reason why the mothers might have obsessed about them. So in only one of these birthmark cases, that of Necip, would I regard maternal impressions as even a possible explanation – and even then there is nothing else in the details of the case to support it.

The birth defect cases are not so clear-cut. Ma Khin Mar Htoo's mother had an announcing dream before she became pregnant, as an acquaintance she presumably knew all about Kalamagyi's death, and because of the nature of her injuries it may well have had a significant effect on her – perhaps even enough to bring maternal impressions into play. Semih Tutusmus' mother had never met Selim Fesli, although she had vaguely heard about his death because her husband knew Selim well; but her announcing dream only occurred two days before Semih's birth, so obsessive maternal impressing seems unlikely in this case. Ma Htwe Win's mother had actually walked past the spot where Nga Than's body was being exhumed; she saw a crowd and noticed the body but apparently did not stop or take much notice. Nevertheless, perhaps she read about the gory details in the newspapers, which caused her to dream about them the following night, when she was only two and a half months pregnant. But nothing else in the case leads us to suppose that she then obsessed about them enough to generate such strong defective impressions on her unborn child.

Even in those cases where we might allow for maternal impressions playing a part, we would have to assume that the childrens' subsequent memories and recognitions were all totally imprinted by their parents, and then adequately covered up or forgotten so that Stevenson could not detect them. Moreover, any intense behavioral traits accompanying such cases would have to be similarly imposed and conditioned. This is not impossible, but it would verge on requiring deliberate and persistent fraud. So, on balance, it seems that maternal impressions might account for only a handful of especially birth defect rather than birthmark cases, and even in these it is hardly a watertight explanation.

In looking elsewhere, Stevenson argues that a related but this time paranormal explanation for birthmark and defect cases – which would now involve reincarnation – might be that the subject was concentrating so intensely on the injury that killed them that they carried a physical reminder over into their current incarnation. We will see in the final chapter that this view is supported by a number of esoteric and religious teachings, which suggest that one's emotional attitude at the time of death is crucial to what happens next. Of course, on the face of it we might not expect karma to be carried from one life to the next in any physical way, especially not in these cases when the subject was usually the innocent party anyway. But we will also see in chapter 7 that in unusual karmic circumstances, especially where there is perhaps a degree of nonacceptance of a traumatic experience in a previous life, some sort of psychological or even physical reminder may indeed be carried forward into the next life.

Such is Stevenson's reputation for scientific objectivity and impartiality that I have been able to locate very little direct criticism of his work and methods. Perhaps many skeptics have found, when they made the effort to study his research properly, that he had already considered the materialistic alternative explanations for his cases in great detail, both individually and collectively.

Having said that, there will always be plenty of skeptics whose views are so entrenched that they refuse to take the time to study the considerable evidence collated by Stevenson. This does not, however, prevent them from picking on easier targets. We have already seen how, for example, Paul Kurtz was prepared to deliver an opinion for ABC News that James Leininger's parents were responsible for his memories by imposing a fantasy of their own making upon him, even though one suspects that he made no effort to study the case properly and meet the people involved. This despite the fact that he is professor emeritus of philosophy at the State University of New York, and the founder and chairman of the highly skeptical Committee for the Scientific Investigation of Claims of the Paranormal, or CSICOP. This all sounds very impressive. But do CSICOP's professional standards even begin to approach those of someone like Stevenson? It appears not.

Which leads us nicely onto Richard Wiseman, a former professional magician turned psychologist from the University of Hertfordshire in the UK, who is also a member of CSICOP – as is Susan Blackmore who we met in the last chapter. It will therefore come as no surprise that he has consistently appeared in the media to debunk supposedly paranormal phenomena. Of particular relevance here is his involvement in a documentary aired on both the Learning and Discovery Channels in 2003, entitled *Past Lives: Stories of Reincarnation*, in which he is shown conducting an experiment where he asked young children simply to make up an imaginary friend, and to describe the things that happened to them. I have been unable to locate any published results for this experiment despite spending some time searching the internet, but one example of a three-year-old girl called Molly is used in the documentary. She came up with a description of another child, called Katy, who was also three. Molly said she had red hair, blue eyes, and was wearing a pink dress with flowers on it when she ran away. This is the relevant excerpt from the experiment:

> *When Katy ran away, Molly, did good or bad things happen? [Pause while Molly is unresponsive to Wiseman] Was there anything bad that happened to Katy?*
> Bad.
> *Bad? What's bad that's happened?*
> The monsters got Katy.
> *What were the monsters like?*
> Ugly.
> *They were ugly monsters? What happened?*
> Don't know.
> *[Molly's mother interjects] What happened to Katy when the monsters got her?*
> The monsters bit her.
> *[Molly's mother again] They bit her? So what happened to Katy?*
> Died.

Wiseman then tried to see if he could find a match for this story by looking through newspaper archives for children that had been abducted and killed, and managed to find one in which he says thirteen of the seventeen statements made by Molly were verified. Triumphantly, he proclaims he has proved that all such cases are based merely on imagination and pure chance: 'If Molly were claiming to have lived before, this would be the reincarnation case of the decade.'

Apart from Wiseman's massive exaggeration that clearly displays his ignorance of the depth of evidence available, was this a valid experiment? We can see that he deliberately led her down a negative or 'bad' route by his emphasis in his opening question. This is hardly objective evidence that children spontaneously evoke bad memories more than good, as he claims in the program. On top of this, he is concentrating entirely upon the idea that such memories arise from imagination and by chance, and completely ignoring the far more prevalent possibility in real cases that they might have been obtained by normal means. Did he check to see if Molly might have heard about the death of his 'matched' child from the television, or her parents? Where are the rigorous scientific controls that Stevenson himself insists upon?

Far more importantly, Molly's responses to questioning are brief and have an obviously childish tone. So where is Wiseman's explanation for the much more detailed memories of people, places, nicknames, private facts and so on that we have seen are so often provided by the children in Stevenson's studies, and indeed in the case of James Leininger? Can these really be so easily dismissed as the products of mere imagination, or even as having been normally acquired? Does he even know about the birthmark and defect cases for which random chance is a totally implausible explanation? Yet again, just as with near-death experiences, we have a supposed expert using reductionism to a ridiculous degree without even attempting to examine the full range of the phenomenon in question.

Fortunately the team that Stevenson has painstakingly built up at the University of Virginia is continuing his good work, and attempting to maintain his high standards of professional, objective investigation of the cases that come their way. And others too, such as psychologist Erlendur Haraldsson of the University of Iceland, have entered the fray.

In *Children Who Remember Previous Lives* Stevenson sums up his position on normal cases with great reserve:

> I may have a duty here to say what interpretation of the cases I myself favor. I have no preferred interpretation for all the cases, and I do not think that any single one of them offers compelling evidence of reincarnation. Yet I can say that I think reincarnation is, for some cases, the best interpretation. I am not claiming that it is the only possible interpretation for these cases,

just that it seems the best one among all those that I have mentioned.

When he later considers his cases of birthmarks and defects in *Where Reincarnation and Biology Intersect* he is somewhat more forthright:

> I accept reincarnation as the best explanation for a case only after I have excluded all others – normal and paranormal. I conclude, however, that all the other interpretations may apply to a few cases, but no more than a few. I believe, therefore, that reincarnation is the best explanation for the stronger cases, by which I mean those in which the two families were unacquainted before the case developed. It may well be the best explanation for many other cases also....
>
> This is a matter about which my opinion should count for little. I regard my contribution as that of presenting the evidence as clearly as I can. Each reader should study the evidence carefully – preferably in the monograph – and then reach his or her own conclusion.

One can only admire Stevenson's professional guardedness, and his humility about his own opinion. What a shame it is that some of the supposed professionals who are skeptical about children's past-life memories are not equally circumspect before denouncing them. But, in any case, I would beg to differ with Stevenson on this one occasion – and suggest that his opinion as the unquestionable leader in his field *should* count for a very great deal.

4

HYPNOTIC REGRESSION
How Reliable Is It?

Martin Gardner, another member of CSICOP, had this to say about hypnotic regression into apparent past lives back in 1957:

> Almost any hypnotic subject capable of going into a deep trance will babble about a previous incarnation if the hypnotist asks him to.... In every case of this sort where there has been adequate checking on the subject's past, it has been found that the subject was weaving together long-forgotten bits of information acquired during his early years.

We can see that Gardner's simplistic rejection has all the hallmarks of other CSICOP members' dismissals of children with spontaneous rather than hypnosis-induced past-life memories. But is it more valid in this case?

His comments came against the backdrop of the previous year's publication of *The Search for Bridey Murphy*, a book that had taken the world by storm and sold nearly 170,000 copies within two months. Its author Morey Bernstein was an amateur hypnotist who, four years earlier, had conducted a series of regression experiments with Virginia Tighe, a housewife from Colorado, who he referred to as Ruth Simmons in an unsuccessful attempt to protect her identity. She was apparently an excellent subject so, rather than just regress her into childhood as most other hypnotists did at the time, he decided on the then relatively novel approach of asking her to go back before that into her previous life.

Immediately she started talking with an Irish brogue and identified herself as Bridey Murphy, who was supposed to have lived in County Cork in Ireland. Over time more details emerged. She was born in 1798 with the full name Bridget Kathleen Murphy, her father Duncan was a barrister, married to Kathleen, and they were Protestants. At twenty she married a Catholic named Sean Brian MacCarthy, and they moved to Belfast where he taught law at Queen's University. Here they had a second wedding ceremony presided over by a priest called John Joseph Gorman, at a St Theresa's Church. She died at the age of sixty-six. More obscurely,

Virginia also sang a number of Irish songs while hypnotized.

Although Bernstein does not appear to have made massive efforts to corroborate her story before first publication, he had at least confirmed that the two grocery shops that 'Bridey' recalled frequenting in Belfast, Farr's and Carrigan's, did indeed exist at that time. But none of the birth, death or marriage details provided have ever been verified because official records do not go back that far in Ireland. Worse still the case was apparently demolished when, within four months of publication, investigative reporters claimed to have established that in her childhood in Wisconsin Virginia had lived across the street from a woman called *Bridie* Murphy, who had grown up in Ireland, used to tell her stories about life there, and had taught her a number of Irish songs.

This exposé gained so much publicity that the case has been widely dismissed ever since. Nevertheless Curt Ducasse, a highly respected professor of philosophy at Brown University on Rhode Island, investigated it thoroughly and in 1960 produced a paper for the *Journal of the American Society for Psychical Research* in which he concluded that the exposé itself was flawed, and that the case stood as one unexplainable by normal means. And in 1965 Bernstein produced an update of his book with reporter William Barker, including a new final chapter refuting the exposé. It certainly appears that a number of facts mentioned in the regressions that were reported to be historically inaccurate in the exposé turned out, on further investigation of more obscure sources, to be true. And based on these two revisions no less an authority than Ian Stevenson – who discusses hypnotic regression at length in *Children Who Remember Previous Lives* and is generally somewhat skeptical about it – believes that this particular case is a strong one that remains unexplained, even if unverified.

Whatever we might make of the Bridey Murphy case, I want to examine some of the issues surrounding past-life regression in general – as opposed to that conducted for therapeutic purposes, which we will consider later in this chapter. Clearly there are problems with validating hypnotic regressions into past lives that do not arise with many of Stevenson's child recall cases. For a start, with adults we have a far greater problem in attempting to establish whether they could have obtained the information through normal sources, perhaps many years ago when they were children, and then forgotten it. Stevenson discusses such source amnesia, and provides an interesting illustration dating back to the early part of the twentieth century. Although it does not involve regression but rather automatic writing while in a self-induced trance, the subject claimed to be channeling a person called Blanche Poynings, providing many details of her life. But in a subsequent trance session, when interrogated about the source of her information, she revealed she had read a novel called *Countess Maud* that was then found to contain all the major details she had recorded. And recent studies into past-life regression in general have shown that source amnesia cannot be discounted.

Nor can we entirely discount the possibility that in some cases more than just amnesia is involved, and the subject is perhaps a specialist in a particular period of history and simply conducting an elaborate and deliberate hoax. But I suspect even most skeptics would accept that such cases are likely to be extremely rare. And, as we will shortly see, a subject that is genuinely hypnotized finds it almost impossible to lie, while most professional hypnotherapists would normally be able to detect when a subject is not really in trance but just pretending.

The other aspect of past-life regression that differs significantly from spontaneous childhood recall is that it often takes the subject back into lives that occurred centuries ago, and in other countries, so attempting to check the details of cases to the extent of identifying the specific deceased personality is usually impossible. Verification is further hampered in that, contrary to popular skeptical opinion, past lives revealed during regression are almost always those of unremarkable rather than famous people. Nevertheless, when specific and verifiable details emerge, how accurate do they tend to be? Some cases have indeed provided obscure details that were subsequently verified by experts, as we will shortly see. But it must be admitted that others have been shown on investigation to contain clear historical anomalies.

Any sensible view of past-life regression in general must take imagination into account, and acknowledge that in many cases *some* aspects of recall may be derived from the subject using their imagination to build on information acquired from normal sources such as books, television or films that they may or may not have forgotten. I have already accepted this when analyzing my own regression in chapter 1. When I subsequently investigated the methods of torture used during the Spanish Inquisition, both the rack and nail-pulling are frequently mentioned; but I have no idea whether my descriptions of the uniforms of the guards in the prison, or of the regalia worn by my religious interrogators, could be appropriate for what I pinpointed as the period when the Inquisition began in Spain – which is normally taken as the latter part of the fifteenth century. In any case, nothing I recalled was outside the realms of what my imagination could easily conjure up based on knowledge I had already gleaned from normal sources. Does that automatically mean it was all a fiction of my own construction? Not at all. But it *proves* nothing one way or another, and this must be accepted as true of many cases of past-life regression when it is undertaken only in a general rather than a therapeutic context.

Stevenson and other critics also discuss the extent to which suggestion on the part of the hypnotist plays a major role in constructing what they regard as past-life fantasies rather than memories. I actually think this aspect is overplayed, and my own experience is perhaps instructive. Before my sessions with Andy Tomlinson I visited another regression therapist who decided not to hypnotize me in any formal sense, but just to let me 'meditate' my way into potential past-life memories while physically guiding me – because my eyes were shut – along an imaginary time-line on the floor of her office. I did have a very vague recall of two, one as a young sailor and the other as a Roman nobleman. But I found this session something of a struggle and, without wishing to denigrate her professional talents in any way, more often than not I had no strong intuitions with which to answer her questions; nevertheless, on a number of occasions I still felt compelled to say something, effectively out of embarrassment. So I had no great confidence that what I had experienced was genuine recall.

By contrast, when Andy hypnotized me properly the experience was completely different. Details came through often without any prompting, and there were only very few occasions in a total of more than four hours spread over two sessions – the second of which we will discuss in chapter 6 – when I was stumped by a question. On those occasions I had no problem admitting that I did not know the answer, or could not 'see' anything. And, as I indicated in chapter 1, there were quite a few instances where I specifically corrected him when he interpreted something wrongly or tried to move me on before I was ready, or in a direction I thought was inappropriate. As far as I can tell from reading the transcripts of many other regressions, the general tenor of my sessions was pretty typical, and most other subjects display a similar attitude. On that basis I would argue that, although suggestions from the hypnotist might sometimes play a part – and probably more with some people than others – in general they have considerably less influence than many skeptics make out. As we will see shortly, most professional hypnotherapists agree with this view and make a point of emphasizing their subjects' impartiality, which is allied to their literal interpretation of questions and inability to lie while in an altered state of consciousness.

Whatever we may think of the majority of general past-life regression cases, there are some in which the memories are so detailed and obscure, and so obviously not derived from normal sources, that when they are subsequently verified they leave us little option but to accept they at least involve paranormal processes – even if further discussion is required to consider whether reincarnation itself is the best explanation.

Some of the finest cases on record come from the diligent research of Australian psychologist Peter Ramster. From the early seventies he used hypnosis in his therapeutic practice to regress patients back into their childhoods, but was initially skeptical when some appeared to be regressing into past lives without any prompting. As with so many of his colleagues, as we will shortly see, when he experimented further the therapeutic results he consistently achieved changed his mind, and he documented a number of cases in his 1980 book *The Truth about Reincarnation*. He then developed an admirable determination to see past-life regression taken seriously as a key tool by the rest of his normally skeptical profession. So he conducted an experiment in which he chose three subjects from his home town of Sydney who had particularly vivid recall of previous lives in Europe, which none had ever been to in their current life, and arranged for them to visit the locations they described on the other side of the world to see whether the facts could be verified. They were accompanied by independent witnesses and a film crew, the results appearing first in a stunning television documentary he produced in 1983, and then seven years later in his second book *The Search for Lives Past*.

One of the subjects involved was Gwen McDonald, who had no particular interest or belief in reincarnation and initially only visited Ramster to accompany a curious friend. But how fortuitous that she did, because over the course of a number of sessions in Australia she proved to be an excellent subject who repeatedly regressed to the eighteenth-century life of a girl called Rose Duncan, who lived with her father Adam and his partner Bessie in a small cottage not far from Glastonbury in Somerset. Speaking apparently with the accent and manner of a relatively uneducated yokel of that time and place, Gwen stated that Rose was born in 1765 and led a happy but relatively uneventful life in the cottage, which formed part of an estate belonging to a Scottish émigré by the name of James Steward Mackenzie. But she ran away from home to spend the night in her favorite haunt, the legendary Glastonbury Abbey, after her father revealed his intention to place her in an arranged marriage; unfortunately she suffered from hypothermia as a result, and died three weeks later aged just seventeen.

In Sydney Ramster was able to confirm some details, such as that the said James Mackenzie had been an influential landowner in Somerset during the period in question. But far more was to come once they traveled to Somerset itself. Among many other remarkable feats, in leading the team to her former home without recourse to any maps Gwen came to a road intersection where she said five houses had previously stood, one being a cider house – and although only one now remained the occupier was able to confirm her story, adding that the houses had been built in 1742. After this she led them across a stream near a fork and a waterfall, later confirmed to have had stepping stones that had recently been removed – all of which she had described. She was then able to locate her former home itself, Rose Cottage, and although it had been enlarged in the interim, the original element that was now part-pigsty, part-garage would have been exactly as she had described once close inspection revealed certain modern alterations to the doors and windows. She also recalled two small pyramids that had been in the grounds of the Abbey, and some feather carvings on a doorway; she identified the names of a number of the surrounding villages from her former life, even though on modern maps one no longer exists and another has changed name; she used certain long-obsolete west country words and slang; and she recalled a number of local Arthurian and Druid legends. Most of these details were so obscure they required confirmation by local historians.

Perhaps most stunning of all, while still in Sydney Gwen had described one of a row of five small cottages near a stream just outside Glastonbury, to which Rose had once been taken when she had injured her foot in the Abbey. She also described and drew the exterior of the 'Pilgrim's Inn' along the way, and some carvings on one of several stone floor slabs in the cottage that the owner had stolen from the Abbey. When she led them on this final part of their exploration, again without maps, the exterior of the now renamed 'George and Pilgrim' remained exactly as she had drawn it. Even more startling, when they arrived at the row of cottages that had by now become a dilapidated chicken shed, they swept the floor free of its layer of droppings for the first time in years. This revealed the floor slabs from the Abbey – and on one the carvings were exactly as she had drawn them while on the other side of the world.

Ramster mentions several other interesting phenomena in passing. He reports that after regression several of his subjects developed bruising in areas where they had recalled being hurt in a previous life, and one who had been guillotined had a prominent red mark across the back of her neck similar to a birthmark. These cases clearly have some psychosomatic similarity to Stevenson's birthmark and defect cases. Another subject pointed out under hypnosis where she had lived in Düsseldorf during World War II on a map, but when asked to repeat the feat after she was brought back to normal consciousness she had to ask for her reading glasses. This is similar to the apparent sightedness of blind people during a near-death experience, and must lead us to wonder whether such sensory improvements somehow extend into all altered states of consciousness. And, perhaps adding just a little validation to my own regression experience, one of his subjects even remembered being tortured as a heretic in Spain in the first half of the fifteenth century: her nails were pulled out, and she too emphasized how her torturers always knew when to stop to keep her just this side of death.

We saw in the last chapter that Swarnlata Mishra was able to perform Bengali songs even though she could not converse in Bengali. However, Stevenson has documented three other cases where this use of a foreign language in recalling a past life is enhanced to the point where the subject actually converses in that language – the technical term for this being responsive, as opposed to recitative, zenoglossy. And, despite his skepticism about regression in general, in fact two of these subjects were adults who did not recall their past life spontaneously like his child cases, but instead only under hypnosis.

Of these cases I will outline here that of Dolores Jay, which is fully recorded in Stevenson's 1984 book *Unlearned Language*. Her husband Carroll was an amateur hypnotist who had begun experimenting with past-life regression in the late sixties, and found his wife was an excellent subject. But he was merely hypnotizing her to relieve some back pain one day when she unexpectedly answered '*nein*', the German for 'no', to one of his questions. Over the course of several sessions, and with the help of a German dictionary, Carroll managed to establish that Dolores was regressing to a past life as a young girl called Gretchen Gottlieb from Eberswalde. But it was only a year later that he invited a friend who spoke German to attend a session with her in which she was questioned in German for the first time, and responded. This was the only session that involved an outsider before Stevenson became involved in 1971, and he attended a number of subsequent sessions with Dolores, accompanied by a variety of other German-speaking witnesses.

After extensive investigations into her childhood Stevenson established to his own satisfaction that Dolores had had no significant exposure to the German language in her current life, and had certainly not been taught to speak it. He even arranged for her to take a lie detector test about this, which she passed. Nor does he think the couple had any motive for fraud, given that they received a good degree of criticism over the case from their local community because Carroll was a Methodist minister. And although Gretchen's German responses to her interrogation were somewhat halting and sparse, and not always grammatically correct, when coupled with her use of a few archaic words that are no longer in use they went far enough to eliminate the possibility of Dolores using pure guesswork or imagination.

She spoke only German in these subsequent sessions, although she was happy to be questioned in German or English. The following extracted highlights come from a session in May 1973 in which she was being questioned primarily in German, but for simplicity I have only shown her responses in German. These are the exact phrases and words she used, and do not incorporate any attempt to amend her German spelling or grammar; but any serious student should be aware that Stevenson provides the full dual-language transcripts of all these sessions in his book. This session opens with Gretchen somewhat irritated that she is being questioned about her rather sad life yet again. She was extremely paranoid about talking to strangers, and from her mention of 'Pope Leo' and other information it appears she was living in the late nineteenth century as part of a persecuted Catholic minority:

> Warum er kommen weider und weider (why does he come over and over again)?
> *Speak up Gretchen, how are you today?*
> Gefährlich (dangerous).
> *Dangerous? Why? What is dangerous?*
> Sie horen (they hear).
> *They listen?*
> Das Bundesrat (the Federal Council).
> *And what will the Federal Council do?*
> Gretchen sache sehr schlecht (things are terrible for Gretchen).
> *How old are you Gretchen?*
> Vierzehn (fourteen)....
> *Where is the Federal Council?*
> Der ist überall (it is everywhere).
> *Everywhere?*
> Ja (yes).
> *Everywhere? They are listening?*
> Ja (yes).
> *That is dangerous?*
> Sehr beschwerlich (very troublesome).

Sadly it appears that Gretchen died aged only sixteen, possibly after being made to hide in the forest by her father.

What are we to make of this? Admittedly there were elements of Dolores' recall that seemed at the very least historically confused: her statement that Gretchen's father Hermann was the mayor was not borne out by a search of local records, and under prompting she alluded to Martin Luther even though he had lived much earlier. But, even if confusion and imagination played some part, Dolores' ability to speak a language unknown to her current personality indubitably seems to point towards some process outside of the normal physical sphere.

Another impressive case is that of Cynthia Henderson, one of Ramster's subjects in *The Search for Lives Past*, who remembered the life of a French aristocrat in the eighteenth century. As Amelie de Cheville she had been brought up in a chateau near Flers in Normandy, and had many happy childhood memories. She married and moved to Paris, but as the Revolution took hold her life became increasingly threatened. Eventually she was taken from her house and guillotined along with many other members of the aristocracy.

Like Gwen Mcdonald, Cynthia was able to direct Ramster's team some distance from the center of Flers to the chateau, without the assistance of any maps and despite a new estate confusing the route. It was still standing, although in a somewhat desolate state having been bombed during World War II, and her description of the exterior of the chateau, its gardens and lake proved accurate. She was able to repeat the feat with a house near Mont St Michel that she had visited regularly on holidays, finding it without maps or mistakes, and describing the exterior correctly as well as a number of unusual interior features of a nearby chapel – such as the diamond-shaped blue-grey tiles on the floor, and a hexagonal stone font. And although she was able to identify that her marital home in Paris was north of a central bend in the Seine on the Rue St George, when the team visited the street it had changed so much that her former home had obviously disappeared.

All of this is impressive enough, but it was Cynthia's ability to speak fluent French when in trance that most interests us here. Ramster had established that at the age of twelve she had received some basic French tuition for two months at the most, but he was intrigued to see how she might get on with the language when reliving Amelie's life under hypnosis. So he arranged for a French volunteer witness called Antoinne to meet with her in Flers, and to speak with her in his native tongue. Although Ramster's book is deliberately not written to the same scholarly standards as Stevenson's, and he provides no detailed transcripts of this session, the results were apparently astonishing:

> To the surprise of everyone in the room, she fully understood what Antoinne had said to her and answered him in fluent French. There ensued a long conversation in French. Sometimes Cynthia answered his questions in French and sometimes in English. Sometimes Antoinne spoke in English and she answered him in French. It was apparent at all times that she was aware of what was being said and was able to answer. Antoinne had gone

off on a tangent asking her all sorts of questions and she correctly answered him. Her knowledge of French seemed to far exceed anything she might have been able to learn from a short period in classes at school.

Antoinne was astonished. He said she spoke French well, as a Frenchwoman spoke it, devoid of any English accent. Furthermore, he said she spoke in a manner more in keeping with the eighteenth century, as some of her words were old-fashioned. Sometimes she hesitated, however, as if the words came easily one minute and only with difficulty the next. Yet, Cynthia displayed that she had enough of a command of the French language to understand all that was said to her. The startling fact was that her French accent was perfect, her English [or presumably Australian] accent disappeared, and even the English she spoke while in trance had a French accent.

When the team went into the market in Flers after this session, it once again became painfully obvious that in her conscious state Cynthia was unable to converse in even the most basic French. As for deliberate fraud, which appears to be the only possible materialist explanation for this case, Cynthia would have had to be so devious, and so adept at hoodwinking Ramster and his team over a lengthy period, that it is scarcely credible.

In fact Ramster regularly directed his subjects to speak or write the language of their previous incarnations, and found that they were often somewhat reluctant because this seemed to require them to identify with their previous personality more than they wanted to – especially if the life in question held unpleasant memories. Nevertheless, by reassuring them he found he was consistently successful in this endeavor. For example, in *The Truth about Reincarnation* he describes how his subject Alexander Cochrane recalled the early twentieth-century life of a Welshman called George Evans. He wrote down several words and a short sentence in the Welsh language when pressurized to do so, all of which were subsequently verified, even though he had apparently had no exposure to it in his current life.

Arguably the most tantalizing of Ramster's cases is that of Jenny Green, who recalled a number of past lives, including that of an ancient Egyptian priestess in a temple dedicated to the goddess Isis some four thousand years ago. Not only did she write down a number of hieroglyphic inscriptions from the temple walls, several parts of which were subsequently verified by an Egyptologist, but on a number of occasions when directed she actually *spoke* the language of the time. Unlike most forms of writing, which use a phonetic alphabet, there is no connection between how a hieroglyphic script appears when written and how it is spoken – so scholars have absolutely no idea how the ancient Egyptian language sounded. But the potential authenticity of Jenny's utterances was apparently enhanced by their extreme fluency:

> Jenny has not learnt any of the languages she can speak under trance and, when awake, is totally unable to understand a word of what she hears herself saying on the tape. Upon waking she suffers complete loss of memory of the language and the topic. She speaks the language of ancient Egypt with surprising fluency. One would expect her speech to be fragmented, or at least very slow. Some of the sounds of the language are very deep and complex, and it would be very hard for most English-speaking people to achieve them; but Jenny rattles off the language as if she had been speaking it all her life. Even very complex combinations of sound are given very quickly and fluently. She pronounces without faltering words that would have my tongue tied up in knots before I could finish uttering the first syllable.

Even though I have no idea what follow-up has occurred in the intervening years, Ramster indicates in his book that he was keen to work more closely with Egyptologists to see if his ten-minute tape – in which Jenny may well be talking in a language that has not been spoken for more than two thousand years – could shed further light on this great enigma. Although, as we will see as we progress through the book, there are a number of more general regression cases from other researchers that date to a similar age or even earlier, one can only wonder how many more lost wonders concerning our earliest periods of history might be uncovered if some regressors were to concentrate specifically on taking subjects back to these early epochs.

To conclude this section on regression subjects who are able to speak and write unlearned languages, Canadian psychiatrist Joel Whitton – who we will meet properly later in this chapter – has documented another intriguing case. His subject Harold Jaworski regressed to the life of a Viking sailor called Thor, and at Whitton's request wrote down twenty-two words and phrases that, when examined by a specialist, were revealed to be primarily nautical terms in Old Norse – the precursor of modern Icelandic – with a smattering of words of Russian, Serbian and Slavic derivation. Perhaps even more impressive was Harold's regression to the life of a Zoroastrian priest in seventh-century Mesopotamia called Xando, under which guise Whitton asked him to write down his version of a number of common words such as 'brother', 'house', 'clothing' and 'village'. A separate expert confirmed that the resulting spidery script was an authentic reproduction of the long-extinct language *Sassanid Pahlavi*, which was used in the area at that time and bears no relation to modern Iranian.

A common misconception is that past-life regressors are all poorly qualified amateurs who already believe in reincarnation, and will do anything they can to prove its validity, which completely compromises their objectivity. This may have some truth in respect of the now significantly expanded community, although considerable efforts are being made to regulate it and ensure professional standards of both training and practice are maintained. But when we look at the background of the pioneering regressors who discovered its *therapeutic* benefits, rather than concentrating on investigating reincarnation in general, we find that nothing could be further from the truth.

These pioneers all published the results of their work, and shared a number of common traits. Nearly all qualified as professional psychiatrists or psychologists, with as scientific a background as that training provides. Nearly all came to use past-life regression more or less by accident, or at least reluctantly, and were previously either Christian, agnostic or atheist. As a result, like Ramster nearly all were profoundly skeptical of the results of their regression therapy at the outset, but gradually became convinced as their work progressed and they could no longer escape the obvious conclusion: that, as a therapeutic tool, past-life regression was able to produce dramatic, rapid and permanent improvements in certain patients who had spent years in conventional therapy with no significant improvement whatsoever. Moreover, they tended to only add past-life therapy to their overall toolkit, so they continued to use more conventional therapies until in particular cases they felt past-life regression would be appropriate. They all also emphasize that their patients' existing religious beliefs, or lack of them, had no impact whatsoever on the success of their therapy. So, it is of course possible that some patients might have concocted past-life scenarios that would explain their symptoms, and might even have obtained a placebo cure as a result. But the general fact that past-life memories are clearly not based entirely on imagination, and that most patients had no prior belief in reincarnation and were usually only seeking general therapy, tends to suggest that this would have been a relatively rare occurrence.

Past-life regression had been attempted sporadically before Bernstein's experiments. As far back as the late nineteenth century, a Parisian military colonel by the name of Albert de Rochas had dabbled with a form of hypnosis based on the 'animal magnetism' techniques first developed by Austrian physician Franz Anton Mesmer in the late eighteenth century, and in regressing his subjects back before birth found that many recalled their death in their previous life. Needless to say he was roundly criticized by a western world to which reincarnation was largely anathema at the time, apart from in theosophical circles, and his work was dismissed as entirely explainable by his suggestive control of his subjects. But we can now see that the results recorded in his 1911 book *Les Vies Successives* are remarkably consistency with modern research.

Then in the mid-twentieth century the man who inspired Bernstein more than any other, British psychiatrist Alexander Cannon, regressed nearly fourteen hundred patients over a lengthy period. He consistently found that symptoms that could not be cured by conventional psychiatry were significantly reduced by past-life therapy, and in his 1950 book *The Power Within* he emphasized his change of stance over time:

> For years the theory of reincarnation was a nightmare to me and I did my best to disprove it and even argued with my trance subjects to the effect that they were talking nonsense, and yet as the years went by one subject after another told me the same story in spite of different and varied conscious beliefs, in effect until now, well over a thousand cases have been so investigated and I have to admit that there is such a thing as reincarnation. It is therefore only right and proper that I should include this study as a branch of psychology, as my text bears witness to the great benefit many have received psychologically from discovering hidden complexes and fears which undoubtedly have been brought over by the astral body from past lives.

Another British pioneer was Denys Kelsey, a medical doctor turned psychiatrist who had been using hypnosis to regress his patients into childhood since the late forties, but had no belief in reincarnation until 1958 when he teamed up with psychic Joan Grant – who had published a number of autobiographies of previous lives in ancient Egypt and elsewhere. Their way of working was unique in that Grant would sit in on Kelsey's hypnosis sessions, and pass him notes to confirm whether or not she too was 'seeing' what the patient was remembering about a past life. In this way they could direct the therapy even more accurately, as an example from their 1967 collaboration *Many Lifetimes* indicates. One patient, who had repeatedly undergone normal age-regression therapy with Kelsey to alleviate feelings of guilt and inferiority about his identification with being a woman, had found his symptoms only partially alleviated. After an intermission of several years he contacted Kelsey again, complaining of a severe recurrence of his problems. By this time Kelsey had teamed up with Grant, so past-life regression was now an option:

Within a few minutes he began to describe scenes in which an elegant young woman appeared, always with a handsome escort. But the scenes changed abruptly: swathed in white ermine she was alighting from a Daimler at the entrance to the Savoy, and then, without any thread of continuity, she was on the deck of a large yacht and then in the paddock at Ascot.

Joan handed me a note. 'This is a genuine recall. But he is not seeing the girl he really was: these are the girl's daydreams of the woman she longed to be. Tell him to see the girl herself.'

Grant subsequently explained that the reason she knew these images were fantasies, albeit real ones that the previous personality had repeatedly focused on, was because they were static descriptions and contained no action indicative of genuine experience. Intriguingly they had also come through in previous sessions but, because neither Kelsey nor his patient had any awareness of past lives at that time, they had been unable to make therapeutic use of them. But this time he went on to describe how his previous personality had fallen pregnant, had been rejected by her high-society lover leaving her dreams in tatters, and had died when a back-street abortion went wrong. Nevertheless, the patient was apparently cured in this single session, reporting no recurrence of his problems for many years after. In common with so many of his successors, it was repeated therapeutic success of this nature that convinced the scientifically trained Kelsey of the reality of reincarnation – on an intellectual and not just an intuitive level – even though he is at pains to point out that past-life regression is not a panacea, and that in many cases the root of a neurosis can be found in the current life.

Despite the success of these early pioneers, it was only really in the seventies that past-life regression came to receive widespread attention. Again in Britain, Joe Keeton became well-known for his lecturing and television appearances. From an early age he discovered he had a gift for hypnotizing people, although he did not take this too seriously for some time. But from the mid-fifties he used his gift to perform more than eight thousand regressions, seven of which were detailed in his 1979 book *Encounters With the Past*, co-authored with Peter Moss. Unusually for our pioneers Keeton was not a qualified psychologist or psychiatrist, nor did he use his gift for therapeutic purposes, but his integrity was proven by the fact that he consistently refused to charge for his services, relying instead on the income from his main job as a catering manager. One of his more intriguing cases arose in 1983 and involved a journalist from the *Evening Post* called Ray Bryant, who had regressed to a past life as a farm laborer in Essex at the turn of the twentieth century. In a subsequent session he was asked by Keeton to go back in time to 22 April 1884, at which point his previous personality would have been only four years old. When he did, he was terrified. He said the house was shaking, and the plates were falling off the shelf. What Bryant did not know was that Keeton had previously found a reference to the 'Great Essex Earthquake' that occurred on that day.

Another European pioneer of past-life regression is Hans TenDam, an eclectic Dutch psychology graduate whose primary occupation as a management consultant has not prevented him from gaining a solid reputation in the field. He has led the way in attempting to standardize training methods in Europe, and has also trained a number of practitioners in Brazil. His book *Exploring Reincarnation*, first published in Dutch in 1983, is one of the seminal works on reincarnation in general. He followed this up in 1996 with a practical guide to regression therapy, *Deep Healing*, which includes information from his own experience with patients.

Apart from Ramster, who was operating in relative isolation in Australia, most of the other practitioners who set the early pace were in America. Morris Netherton was raised as a Methodist with no belief or interest in reincarnation. But he trained as a counseling psychologist and by the late sixties decided to experiment with past-life regression after some interesting experiences with self-analysis. Over the next ten years he regressed many thousands of patients, although rather than using formal hypnosis he adapted Gestalt therapy – which had been developed previously by Fritz Perls, and relies on picking up on trigger phrases patients use repeatedly when describing their current problems. Although some lingering skepticism about reincarnation remained with him for some time, it had been completely dispelled by 1978 when his book *Past Lives Therapy* was published. Based on the concrete evidence of the success of his therapy at effecting lasting cures for his patients, he had this to say:

> Patients recreate scenes in past lives for the purpose of understanding certain problems they have in the present; it would be pointless to question the veracity of the material they are reporting. Past-lives therapy does not depend on the 'truth' of reincarnation, but on putting aside the question of 'truth' in order to work toward curing the patient's behavioral problem.
>
> Having made this point, I must state my own belief at once, which is that reincarnation does in fact take place. I have been influenced in this belief by neither occultism nor eastern religion, however. The belief has evolved by following my own observations to their logical conclusions. On the basis of the cases I have handled personally, and the independent research I have done, I feel that the theory of reincarnation *most logically* explains the phenomena I have witnessed....
>
> As far as my patients are concerned, the success of their therapy is

unaffected whether they embrace a belief in reincarnation or remain skeptical throughout.

Edith Fiore was brought up attending various branches of the Protestant church, but became an agnostic while gaining her doctorate in clinical psychology because it was more in keeping with her scientific bent. In her 1978 book *You Have Been Here Before* she describes how she had been in psychiatric practice for many years before she moved to California and started to use hypnotherapy in 1974, and it was another two years before she stumbled upon past-life regression. But when she did she quickly began to question her agnosticism:

> Until two years ago I was totally uninterested in the idea of reincarnation. Then one afternoon, while using hypnosis with a male patient, I witnessed something that radically affected both my professional life and my personal beliefs. He had come to me because of crippling sexual inhibitions. When I asked him, while he was under hypnosis, to go back to the origin of his problems, he said, 'Two or three lifetimes ago I was a Catholic priest.' We traced through this seventeenth-century lifetime, looking at his sexual attitudes as an Italian priest, and found the source of his sexual difficulties. I was aware that the patient believed in reincarnation. Therefore, I felt his vivid description of his past life, colored by a great deal of emotionality, was a fantasy. However, the next time I saw him, he told me he was not only free of his sexual problems, but felt better about himself in general.

When two similar cases arose shortly afterwards, Fiore decided she would use past-life regression routinely as part of her psychologists' toolkit, whenever a patient's own subconscious mind indicated that the origin of a problem was to be found in a previous life – while at the same time accepting that many patients' problems still stem primarily from experiences in this life. These were her early conclusions:

> Actually, whether the former lifetimes that are 'relived' are fantasies or actual experiences lived in a bygone era does not matter to me as a therapist – getting results is important. I have found past-life regression consistently helpful, often resulting in immediate remission of chronic symptoms that do not return, even after months and years.

As her practice progressed to the point where she had performed over twenty thousand past-life regressions, Fiore became increasingly convinced that some of her subjects, although by no means all, were possessed by earthbound spirits that were responsible for their symptoms and memories of past lives. This resulted in the publication in 1988 of her second book, *The Unquiet Dead*. We will return to this aspect of her work in chapter 9, but for now this is how her attitude to reincarnation had firmed up by then:

> Throughout the years, I have evolved from a disbelief of – but fascination with – the 'supernatural' to intellectually accepting the concepts of reincarnation and the continuation of personality. I am still not totally convinced of these at an emotional level and find myself at times questioning and pondering whether it is all fantasy. However, I must admit to myself that the therapy works! Why? Then I intellectually acknowledge the concepts as within the realm of reality again. And so it goes!

Helen Wambach qualified as a psychologist in the mid-fifties. She remembers the Bridey Murphy case being treated with disdain by her college professors, and she went along with that. She had been in practice for many years when a vivid *déjà vu* experience in 1966 piqued her interest, followed by several encounters with children who appeared to have spontaneous past-life recall. She became determined to research past lives in general, initially investigating individual patients' recall and examining the extent to which it could be verified from a historical perspective. But she gradually decided that such research would never prove anything conclusive about reincarnation one way or the other, and that a better direction would be to regress *groups* of volunteers in order to gain statistical data that might or might not suggest reincarnation as the best explanation for their past-life memories. So between 1974 and 1978, in a temporary departure from her therapeutic practice, she undertook a series of group regressions with some eleven hundred volunteers, not just from her base in California but from across the midwest of America.

Once Wambach had refined her methods she found that of the order of ninety per cent would experience some sort of recall, and that a further six per cent responded to individual hypnosis, especially when their psychological blockages were removed. She took three sessions with each group so that most recalled at least three past lives, offering them several options as to the periods they might want to regress into in each session, going as far back as 2000 BC. And her findings from such a large and controlled survey, as reported in her 1978 book *Reliving Past Lives*, were impressive.

Over the four millennia, almost half of her subjects' past lives were lived as a male and half as a female, exactly as we would biologically expect – and this held true even though her sample was considerably biased towards female volunteers. Between sixty and eighty per cent of past lives involved the lowest social class of the time, suggesting that imagination and ego were not significant factors – and nonmaterialists will be gratified to learn that the lower-class lives were universally reported as happier than the upper-class ones. Her subjects' descriptions of their race, geographical location, clothing, footwear, food and eating utensils in the different eras all conformed to historical patterns that certainly make logical sense, even if they were difficult for Wambach to verify with any great accuracy. As for their deaths in previous lives, consistently across the different eras more or less eighty per cent died naturally or accidentally, with the remaining twenty per cent of violent deaths only rising to thirty per cent for the start of the twentieth century – coincident with World War I. Again, it appeared that imagination of a violent and heroic death was not playing a significant role. And, as with the near-death experience, death was universally reported as a positive experience of peace and release.

Some specific cases in Wambach's survey lend further support to the idea that her subjects' past-life memories were not culled primarily from a combination of imagination and known historical data. On a number of occasions detailed investigation proved they had more accurate information than that provided by general history books, which was only subsequently confirmed by specialists. In fact I can add something to this aspect of her research, because one particular case involved a subject living in Mesopotamia in 1700 BC who referred to teaching the 'code of Hammurabi', which Wambach rejected because her further research apparently indicated this code was not developed until 1300 BC. But because I have some knowledge of this subject I can reveal that specialist sources available even at the time of her survey – as well as more modern ones – universally indicate that Hammurabi ruled Babylon, and developed his well-known law code, in the first half of the eighteenth century BC.

In common with all of our pioneers, Wambach also emphasizes that most subjects are fiercely determined to maintain the accuracy of their recall, which again indicates that suggestions of subjective control by the hypnotist are significantly overplayed by skeptics:

> Certainly, their responses are the result of the hypnotist's suggestions and they do respond immediately when you tell them to see something. But when I have misunderstood what my subjects have said, or my questioning is not clear, they will not change the image to suit my interpretation of what it is they are doing.... Subjects have a strong desire to tell the truth under hypnosis. They become very concerned about the truthfulness of their answers, and will cling stubbornly and literally to whatever it is they are experiencing.

British-born psychologist Brian Woolger had studied comparative religion as a postgraduate, but was no believer in reincarnation when he set up his psychotherapy practice in Vermont in 1976. So he was somewhat skeptical when, three years later, a colleague suggested he should experiment with a technique for self-regression into a past life – but he was professionally curious enough to try it. What he did not expect was to recall vividly and in detail the life of a mercenary involved in the brutal repression of the Cathars in southern France in the thirteenth century, who then changed sides and ended up being burned at the stake. Indeed there was a supreme irony to this, in that eight years earlier he had reviewed a book called *The Cathars and Reincarnation* by British psychiatrist Arthur Guirdham, in which he describes how a patient had recalled obscure and subsequently verified details of the life of a repressed Cathar – which eventually led to Guirdham believing he too was involved as her lover. At the time Woolger had dismissed this case as 'transference' between patient and therapist, but he now realized that his own experience was related – although markedly different – to Guirdham's. And because he had always had a fear of fire, a total distaste for orthodox religion and especially Christianity, strong pacifistic tendencies based on the deliberate repression of a violent streak, and regular dreams about torture and killing – none of which he had ever been able to properly explain, despite his own vocation – he knew his own experience could not be dismissed so lightly.

From that point on he began to experiment with past-life regression in his practice, and by the time he wrote his 1988 book *Other Lives, Other Selves* he had reached the following conclusion:

> From nearly a decade of taking clients and colleagues through past-life experiences and continuing my own personal explorations, I have come to regard this technique as one of the most concentrated and powerful tools available to psychotherapy short of psychedelic drugs.

One of the finest case studies of the power of past-life regression, and of how it can creep up on and convert a complete skeptic, is provided by Brian Weiss, who we met briefly in chapter 2. In his 1988 book *Many Lives, Many Masters* he describes his initial skepticism as the Head of Psychiatry at a university-affiliated hospital in Miami:

> Years of disciplined study had trained me to think as a scientist and physician, molding me along the narrow paths of conservatism in my profession. I distrusted anything that could not be proved by traditional scientific methods. I was aware of some of the studies in parapsychology that were being conducted at major universities across the country, but they

did not hold my attention. It all seemed too farfetched to me.

But he goes on to describe what happened when, in 1980, he started to treat a new patient called Catherine. Although an outwardly attractive woman of twenty-seven, she suffered from a mass of phobias – of water, of choking, of the dark and of death. She was an insomniac who often spent the night in a cupboard to feel safe, and when she did sleep fitfully she had terrible nightmares. She was deeply depressed, and suffering increasingly from acute anxiety and panic attacks.

Throughout eighteen months of weekly appointments Weiss tried everything he knew, but could make no real progress with Catherine. Finally he persuaded her to overcome her fear of hypnosis, and regressed her back into her childhood. At the age of five she recalled having been pushed into a swimming pool and having nearly drowned. At the age of three she recalled having been abused late at night by her drunken father. Weiss was confident he had finally cracked her case. But she returned a week later with her symptoms stubbornly intact. He wondered if he could have missed something from even earlier in her childhood, and took her back again. When nothing emerged at age two, somewhat in desperation he told her to go back to the time from which her symptoms arose. His scientific mind was not prepared for her to suddenly start describing a big white building with pillars and steps, and to tell him that the year was 1863 BC. As a girl in her mid-twenties called Aronda she had drowned, clutching her baby daughter, when a natural catastrophe engulfed her village in a tidal wave. Although still skeptical, when Catherine returned a week later looking far more radiant, and announced that she now had no fear of drowning and that her nightmares had lessened, he knew that he had to take her experience seriously.

Over the next few months Catherine regressed into a number of other past lives out of which various traumas emerged, each one seeming to work its magic on her current personality so that her initial phobias and anxieties were mere shadows of what they had been. But the real shock was still waiting for Weiss. It was not long before Catherine began to regularly enter the interlife *after* her various deaths in previous incarnations. And when she did, some seriously startling messages started to emerge – not least a personal one for Weiss that left him reeling:

Your father is here, and your son, who is a small child. Your father says you will know him because his name is Avrom, and your daughter is named after him. Also, his death was due to his heart. Your son's heart was also important, for it was backward, like a chicken's.

Weiss had always been careful to maintain a professional distance from his patients, and Catherine was no exception. He felt it was almost inconceivable that she could have known his young son Adam had died nine years earlier, when only twenty-three days old, because he had a one-in-ten-million defect whereby the pulmonary veins entered his heart on the wrong side. Nor did he think it likely she had learned from any normal source that his daughter Amy had been given the same Hebrew name as his father. This was Weiss's reaction:

> My life would never be the same again. A hand had reached down and irreversibly altered the course of my life. All of my reading, which had been done with careful scrutiny and skeptical detachment, fell into place. Catherine's memories and messages were true. My intuitions about the accuracy of her experiences had been correct. I had the facts. I had the proof.

It is possible to suggest that, for all his scientific training, Weiss became unduly influenced by and personally involved in this case after these initial disclosures. This becomes even more likely when we learn that, with some similarity to Guirdham's experience, many of Catherine's subsequent sessions revealed Weiss to have been a great teacher in a number of previous incarnations with her. And the messages from the 'Masters' as she called them were more for him than they were for her, and related to his personal calling to write this and other books. In fact many of these messages read very much like channeled material from external spiritual sources, but in fact it is clear that they do derive from hypnotic regression whereby Catherine was speaking on her own behalf – and we will return to this distinction in chapter 7. In any case, arguably Weiss's work does lay itself open to charges of egotism – or at least transference – from skeptics. However, as we will shortly find out, most research into the interlife does not involve only one case, or the passing on of messages for the regressors themselves so that they remain professionally detached and are not subjectively involved in their patients' experiences.

We have seen that, on closer inspection, past-life regression is perhaps not as unreliable as it might at first appear. There are some excellent general cases that stand up to close scrutiny in terms of obscure and subsequently verified details. And, although we must accept that source amnesia, imagination and subjective leading may sometimes play a part, it would once again be simplistic and reductionist to attempt to use these factors alone to explain every aspect of every one of the now tens of thousands of past-life regression cases on record.

As we did with childhood recall, we should briefly consider the possibility that these past-life memories are somehow passed down physically through the genes of the subjects' ancestors. Even more here we can see that this cannot be so, because too many hypnosis-induced past lives result in the subject dying childless – quite apart from the fact that most subjects have lives all over the world and as different racial types, some quite close together in time, rendering any ancestral link virtually inconceivable. Moreover, subjects rarely if ever demonstrate recall of their parents' or grandparents' lives, which is surely what we would expect if genetic memory were responsible. And, in any case, as an attempt at a materialist explanation genetics cannot account for memories of events after death or before birth.

If we turn to the paranormal explanations, we need to assess these against each of the three types of case I have described above: general, zenoglossy and therapeutic. The use of extrasensory perception to tap into a universal etheric memory could once more be put forward as a possible explanation for the general cases. But it cannot account for the cases of zenoglossy because foreign languages need to be *personally* learned and practiced, nor for the therapeutic cases because in the majority of these it is clear that the *personal* karmic links between a past life and the current one are what renders the therapy so successful. Tapping into the individual memories of the discarnate souls of the deceased might account for the general cases, and is potentially a more personalized explanation for the therapeutic cases, even if it does not hold for those involving zenoglossy – but because therapeutic cases tend to involve unusual psychological traits, such an explanation should probably be considered under the heading of possession by earthbound spirits anyway.

So, while possession is unlikely to account for the general or zenoglossy cases in which the subjects display no unusual behavioral traits, can it account for the therapeutic cases? It is clear that we must now distinguish between the past-life therapy conducted by the majority of professionals whose work we have just reviewed, and the spirit-releasement therapy in which a few of them such as Fiore have gone on to specialize. Although both have produced impressive evidence that they can be used to cure psychological and sometimes related physical problems that stubbornly refuse to respond to conventional medicine or psychotherapy, even the champions of spirit-releasement therapy do not suggest that it is a complete substitute for past-life therapy – they see it instead as an additional element in their toolkit. They might argue that possession is more commonplace than is normally recognized but, as we will see in chapter 9, possession cases have entirely different characteristics – and especially do not involve the elements of personalized karma that are clearly involved in past-life, and indeed interlife, therapy.

So, I would argue that reincarnation is still an overriding explanation for the vast majority of the huge number of documented cases of therapeutic past-life regression, and also for the smaller number of cases of zenoglossy. And if it is the best explanation for the bulk of these, simple logic suggests that it is likely to be the best explanation for the general cases as well – even if *some* of these might involve telepathic contact with either universal memory or the soul of some other deceased person.

Having reached this conclusion, we might also consider an important criticism of normal childhood-regression therapy in a somewhat different light – that of 'false memory syndrome', in which supposed memories cannot be correlated with any known facts of the patient's early life. We can now suggest that in some cases these memories may indeed be real but related to a previous life, a possibility that the therapists concerned may have failed to appreciate or even consider.

As the founder of modern psychoanalysis who, to his everlasting credit, concentrated heavily on unlocking the secrets of the unconscious mind, Sigmund Freud held that infant sexual impulses were the prime source of psychological problems in adulthood. But his one-time protégé Carl Gustav Jung was ultimately to prove far more open to nonmaterialist ideas, and was arguably the founder of what is now referred to as the 'transpersonal psychology' movement, which attempts to bring together modern western psychology with traditional eastern spiritual wisdom. He coined the term 'collective unconscious' to describe what he regarded as a repository of archetypal images built up over thousands of years of human history that recurred frequently in his subjects' dreams, and which he claimed could be analyzed to ascertain their state of mental health. There are, of course, certain similarities between this and the idea of universal memory to which I have previously referred.

But an insight into Freud's own state of mind can be gained from Jung's memoirs, in which he claims that Freud urged him to 'make a dogma... an unshakable bulwark' of his own theories of infant sexuality 'against the black tide of mud – of occultism'. In fact Freud had experimented with using hypnosis to regress his patients into childhood early in his career, but dismissed the results when details could not be corroborated. Perhaps he might have continued along this path if only he had allowed for the possibility that his patients' memories might have come from past lives instead. And it is surely highly regrettable that his profound influence ensured that the majority of his professional colleagues would continue for so long in a vacuum that would largely ignore the possibility of past-life traumas being able to exercise a significant influence on a patient's current psychological state.

All of that having been said, this book's primary aim is not to prove the phenomenon of reincarnation per se, or the value of past-life regression as a therapeutic tool. So at last we can now get to the hub of what I regard as the pioneering regressors' most crucial breakthrough – into the interlife experience. I indicated in the opening chapter that I discovered Michael Newton's work some time ago, and that I have since found that a number of other professionals have engaged in this type of research, many of them in fact before he did. I also indicated that it is the consistency of their subjects' reports of the interlife experience that had such a profound effect on me, and led me to write this book. Crucially, this consistency would count for little if it derived from them all taking their lead from each other, and then leading their subjects on. Or if their work had been so widely publicized that there was a likelihood their subjects' conscious exposure to it had subjectively preconditioned their experience. But, as we will now see, close scrutiny of the background to their research reveals that neither of these possibilities is likely to have played a major part.

Of those practitioners I have already mentioned, as early as 1976 Fiore found that a number of her patients could progress on from their death in a previous life into the interlife, about which they apparently provided incredible descriptions, although unfortunately she provides only sparse details of these in her existing books. At about the same time Wambach, spurred on by her initial past-life research results, was concentrating specifically on pre-birth questions with 750 of her volunteers, publishing her results in 1979 in her second book *Life Before Life*. In the late seventies Ramster too made some interesting discoveries about what happens after death, while I have already referred to Weiss's discoveries through his patient Catherine in the early eighties.

There are also a number of pioneers I have not mentioned so far, either because they specialized in the interlife or because their discoveries came somewhat later. Joel Whitton, who we met briefly earlier in the chapter, is something of an exception among them in that he had dabbled with hypnosis from an early age, and openly admits that reincarnation had always been part of his worldview, although he allied himself to no particular religious sect or creed. So by the time he was a leading psychiatrist at the University of Toronto it was natural that he would use past-life regression therapy in his practice, which he did from the early seventies, and with such success that he became known locally as the 'Lost Cause Doctor'. But Whitton stumbled upon the interlife entirely by accident. The Toronto Society for Psychical Research had agreed to his proposal to conduct a scientifically controlled, long-term study of past-life regression, and after interviewing over fifty candidates he chose Paula Considine – a temperamentally stable and unexceptional forty-two-year-old housewife, who was deeply hypnotizable and had no particular feelings about reincarnation one way or another. In their weekly sessions she regressed into a number of different lives in different eras when, as his co-author Joe Fisher reports in their 1986 collaboration *Life Between Life*, events took a most unexpected twist:

Paula's inventory of lives had been traced back to an existence of a slave girl in ancient Egypt when, unpredictably, her hypnotic traveling suddenly changed course. One Tuesday evening in April 1974, as she was talking in a deep trance about Martha Paine's life on the farm [an incarnation in the early nineteenth century], Dr Whitton remembered there were further details he wished to learn about the last days of Margaret Campbell [the previous incarnation in the early eighteenth century]. First he interrupted his garrulous subject. Then he told her:

'Go to the life before you were Martha.'

Expecting Martha's childlike voice to be exchanged for that of the elderly Canadian housekeeper, Dr Whitton waited several minutes for the familiar French-accented enunciation. But no sound, save the occasional sigh, came from Paula's mouth. Her lips moved only with a constantly shifting facial expression which indicated she was watching events unfold. But what events were these? Not knowing where she was in time, Dr Whitton was wondering where he had erred when Paula interrupted his bewilderment with a rapid flickering of her eyelids. Her lips, too, puckered repeatedly as if she were searching for words and not finding them. Then, slowly and with great difficulty, she announced in a dreamy monotone:

'I'm in the sky. I can see a farmhouse and a barn. It's early... early morning. The sun... is low and making, making... making long shadows across the burnt fields... stubby fields.'

Dr Whitton could barely believe what he was hearing. Paula wasn't supposed to be 'in the sky'. So he must have made a technical error; but which one? Hypnotic subjects have much in common with computer programs in that their wondrous responses rest upon the most literal commands. They must be told exactly what to do. Make one mistake and the show won't go on – at least not the show anticipated by the hypnotist. Dr Whitton had told Paula, 'Go to the life before you were Martha.' Normally, he would have commanded, 'Go to the incarnation before you were Martha.' Clearly there was a difference between the two.

'What are you doing up in the air?' asked the puzzled hypnotist.

'I'm… waiting… to… be… born. I'm watching… watching what my mother does.'

'Where is your mother?'

'She's… out at the pump and she's having great difficulty… difficulty filling the bucket.'

'Why is she having great difficulty?'

'Because my body is weighing her down… I want… I want to tell her to take care. For her sake and for mine.'

'What is your name?'

'I… have… no… name.'

This is well worth recounting in detail, because it is typical of the way in which several other pioneering hypnotherapists' imprecise commands have led to their discovery of the interlife, as we will shortly see. As for Whitton, with commendable professionalism he restricted the remainder of his study with Paula to her past lives alone, and objectively concluded in his report: 'There is no reason as yet to suspect that hypnosis will successfully carry the burden of proof of reincarnation.' However, once that was completed his curiosity had been so aroused that he decided to specifically devote a proportion of his practice to interlife research, and over the next decade he repeatedly regressed more than thirty new subjects into that realm.

Dolores Cannon is also something of an exception in that she is the only pioneering interlife researcher who does not have a professional background in psychology or psychiatry, but she did qualify as a hypnotherapist and set up her practice in Arkansas in 1979. It is also the case that she did have an interest and belief in reincarnation at this point, and that rather than work as a therapist she was specifically motivated to undertake general research into her subjects' past lives. In addition she claims to have a fair degree of personal psychic ability. But I do not believe any of this should automatically disqualify her work from being taken into account in this study – in particular because, as she relates in her 1993 book *Between Death and Life*, she too appears to have stumbled upon the interlife by pure accident:

I can still remember the first time I stumbled through the door and spoke to the 'dead'. It was during a past-life regression and when the subject 'died' on me – it happened so quickly and spontaneously that I was taken off guard. I was not fully aware of what had happened. I don't know what I expected would occur if someone were to go through a death experience. But as I said, it happened so quickly there was no time to stop it. The person was looking down at their body and saying they looked just like any other corpse.…

When I overcame my shock and wonder of being able to speak with someone after they had died, my curiosity took over and I was filled with questions I had always wondered about. From that time forward, each time I found a subject who could go into the deeper states of hypnosis required for this type of research, I made a practice of asking some of the same questions. Religious beliefs seem to have no influence on what they reported. Their answers were basically identical each time. Although worded differently, they were all saying the same thing – a phenomenon in itself.

We can see from this that Cannon was deliberately asking her more receptive subjects some highly philosophical questions, and for that reason her work has some similarities to Weiss's in that some of her session transcripts that fill the book almost read like channeled material. Her own commentary is minimal, mainly coming through in her questions to her subjects, and in most cases she does not mention their names or circumstances, so it is impossible to know how many different subjects she used in writing this book. But, despite these additional differences from most of our other interlife pioneers, it is clear that her material does come from multiple regression sources rather than any sort of channeling.

Shakuntala Modi is a qualified psychiatrist with a practice in West Virginia. She quickly realized that hypnotherapy paid great dividends where other treatments failed, so for many years she regressed her patients into childhood, but knew nothing about past lives. Like so many others before her, she was completely taken aback when one day in 1986 she instructed a patient suffering from claustrophobia and crippling panic attacks to go back to the time when these problems arose – and the patient reported that she was a young girl who had been buried alive. As usual, she was even more stunned when she found that the patient was almost immediately cured, a speed of remission that Modi had never before even come close to achieving. Like Fiore before her, she would go on to concentrate heavily on the phenomenon of spirit possession as a potential source of the ailments of many of her patients, as we will see in chapter 9. But in her 1997 book *Remarkable Healings*, although she does not talk about stumbling upon it in a similar way, she makes it clear that in the intervening decade she had also taken hundreds of her patients through the death experience and into the interlife proper.

And so we finally come back to Newton. He gained a doctorate in counseling psychology and became a master hypnotherapist, setting up in practice in Los Angeles in the early eighties. Although he regularly regressed patients into their childhoods, for a long time he resisted the use of past-life therapy – regarding it as 'unorthodox and non-clinical'. This is how he takes up the story in his 1994 book *Journey of Souls*:

> My interest in reincarnation and metaphysics was only intellectual curiosity until I worked with a young man on pain management. This client complained of a lifetime of chronic pain on his right side. One of the tools of hypnotherapy to manage pain is directing the subject to make the pain worse so he or she can also learn to lessen the aching and thus acquire control. In one of our sessions involving pain intensification, this man used the imagery of being stabbed to recreate his torment. Searching for the origins of this image, I eventually uncovered his former life as a World War I soldier who was killed by a bayonet in France, and we were able to eliminate the pain altogether.
>
> With encouragement from my clients, I began to experiment with moving some of them further back in time before their last birth on earth.... I came to appreciate just how therapeutically important the link is between the bodies and events of our former lives and who we are today.

But it was not long before Newton, too, chanced upon the interlife as well:

> Then I stumbled on to a discovery of enormous proportions. I found it was possible to see into the spirit world through the mind's eye of a hypnotized subject who could report back to me of life *between* lives on earth.
>
> The case that opened the door to the spirit world for me was a middle-aged woman who was an especially receptive hypnosis subject. She had been talking to me about her feelings of loneliness and isolation in that delicate stage when a subject has finished recalling their most recent past life. This unusual individual slipped into the highest state of altered consciousness almost by herself. Without realizing I had initiated an overly short command for this action, I suggested she go to the source of her loss of companionship. At the same moment I inadvertently used one of the trigger words to spiritual recall. I also asked if she had a specific *group* of friends whom she missed.
>
> Suddenly, my client started to cry. When I directed her to tell me what was wrong, she blurted out, 'I miss some friends in my group and that's why I get so lonely on earth.' I was confused and questioned her further about where this group of friends was actually located. 'Here, in my permanent home,' she answered simply, 'and I'm looking at all of them right now!'

From this point on Newton realized he wanted to find out as much as he could about the interlife, and he worked with many of his patients for over a decade to elicit some of the finest material we have available at present. He presented more of his interlife research in 2000 in his second book, *Destiny of Souls*.

Crucially, virtually none of these interlife pioneers explicitly mention any prior knowledge of the others' work. We have seen that they all seemed to stumble upon the interlife by accident, much as most of them did with past lives in general. Bear in mind that much of this pioneering work was performed before widespread use of the internet revolutionized the communication in any line of research. And even if we allow for the possibility that later researchers like Cannon, Modi and Newton might have come across some of the earlier studies during the course of their own work, but simply do not mention this fact in their books, they all still seem to have developed their own distinct methodologies and approaches quite separately. In particular there are potential psychological dangers inherent in regressing subjects into the interlife that are even greater than those in ordinary past-life therapy, and these professionals have all developed their own key phrases, trigger words, protection instructions and other techniques needed to elicit the memories but at the same time keep their subjects safe and well.

There are two exceptions in respect of prior knowledge. First, Weiss admits that in the early stages of Catherine's treatment he avidly read up on other general past-life research, and specifically mentions the work of Fiore and Wambach, but his subsequent exposure to the interlife still appears to have come as a complete surprise. Second, Modi specifically mentions consulting the work of Wambach and Whitton among others after she had stumbled across past lives in general and, because she provides no details of how she came across the interlife, it is arguable that her material in this specific area might be considered less objective. I should also point out that both Weiss and Modi mention Stevenson's non-interlife-related work, and that both Wambach and Whitton admit to studying Raymond Moody's contemporary and highly publicized work on near-death experiences – but this latter is only the tip of the iceberg in terms of the interlife experience, so it does little to compromise the independence of their early research. Meanwhile Ramster also mentions Stevenson's work, and alludes to near-death experiences in general, but that is all.

Equally crucially, how much general public exposure has this interlife research received? If we start with the most recent and work backwards, certainly Cannon's and Newton's books have sold extremely well, with Modi's perhaps somewhat behind, but none of them is exactly a household name. And even if their recent work has had some widespread cultural influence, it does not discount the experiences of their own subjects that arose before their work was published more or less simultaneously in the mid-nineties. As for the research that went before, although Weiss's book sold well when it was published in the late eighties, it was based on a single case that is not exactly fully representative of the interlife experience anyway. Whitton's work, published in the mid-eighties, was far more representative but did not gain widespread public exposure, the same being true of Wambach's work from the late seventies. Meanwhile, as we have already seen Fiore published few details of her interlife research in any of her books, and Ramster's work has always remained little known outside of Australia.

In addition, these researchers invariably highlight the fact that their subjects come from highly varied educational and religious backgrounds, and that many had an initial attitude of total skepticism towards reincarnation. This is apparently true even of those practitioners that we might expect to have attracted subjects who were more inclined to a belief in reincarnation such as, for example, Whitton and Newton – who both appear to have gained some at least local renown for their specialism in past-life and even interlife regression. The only exception to this is probably Wambach's group volunteers. Nevertheless, as far as interlife research in particular is concerned, it is highly improbable that anything more than a tiny handful of all of these researchers' subjects had any significant prior knowledge of the subject that could have conditioned their own experiences.

Of course, skeptics might still argue that subjective leading by each individual practitioner with their own subjects is likely to be far more prevalent in interlife than in general past-life research, precisely because of the potential consistency of the experience. This is to some extent a valid argument, and we will see from the transcripts that subjects are often deliberately pushed to answer specific important questions, because only in this way can the researchers attempt to evaluate the consistency of their answers. But we will also see that the possibility of this being a significant factor is once again proved remote by the regularity with which they correct, scold or even laugh at their interrogators for their lack of knowledge or perception. Indeed, if interlife regressions relied upon subjective leading alone we would never have known anything about it – because, as we have seen, the interlife experience was only independently discovered by our pioneers precisely because their early subjects took them somewhere they were not expecting to go, and about which they knew nothing. We also have the undoubted and universally reported fact that, in the main, subjects under hypnosis simply cannot be *told* to experience something – they have to feel it is real for themselves. As for subjects being prompted and then using their imagination, they could only do this if they had existing knowledge to work with – and I have already proved that very few of them are likely to have had any exposure to even scant details of the interlife experiences of other subjects, let alone the fuller details that would be required for them to come up with similarly detailed descriptions themselves.

How many subjects were involved in this research, and what proportion of the population can access the interlife? If we look at the researchers that were deliberately concentrating on the interlife, at least for a period of time and in one aspect of their practice, Wambach's statistical sample of 750 subjects who could access and then recall their pre-birth experiences represented only about forty per cent of her total volunteers. But we should remember that hers was a unique group situation in which she was deliberately attempting to take everyone to the deepest state of hypnosis in which they *should* still have had conscious recall, which would be required for them to then record their experiences; and it would appear that this blanket level of deep hypnosis was probably just too deep for quite a few of her subjects to have any conscious recall. Whitton conducted a number of sessions over several years with each of the thirty-plus subjects with whom he decided to concentrate on the interlife, but these represented only a small proportion of his therapeutic practice. Cannon reports that she took hundreds of subjects through the death experience and into the interlife. And although Newton selected only twenty-nine subjects as the case studies for his first book, and sixty-seven for his second, he reports that these came from a much larger total that had had similar experiences. None of these last three appears to suggest they had any great difficulty in regressing many of their subjects into the interlife in individual sessions, although all four report that a deeper state of hypnosis is required for this than for general past-life regression, and that not all subjects can achieve it. Whitton refers to accessing the *metaconscious*, and Wambach and Newton the *superconscious*, state.

As for those researchers who were not expressly concentrating on the interlife, Fiore is somewhat vague but seems to suggest that, of over one thousand subjects she took through the death experience in a previous life, most were able to achieve some sort of interlife recall. Modi and Ramster are similarly vague, but again the suggestion appears to be that both treated hundreds of subjects and that most had a common interlife experience. Weiss is the only real exception, finding that only one out of a further twelve subjects that he regressed into past lives before 1988 could access the interlife.

I should also point out that pioneers such as Netherton and Woolger regularly refer to their patients having a 'blank' interlife experience, and we will establish the reasons for this in later chapters. But for now it is worth emphasizing that any regressor who is not familiar with the possibility of two entirely different types of interlife experience might confuse someone who is having a blank experience with someone who is not able to have them at all, and vice versa, when clearly there is a difference between the two.

With that, let us finally turn to what our pioneers' subjects have to say about the interlife. Wherever possible I will quote directly from the transcripts of the hypnosis sessions, as do many of the pioneers in their own work, because only this can provide a proper flavor – not only of the independence of thought of the subjects and the extent to which they are not led on, but also of their animation, and of the extraordinary knowledge and insight they seem to possess when regressed into the interlife.

5

PAST-LIFE REVIEWS
Are We Judged?

A man arrives at the Pearly Gates, waiting to be admitted. St Peter is reading through the Big Book to see if his name is written in it. After several minutes, St Peter closes the book, furrows his brow, and says, 'I'm sorry, but I don't see your name written in the Book.'

'How current is your copy?' the man asks.

'I get a download every ten minutes,' St Peter replies. 'Why do you ask?'

'I'm embarrassed to admit it, but I was always the stubborn type. It was not until my death was imminent that I cried out to God, so my name probably hasn't arrived on your copy yet.'

'I'm glad to hear that,' says St Peter, 'but while we're waiting for the update to come through, can you tell me about a really good deed that you did in your life?'

The man thinks for a moment and says, 'Hmmm, well there was this one time when I was driving down a road and I saw a group of bikers harassing this poor girl. Infuriated, I got out of my car, grabbed a tire lever out of the boot, and walked up to the leader of the gang. He was a huge guy; six-foot-four, 260 pounds, with a studded leather jacket and a chain running from his nose to his ears. As I walked up to him, the other bikers formed a circle around me and told me to get lost or I'd be next. So I ripped the leader's chain out of his face and smashed him over the head with the tire lever. Then I turned around and yelled to the rest of them, "Leave this poor innocent girl alone! You're all a bunch of sick, deranged animals! Go home before I really teach you a lesson in pain!"'

'Wow!' says St Peter, duly impressed. 'When did this happen?'

'About three minutes ago.'

We are all familiar with the Christian idea that our actions in earthly life are judged after death, so much so that jokes about St Peter and the Pearly Gates of heaven abound. But this idea has a lengthy provenance that we can trace right back to the supposed birth of civilization in Mesopotamia – or modern-day Iraq – in the latter half of the fifth millennium BC. A Sumerian elegy entitled *On the Death of Nannaya* describes how:

Utu, the great lord of the netherworld, after turning the dark places to light, will judge your case. May Nanna decree your fate on the day of sleep.

The ancient Egyptians were more explicit and believed that after death, as well as undergoing many trials and tribulations, they would come to the 'Judgment Hall of Osiris' in which they would be subjected to the 'weighing of the heart' ceremony. This is how one expert commentary on what are loosely called the various Egyptian *Books of the Dead* describes it:

In the ordinary judgment scenes we find that the heart of the deceased is weighed in the balance against the feather symbolic of Ma'at or righteousness, that the operation of weighing is carried out by Thoth and Anubis in the presence of the great gods, the owner of the heart himself sometimes looking on, that the gods accept and ratify the verdict of Thoth, and that the deceased is then led into the presence of Osiris by Horus. Sometimes the heart of the deceased is weighed against his whole body... and at other times the pans of the scales only contain weights.... [In an alternative scene] the object in the pan is being weighed against the symbol of 'evil', which it seems to counterbalance exactly. This being so, it seems that the wickedness of the deceased did not go beyond a recognized limit.

In fact, although there is much confusion and speculation about this issue from uninformed sources, neither the ancient Egyptians, or for that matter their Mesopotamian counterparts, believed in reincarnation. Indeed, contrary to popular belief, the former's conceptions of the afterlife appear to be, at least on the face of it, somewhat philosophically primitive. After all, not only did they have a questionable preoccupation with the need to preserve the physical body by mummification, and hold the somewhat elitist view that only those who could afford to have a version of the *Book of the Dead* inscribed in their tomb could achieve eternal life, but they even devised all sorts of prosaic tricks in their attempts to hide their crimes from Osiris. Nevertheless, these ideas on judgment after death passed on first into Zoroastrian and then into Judaic belief systems, which also contain the idea of 'the balance in which every man's actions will be weighed on the day of judgment'.

So is this age-old idea that our lives are formally examined by various divine judges after death, thus determining our fate in the afterlife, borne out by modern research?

When we consider the full scope of the interlife experience proper there are many different stages and associated activities, of which the past-life review and next-life planning elements with which we are primarily concerned in this chapter and the next form only two. In order to attempt to present a coherent description of these various stages I intend to use Michael Newton's highly detailed *Journey of Souls* as my primary source, with some additional information from *Destiny of Souls*, and then we can compare his findings with those of other researchers. When I later refer to them corroborating his research, I am not ignoring the fact that many of them made their discoveries before he did – I merely use his work as a starting point because it is the most detailed. We should also note that the level of karmic advancement of souls, and their state of mind, can have a significant impact on the nature of the interlife experience. So we must bear in mind their individuality, while at the same time trying to establish some common patterns.

Without exception, all interlife researchers indicate that the death experience itself is normally entirely consistent with that commonly described in near-death experiences, with subjects universally reporting a sense of hovering over the physical body, and a feeling of great freedom and release. Many souls also try to comfort the loved ones they have left behind, and to let them know they are not really 'dead'. But Newton's subjects indicate this is a difficult task that requires much practice, made harder because the grief of friends and family tends to block their ability to receive telepathic contact from the deceased. There is also a suggestion that if grief is excessive it can prevent, or at least hinder, the deceased soul's proper transition into the ethereal realms. So we on earth might benefit all parties by being less concerned with our own grief at the death of someone close to us and, in opening ourselves up to communication from beyond the grave, gain solace that our loved ones are still thinking of us while in a far better place – indeed that we will almost certainly meet them again in happier circumstances in our proper spiritual home.

Most departed souls feel a 'pulling sensation' guiding them towards the ubiquitous tunnel, which they accede to sooner or later. Generally speaking more advanced souls seem to have little desire to hang around in the 'astral plane' of the physical world, and they enter the tunnel with a sense of relief that they are returning to what they instantly recognize as their 'proper home'. By contrast less advanced souls, especially those that have suffered a sudden or traumatic death, may be a little disorientated at first and require some assistance from their spirit guide.

Once souls enter the tunnel they all perceive the bright light at the end into which they emerge without apparent delay. As we saw with the near-death experience, Newton's subjects vary in their descriptions of the ethereal realms they then encounter, but in general they confirm that less advanced souls are more likely to perceive them in familiar physical terms – perhaps seeing great crystalline castles, or rivers and meadows and rainbows – because this makes them feel more at home and relaxed. The same is true of their perceptions of the other souls that come to greet them, with less advanced souls recognizing a familiar human-type form, either from the waist up or perhaps just as a face, again to make them feel more at home and render the transition less traumatic. Indeed, one of the refreshingly comical aspects of Newton's subjects' reports – which only adds to their likely reliability – is that some less advanced souls apparently show a high degree of vanity in choosing what physical form to project themselves, even to the extent of choosing one they have never actually had on earth, without realizing that other souls can see through their disguise immediately and are laughing at them in a good-natured way.

Nevertheless, even less advanced souls seem to appreciate that all souls in the ethereal realms are really just 'balls of intense energy', and they have an immediate appreciation of the other incarnations they have shared as friends and family of the soul mates that come to meet them. When pressed on what she meant when she said she was 'hugging' one of her closest soul mates, one subject described it as 'two masses of bright light whirling around each other'. Newton's subjects also confirm the suggestion from near-death experiences that communication in the ethereal realms is by telepathy, although especially private communications are effected by 'touch which passes between the two souls as electrical sound impulses'.

Even those less advanced souls who have managed to make the transition through the tunnel and into the ethereal realms by themselves tend to require more time to orientate themselves once there, so again, especially for those who are somewhat traumatized, their spirit guide will be the first to greet them to lessen their confusion or bear the brunt of their frustration; and even when they are not the first point of contact, they are usually around keeping an eye on things. On the other hand more advanced souls may be met by no one straight away, and may even bypass most of the early transition stages. One such subject who was keen to reach his appointed home in the ethereal realms described his mode of travel as like being on a 'homing beacon of sound and light' that was part of his own unique 'tonal pattern or frequency'. This fits in entirely with the idea that harmonics and energy vibrations lie at the core of all realms and, in common with many near-death experiences, even less advanced souls describe hearing 'musical vibrations' straight after death that become more harmonious as they enter the light.

Many of Newton's subjects also report that at some point early on in their interlife experience they are taken to a place where they receive a 'healing shower of energy', which washes away all the negative emotional influences of physical incarnation as a human, allowing them to 'become whole again'. The implication seems to be that this process allows souls to clear excessive emotional blockages, even if memories of the causes must remain intact – at least in the ethereal realms – for karmic learning and advancement to work effectively. It appears that more advanced souls make better use of this cleansing energy, while the less advanced are less adept at using it to clear their negative karmic debris, and so tend to carry more of it forward. In fact, as we will see in chapter 7, the effectiveness of this and other interlife processes designed to clear intense emotions can have a huge impact on future incarnations.

Newton's subjects report that there are three types of soul who do not conform to these standard transitional patterns. The first are what we might term 'ghosts', who are usually immature souls that have suffered a sudden and sometimes traumatic death. They are so focused on unfinished business in the earthly realm, or so aggrieved by what they perceive as a great injustice, that they simply refuse to go with their spirit guide – or may not even be able to perceive them because of their failure to adjust themselves to the higher vibrations of the ethereal plane. Some may not even realize, or at least accept, that they are dead, while others know they have passed on but are expecting to return to a physical body straight away. They continue to hang around earth's astral plane, tending to remain attracted to the geographical location of their home or death, and because of their confusion and frustration they can make a nuisance of themselves to incarnate humans. However, Newton's subjects report that these cases are relatively rare, and that above all such souls are not in any sense evil or demonic, so that sooner or later they will normally go into the light with their spirit guide – even if sometimes only after assistance from a professional psychic, with whom they may be more in touch than ethereal entities.

In this context, we have seen that some researchers suggest that some souls are so immature or disoriented that, in their haste to return to incarnation, they do not go through the normal interlife processes at all. This might involve a blank interlife experience in the ethereal realms proper, or they might never even make the transition and remain in the astral plane only, perhaps even for an extremely short time before effectively jumping straight into another fetus. It seems this latter scenario may be true of at least some of Ian Stevenson's child cases. By contrast, some researchers believe that earthbound spirits may try to take possession of other incarnate humans. We will return to these possibilities in chapters 7 and 9.

The second exceptional type of soul is one that is not damaged per se, but is sufficiently tired or traumatized by earthly life that it needs a period of rest and seclusion before joining in with normal interlife activities. For less advanced souls this will be arranged and supervised by their spirit guide, while more advanced souls seclude themselves voluntarily for as long as they feel is appropriate to restore their energy. This requirement for an initial period of rest or seclusion before rejoining the normal interlife flow is not to be confused with the general rest and recreational activities enjoyed by all souls during the interlife, which we will consider shortly, nor with the blank type of interlife experience.

The final type of exceptional soul is one that has repeatedly committed serious crimes against others in various incarnate lives, with deliberately malicious intent and little apparent remorse. These are immediately taken to a secluded part of the ethereal realms where they undergo a process of isolation and rehabilitation. Newton's subjects also report that no matter how much an individual soul may repeat the same mistakes, it is never annihilated because its energy cannot be destroyed, even though it may ultimately be 'remodeled' by an infusion of new and pure soul energy. Again, a few of our pioneers take a different view on demonic forces, which we will consider in chapter 9. But certainly Newton's conclusion is that there is no such thing as an inherently evil soul, and nor is there a hell into which such souls are cast for eternity – even if they may *project* their own mental torments onto their surroundings while in seclusion.

Although we should remember that time is not necessarily perceived as sequential in the ethereal realms, a number of Newton's subjects report that at some point not long after death they participate in an 'orientation' with their spirit guide. This appears to be part of the process designed to ease the transition into the ethereal realms for less advanced and especially traumatized souls, and as such it not only allows them to be comforted and reoriented, but it may also include a relatively informal review of the life just completed. And this is where we first find that modern research departs significantly from the judgmental ethos of so many formal religions. Because this process is universally described as nonjudgmental, and the review is an instantaneous, panoramic one that is largely conducted by the discarnate soul itself. The guide is in no sense strict or unkind, acting more as a benevolent counselor, but at the same time everything is laid bare, there are no secrets, and any harshness appears to come from the subject being forced to analyze both the good and bad aspects of the life they have just led – including especially any important things they did not achieve but had intended to.

So, while for the most part any such initial review appears to be fairly good-natured, and the subject is then able to move on to other stages without undue worry, their guide is persistent in pushing them to take responsibility for, and fully understand, their actions. Moreover, some subjects undoubtedly feel apprehension. One in particular, who had committed suicide in her life just completed, already realized as she approached her initial orientation that she had 'blown it' and would have to reincarnate to do it all over again, wasting a lot of time.

Whether or not they participate in this initial orientation, most subjects report being transferred to a 'staging area' that might be thought of as the hub of a huge travel station, in which many incoming souls are in transit to their proper home in the ethereal realms. When they leave this area they travel along corridors that bulge in places with other 'soul groups' who belong and work together, while they are themselves in transit to their own soul group. These groups, which Newton refers to as 'primary', usually contain between three and twenty-five souls, with the numbers increasing with the degree of advancement. All members of the group are the most intimate soul mates, and will have known each other from the start of their existence and lived together in various different relationships to each other over the course of many incarnations. So subjects realize they are now 'going home', and in looking forward to the rapture of seeing those really closest to them again describe themselves as 'like salmon swimming upstream to the place of their birth to spawn'. Of course, if we transfer this to an earthly setting, it is the idea of close soul mates from our primary group – or perhaps from a 'secondary' pool of other affiliated groups with whom souls have less regular contact in the ethereal realms – that explains the immediate chemistry all of us sometimes experience on meeting someone new for the first time.

On arrival, less advanced souls again report seeing their home in familiar earthly terms, as a favored house, school or temple from a particular incarnation. Here souls are formally greeted by the other members of their group, especially if they were not present during the initial transition, and interestingly even those members still in incarnation on earth are present in a more dormant way, appearing as lower-energy light emissions. This indicates that all souls leave a portion of their energy make-up back in the ethereal realms at all times, and the idea that souls can 'split' to some extent is reinforced when we find that they can lead two, and in rare cases three, concurrent lives on earth. Subjects report that this is not easy or normal, but it is a method chosen sometimes to speed up karmic development. More advanced souls even report that the word *split* is misleading, because each part 'remains whole'. This of course means that at some point early in the interlife experience all souls must go through the process of reintegrating with the energy they left behind. Again we will return to these issues in chapter 9.

Not long after their arrival home, all of Newton's subjects report that they participate in a formal life review with a 'council of elders', who tend to be more spiritually advanced than spirit guides and may no longer be incarnating on earth. The number of elders varies between three and seven for most souls, but sometimes as many as twelve are present for the more advanced. The composition of this review council is different for each soul, even for those in the same soul group, and appears to relate very specifically to the needs of each individual soul. It can even change for any given soul from one interlife experience to the next. Here is how one subject describes her review:

> After I meet with my friends, my [younger] guide Veronica takes me to another place to meet with my panel of elders. She is at my side as an interpreter for what I don't understand and to provide support for my explanations of my conduct in the last life. At times, she speaks on my behalf as a kind of defense advocate but Quazel [the subject's older guide who is already in attendance] carries the most weight with the panel. There are always the same six elders in front of me who wear long white robes. Their faces are kindly, and they evaluate my perceptions of the life I have just lived and how I could have done better with my talents and what I did that was beneficial. I am freely allowed to express my frustrations and desires. All the elders are familiar to me, especially two of them who address me more than the others and who look younger than the rest. I think I can distinguish appearances which are male or female. Each has a special aspect in the way they question me but they are honest and truthful, and I am always treated fairly. I can hide nothing from them, but sometimes I get lost when their thoughts are transmitted back and forth in the rapid communication between them. When it is more than I can handle, Veronica translates what they are saying about me, although I have the feeling she does not tell me everything. Before I return to earth, they will want to see me a second time.

It is the telepathy between all attendants at the council review that makes it so unlike a courtroom trial, because nothing can be fudged or hidden. But far from being judged by higher beings, the overriding impression Newton has obtained from his many subjects is that our own souls themselves are by far the most severe critics of our behavior in past lives. By contrast the elders show infinite patience, and care only about us gaining a proper perspective on our past actions to help us to learn from our mistakes. So, although this is a more in-depth process than any initial review during orientation, it is still far removed from the judgmental trial portrayed by most formalized religions. But even more than during an initial orientation, council reviews have a panoramic aspect that assesses progress and trends throughout all of our past lives, and the elders are also probing for information that will help them to assist us in choosing our next life when the time comes.

Another of Newton's subjects provides us with specific details of the analytical content of his review in this extract that I have deliberately condensed in places:

Give me an idea of how things proceed from here?
We start with what I did right. I had a successful company which employed many people in my past life. I'm turning this over in my mind. I want to make a good impression by telling them about my charity contributions – you know, my good acts. Then things drift into the way I ran my company... my inability to avoid conflicts – disagreements and anger with my employees. It's so frustrating... and I'm working on this....

I'm trying to anticipate their questions. I know I enjoyed accumulating material possessions in my life. They want me to tell them why and I say it made me feel valuable as a person, but I stepped on people. Then they bring up similar actions on my part from former lives... and if I feel I am doing better....

This is what I hear in my mind: 'Emmanuel, we are not here to judge you, punish you, or to override your thoughts. We want you to look at yourself through our eyes, if you can. That means to forgive yourself. This is the most challenging aspect of your time with us because it is our desire that you accept yourself for who you are with the same unconditional love we have for you. We are here to support you in your work on earth. Toward that end, we would remind you of the bus stop incident.'
The bus stop incident – what does that mean?
I was confused myself when he said it. I look back at Joaquin [the subject's guide] for assistance.
Explain what happens then Emmanuel.
The Wise One in the center... his thoughts come to me once more: 'You do not remember this incident? The woman who you helped one day while she was sitting at the bus stop?' I said, 'No, I don't.' Then, they wait for my memories to kick in and someone sends a picture into my mind. I'm beginning to see... there was a woman once... I was walking toward my office with my briefcase. I was in a hurry. Then I heard this woman crying softly to my left. She was sitting at a bus stop next to the sidewalk. It was during the Depression, people were desperate. I stopped. Then on an impulse, I sat down next to her and put my arm around her, trying to

comfort her. This was a very unnatural thing for me to do. My god, is this what they are interested in? I was with this woman for only a few minutes before the bus came. I never saw her again.

How do you feel now about the Wise One bringing up this incident during your hearing?

It's so crazy! An entire lifetime of giving money to charity and they are interested in this! I gave this woman no money, we only talked.

Again we see the stress from the review council is on learning, forgiveness – especially of oneself – and unconditional love, rather than judgment. Not to mention providing confirmation of the truth of the old saying, 'it's the little things that count'.

After this formal review subjects rejoin their group, and it is in this setting that most of their time in the ethereal realms is spent. Contrary to the image of the afterlife presented in many popular accounts, Newton's subjects report that they do not just sit around in a blissful state all the time, even though some time is set aside for a variety of rest and recreational activities. But for the most part they are pretty constantly engaged in further discussion of their former lives – of the lessons they have learned and the good and bad choices they have made, and of the things they have not yet properly learned or mastered – with the other members of their group. This is consistently described as an educational setting, and the members of a primary group can be regarded as a particular class who have a similar level of experience. These classes also have a teacher inasmuch as the members of the group all share the same spirit guide, although much of the learning process is by good-natured and often humorous criticism between peers. The teacher is present less often the more advanced the group, and some groups have two guides – a junior who is still under 'teacher-training', and a more senior one that appears less often and looks after a number of groups.

Another method of evaluating and learning from past lives involves the regular use of what Newton's subjects consistently describe as the library of 'life books'. This aspect of the ethereal realms bears all the hallmarks of the universal etheric memory that I have discussed previously, or of the 'akashic records' as it is commonly known in esoteric circles. Subjects visit this library either alone or with their spirit guide, and are usually assisted, at least initially, by one of a number of librarian guides who help them locate the correct life book from their own collection.

When opened the life books take on a three-dimensional screen quality that allows the subject to replay scenes from past lives in total detail.

They can be used to show alternative courses of action, which can then be played out so that the subject can observe how their life would have evolved if they had taken alternative paths at particular karmic forks in the road. For example, one subject committed suicide as a young pregnant farmgirl in rural Victorian England because her young lover had just died, and she was unable to face telling her parents that she was about to be an unmarried mother, or face the horrors of running away to London to a life of almost certain prostitution. Her librarian guide showed her a number of alternatives, one of which was indeed a pretty wretched life in London as a prostitute who died young, but also others in which her parents, although angry, helped her to have as normal a life as possible with her child.

Alternatively these books can be used to allow the subject to actually enter a scene from a past life as a full participant. For example, another of Newton's subjects was shown scenes from his early childhood when he had been a bully at school, and as well as reliving these events as himself, he also switched and entered the role of another young child who was on the receiving end of his bullying. Nothing could have better shown him the pain he caused others at this time. It appears that subjects can even alter the events completely to gain a different perspective.

A similar theme is encountered when Newton's subjects discuss how they role-play their lives in their soul study groups. In these sessions soul mates take on different roles from the 'play' of the past lives they led together, and in this way they see how each of them could have reacted differently to various circumstances – which in turn helps them to see how they might behave differently in future lives. This is apparently an enjoyable as well as educational pastime, and it is one of the factors that leads subjects to describe the process of incarnate life as the playing of a 'game' – albeit one that can be very real and painful at times. But we can see from this that if in incarnate life we were sometimes able to stand back and see ourselves as just playing another character in a lengthy play, or another role in the game of life, it could help us to put our apparent earthly burdens into better perspective.

All of this suggests that the different learning environments in the ethereal realms are actually far more interwoven than Newton sometimes suggests. In particular, both group classroom learning and the formal council review seem to require access to the library of life books – or what we might refer to as the 'library of life books and films' to ensure that its full scope is properly understood.

Before we leave Newton's descriptions of the transition and review stages of the interlife experience, we should say a few words about recreational and other activities consistently reported by his subjects. I have already indicated that ample time is provided for rest and recreation, and this can include a whole variety of activities from dancing and music to various games, although even many of these can have a learning aspect that may be further developed later on. Souls can visit a 'space of transformation' in which they adjust their energy wavelength to experience what it is like to become any animate or inanimate form, and a 'place of projection' where they can make contact with incarnate souls to provide energy or other assistance – although this is in contrast to the constant activities of spirit guides, who keep a regular eye on their group members while they are on earth, and can contact them either to prod their intuition when awake or alternatively via their dreams while sleep, or even be contacted by them usually during meditation. Souls can also visit earth's astral plane, not to make any sort of contact but, for example, to return to and enjoy a favorite place for a while, because for some this is more rewarding than recreating a simulation of the experience in the ethereal realms.

His subjects also report a range of ethereal specialisms for which advancing souls can be in training. We will discuss the possibility of souls incarnating on other planets in the final chapter, but 'explorers' regularly visit the astral realms of other planets throughout the universe without fully incarnating on them. Some of these planets are physical, and some more nonphysical or 'mental' worlds, and although subjects initially do this for relaxation, as they progress their visits may become part of their training for exploring new planets that have yet to be inhabited. Other specialisms include 'designers' who assist the evolution of life on appropriate planets, 'harmonizers' who help to heal large-scale disruptive energy patterns on them, and 'ethicists' who study the way moral codes develop in various intelligent life forms. Plus, of course, many souls undergo teacher-training to become spirit guides themselves.

We all know that there is a common perception that our lives 'flash before us' when we face death, and we can start the process of corroborating the concept of the life review by seeing how this observation is borne out by a number of near-death experience researchers. For example, in *Life after Life* Raymond Moody describes the instantaneous, panoramic life reviews that occur not infrequently in conjunction with a near-death experience:

> This review can only be described in terms of memory, since that is the closest familiar phenomenon to it, but it has characteristics which set it

apart from any normal type of remembering. First of all, it is extraordinarily rapid. The memories, when they are described in temporal terms, are said to follow one another swiftly, in chronological order. Others recall no awareness of temporal order at all. The remembrance was instantaneous; everything appeared at once, and they could take it all in with one mental glance. However it is expressed, all seem in agreement that the experience was over in an instant of earthly time.

Yet, despite its rapidity, my informants agree that the review, almost always described as a display of visual imagery, is incredibly vivid and real. In some cases, the images are reported to be in vibrant color, three-dimensional, and even moving. And even if they are flickering rapidly by, each image is perceived and recognized. Even the emotions and feelings associated with the images may be reexperienced as one is viewing them.

Some of those I interviewed claim that, while they cannot adequately explain it, everything they had ever done was there in this review – from the most insignificant to the most meaningful. Others explain that what they saw were mainly the highlights of their lives. Some have stated to me that even for a period of time following their experience of the review they could recall the events of their lives in incredible detail.

Many of Moody's subjects also placed the review in the context of being educated by a 'being of light', in particular about love and knowledge, as the following case shows:

All through this, he kept stressing the importance of love. The places where he showed it best involved my sister; I have always been very close to her. He showed me some instances where I had been selfish to my sister, but then just as many times where I had really shown love to her and had shared with her. He pointed out to me that I should try to do things for other people, to try my best. There wasn't any accusation in any of this, though. When he came across times when I had been selfish, his attitude was only that I had been learning from them, too.

He seemed very interested in things concerning knowledge, too. He kept on pointing out things that had to do with learning, and he did say that I was going to continue learning, and he said that even when he comes back for me (because by this time he had told me that I was going back) that there will always be a quest for knowledge. He said that it is a continuous process, so I got the feeling that it goes on after death. I think that he was trying to teach me, as we went through those flashbacks.

In *Life at Death* Kenneth Ring reports similar experiences of the review phenomenon:

A person may experience the whole or selected aspects of his life in the form of vivid and nearly instantaneous visual images. These images usually appear in no definite sequence (though they sometimes do), but rather as a simultaneous matrix of impressions, like a hologram…. They are usually overwhelmingly positive in emotional tone, even though the individual viewing them ordinarily (but not always) experiences them with a sense of detachment.

And in *The Truth in the Light* Peter Fenwick adds some important observations:

In the 'classical' life review the person is shown his or her whole life in a panoramic fashion. Although actions which have been carried out are often seen as shabby and self-interested, the person does not feel judged; guilt is made more tolerable by the supportive quality of the surrounding light of love. Often the person experiences himself the emotional or physical pain that he has caused to others. Usually he is left with a feeling that he has learned from this and a determination to change and do better.

This provides specific confirmation of Newton's assertions concerning both the lack of judgment in life reviews, and the idea that the discarnate soul can experience their past-life actions from the perspective of those they have wronged. And Fenwick reports on another case in which the subject emphasized that it was not just his actions, but also his innermost thoughts and intentions, which were under review:

After the life review I spent some time resting and considering the implications of what had happened. I did not feel that I had been judged except by myself. There was no denying the facts because they were all there, including my innermost thoughts, emotions and motives. I knew that my life was over [wrongly as it turns out] and whatever came next would be a direct consequence of not only what I had done in my life, but what I had thought and what had been my true feeling at the time.

Near-death-experience researchers suggest that only about a quarter to a third of their subjects experience life reviews – indeed in some studies the figure is far less – and that they seem to be more prevalent in cases of accidents, such as falls or drowning or vehicle crashes, when the brush with death was sudden and unforeseen. Materialists suggest that the phenomenon is triggered because the brain is searching through its memory banks for some way to cope with the trauma, but as usual this seems to be a highly simplistic explanation for the variety and richness of the review experiences recorded – and especially the *new* insights that are derived from them. On the other hand we might naturally expect anyone with a fatal illness, or an older person who knows they are going to die, to spend some time contemplating their life and what they have achieved. So perhaps in some way the condensed and automatic life review in cases of sudden potential death acts as a substitute to help the person to come to terms with their life before they die. Nevertheless, there are sufficient similarities between the life reviews that occur during near-death and interlife experiences – such as their instantaneous and holographic nature that transcends the normal physical constraints of time and space, the lack of judgment except perhaps from oneself, and the emphasis on spiritual education in matters such as love and knowledge – that they must surely be regarded as related paranormal phenomena.

If we now turn to the research of our other interlife pioneers, apart from the common aspects of the immediate post-death experience that I have already commented upon, I will attempt to summarize their most relevant findings concerning not only past-life reviews, but also the transition into the interlife and other more general activities in and aspects of it.

This is how Peter Ramster's subject Jenny Green, who we met in the last chapter, describes certain parts of her interlife experience in *The Truth about Reincarnation*:

> *I want you just to think about the inbetween lives after each incarnation. Did the inbetween lives change at all after each successive life on earth? Was there a different inbetween life each time or was it all the same? Did you go back to the same place after each life or did you go back somewhere different?*
> Somewhere different.
> *Were the people different each time or were they the same?*
> Some were the same, and some were different.
> *Did you ever keep track of any people from earlier lives – people who may have lived in incarnation with you?*
> Yes.
> *Just before you were reincarnated into this life, what did you spend most of your time doing?*
> Talking to people, sharing ideas.

We have already seen that Newton suggests the composition of the review council can change for any given soul from one interlife experience to the next, and here Ramster is generally confirming that the interlife experience is different between each set of incarnations for any one soul. This is what we would expect, because their recuperation, life review, training and planning requirements will depend heavily on the specific nature of the incarnations on either side – even if there may be certain consistent karmic threads running through a series of lives.

Ramster then turns to the issue of consciousness in the ethereal realms, and Jenny's responses show great perception concerning not only the separation of consciousness from the physical brain, but also the extent to which the latter acts as a hindrance:

> *Can you describe to me what is the different form of consciousness you have after you die? What is the difference between being consciously awake after you die, and awake before you die?*
> Don't have to function through a physical brain. Don't have the limitations of a physical brain.
> *What are the limitations of a physical brain?*
> A physical brain has to relate to a physical world. It has so little concept of other things outside of the physical world. Without the physical brain, you are more aware of both worlds. You are more aware of different states of consciousness.
> *Is there any similarity between being asleep and being dead?*
> It's similar. In sleep you are still bound to the physical, but you have more awareness than you do when you're awake.
> *At certain stages of sleep your mind is full of unrealities such as dreams, or the realities of a dream are clouded in symbolism. Do you have the same sort of thing after death in the consciousness of another life?*
> No. The clouding of the memory is the lack of communication between the consciousness and the physical brain. That's where things get muddled up.
> *Is there any way that one can overcome the limitations of one's physical brain?*
> Yes… by recognizing where the mix-ups occur and going behind them.
> *How do you recognize where the mix-ups occur?*
> You should just know, like an instinct.

Ramster also emphasizes that his subjects consistently report having a rest period after death because they were tired. In *The Search for Lives Past* he goes on to describe his subjects' views on the different 'levels' experienced in the ethereal realms:

> It seems from all the accounts of past-life recall, that the number of places one may go after death are many, as if the world on the other side of death is composed of various levels. The level to which one belongs is determined by one's advancement. It seems that each person goes to a plane of existence where they find people similar to themselves. The people on each plane

will be such that each has a great affinity with the other people on that same plane. Sometimes they will meet dead relatives or friends after they die, however, this seems to depend upon the level to which those relatives and friends belong.

More complex notions of different levels of the ethereal realms that are related to soul advancement are discussed in other esoteric teachings, and we will return to this idea in the final chapter. But for now we can still see that the general idea being expressed by Ramster's subjects is that of soul groups at similar stages of spiritual advancement. This corroborates Newton's findings, even to the extent that while our closest friends and family from our past life will almost certainly be at the same stage of advancement – and therefore members of our primary, or at least secondary, soul group – some others may not; so we would be unlikely to encounter these latter souls in the ethereal realms.

As for past-life reviews, although Ramster's subjects do not specifically mention the formal council review, they consistently refer to visiting a 'Hall of Records', which is entirely consistent with the idea of the library of life books and films. It is worth pointing out that this bears out the view I expressed in *Genesis Unveiled*, and to a lesser extent *Giza: The Truth*, that the Hall of Records should be thought of as an ethereal construct that helps us to gain inner wisdom, rather than any sort of physical treasure trove of lost documents still waiting to be discovered on earth. Ramster's subject Gwen McDonald, who we also met in the last chapter, describes visiting it after her life as Rose Duncan – and it may or may not be cultural conditioning that makes her associate it with an Egyptian librarian, given that many people believe a physical Hall of Records is located somewhere in the vicinity of the Great Sphinx of Giza:

We walked to the Hall of Records and that was where I met the Egyptian. He was so kind, he showed me all I had done, things I should have done but didn't do. The place was like a library and it's full of records. It was a big place, a very big place. It had a long corridor with a sort of gold light everywhere inside. He showed me my life… but I could see it in my mind, not on paper, all the things I'd done, things I needed to do and didn't do.

The thing I needed to do was to be more conscious of other people. I was selfish, I only thought about myself and where I lived, my home and not the poor people in the village and the poor children. I should have helped, but I didn't. His voice is almost music, and there is a light that shines around him… when he looks at you his eyes seem to read what you are thinking… he seems to know.

I was told that in the Hall of Records there is a file on every living soul that ever incarnated and each time we have to see what fools we've been, what mistakes we've made. We have two paths to choose... if you take the wrong path it's all against you... if you take the right path it's all for you, and it's balanced out in the Hall of Records, and it's all there... every page, almost every thought and every deed is there... every book... every spoken word you can find. It's gold inside... lit up with a gold light, pure light. Everything in there is knowledge, and the keeper, the Egyptian in this plane, looks after and controls the records....

When we leave the Hall of Records the Egyptian bows, puts his hands together and smiles. When the door shuts, you know what you have to do, it's all in your mind without him having to say a lot. It's in your mind... it's there.

Joel Whitton provides some of the finest corroboration of Newton's interlife findings. In *Life Between Life* he and his co-author describe how his subjects make the transition from the physical to the ethereal plane:

The smoothest transition from the incarnate to the discarnate state is accomplished by those individuals who have spent their lives molding an outer character in accordance with the soul's highest impulses. They rejoice over the body's disintegration and are exhilarated at the prospect of being free from encasement. A person of advanced development who has a sense of incompletion about the life just passed will feel remorse at his or her inadequacy even while longing for the opportunity to rejoin the sublimity of the *bardo* state [the Tibetan word for the interlife]. Less-developed personalities usually adopt one of two stances. Fearing what death may bring, they may struggle in vain to remain in the body. Or, particularly if they are in poor health, they may wish to exchange their bodily vehicles as quickly as possible for a new 'suit', and rapid reentry into physical existence. The shock of violent death often causes the disembodied soul to linger on the earthbound plane, perhaps out of bafflement, fury, self-pity, or the desire for vengeance....

The much publicized 'tunnel' experience – an archetype of transition – is a common feature of the withdrawal from earthbound existence. Time and time again, Dr Whitton's subjects have told of 'seeing' their bodies lying beneath them before being pulled rapidly through a high, cylindrical passageway. They then discover they have left their physical bodies and cannot comfort and reassure relatives and friends who have been left behind. In most cases, however, the onset of strange and wonderful experiences soon dissipates all earthbound attachment.

The tube or tunnel appears to serve as the channel of conveyance to the afterworld. Some people are met by 'guides' while still in transit and escorted into the interlife, but most subjects tell of traveling alone and merging with a multitude of strangers at the end of the journey. Whoever eventually receives the new arrival into the *bardo* – a deceased relative or friend, a conductor, or a guide who has been watching over its 'charge' during the last life – is often seen to be carrying a torch to light the way.

We can see that Whitton does make the suggestion that some less advanced and confused souls may attempt to return into incarnation immediately, and this is a point we will pick up on in chapter 7. But he then goes on to confirm Newton's suggestion that each soul perceives the ethereal realms differently, based it would seem in part on their level of advancement, in part on their initial state of mind after death, and in part on their general expectations. Again, some describe palaces and gardens and oceans, while others report no physically oriented perceptions at all. He also corroborates the idea of soul mates from our group with whom we share many incarnations, and of each interlife experience being unique – indicating that one of his subjects had been regressed into seven separate interlives between incarnations.

As for life reviews, Whitton provides excellent corroboration for the idea of a review council that is worth quoting in albeit-abridged detail:

Nearly all who ventured into metaconsciousness have found themselves appearing before a group of wise, elderly beings – usually three in number, occasionally four, and in rare instances as many as seven – perceived in a variety of guises. They can be of indeterminate identity or they may take on the appearance of mythological gods or religious masters....

The members of this etheric tribunal are highly advanced spiritually and may even have completed their cycle of earthly incarnations. Knowing intuitively everything there is to be known about the person who stands before them, their role is to assist that individual in evaluating the life that has just passed and, eventually, to make recommendations concerning the next incarnation.

If there is a private hell in the life between life, it is the moment when the soul presents itself for review. This is when remorse, guilt, and self-recrimination for failings in the last incarnation are vented with a visceral intensity that produces anguish and bitter tears on a scale that can be quite unsettling to witness. While incarnate, one's negative actions can be rationalized and repressed; there are always plenty of excuses available. In the interlife the emotions generated by these actions emerge raw and irreconcilable. Any emotional suffering that was inflicted on others is felt as keenly as if it were inflicted on oneself....

The judges radiate a restorative, healing energy that abolishes any handicaps and assuages all guilt.... Rather than confirm the self-loathing and dissatisfaction of the contrite soul, the board of judgment expresses encouragement, pointing out where the life has been positive and progressive. It's as if they are saying, 'Come on now, your life wasn't *that* bad'....

For the purposes of self-assessment, the soul is confronted with an instantaneous panoramic flashback which contains every single detail of the last incarnation.... Said one subject: 'It's like climbing inside a movie of your life. Every moment from every year of your life is played back in complete sensory detail. Total, total recall. And it all happens in an instant.'

The review tells the soul more about the last life than the individual alone could ever hope to realize, even with full restoration of memory. An entire world of which the individual was not aware is given expression. The larger picture is etched in vivid detail so that the soul realizes for the first time when happiness was thrown away or when thoughtlessness caused pain in another or when life-threatening danger was just around the corner.

The soul absorbs every jot of meaning from this personalized videotape and this precipitates a rigorous exercise in self-analysis. This is the soul's moment of truth and, as it proceeds, the judges tend to remain in the background. They do not, according to Dr Whitton's subjects, act in the authoritarian manner suggested by cultural tradition. Rather, they behave more like loving teachers whose aim is to encourage their student to learn and benefit from past mistakes. The board of judgment frequently initiates discussion of critical episodes in the last life, offers retrospective counsel, and instills reassurance that each experience, no matter how unsavory, promotes personal development.

The individual's hopes, friendships, ideals, esthetic inclinations, and mental processes all form part of the review. Emotionalism is kept to a minimum as the judges gently assist the soul in an objective understanding of its actions within the larger context of many lives. Only by observing karmic trends and patterns – always difficult to discern within a single lifetime – can the soul gain some measure of its progress on the long, long journey of spiritual evolution.

We can see that, once again, love, self-forgiveness and learning are emphasized by the review council, rather than punishment. Whitton also corroborates the idea of ongoing learning in a mixed classroom-library environment, and of training in a variety of ethereal specialisms:

Most of Dr Whitton's subjects have found themselves hard at work in vast halls of learning equipped with libraries and seminar rooms. Doctors and lawyers, for example, have spoken of studying their respective disciplines during the interlife while others remember applying themselves to such subjects as 'the laws of the universe' and other metaphysical topics.

Dolores Cannon provides similarly valuable corroboration of a number of aspects of the interlife experience in *Between Death and Life*. With respect to the transition from the physical to the ethereal realms, her subjects confirm that they are normally met by friends or family members, that they quickly become aware of the karmic connections with these from various past lives, and that the expectations of the deceased play a significant part in modeling their surroundings in the ethereal realms. She confirms that those souls who are traumatized or confused are given special treatment by their spirit guide to reorientate them – or may even remain for a while as ghosts on earth's astral plane – and that seriously damaged souls are taken to a special place of seclusion for rehabilitation, where they will stay for varying lengths of time before rejoining the normal flow. Particular emphasis is given to the 'temple of healing', which appears to be the equivalent of Newton's healing shower of energy.

Cannon's subjects report on a variety of 'general councils' performing different tasks. The one she uses as a detailed example is reported to be involved in overseeing and regulating 'overall energy patterns' on earth, which sounds very much akin to the work of Newton's harmonizers; but she also corroborates his idea of masters of design when she refers to councils that work on the 'creator level'. In general her subjects appear to confirm the idea of ethereal specialisms for which advancing souls can be in training. As far as life reviews are concerned, she reports that one type of council is involved with reviewing former lives with individual souls, in conjunction with their spirit guide and with the assistance of 'holographic projection'. She also mentions the review council experience of one woman who described a near-death experience to her without hypnosis:

> Instantly I was in another place. I wasn't in the tunnel any more. It was kind of like a backyard, and there was a circle of people. I've tried since then to guess how many were in that circle of people sitting around in chairs. I would guess maybe eight, ten men and women. I perceived that they were my council. And I knew that every single person has a council that has a responsibility for each soul down here.

Cannon's subjects also corroborate the two other main aspects of learning discussed by Newton. On the one hand, this is how one describes the educational classes he attended on an ongoing basis with the other members of his soul group:

> It is the school of knowledge. I see the hall. It has tall pillars and it's all in white.... It has classrooms off of it. This is a kind of main walkway, I guess. You can see anything that you want to see here. Just by visualizing

it, it occurs. You can make it as nice or as bad as you wish. If you're dealing with a guilty conscience and want to make yourself suffer, you can make yourself do that also. You can make the surroundings look like you want them, or the way you have visualized it....

Is there anyone else there with you at the school?
There are about fifty people just in my class. There are others here, but we don't have much to do with them. They are working out other problems. They have different lessons that they have to learn, and they must come to terms with it within their own selves....

When you learn, do you do it all by yourself or does someone help you?
No. I get help if I need it. If I search or if I ask or I question, all things come and it's there.

Who is teaching you?
The masters. Each class has several. They teach you to study one's self....

What are you learning at the school?
I'm studying life experiences and effects. I study long and hard in order to learn and to know. I put the pieces of my experiences together and compile them to make sense of my existence.... I try to understand why I acted and reacted in such a way so as not to repeat previous errors. We amass great knowledge here of lessons to be learned, karma to be dealt with.

Because this subject seems to spend a great deal of time studying alone, and his soul group is a large one, we might suspect that in Newton's terms he is relatively advanced – but as I noted in the last chapter this seems to be true of most of the subjects Cannon uses to source the material for her book. And because the idea of replaying events from different perspectives is mentioned in this classroom context, arguably it again emphasizes the interconnection between the library and classroom environments. This is confirmed by another of Cannon's subjects' description of the library itself:

I'm in a huge study. There are books and scrolls on everything, and all types of manuscripts on the shelves.... It's a big area; almost cathedral size. There's a man there – he's a spirit, and he's just luminous.... He is showing me around. There's the library with the huge rotunda where people are gathered in groups and studying and discussing issues. They are able to go into viewing rooms around the perimeter of this room to view things if they wish. All knowledge is stored in these but it's not like a computer.... And he says we could go into the scriptorium. This is where things are read. This is where people who can relate to writing and reading like to go.... It's for people that are not very advanced souls. They're medium advanced souls that still need the written word to make sense of their consciousness....

Low level energy souls find it very hard to step into this realm. They feel frightened or afraid of this area.... They still carry most of the negative

115

qualities of their former existences.

We can see that this subject particularly emphasizes that some souls are more comfortable with book than film-type learning, and that less advanced souls might tend to avoid this learning environment altogether – which again we will pick up on in chapter 7. In addition to this, the same subject then goes on to describe a 'tapestry room' that apparently has a similar function but can only be used by more advanced souls:

> The guardian is explaining that every life that has ever been lived is represented as a thread in this tapestry. This is where all the threads of human life, the souls that incarnate are connected. It illustrates perfectly how each life is interwoven, crossing and touching all these other lives until eventually all of humanity is affected. The absolute oneness of humanity is represented by the tapestry. It is one but composed of all these many parts. Each cannot exist without the other and they all intertwine and influence each other....
>
> It's like looking at the most beautiful creation of art. It's made up of strands that range from a tiny piece of string all the way up to cable size, as thick as your wrist.... Most of them are kind of rope size and then they get thicker and thicker as they go along....
>
> This is what the ancients call the 'akashic records'. These are the akashic records that advanced souls understand. He says some of the records are kept in book form, but those are for souls who are not as highly advanced.

Admittedly this idea bears some similarity to the 'three fates' of Greek mythology, who looked after the 'threads' that governed each person's life, and this might even have influenced this subject's description. Nevertheless this modern tapestry concerns the past as much as the future, has nothing to with predetermined fate, and is also an extremely useful metaphor as we will see in chapter 8. Meanwhile, as we saw with one of Newton's subjects, another of Cannon's also emphasizes the overriding importance of unconditional love as the main attribute we should try to develop as incarnate souls, along with tolerance and patience.

In *Remarkable Healings* Shakuntala Modi uses somewhat Christianized language, despite her clear acceptance of reincarnation, which is not to everyone's taste. But, although her descriptions of her patients' interlife experiences are not necessarily in the same chronological order as Newton's, they corroborate a number of important points. With respect to the transition stage, they suggest that they all recognize their soul mates and the part they played in previous lives; that all souls go through a 'cleansing' process just like Newton's healing shower of energy to remove negative emotions and attitudes – although, again, not the associated memories; and that souls who have had a particularly traumatic time in their last life are met by their spirit guide early on and allowed to 'ventilate' their feelings. They also consistently report a 'resting phase', after which they enter the 'inner sanctum of heaven'.

As for life reviews, Modi makes a brief reference to ongoing learning within our soul groups, but this is her detailed description of her patients' review council experiences:

> Patients describe going to another room after cleansing, where there are one to five or even more beings waiting for them. Patients say that if they are at a very high level spiritually, in the Light, then there are usually a master and other very high beings. If the patients are less developed spiritually, there may be angels or other wise beings of heaven. These beings serve as counselors who help in reviewing the life. They usually have a broader perspective and clear understanding of the nature of the Light and the universe.
>
> Patients describe reviewing their whole life with the help of these counselors. Together they review their purpose for that life and the lessons they learned or failed to learn. They also evaluate their spiritual achievements.
>
> According to patients, the function of the Light beings who help them review their life is not to judge or condemn them. Their function is to help them get the information out in such a way that the patients can see and understand it clearly. Patients usually say this is the most difficult stage, because it is they who judge themselves. There is no judgment or punishment by God or the Light beings who are helping them. Patients are their own harshest judge and jury.
>
> Patients often describe this as a process of self-analysis and evaluation of the life they just lived. They alone interpret their success or failure in meeting the goals they set in the Light for that life. Their feelings of disappointment and bitterness over lost opportunities and wrong actions cannot be adequately described. Their feelings of success and triumph about goals they achieved and good acts are just as remarkable and hard to convey. This is the stage in which patients come to grips with the harm they did to themselves and others by suicide, murder, and other negative actions.
>
> During the review, patients not only assess every good and bad thing they did, but also experience other people's feelings. In heaven, patients describe themselves as nonphysical spirits. There are no barriers of time and space. Patients can return to any moment in the lifetime they just departed and observe the events from different points of view.

We can see this description emphasizes the usual factors of learning and absence of judgment except from ourselves, as well as corroborating Newton's idea that the make-up of the review council varies depending on the subject's level of spiritual advancement. And in suggesting that souls are able to replay past events as an observer from different perspectives, it even implicitly corroborates the idea of the library of life books and films.

In *You Have Been Here Before* Edith Fiore tantalizes us with the following statement:

> A description of the interim between lifetimes, taken from my patients' fascinating accounts, will have to wait for a future publication. It is a book in itself!

This separate work has never appeared, so I contacted Fiore to check the status of this material. It seems that, unfortunately, certain tragic circumstances around that time prevented her from completing a book called *The Interim* that she was in the process of writing next; and now, even more unfortunately, she no longer has all her drafts and case notes from that time. Nevertheless, in her first book she does describe how our transition after death is aided by spirit guides and other former friends or family members. And this is how one of her patients describes the concept of the past-life review, as revealed under hypnosis when she was reliving how a discarnate voice spoke to her during the intensely emotional experience of her son's birth:

> It explained why we're here – the reason why we're here, what life is all about, the truth. And the truth is that we're all on a path back to God and we live many lifetimes. We live by the law of karma which dictates, in effect, that we have to pay off our debts from our past lives. Once we die, we look back on how we lived that life... *we* are the judges of how we lived that life. We look to see where we failed. Maybe it's like a stylus constantly recording. Our soul is constantly having the stylus going, recording our deeds, our thoughts, our actions, whether or not we're hurting anybody – and that's what it's all about. Love is how we treat others, by word and by deed. After we cross over, we examine how we lived our last lives. We see where we failed and where we maybe made some gains.

Again the emphasis is on us being our own worst judges, and on thoughts and intentions being just as important as actions – and Fiore reports that many of her patients confirm this understanding of the life review. She also briefly corroborates the idea of the review council, and of life films, in *The Unquiet Dead*:

If the regression continued, they reported experiences of a rich, full existence in another world. At one point, with wise counselors, they reviewed the life they had left and saw it all as though watching a film…. It was clear to them that the purpose of this review was to enable them to see where they passed key challenges and failed others.

In *Many Lives, Many Masters* Brian Weiss, through his subject Catherine, confirms the idea of initial rest and reorientation by referring to souls that are burned out going to the 'plane of renewal'. She also confirms Newton's idea of the place of projection: 'In spiritual form you can always contact those that are in physical state if you choose to. But only if there is importance there… if you have to tell them something they must know.' As for life reviews, these are referred to as occurring on the 'plane of recollection', and the implication appears to be that this contains something similar to the library of life books and films:

> There are seven planes in all, seven planes, each one consisting of many levels, one of them being the plane of recollection. On that plane you are allowed to collect your thoughts. You are allowed to see your life that has just passed. Those of the higher levels are allowed to see history. They can go back and teach us by learning about history. But we of the lower levels are only allowed to see our own life… that has just passed.

I have not so far mentioned Helen Wambach, and this is because she does not mention past-life reviews at all in *Life Before Life*. But there is a very good reason for this, and that is that the 'pre-birth' questions she put to her groups did not cover this area at all. We will gain far more from her material in the next chapter, but for now it is worth pointing out that she did ask her subjects to visualize whether in their past lives they had been associated with anyone they knew in their current life:

> Eighty-seven per cent of all my subjects reported being aware of how they had known important people in their current life from past lives. These relationships were quite varied [with friends and family members being mixed up again and again]…. My subjects all tell the same story. We come back with the same souls, but in different relationships. We live again not only with those we love, but with those we hate and fear. Only when we feel only compassion and affection are we freed from the need to live over and over with the same spirits, who are also forced to live with us!

Although other researchers corroborate the idea that our relationships with soul mates are not always completely harmonious, and for good karmic reasons, as we will see in chapter 7 it is only in unusual karmic circumstances that we are likely to 'hate and fear' them with any sort of regularity. But, in any case, Wambach's research certainly supports the idea of the soul group – as, for that matter, does that of many other past-life practitioners who I have not discussed at all.

There remains, however, one last researcher whose comments on the interlife should be considered, and that is Morris Netherton. He has this to say in *Past Lives Therapy*:

> My experience with this 'space' has been far too shallow to make any definitive statements. Patients describe a life outside the body as easily as they describe their births and deaths. I rarely let patients linger in this area, however, although it is very tempting, with its mysteries and promises of sudden revelation. In fact, in my experience, life outside the body reveals very little. It does not seem to be a state of exalted wisdom or extraordinary perception at all. The problems that plague a particular life are carried into the space between lives. Our inability to deal with these problems influences our choice of the next body we enter.

Netherton's findings are somewhat disconcerting, in that all his patients seem to repeat the same patterns over countless lives. In fact if his case studies are indicative of his general experience, then it is little wonder that he is so jaundiced in his views. However, we must remember that he was operating entirely in a therapeutic capacity with people suffering from reasonably severe psychological and psychosomatic problems. So for the moment we must fall back on the explanation proffered in chapter 3 to account for Stevenson's birth defect cases, and which we will discuss properly in chapter 7: that these are abnormal karmic circumstances in which the patients repeat behavioral patterns because of nonacceptance of a previous experience.

As for the interlife, Netherton admits that he actively shied away from investigating it, and he would certainly not have been regularly asking probing questions about it as most of our other researchers were. Moreover, given that the bulk of his book is devoted to therapeutic case studies in which he personally helped his patients to remove karmic blockages from past lives, under his bleak assessment only these lucky people would ever be able to escape an endless cycle of worsening karma. This would, of course, be a nonsense. Even most people with psychological problems never receive past-life therapy while in incarnation, and instead obtain assistance and insight during the interlife – especially when reviewing their past lives and choosing their next ones with spiritual counselors.

By combining all this research we can summarize the major, consistent elements of the transition and review stages of the interlife experience proper as follows. After making the transition from the physical plane via the tunnel and into the light of the ethereal realms, less advanced souls tend to be met by their spirit guide, or by friends or family members – in which case they quickly become aware of their karmic connections with them in various past lives. Our expectations and level of advancement play a significant part in modeling our surroundings in the ethereal realms, and less advanced souls will tend to perceive people and places as having physical traits.

Some of us spend a little time just resting and restoring our energy, and most of us receive a healing shower of energy that removes excess negative emotions. Less advanced souls who are particularly confused or traumatized are given special treatment by their spirit guide to reorientate them, and this may involve an element of initial life review as well as a period of rest and seclusion. More seriously damaged souls are taken to a special place of seclusion for rehabilitation, where they stay for varying lengths of time before rejoining the normal flow.

The life review and more general learning process takes a number of forms. It would appear that most of us are involved in a formal review with a council of elders, whose composition varies according to our individual requirements and experience. Most of us also have access to a library containing life books and films, which can be used to replay past events either as observers or as participants, either in their original form or by changing our decisions, or even by taking the role of others – especially those we have wronged. Ongoing learning and past-life analysis also takes place in the context of classrooms, where we are involved with other members of our soul group who are at a similar stage of karmic advancement. Both our council review and educational classes will tend to make use of the library of life books and films. More advanced souls may even be in training for a number of ethereal specialisms.

Whatever form our life reviews take, they include all of our thoughts and intentions as well as our actions, and also the main karmic threads running through our multiple past lives. We are never judged during our life reviews, only helped to see our past lives and their karmic patterns as objectively as possible. Above all, the more advanced souls that assist us in this process show great patience, love and understanding – while we ourselves are ultimately our own harshest critics.

	Newton	Ramster	Whitton	Cannon	Modi	Fiore	Weiss
Transition via tunnel and light	●	●	●	●	●	●	
Met by friends and family or spirit guide	●	●	●	●	●	●	
Varied perception of surroundings	●		●	●			
Healing shower of energy	●			●	●		
Initial rest and energy restoration	●	●			●		●
Reorientation for traumatized souls	●			●	●		●
Rehabilitation for more damaged souls	●			●			
Soul group members at similar level	●	●	●	●	●		
Review with council of elders	●		●	●	●	●	
Replays/role-plays via life books and films	●	●	●	●	●		●
Ongoing classroom learning with group	●	●	●	●	●		
Nonjudgmental nature of reviews	●	●	●	●	●	●	
Training in ethereal specialisms	●		●	●			

In the grid above I have summarized these major elements and shown which ones are corroborated by which interlife regressors. I have omitted the relevant near-death-experience research findings because these only provide generalized corroboration of the initial transition and the panoramic life review, and also Wambach's and Netherton's findings for the reasons already given.

This grid helps to confirm that there is a great deal of commonality in the findings of these pioneering researchers in respect of the basic transition and life review stages. We should also remember that some of these researchers were not concentrating on the interlife experience per se, and really only commenting on it in passing. To that extent, a gap in the grid may well mean either that the given researcher encountered the element in question but does not bother to mention it, or that they failed to ask their subjects any pertinent questions about it. In no instance can a gap be taken as a direct contradiction of the findings of the other researchers – especially when, as I have already indicated, we must also accept that there is an unavoidable element of uniqueness to interlife experiences. The only exception to this would be if I were to include Netherton's and Woolger's reports of the completely blank interlife experience – but I will deal with this complication in chapter 7. In any case, above all else our interlife pioneers universally emphasize that we are *not* judged by power-wielding higher beings after death, as so many formal religions would have us believe. Instead, the only judgment comes from ourselves.

In closing, let us consider an important point made by Ramster. Very few of us have any conscious memories of our current life before the age of about two or three, and certainly not of our birth. And yet we do not deny that we were alive then. So if unconscious memories of this period are unlocked under hypnosis, even skeptics have little trouble in accepting they may well be real memories. On that basis, it is surely illogical to be so distrustful of memories of earlier incarnations – even if, for some of us, the further back we go the less detailed and accurate the recall, and even if we must accept that some elements may be tinged with pure imagination. Can we not, therefore, say the same thing about memories of the interlife – especially when there is so much consistency in the reports of so many different subjects via such a variety of different regressors?

6

LIFE PLANS AND CHOICES
Are We In Control?

OK, well we'll leave your soul group right now, and I want you to move to that time when you need to go to the wise spirits of light who plan with you every new incarnation. Go to that place, and then just describe what it is you see and experience.
Yes. We're talking about me coming back.
OK, well just describe what it looks like, this particular place you've gone to. Are there any figures you can see?
I'm not seeing it visually, I'm just aware there's two or three…
Just be careful, look at them carefully, just check out whether there's two or three. Just look at them.
Three.
Are they showing themselves in energy form, or human?
Just energy form.
Are you comfortable with that, or would you like them to show themselves in human form?
No, I'm happy with that… my spirit guide's with me as well.
And what's his position relative to you, is he by your side or behind you?
Kind of to one side but behind, and they're kind of in front of me.
And are you aware of what this place is like, where these three spirits of light are? Just describe this special place.
Well, I know they're… they're much higher than us… I've seen them before.
Has this place that you're in got any earthly features to it, or is this just an energy place that you're in?
I'm really seeing it just as an energy place.
And how would you describe this energy place?
It's not much different from any other, the difference is the other people you're with. I know I'm here to talk about what I'm going to do next time, and I know who the three are… they've done this with me before… so, it's kind of familiar.
And tell me, what colors do you notice these spirits of light are?
They're darker… a deep blue color.
And are you aware of any other presence at all in this place?
No… I don't think there is anyone else there… I think this is kind of a

preliminary chat.

OK, well tell me about this preliminary chat, and is this done telepathically or do they communicate in some other way to you?

No, it's all telepathic… and it's straight away understood that I had a pretty easy life last time… and… even that time, when we planned that last one, it was agreed that if I took that somewhat easier one I'd have a couple of harder ones coming up… so we start by reminding ourselves of that plan anyway, and I say, yes, I know all about that… so they say are you ready for a harder one, and I say yes… I think I say what kind of hard are we talking about?

And what kind of hard is that?

I think they're saying that you need to… you're not going to get the same kind of support you got last time… you need to learn to do it on your own.

Do you agree with that?

Yes… because ultimately I know that we're all completely alone, but at the same time we're all completely one… and I need to live that, we agree that I need to live that and experience that.

Do they do any preparation for this life, or do you have to go to another place… to try out different types of bodies?

Another place.

OK, we'll leave them for a moment, and come back later.

OK.

Alright, now I want you to go back to that special place where you can try out different bodies, describe what it's like.

Images.

Are there any spirits there that are looking after this place?

No, I'm on my own.

How do you go about experimenting with different bodies?

I think they've got three for me to look at.

Just describe these different options other than the one you're in.

I think in one of them… I end up traveling from quite an early age.

Is that a male or a female body?

I think they're all male again.

Is it a strong or a weak body?

Strong… I think all my options are strong-bodied ones this time, I've had weak bodies in the past… so the first option is somebody who travels around a lot, and never really settles down.

OK, how do you find out about this, does it telepathically come to you, or do you try out the bodies somehow?

I'm seeing it as just flashed images.

Is this like a summary of the whole life, or just bits?

Bits.

So you have one body as a strong man who travels a lot and never settles.

What's the next body you have a choice of?
I think it's somebody who's going to be in the Church.
What sort of life would that be like?
Again, he'd be alone a lot... no wife and family... but there are other securities.
And the third body, is this the one you're in now?
Yes.
And what are the images that are flashed in front of you about selecting this body?
I would end up writing... all three options had a loneliness aspect, but they also all had a... a goal in terms of some sort of spiritual quest, and possibly even teaching, just in different ways... those were the two things, and there were three different options of how to go about that.
And, what is it that as a soul makes you decide to pick the body you're in now?
I think I like the idea of writing... I haven't done it before... I don't... both of the others would have involved putting a message across by talking really... this one didn't, and I liked that.
Is there any aspect about selecting this body other than loneliness that you would experience? See if that information is available.
The loneliness bit is not simple... it's not necessarily there all the time... I knew I was going to get an easy childhood, and a good education which I was going to need... but the tests would come later... but they're not necessarily there all the time.
Do you get a choice of the type of mind you would have with these bodies?
Well there's different characteristics in each... my fundamental... my underlying mind is obviously going to be the driving force in each of them... but there would have been slightly different characteristics in each.
So it's like three packages. Mind, emotions, and body come as a package with each of those characters you would have.
Yes... the bodies wouldn't have been that dissimilar because we'd agreed there were enough other things for me to do without worrying unduly about bodily affliction, so the bodies weren't a major problem, it was more a case of different styles to achieve certain results... so maybe the one I've chosen is... a more intellectual style. The other two might have been more...
OK, well just be aware that you made that decision. Have you finished at this place now, or do you have to stay for any other reason?
No.

OK, we'll go back to that meeting with the three spirits of light and, being aware that you've picked this particular body, do they have anything else to say to you about this particular life you're going to be in?
I'm asking about in exactly what way it's going to be made difficult for me.

And are they able to tell you at this preliminary meeting, or does that happen at the full meeting later?
I'm at the full meeting now.
Is that with the same three spirits of light?
Yes... and with my spirit guide as well.
OK, and you're discussing how it's going to be made difficult.
I told them that I like the person who's going to write the books option... and they say that's fine... then I ask them in what way is it going to be made difficult for me in terms of both getting the job done, and the loneliness bit of it, the not having support bit of it... I tell them that I'm... depending on what happens those things could make it a lot harder than... I mean I accept that it's not going to be an easy life.
Are they going to show you any past lives to help you understand what areas need to be made difficult in this life?
Don't think so.
OK, well just tell me what is it they say to you.
I think they're just saying that you know enough about the option you've just chosen, you will be able to do it, and you won't suffer any more than is appropriate... and I've got to trust that.
Just ask the spirits of light what the purpose of this life as the writer is. What's it to achieve, spiritually and karmically?
Well, I've got a load of basic personal spiritual growth to do in this one, on a very literal level... in other words consciously studying it in a way I haven't before.
And this is about the types of books you're going to be writing is it?
Yes, it's known that that's going to be the nature of them.
And is it planned that you are going to write lots of books, or will there just be a few... are they able to tell you?
Right at the outset, it was just agreed that I was going to be writing a few that would have enough importance to merit me doing them, and then it was left open after that.
[The regression now switches emphasis into the present to allow me to reevaluate and question my original life plan]
So this is where it's your opportunity to choose whether you develop the spiritual theme, or whether you just write the few books that were initially planned?
Yes.
And do you know what those books were that were initially planned? Are they the ones you've done already?
Probably.
See if the spirits help us with this.
They are saying yes, it was those two.
And will continuing to write these books be a way of spiritually growing that you choose to do yourself?
I think we're agreed that I don't have to write any more to grow personally,

so the question is whether I write… in the hope it will help others. My personal growth can be done without writing now… but my hope is that I can help others if I carry on, otherwise it's not worth doing it.

And are there some spiritual paths of helping others that were discussed that you could choose from… are they permitted to tell you that information?

They're telling me that if I want to help others, this is the option, it's this or nothing. This is the talent I've been given.

OK, and how will you know whether the thing you're doing is the right path?

They're telling me that… what I've done so far has been right… ish, at least, and that what I'm planning to do at the moment is… yes, that's also right. I can't get any guarantees after that.

Will you have a feeling inside, an intuition, to tell you you're doing the right thing, or will other guides be given to help you?

Yes, I will have an intuition, it's more a case of… I'm trying to explain to them that it was made pretty hard for me already, and it's when it's made hard for me that it's difficult to be sure and to trust my intuition… they're saying that they understand that, and that there was good reason to make the last bit hard, partly to test my own resolve, which I needed.

And how well did you do that? Ask them for feedback.

They're pleased that I stuck at it when I could have walked away… but I need to tell them that if it keeps being made that hard then it's going to be difficult for me to keep the faith that I'm doing the right thing… and I'm telling them that… they're saying they understand that, and they're not promising it's all going to be a piece of cake, but I'm not going to be tested as much as I was. And that's fair enough.

Are you happy with that, or do you need any more specific information? You know the worst is past, in terms of difficulty.

I'm accepting that from the point of view of… that I'm on the right path from that point of view, but I need to talk to them more about whether I'm going to be OK financially.

Well let's talk about the financial side, and we'll ask them whether there's any help that can be given to you at this point, now you've completed that important test.

Well, we're agreeing that I don't need it right now, it's more the worry for the long-term future… and they're saying we've looked after you OK one way or another up until now, haven't we? And I have to agree… I think the implication is, of course we'll make sure you're OK.

Because if you're on a spiritual path, doing spiritual work, if you're not OK financially it will stop you doing that work.

Yes, I know!

They'll understand, they know.

OK, I think what they're saying is you've got to just trust more, and I accept that… I will.

By now you might have guessed that this is an extract from another personal regression session with Andy Tomlinson, which he conducted two days after the one I quoted from in the opening chapter. I have omitted the opening section that deals with my most recent past life as a poor farmer, and also a section from the middle that deals with some rather more personal issues. Otherwise this is, again, a verbatim transcript.

Of course, this attempt to revisit my own last interlife, and in particular the choice and planning of my current life, 'proves' even less than my earlier past-life memories of life during the Inquisition. I had already studied Michael Newton's work in some detail, so in my case it is perfectly possible that I concocted the whole thing from a combination of my existing knowledge and imagination. But, again, there are some elements that suggest to me this is not entirely the case. This was not a normal session inasmuch as I was deliberately trying to revisit this planning stage with Andy, not just as part of my research *for* this book, but in an attempt to establish whether I should be attempting to continue with my writing *at all* in the face of no little adversity. To clarify, many regressors suggest we can revisit the interlife planning stage for this life to reevaluate our life 'contract', and if appropriate reaffirm it but perhaps asking for additional help from our guides or elders at the same time. To that extent I was given a renewed determination to trust my intuition and to accept that, if I was on the right path, I would be looked after one way or another. And even if that proves nothing at all to anyone else, it still had a deep personal resonance for me.

The whole idea that we might be actively engaged in planning our own incarnations, including all the trials and tribulations that we all encounter to varying degrees, has massive implications. It is arguably the most important aspect of this book, not least because of the enormity of its revelation of the extent to which we, as individual souls, are in control of our own destiny. The implications of this are *so* wide-reaching that some people struggle with the idea when they first encounter it, and we will examine them far more in the next chapter – at the end of which I hope I will have gone some way to proving that it is one of the most individually empowering ideas ever presented to humanity. But, for now, I want to concentrate on demonstrating the extent to which our pioneers' research indicates that we do indeed have such control, and to provide examples of the mechanics of the process.

The other reason why this concept is so startling is that, unlike the past-life review, it is one with little historical provenance. I have not been able to trace any real references to it in ancient literature, however obscure. In fact the first time I personally came across the idea of life plans was a brief allusion to it in James Redfield's seminal novel *The Celestine Prophecy*. Although this book is not to everyone's taste, it has been responsible for introducing many tens of thousands of people around the world, including myself, to a more spiritual worldview; one based primarily on enhancing our awareness of energy interchanges, intuition and synchronicities – a term coined by Jung to emphasize the fact that most apparent coincidences do not happen by chance, and usually have an important underlying message for us. Of course, to some extent the idea of a life plan is merely a confirmation of the vague intuition many of us have that our life has some sort of specific purpose and meaning, an important destiny to be fulfilled, but personally I was always rather skeptical of this idea because it seemed to pander to the ego. Nevertheless, when I reencountered it in Newton's work some years later, the details impressed me sufficiently to believe that we do indeed make such plans – it is just that we may deliberately include unpleasant as well as pleasant elements in them, which is a far less self-aggrandizing concept. So, again I will use his research from *Journey of Souls* and *Destiny of Souls* to map out the details, and this will set us up to compare it with the findings of our other pioneers.

Newton's subjects report that souls reach a point where they either decide themselves, or are 'made aware' by their spirit guide, that it is time for them to return into incarnation. And although it appears that souls may show a degree of resistance to leaving the love, security and comfort of their real home for the uncertainty and harshness of earthly incarnation, they all agree sooner or later, and forceful coercion is never required. One particular issue stressed to reluctant souls is that they do not *have* to go back into incarnation on earth, but that their learning processes would take an awful lot longer if they did not – and we will return to why physical incarnation is important later.

In fact, during their classroom discussions with their soul group, and indeed throughout the interlife experience, souls have not only been considering the progress and mistakes they made in past lives, but also teeing themselves up for the lessons they would like to learn and the sort of experiences they will need in the next one. And once the decision to return has been made, the first stage will tend to involve the subject having more concrete discussions – usually with their guide although sometimes with their elders – about the potential circumstances for their next life.

Of course, two of the primary considerations will be where to reincarnate, and into what family. Newton's subjects report that affiliations to particular countries or races are rare and, if they do exist, relatively short-lived – after all, the whole point of repeated reincarnation is variety of experience. They further suggest that only in exceptional circumstances might souls choose to come back in more or less the same location as that of their last life, or in even more exceptional circumstances into the same family. I would argue that the most obvious reason for this would be if souls were in a hurry to come back, and especially if they did not actually have a proper interlife experience; for example, most of Ian Stevenson's child cases had a tendency to incarnate in the geographical vicinity of where they previously died, but I have already suggested that they are karmically unusual. Nevertheless, we should also acknowledge, as both Newton and Stevenson do, that certain especially native cultures around the world believe that their souls repeatedly reincarnate into the same tribe, often with some sort of ongoing family ties. I would suggest that it is not beyond the bounds of possibility that such soul groupings represent a special case, and perhaps even a throwback to a time when the tribal way of life was far more prevalent across the world – although in using this term I do not mean to imply that such soul behavior would be in any way inferior, except that it would tend to limit a soul's experience when there is now such variety available in the modern world. Newton also suggests that the soul of a child that has died young might return to the same parents as a subsequent child – and we will discuss the karma behind such actions in the next chapter.

In any case, Newton's subjects report that after any initial planning discussions their guide will have some sort of behind-the-scenes communication with 'coordinators' who set up a session in the 'place of life selection' – which they compare to a giant movie theater with screens all around. Here souls are able to review the various options available to them in terms of a selection of human beings that will be incarnate with more or less the right sort of aptitudes, circumstances and environment, at about the right time, perhaps in a number of geographic locations. So effectively this place is one where the subject can manipulate time and control the movie telepathically as if it were a video playback, fast-forwarding where necessary and even pausing the scene to enter it temporarily and gain direct experience of that particular incarnation. The formative period between the ages of about eight to twenty is most regularly viewed, but major events after that may also be seen. This is how one subject describes the experience in some detail:

Continue to report everything. What do you see next?
The ring is surrounded by banks of screens – I am looking at them.
Screens on walls?
They appear as walls themselves, but nothing is really solid... it's all...

elastic... the screens curve around me... moving.

Tell me more about the screens.

They are blank... not reflecting anything yet... they shimmer as sheets of glass... mirrors.

What happens next?

I feel a moment of quietness – it's always like this – then it's as if someone flipped a switch on the projector in a panoramic movie theater. The screen comes alive with images and there is color... action... full of light and sound.

Keep reporting to me. Where is your soul in relation to the screens?

I am hovering in the middle, watching the panorama of life all around me... places... people... I *know* this city!

What do you see?

New York.

Did you ask to see New York City?

We talked about my going back there. Gee – it's changed – more buildings... and the cars... it's as noisy as ever.

I'll come back to New York in a minute. Right now I want you to tell me what is expected of you in the ring.

I'm going to mentally operate the panel.

What's that?

A scanning device in front of the screens. I see it as a mass of lights and buttons. It's as if I'm in the cockpit of an airplane.... I know it sounds crazy but this is what is coming through to me so I can explain to you what I am doing.... I will help the controllers change the images on the screens by operating the scanner with my mind.

Oh, you are going to operate the projector as if you were working in a movie theater?

[Laughs] Not the projector, the scanner. Anyway, they aren't really movies. I am watching life actually going on in the streets of New York. My mind connects with the scanner to control the movement of the scenes I am watching....

Position yourself at the panel and become the operator while continuing to explain everything to me.

I have assumed control. I see... lines converging along various points in a series of scenes... I'm traveling through time now on the lines and watching the images on the screens change.

And the scenes are constantly moving around you?

Yes, then the points light up on the lines when I want the scene to stop.

Why are you doing all this?

I'm scanning. The stops are major turning points on life's pathways involving important decisions... possibilities... events which make it necessary to consider alternate choices in time....

Do you create the scenes of life while you track?

Oh no! I simply control their movement through time on the lines.... The lines of energy are… roads with points of colored light as guideposts which I can move forward, backward, or stop.

As if you were running a video tape with start, fast-forward, stop and rewind buttons?

[Laughs] That's the idea.

All right, you are moving along the track, scanning scenes and you decide to stop. Tell me what you do then.

I suspend the scene on the screens so I can enter it.

What? Are you saying you become part of the scene yourself?

Yes, now I have direct access to the action.

In what way? Do you become a person in the scene, or does your soul hover overhead while people move around?

Both. I can experience what life is like with anyone in the scene, or just watch them from any vantage point.

Now this raises some interesting questions, because at first sight it might appear that once we have made our life choice everything else is predetermined. This idea is reinforced by this subject referring to the place of life selection as the 'ring of destiny'. However, nothing could be further from the truth, and in fact what they appear to see are merely snippets of a number of major *probabilities* on the primary timeline of each future life of their potential incarnations, combined with some less likely or indeed beneficial alternatives based on different choices that might be made, which are then additional *possibilities* for each life. Apparently, though, these alternatives are not unlimited, because after a certain point adding choices does not productively enhance the potential for us to learn lessons. The overall emphasis is that incarnate life involves personal responsibility for karmic choice in a climate of free will. This is how Newton himself describes the planning process:

As they view specific scenes of what the Timemasters want them to see, some souls feel they are playing a chess game where they don't yet know all the possible moves available for a desired ending. Usually, souls look at parts of a future life on a base line, or ring line, as some clients call it. The ring line represents the greatest probable course of a life for each body examined. The soul preparing for incarnation knows that one chess move, one minute change in the game they are watching, could alter the outcome. I find it intriguing that most of the time souls are not shown any in-depth probable future outcomes. They know there are many other possible moves on the chessboard of life which can change at any moment of play. Frankly, this is what makes the game interesting for most souls. Changes in life are conditional on our free will toward a certain action. This causality is part of the laws of karma. Karma is opportunity but it also involves fortitude and endurance because the game will bring setbacks and losses along with personal victories.

Newton provides a prime example of this with a subject whose previous life had been cut short aged sixteen when, on the spur of the moment and in a quest for adventure, he volunteered as a Union messenger for the Battle of Gettysburg in 1863. He had no chance to say goodbye to anyone, and was killed in action the next day. When he returned to his soul group after death, that portion of his young sweetheart's soul energy that remained in the ethereal realms cried out: 'Why are you back here? We were supposed to be married!' He immediately realized this was a totally unforeseen action in his life plan, indicating the extent to which we can exercise free will.

The previous subject goes on to discuss his various next-life choices in some detail. He had requested that he be allowed to train as a classical pianist, because his musical interests were thwarted by an early death and lack of financial opportunity in his previous life in New York. He was also allowed to look at similar possible lives in Los Angeles, Buenos Aires and Oslo. In all these places he watched the students practicing in various musical academies, even making brief contact with their minds to experience their thoughts and feelings. He was particularly studying them in 1956 when they were in their teens, which in earth time meant that he was fast-forwarding from some time just before his birth in 1937. In this case, he did actually choose to return to the same city:

I want New York.
Do you think you have looked at the other cities carefully enough?
[Impatiently] Yes, I did that, but I don't want them.
Wait a minute. What if you liked a music student in Oslo, but wanted to live in New York City?
[Laughs] As a matter of fact, there is a promising girl in Los Angeles, but I still want New York.
All right, move forward. As your time in the ring draws to a close, give me the details of your probable life selection.
I am going to New York to be a musician. I'm still trying to make up my mind between a couple of people, but I think I will choose [stops to laugh] a dumpy kid with a lot of talent. His body won't have the stamina of my last one, but I'll have the advantage of parents with some money who will encourage me to practice, practice, practice.
Money is important?
I know I sound... grasping... selfish... but there was no money in my last life. If I want to express the beauty of music and give pleasure to myself and others, I need proper training and supportive parents, otherwise I'll get sidetracked... I know myself.

We can see that this subject was not only offered a choice of four different cities, but apparently also several options of different students in each of them. This is perhaps rather more than the norm, and certainly in my own example I seemed to have only three life options – albeit rather more contrasting ones. But if this subject's life planning sounds a little too easy and comfortable, we should remind ourselves that his previous life had been a hard one. By contrast, here is the report of another subject whose previous life was that of a wealthy and pampered Chinese empress – and who also only had three options from which to choose

> Of my three choices, two were women and one was a handsome young man who, I was told, 'was feminine inside'. One woman was very thin, almost frail-looking, who was to live a quiet life of a devoted wife and mother. The other woman was chic, kind of flashy, and destined to be a society gadfly. She was also emotionally cold. I chose the man because I would have to cope with a life of homosexuality. I knew if I could overcome the shame of society it would offset my life of adulation as an empress.

He could have chosen to have more fun as a society girl, but in a life so similar to that of the empress that his karma would have been little advanced. He could have chosen the quiet and devoted wife, which arguably would have been more or less a halfway-house choice in terms of adding to his karmic experience. But instead he chose the hardest option for the swiftest possible karmic progression and balancing. This was his choice, and he makes no suggestion that he was coerced. We will consider hard life choices in far more detail in the next chapter.

Of course, while we are learning our own lessons we are also playing a part in the lessons learned by others around us, so another part of the life-planning process involves subjects coordinating them with other members of their soul group. There is clear deliberation about coming back as people who will be part of each other's lives to a greater or lesser degree. We can only assume therefore that the coordinators actually program the life choices each member sees in the place of life selection to have certain probable interactions already built in.

However this underlying process works, the outcome reported by Newton's subjects is that a whole host of souls finally meet in the 'place of recognition' prior to their rebirth. Those present will not only be other members of the primary soul group, but also others from the broader secondary group, and maybe even some others outside of this.

The overriding principle is that all of these souls plan to impact on each other's lives to a greater or lesser extent in a complex web of probable or only partially predefined interactions, which combine to best allow for the potential fulfillment of a number of mutual life goals for each of the participants. Moreover, it is not necessarily the *length* of the potential interaction that defines the strength of the bond between the two souls, but rather the importance of its *impact*.

Of course, the idea that all of these souls come together before incarnating would seem to suggest that they all come down at exactly the same time, whereas in reality this is clearly not the case. Needless to say we must remember that time does not operate in the same way in the ethereal realms, so that – even though I believe that the concept of elapsed time still has a part to play in them – a delay of, say, ten years before one soul reincarnated might seem like the blink of an eye to them. But another way in which the logistics of so many people planning together could be assisted – although this is a complex issue and I am only speculating – is by souls that are already in incarnation letting their soul energy that they left behind in the ethereal realms be involved in 'secondary' planning on a limited ongoing basis. This non-incarnating soul energy is, after all, an integral part of our higher self. It may even be that our incarnating soul energy can get involved in such planning, for example when we sleep, but my feeling is that this portion may be somewhat more restricted to the astral plane. Having said that, perhaps attempting to make such distinctions unnecessarily complicates the general argument.

Newton suggests that our parents tend to come from the broader secondary group, and by implication this would mean that our children do likewise. One reason for this might be that to some extent members of the same primary soul group will try to reincarnate at more or less the same time, or at least in the same human generation – so on that basis they would tend to be our partners or spouses, siblings or friends. However, it appears this is not a hard and fast rule, and Newton provides one case study where he maps the human relationships of one subject over a number of lives against the individual souls involved, noting whether they are from that subject's primary or secondary group. At least in this case the other members of the primary group regularly swapped generations from one incarnation to the next, sometimes being a spouse, sibling or friend to the main subject, sometimes being a parent, child, nephew or niece.

I can only assume that the logistics of planning for such primary cross-generation interactions would have to involve the non-incarnating element of the subjects' soul energy if relatively short interlife durations were involved. For example, if I were to assume that my father was a member of my primary soul group, I may live for as much as fifty or so years after his death. If he were to reincarnate again within that time, but we were still due to have some sort if interaction in our next lives, we would have no obvious interlife overlap in which to plan together. And, as we will see in the final chapter, there is a strong suggestion that in the modern world intervals between incarnations are that short. So it might even be that my non-incarnate soul energy is planning another interaction with him right now, even while I am still in this one.

In any case, the nature of the revision program in the place of recognition is that a number of coordinating prompters provide each group with details of important 'triggers' they should remember once they are incarnate in the next life. Despite the general amnesia that progressively overtakes us when we return to incarnation, these recognition triggers are left with us to prompt us at certain points in our lives that something or someone is crucial to our life plan. They will most likely come through to us as strong intuitions in incarnate life, even though they may just be small and ostensibly insignificant details about other people we meet along the way. These triggers might provide a signal for us to recognize our intended partner, or for a brief but highly significant meeting with a stranger who has some other important role – such as initiating a change of career, or acting as a stimulus to move to another area or country. Subjects report that clearly we can miss these signs, as no doubt many of us do, and that there may even be contingency plans to provide us with another chance for important interactions. But at the end of the day if we completely miss any given set of signs, life goes on but in a different direction from that originally planned – and we may fail to learn our chosen lessons as effectively as we had hoped.

Whether or not souls have a preliminary meeting about their next life with their elders – as I reported doing at the beginning of this chapter – in most cases they will have a formal meeting with them after their visits to the places of life selection and recognition, and just before they return into incarnation. The planning council is restricted to fewer elders, often only three, and these will normally be the prime members of that soul's review council – although sometimes one or even two are unknown specialists. Here is how another of Newton's subjects describes her final planning meeting, which she attends with her guide Magra:

> They want my input to assess my motivations and the strength of my resolve towards working in my new body. I am sure they have had a hand

in the body choices I was given for the life to come because I feel they are skilled strategists in life selection. The committee wants me to honor my contract. They stress the benefits of persistence and holding to my values under adversity. I often give in too easily to anger and they remind me of this while reviewing my past actions and reactions towards events and people. The elders and Magra give me inspiration, hope and encouragement to trust myself more in bad situations and not let things get out of hand. And then, as a final act to bolster my confidence when I am about to leave, they raise their arms and send a power bolt of positive energy into my mind to take with me.

This last act bears some similarity to the 'nurturing with sparkles' that Pam Reynolds reported receiving before her return to life during her near-death experience, as we saw in chapter 2. I would also suggest that these planning meetings with our elders might be more likely to occur if the next life we have just chosen is a difficult and challenging one.

Newton's subjects show us that a whole range of souls, including our soul mates, guides, elders and other expert coordinators, have a hand in setting the stage for the dramatic potential interactions of our next-life play. But we ourselves have the greatest input to the choices involved in this planning process.

So what do our other pioneering researchers have to say about the way in which we choose and plan our next lives? In *Life Between Life* Joel Whitton and his co-author confirm Newton's suggestion that souls are often reluctant to leave their real home and return into incarnation, and provide excellent corroboration of his findings as regards a final appearance before a planning council:

> The most significant finding of Dr Whitton's research is the discovery that many people plan their forthcoming lives while discarnate. The knowledge of self gleaned from the review process equips the soul to make the vital decisions that will determine the form of its next incarnation. But the soul does not act alone. The decision making is heavily influenced by the members of the judgment board who, mindful of the soul's karmic debts and its need for specific lessons, give wide-ranging counsel.... The choice of one's parents, in establishing the setting and direction of the lifetime to come, is immensely important.
>
> The judges' recommendations are made according to what the soul needs, not what it wants. So they tend to be received with mixed feelings unless the soul happens to be fanatical about pursuing its development at any cost.

This suggests that initially some souls may not perceive the life choices offered to them as attractive propositions, although on reflection they will normally recognize the underlying opportunity for karmic advancement. Whitton continues by corroborating the extent to which we make our life plans in conjunction with other close soul mates:

Planning for the next life is frequently undertaken in consultation with other souls with whom bonds have been established over many lifetimes. Which is to say the choice of the time and place of birth is of paramount importance; to choose wrongly is to miss the opportunity for a productive reunion.

Whitton also makes an interesting observation concerning the extent of planning being dependant upon a soul's advancement:

Less-developed personalities seem to require the guidance of a detailed blueprint, while more evolved souls provide themselves with only a general outline, so that they must then act more creatively in challenging situations.

He follows this up with the suggestion that more advanced souls may have a rough plan that extends several lives in advance, while some rebellious or impatient souls may occasionally decide to reject all advice and return into incarnation with no real plan – but apparently these are wasted lives that serve no real purpose:

Occasionally a trance subject has learned that he or she made no plan in the between-life state – knowledge that is invariably communicated to Dr Whitton in fear. Those who have recourse to a karmic script, on the other hand, respond unemotionally under hypnosis even when they describe a life plan filled with hardship. Nothing could be worse, or so it seems, than to have an open future.

Dolores Cannon also provides excellent corroboration of the life-planning process in *Between Death and Life*:

Before beginning the return trip into the physical life the spirit not only goes through the planning sessions with the masters and teachers and consults with the other people they will be trying to work karma with, but they also check out the family they are considering being born into.

Like Whitton's subjects, Cannon's seem to stress the importance

of the family they may be born into, and how they study them from the
ethereal realms, rather than describing a full-on preview of the life of the
adult individual they may choose to become. Here is one describing her
experience:

> I watch the woman who is to be my mother. In this manner I will know
> what to expect.
> *What do you think of the family?*
> I am very unsure. They are very demanding. They have definite ideas of
> what they wish to do. The final decision hasn't been made.
> *When will it be made?*
> Soon. I have a choice. I have to decide whether the lessons I feel I need to
> learn can be taught in this particular existence.
> *How long do you watch them before the decision is made?*
> Sometimes a few days, sometimes longer.
> *If you decided you didn't want to be born there, would another spirit
> come?*
> Yes, but there is a need for me in this situation. I could learn much from
> this.

They also repeatedly stress that the timing of their incarnation must
be right, as much as anything else because of the way they will need to
interact with other affiliated souls. This is how another describes a planning
meeting with other souls and their guides:

> I am with other spirit entities. There is a group of us gathered together.
> You could call it a sort of discussion and planning group. The majority of
> us here have been linked karmically in our past lives. There is one here
> who is our main guide for the group in general, and our individual guides
> are nearby. We are discussing and planning what karmic problems we will
> be working on during this next upcoming life, the one that this subject is
> currently living. And we are discussing and planning how our lives and
> our karmas will interweave and interrelate and what we hope to work out
> karmically.

She then carries on to discuss what such planning means as far as choice
versus destiny is concerned:

> We discuss how we are going to interact with each other. We have our free
> will on such things from the physical viewpoint when we get there. But if
> we work out these things ahead of time we are more apt to be open to our
> spiritual guides as they try to guide us through. It is a way of not being quite
> so haphazard about working our karma.

This suggests that, rather than relying on Newton's triggers, we may instead be actively prompted to take a certain path by our spirit guides as we go along – although both types of assistance would come through our intuition. But this subject goes on to suggest that some souls have less opportunity to plan, partly because the other souls they hope to interact with may already be in incarnation – whereas I have already suggested that our higher selves in one form or another can probably overcome this problem. And to counterbalance this view another of Cannon's subjects reports that souls do regularly get together in pairs, trios or in larger groups to plan their lives, without apparent restriction of opportunity.

As for planning with our elders, another subject – who appears to be relatively advanced, as we have seen are most of the subjects she quotes – describes how these meetings operate from the perspective of someone who is actually on the planning council:

> Others who are in-between lives right now, but not as advanced as we are, will often need help planning for future lives so as to continue progressing their karma. We give them advice and suggestions from our experiences, and then they can make their own decisions – just as the ones who are on higher planes do for us.

This perhaps goes against Newton's general inference that elders are sufficiently advanced that they no longer tend to incarnate on earth, but as always we should be wary of making hard and fast rules about such things, and clearly elders themselves are at different stages of advancement. In any case, another of Cannon's subjects confirms Newton's suggestion that even when souls appear to be placed under pressure to return into incarnation against their will, they are never *forced* to do anything they do not want to do, and sooner or later see the wisdom of the advice given to them:

> A soul might have to go back if they are not looking at something from the right perspective. They would be shown what perspective they need to look at it from, by living through it. Before anyone comes into a life they observe the balance of karma and they observe how it is [she appears to be suggesting they are given some sort of preview of that life]. And they see what aspects of their karma would be worked out best in this particular situation and this particular balance of karma. Their spiritual masters might give some suggestions to help them figure out what they want to accomplish in this life. But no one is ever made to go into a situation they absolutely abhor. It's generally done by a consensus of opinion between the person and their spiritual masters. They won't like many aspects of the life in particular, but the majority of the life will be something they can handle.

And these extra things they're not too fond of are looked upon as spiritual challenges, something for them to accomplish and to work for. How well they handle these things that they don't care for is one of the things that helps them work off some of their karma. On the spiritual plane when they come back and it is seen that they handled it well, that reflects good upon their karma....

The people who are seemingly forced to come back know it's for their own good. After they are given time to think about it they realize that they really do need to come back or they'll be stuck in that one position for ever, and they would never progress. Never progressing is the closest thing there is to the Christian concept of hell.

Another of Cannon's subjects confirms Newton's suggestion that we need to incarnate to learn properly – comparing any attempt to learn in the ethereal realms alone with reading a book but never converting this mere information into real knowledge by practical, hands-on experience. But yet another agrees with Whitton that some impatient souls are in such a hurry to return into incarnation that they make no real plans in the interlife, and then inevitably find that their lives are 'messed up and confused'.

If we now turn to Helen Wambach's group hypnosis results, we must remember that she asked her subjects general questions concerning whether they chose to return in their current life, whether anyone assisted them in this choice, and how they felt about reincarnating on earth. They then filled out answer sheets after the hypnosis sessions had finished, and their answers to any given question – and there were a number of others that do not concern us here – are not particularly detailed or lengthy. But in *Life Before Life* she reports that eighty-one per cent of her subjects confirmed that they did actively choose to be born, and that they received assistance with this process.

A significant number reported discussions with one or more counselors: 'There was a council of twelve who helped me choose, and I did choose freely.' 'Yes, I chose to be born, but a high council seemed to be helping me to make the decision.' Others were clearly referring to assistance from a planning council without actually using that terminology: 'There was a group helping me choose. They listened to what I had planned and made some suggestions.' 'Yes, I chose to be born, and there seemed to be a board or committee – a group of authorities to help me choose.' Others still identified a single individual helping them, who was most likely their spirit guide, even if only a few of them used the expression. And a huge majority indicated that they planned their incarnations carefully with other members of their soul group with whom they would interact, even though they sometimes referred to them merely as 'friends'.

Again we must remember that these subjects were only asked one question about who was assisting them, so they would tend to concentrate on only that aspect of next-life planning that most impressed itself on them – be that discussions with other members of their soul group, with their spirit guide, or with a council of elders. This does not necessarily mean that other life-planning discussions did not take place, only that they were not encouraged to explore them during the group sessions. Similarly Wambach did not explicitly ask her subjects to recall if they were offered a choice of different lives, but several subjects provided this information anyway: 'I did choose to be born, and I had others helping me choose. I had the choice of several entities.' 'I chose this life amidst some kind of assemblage. I had a few choices but they were not unlimited.' However, the extent to which her subjects might have seen full-on previews of their possible life choices is not clear. One interesting aside was their insistence that most souls who were adopted knew in advance this would happen, and chose to have the closest karmic ties with their adoptive rather than natural parents – although this finding should not belittle the karmic impact that giving a child up for adoption clearly has.

Some of the most revealing of Wambach's responses confirm Whitton's suggestion that a small minority of subjects – in her survey less than three per cent – do not listen to the advice of their counselors or guides. Here is a selection of their comments:

But when you asked about the prospect of living the coming lifetime, I became aware that I should have been more selective and waited a few years.

When you asked about the prospect of being born, someone kept saying, 'Wait till a better time. A smaller family would have more time for you.' But I felt, 'No, it has to be now.'

Yes I chose to be born, but I was in a hurry, and I wasn't sure of my choice. When you asked if anyone helped me choose, I became aware that someone, I'm not sure who, gave me a warning, but I felt that I had to get something done and solve something.

Yes, very clearly, I chose to be born. Some entities were trying to advise me, but I didn't listen. I was impatient to finish something I had started.

Yes, I chose to be born, but it was in panic. It was not a decision made at leisure. When you asked if anyone helped me choose, I was aware of guides that seemed to be large light beams, guiding me not to be born now – but I was determined.

These responses do implicitly support the idea that we choose the time, location and circumstances of our next incarnation. But they also indicate that some souls do not always choose wisely, and can be so impatient to return that they make no proper plan – even though advice is clearly available to them in the ethereal realms. This confirms the reports made by some of Whitton's and Cannon's subjects, and I would suggest that it is most likely to be true of less advanced souls. Again we will return to this issue in the next chapter.

The remaining nineteen per cent of Wambach's subjects were either unaware of the choice to come back or received no clear answer to the question, while a few even asserted they had no choice in the matter at all and were coerced. But at the same time a full sixty-eight per cent of the total subjects reported that they were reluctant to leave their real spiritual home and return into incarnation on earth, which – although in contrast to the minority of impatient subjects above – is not inconsistent with Newton's and Whitton's observations. According to Cannon's subjects the minority of souls who feel coerced into coming back are less advanced, and their perception of the process is clouded by their general reluctance and lack of higher judgment.

In *The Search for Lives Past* Ramster suggests rather more strongly that we may not be in full control of our decision to reincarnate:

> My research findings show that in regard to the place and time one is born into there is only a limited choice, sometimes none. People nearly always recall being told when to come back. I have seen grown men cry in trance, insisting that they don't want to come back to earth. The time of birth seems to be very important and not necessarily the choice of the person reincarnating. It seems that the ability to choose a kind mother, or an easy father, a wealthy family, or a scientific family, is not ours.
>
> People recall being born into a family that suits the specific purpose coming and that could be one of many. If it is to learn humility, then it is unlikely one will be born into a kind and rich family, more likely into a harsh, poor one, possibly a family of slaves or prisoners. In those cases people recall the choice being made by a superior being (or beings) as one is usually not likely to see one's own need for humility. 'The purpose of life is to learn,' people under hypnosis report. Whoever comprises the hierarchy for the decision making I don't profess to know. However, according to testimonies, they play a large part in the choice of the family one is born into and the opportunities that confront one during the course of life.
>
> It seems that one's life, therefore, may not be by chance, but instead may be predestined and not necessarily self-chosen. These are the findings as I can determine from the present stage of my research. According to the memory of those regressed, the spirit has little choice but to take part in

whatever lessons are necessary to achieve advancement.

Despite the general tenor of this summary, Ramster does accept that certain superior beings – in Newton's terms these would be guides, elders and coordinators – are involved in our life choices. And as far as supposed predestiny is concerned, in fact we find several of his subjects contradict this by reporting that there was indeed an element of personal choice involved in their life plans. For example, despite her apparent reluctance to return, his subject Gwen McDonald concludes her interlife recall with a reference to her having to make a choice between two families:

> Finally, a man came, he said I must go back to earth. I didn't want to go back, but I had to. He said there were people who needed me and I must help. There were two families who needed me… I had to choose. I could do what I had to do with both families, but I had to choose… and I must go back.

Meanwhile, in *The Truth About Reincarnation* another of Ramster's subjects reports that when it was first suggested that he might return he flatly refused, and instead of being coerced was given more time to ready himself:

> He showed me pictures, the man showed me pictures of earth, people, places, and I said to him, am I to go back? He said it was my decision. He said I had to understand the life that I would live and then I had to decide whether I wanted it or not. He told me all the things that I'd learnt through my last life and explained some of the things I could learn through another life. I asked why couldn't I learn those things where I was, and he said it was because I didn't have a physical body, and for the lessons I needed to learn I needed a physical body. I told him I didn't want to go back and he said I didn't have to if I didn't want to. He asked me why I didn't want to go back, and I said because I thought it was too hard. He said I would know when the time was right whether I wanted to go back or not. Then things just seemed to stay the same for a long time. We'd meet people and we'd talk. After a while I decided I wanted to come back. Lots of people came and we talked about it. We talked about the things I needed to learn and the things I didn't need to learn, and how I would work out and learn the things I needed to learn and didn't relearn the things I already knew, and what best the situation would be that I be born in. It seemed to take a long time. Just before I did come back I wanted it to be quick. I felt that the sooner it was over with the better, the sooner it was started the sooner it would finish. But they said the time had to be right.

We can see that there is a clear element of life preview at the outset of this report that has echoes of Newton's place of life selection, and that the subject is involved in lengthy discussions – probably with his guide and other members of his soul group, maybe even with his elders – about the lessons he will need to learn. Overall, therefore, it appears that Ramster's own commentary about coercion to return and lack of choice is certainly not representative of all his subjects. But to the extent that it is we must remember that he – like Morris Netherton and Brian Woolger – was primarily working with patients in therapy, rather than attempting to research the interlife per se; almost certainly this will have distorted his findings.

In *Remarkable Healings* Shakuntala Modi provides this brief corroboration:

> All my patients describe the same cycle of life. They exist first as a spiritual being. They incarnate into a physical body, not blindly, not randomly, but with a definite plan in mind. In the Light, they describe planning their life in detail. They claim to choose their parents, spouses, children, and other key people in their lives. Patients also remember choosing their occupation, skills, and talents.
>
> They plan in detail all the important events. Over and over, my patients tell me that not only do they plan happy, good, and productive events, but they also choose negative events, circumstances, and tragedies, to balance their negative actions from the past lives or because they need to learn something from them to grow spiritually.

I would not necessarily agree with Modi's use of the pejorative word 'negative', but at least she balances this with the idea that choosing less pleasant experiences or circumstances may stem from a desire to learn rather than representing any sort of punishment, and we will of course return to this issue in the next chapter.

This is how Edith Fiore's patient that I quoted in the last chapter continues her description of the interlife experience in *You Have Been Here Before*: 'Then we choose our next life. *We* choose our next life, how we are going to be able to make up for where we didn't quite make it in our last lives.' And Fiore's own description of her patients' interlife experiences in *The Unquiet Dead* continues on from the quote in the last chapter in the same vein: 'Spirit counselors pointed out what they still had to learn to make the necessary spiritual progress. The next incarnation was planned, based on this knowledge.'

In *Many Lives, Many Masters* Brian Weiss, via Catherine, also briefly confirms the idea of life planning when she reports:

When we get to the spiritual plane, we keep growing there, too. We go through different stages of development. When we arrive, we're burned out. We have to go through a renewal stage, a learning stage, and a stage of decision. We decide when we want to return, where, and for what reasons.

Later on she reconfirms this when discussing the 'plane of transition':

There are seven planes… seven through which we must pass before we are returned. One of them is the plane of transition. There you wait. In that plane is determined what you will take back with you into the next life…. So you choose what life you will have. In the next phase, you are responsible for the life you have. You choose it.

We can see that Catherine's definitive statements about the extent to which we are in control of our lives, both in the ethereal and physical realms, are entirely in accordance with the opinion of the majority of our pioneers' subjects. Even Netherton ends his brief comments about the interlife that I quoted in the last chapter with confirmation that we choose the next body we enter – which arguably contradicts his predominant skepticism about the repetitiveness of all souls' incarnate lives.

As I did with the transition and review stages in the last chapter, I will now summarize the main elements of the life choice and planning stage of the interlife proper as reported by our pioneering researchers. If we commence with the process of choosing the life we are about to come into, Whitton and Cannon both stress that our choice of parents is crucial, as is the timing of our return – although because of our need to interact with other key souls, rather than any sort of astrological influence. Whitton, like Newton, also stresses the importance of the location we choose, for similar interaction reasons. Wambach did not ask whether her subjects had a choice of bodies at all, although at least two volunteered this information, and while Ramster suggests that the choice may be limited and in some cases nonexistent, at least one of his subjects reported being given a choice of two families. Modi again reports that we choose our parents, Weiss mentions the combination of location and timing, while Fiore merely asserts that we choose our next life. So, apart from Wambach and Ramster, all the others might be thought to infer that we only see one choice at a time. This is clearly far removed from the place of life selection reported by Newton – although balancing this Cannon and Ramster explicitly report the idea of seeing visual previews of at least some aspects of the life under consideration, most of the others implicitly support the general idea of some sort of preview merely by reporting on the extent to which we choose and discuss the life to come. I would also argue that our choice of parents, timing and location are inextricably linked and implicit to any life choice or planning discussions.

It is clear from this that the full multiple-choice preview suggested by Newton is not necessarily a universal experience. I would suggest that in some cases we are only offered one choice of life at a time, which we may only be told about rather than seeing it in full preview – and, as we will see in the next chapter, such differences may well be related to our level of advancement. However, it may also be that Newton's concentration on the interlife has revealed a fuller planning experience than most of our other pioneers, and one that is in fact more widespread than their reports suggest. Meanwhile, not only do Newton, Whitton, Wambach and Ramster report a degree of reticence to leave our natural home in the ethereal realms, but also Whitton and Cannon emphasize that this choice may not be immediately attractive to us, precisely because we only learn by experiencing at least some degree of difficulty. However, what all our pioneers report with some certainty is that we are at liberty to reject any option offered to us – which is why personal choice does universally underlie this process – but that, even where initially unattractive lives are offered, most of us sooner or later see the wisdom of the choice and accept it. Ramster alone suggests that coercion is widespread, arguably misinterpreting his own subjects' evidence, while the very few of Wambach's subjects who suggested they had no choice in their return are clearly exceptional cases.

Turning to the process of planning our incarnation with other souls, Whitton, Cannon and Wambach all explicitly corroborate Newton's suggestion that we plan our interactions with them, and the lessons we will each attempt to learn, in great detail. Ramster hints at the idea by reporting extensive discussions, while it is also implicit in Modi's findings because of her emphasis on how we plan all the important events and all the key people in our lives. Fiore and Weiss are silent on this matter, perhaps only because of the brevity of their reports. Again, none of them goes into anything like Newton's detail, especially in respect of the place of recognition in which he suggests we agree recognition triggers. But, except in the case of immediate family interactions, it is arguable that some sort of similar process would be a logical necessity if more tenuous interactions are going to stand a strong chance of coming to fruition. The other possibility, as Cannon suggests, is that our spirit guides prompt us as we go along.

As regards Newton's description of a final planning meeting with our council of elders – also attended by our spirit guide with whom we will have had extensive previous discussions – again Whitton, Cannon and

Wambach explicitly corroborate this idea. Ramster reports the planning involvement of superior beings and Fiore of spirit counselors, who we can at the very least assume are our guides, while Modi and Weiss are silent on the subject but again perhaps only because of the brevity of their reports.

What do our pioneers have to say about the thorny issue of choice versus predestiny once we are in incarnate life in the physical realm, given that our life plans are presumably in place? Most of them do not really discuss this issue, but Cannon and Weiss certainly affirm Newton's suggestion that we still have karmic free will when in incarnation, and that nothing in our lives is completely predestined. Ramster talks about predestiny, but again he is arguably using the word somewhat loosely. Moreover, all our pioneers confirm that we engage in extensive reviews of our past lives in one form or another, and that the purpose of these reviews is to see where we went right and where we went wrong. Implicit in this process is the idea that we have free will in the actions we take once in incarnation. If everything were predetermined for us, we would learn absolutely nothing and make no progress whatever.

We might also remind ourselves that Whitton reports that more advanced souls have less detailed life plans, but conversely he, Cannon and Wambach suggest that some certainly impatient and arguably less advanced souls may sometimes disregard their guides' and counselors' advice, and return hastily into incarnation without a proper plan at all. These are likely to be somewhat wasted and confused lives that serve no purpose other than perhaps to teach the soul that such impetuousness is inadvisable.

	Newton	Whitton	Cannon	Wambach	Ramster	Modi	Fiore	Weiss
Choice of parents/location/timing	●	●	●	○	○	●	○	●
Multiple choice of lives	●			●	●			
Detailed life preview	●	○	●	○	●	○	○	○
Choice to reject life offered	●	●	●	●	●	●	●	●
Planning with other souls	●	●	●	●	●	●		
Planning with elders/guides	●	●	●	●	●		●	
Choice to deviate from plan in life	●	○	●	○	○	○	○	○

Again I have attempted to summarize these findings in grid form, although I have again omitted Netherton because of the extreme brevity of his report. In this case it is not an exact process, but I believe it presents a reasonable summary given the detailed analysis I have just provided.

In particular, I have inserted circles rather than dots where I think it is reasonable to assume that the element in question is strongly implied by that researcher, for the reasons given above, even if it is not explicitly mentioned by them. And for the most part even the remaining gaps on the grid are, as before, not indicative of active rejection of that element by the researcher. This indicates that, once again, there is a good deal of consistency in the findings of our pioneers as regards next-life choices and planning in the interlife. And the general conclusion is that under normal circumstances, no matter how much help we have, or from whom, or via what mechanisms, *we ourselves* choose, and to a greater or lesser extent plan, the lives we incarnate into – and are the masters of our own fate.

The extent of our control is summarized succinctly by one of Cannon's advanced subjects:

> In these times of distress and urgency, we would ask that you always remember that your experiences are given to you by yourself. You, yourself, choose what is to be experienced, so that you may learn those lessons which you need. Thus through these painful experiences you will indeed begin to know yourself. And if you learn something from these experiences, then they will not have been in vain.
>
> You truly are the master of your own fate and destiny. You, yourself are in complete control of what you call your lifetime. You are the one who is making decisions as to when and where and how. We, from our point of view, can see all the options spread out before you. But it is you, yourself who must make the final decisions.

Before we move on, I would like to say a few words about our return into incarnation. Even many therapists who have no interest in past lives or the interlife have consistently indicated that, under hypnosis and in other altered states of consciousness, we are able to remember astonishing details both of our time in the womb and of the first few years of life. This in turn suggests that we have a surprising degree of awareness during this time, and that the common mistake of underestimating the capabilities and understanding of even very young children is a grave one. In *Many Lifetimes* Joan Grant, who we met in chapter 4, reveals some amazing memories of the intricacy of her thought processes from as early as four months old – while it was one patient's memory of her incarnation right back at the point of conception that first convinced her partner Denys Kelsey that the soul must be separate from the physical body. It seems clear that, despite the relative youth of our physical bodies and brain at this time, the soul that has lived perhaps many times before has not completely lost its experience.

As we might expect, our interlife pioneers have much to say on the issue of our return. Newton's subjects report that, when they are finally ready for rebirth into their chosen human body, the process is similar to that of death inasmuch as they travel quickly down a dark tunnel and suddenly find themselves in the womb. They indicate that the process of assimilating the soul with the impressionable and developing human brain of the unborn child takes some time, and must be carefully handled. Some immature souls go at it 'like a bull in a china shop' and cause significant disorientation, while more advanced souls are very careful about gradually matching their unique energy vibrations to the unique circuitry and wave patterns of their host's brain. But they suggest that some brains are more 'dense' and difficult to work with than others. Moreover, if the characteristics of the ethereal soul and physical brain are not well-matched, and the soul is unable to effect a proper merger, this can have a huge bearing on the subsequent development of the person as a whole and on their future life.

As to the timing of incarnation, Newton's subjects report entering the fetus usually from somewhere between five months into pregnancy right up until just before birth, with the onus on the soul itself to choose the timing. Wambach provides considerable details in her survey, finding that eighty-nine per cent of her subjects did not enter the fetus until six months into pregnancy, while thirty-three per cent of these delayed until just before, or even during, birth. Of the other eleven per cent, quite a few suggested they entered as early as the point of conception. She also found that souls appear to know if a child is going to be born prematurely, and make sure they enter in time, even if in something of a rush. Whitton's subjects report that they enter between several months before birth to as late as just after it, while Cannon's subjects report entering any time from conception right up until some days after birth. Perhaps the most balanced view is Modi's, whose patients describe entering properly at any time between conception and the birth itself, but also suggest that they place at least a portion of their soul energy into the fetus at conception.

With some similarity, Newton's subjects report that they can 'absent' themselves from their host body while it is still in the womb, and indeed for some years after birth, usually up until the time when the child goes to school and becomes more constantly active. They report that they stay in earth's astral plane to be nearby in case of emergency, but one even describes these early years as the one time they can 'goof off' and just have fun with other souls without too much responsibility. Most of Wambach's subjects confirm the ability to leave the fetus – some even seeming to feel that they hovered around the mother's body for a long time before actually entering. Cannon too confirms this, reporting that her subjects absent themselves for short periods not only before birth but also for some years after – although this will usually be when the child is asleep, and must not be for too long. They suggest that such regular absences should cease by the age of about one, but can carry on on an occasional basis until as much as age five. All this is to some extent related to the idea that, even as adults, when we sleep, meditate, are unconscious or in coma, our incarnate soul energy can leave the physical body encased within the astral body – and we will return to this issue in the final chapter.

Newton's subjects indicate that they are fully aware of their mother's feelings while in the womb, and can even attempt to influence them to some extent. Eighty-six per cent of Wambach's subjects confirm an awareness of their mother's emotions, as do most of Cannon's, Netherton's and Modi's. In particular, they all report that the knowledge of whether they are loved and wanted or not can have a profound impact on their subsequent development.

Meanwhile, Cannon also discusses the onset of amnesia after birth:

> The first cries are in frustration at being unable to communicate with these strange creatures in this new environment. Then softly a wave of forgetfulness seems to sweep over them as their responses dull and the memories of other planes and other existences fade away.

In fact many of our pioneers suggest that this amnesia concerning past lives and the ethereal realms is rather more progressive, so that babies and young children have far greater ability to tap into such memories than adults but increasingly lose it over time. This ties in well with Stevenson's research, and with the evidence of George Rodonaia's ability to communicate with his neighbors' baby during his near-death experience, which we discussed in chapter 2. It may even be that when babies sleep for much of the time, rather than forgetting their experiences in the ethereal realms as some people suggest, they are still remembering it at least for a while to make their transition into the physical more gradual and less traumatic. As to why the gradual onset of ethereal amnesia is so important, Newton's subjects indicate it ensures that we do not allow preconceptions from memories of past lives, and of our current life plan, to limit our potential for learning and freedom of choice in the current life. Whitton confirms this, likening it to ensuring we do not have all the answers before we take an exam, but he emphasizes that it is also important for us to forget our natural spiritual home otherwise we would constantly pine to return to it. Modi adds that to keep so many often-traumatic memories of past lives in ready recall would overwhelm us and stop us functioning on an everyday basis, so that some repression is necessary just as with memories of this life; and Cannon agrees with this view. We will discuss amnesia in considerably more detail in the final chapter.

In her quote concerning the birth experience Cannon hints that the soul finds its reemergence into the physical world proper at birth somewhat traumatic, and this idea is given fuller expression by Wambach's subjects:

> Most impressive in the reports was the degree of sadness experienced about emerging into the world. Even though for many of my subjects the actual birth was not physically traumatic, a sense of sorrow pervaded the experience…. Many subjects reported that the onrush of physical sensations on emerging from the birth canal was disturbing and very unpleasant. Apparently the soul exists in a quite different environment in the between-life state. The physical senses bring so much vivid input that the soul feels almost 'drowned' in light, cold air, sounds. Surprising to me was the frequent report that the soul in the new-born infant feels cut-off, diminished, alone compared to the between-life state. To be alive in a body is to be alone and unconnected.

Apparently this deep sense of isolation was made worse if there was any delay in the newborn child being held and comforted by their mother, and these views echo the findings of numerous other researchers.

So it would appear that being born again into a physical body is, in most cases, far more traumatic than the mostly pleasant experience of dying and passing once again into our real spiritual home – even if the physical death itself involves unpleasant circumstances. Much of the reason for this contrast appears to be the lightness and freedom of movement, the heightened awareness and wisdom, and above all the companionship and universal and unconditional love that we experience in our natural home in the ethereal realms. Perhaps if more of us appreciated this contrast we might be far less scared of shuffling off our mortal coil, and far less obsessed with hanging on to physical life at all costs – and especially with attempting to prolong it by any artificial means available when old age or severe illness has reduced its quality to near zero, rather than letting nature take its proper course.

7

THE DYNAMICS OF KARMA
Are We Punished?

The concept of karma has been around for millennia, emerging first in the East. It is nearly always portrayed in the 'revealed wisdom' of Hindu and Buddhist theology as involving 'action and reaction', which is then variously translated into ideas of 'cause and effect', 'what goes around comes around', or 'as you sow, so shall you reap'. But how much do our pioneers agree with this view? And, even more important, does the evidence of their case studies support their interpretations? To answer these questions we will need to examine not only the extraordinary insights of *interlife* subjects, but also the intriguing karmic patterns that emerge from *therapy* patients' past lives. And one thing that becomes crystal clear when we do this is that karma operates in anything but a mechanistically predictable way – which is why it is so inappropriate to talk about the 'laws of karma'.

If we start by looking at our pioneers' general views of karma, there is a distinct contrast between those who were concentrating primarily on past-life therapy and those who were more interlife oriented. In the former group, for example, Helen Wambach and Shakuntala Modi tend towards the classical eastern view of cause and effect. This would encompass both apparently positive and negative aspects of reaping what we sow. But others who were mainly concentrating on therapy tend to emphasize the negative version of this alone, which is usually expressed as 'paying off karmic debts'. Edith Fiore makes no real comment about karma but she does record the insight of one of her patients, as quoted in chapter 5, which is expressed in exactly these terms. Morris Netherton is perhaps slightly more perceptive when he suggests that karma is the 'paying off of debts to ourselves', while Roger Woolger – who says little about the interlife experience, which is why I have not mentioned him in the last two chapters, but does make an important contribution to our study of karma – tends to go along with this view. Meanwhile, in line with his somewhat negative comments about our lack of choice of future incarnations, Peter Ramster is the most hardline of them all, suggesting that karma involves 'exact retribution for past misdemeanors' – which tends to suggest justice of the 'eye for an eye' variety; but, in truth, even his own case studies show far more complexity than can be accounted for by this rather black-and-white approach.

Those pioneers whose research has a somewhat broader perspective display what are in my opinion somewhat more perceptive views. Joel Whitton suggests that there can be elements of directly retributive karma, especially in the earliest stages of an individual soul's development, and also of compensatory karma in which the soul has to make amends for past wrongs in one way or another – that is, to pay off karmic debts. But he adds that especially more advanced souls perceive karma as a learning process that allows them to grow and develop by refining their nature. Several of Dolores Cannon's subjects also stress the learning and growth aspect of karma, indicating that only less advanced souls tend to perceive it in terms of retribution and compensation. Although Brian Weiss's patient Catherine suggests that sometimes we do have to pay off karmic debts, she too indicates that karma should primarily be about refining ourselves by leaving our vices behind, and about learning by experiencing all sides of life. And Michael Newton emphasizes that unpleasant circumstances are normally chosen as part of a learning process.

I indicated in the opening chapter that my preference is for the idea that karma involves 'balancing experiences so that we see both sides of every coin'. This tends to emphasize the learning aspect of *progressive* karma that is favored by this latter group. But it is clear that the reason the former group seem to cling on primarily to the negative version of a more classical view of karma is precisely that they are concentrating on therapy with patients who have psychological or psychosomatic problems of varying severity. I am certainly not convinced that these patients are paying off karmic debts as most of these therapists seem to assume, but what is clear is that they are stuck in cycles of *repetitive* karma. Indeed, having spent several weeks reading through the mass of therapeutic case studies provided by especially Fiore, Netherton, Woolger and even Whitton, I can safely say that it was one of the most harrowing experiences I have ever been through. Certainly if we were all destined for the types of repeatedly unpleasant lives revealed in therapy – whether as predominantly victims, perpetrators or in alternating patterns – it would be a grim prospect indeed. So the first key question is this: are these therapy patients unusual, or do we all go through the same repetitive patterns at some stage?

Most of our pioneers do not directly answer this question. Indeed, quite a few fail to make any proper distinction between progressive and repetitive karma at all. But the real key lies in what some of our pioneers hint at but fail to take to its logical conclusion. That is, to use the *differences* in interlife experiences that appear to be related to karmic advancement to produce a generalized model of soul evolution – which, among other things, must include both repetitive and progressive karmic stages.

We have just seen that Whitton and Cannon suggest that karma is perceived and even regulated differently by souls dependant on their level of advancement. We also saw in the last chapter that both these two and Wambach suggest that less advanced souls may not follow the advice of their guides and elders in planning their incarnations, and may decide to return with undue haste and no real plan. While in chapter 5 we saw that Cannon suggests less advanced souls may not make proper use of the learning facilities available in the interlife. With some similarity, Stevenson's child subjects rarely have any memories of an interlife in the ethereal realms at all, some specifically reporting that they merely hung around the astral plane near their place of death before choosing their new parents and incarnating again relatively swiftly – albeit sometimes assisted by a guide of some sort. Whitton actually goes further by suggesting that some souls merely sleep for lengthy periods between lives:

> Just how much self-consciousness is exhibited in the *bardo* appears to vary greatly from person to person. Those who are keen to proceed vigorously with their spiritual development tend to be most consciously active between incarnations. Those who show little interest in the evolutionary process are inclined to 'sleep' for the equivalent of huge tracts of earthbound time.

Such periods of lengthy 'sleep' are indicative of what I have previously referred to as the blank interlife experience reported by Netherton and Woolger. In this context, the latter asserts that the majority of his patients reported no real interlife experience after death and seemed to come straight back – although again we should be wary of these findings because, like Netherton, he expresses a degree of reluctance to take patients into their life between lives in the first place. However, a minority of Woolger's patients did spontaneously regress into the interlife without his direction, where they recalled a number of our common experiences: of being met by familiar figures from past lives, or by a guide; of reviewing their last life with what he refers to as a 'karmic committee'; and of having access to life books, or in the case of one patient a 'tapestry that represented her many interwoven lives' – which has some similarity to Cannon's subject's idea in chapter 5, but on a less collective scale.

It is interesting that Woolger and his wife did conduct some group regression workshops in addition to his therapeutic work, although he provides no details about how these different environments affected his findings. But it is surely no coincidence that the majority of his subjects were patients under therapy, most of whom were clearly stuck in a cycle of repetitive karma, and that a majority also had no real interlife experience to report. I would not be surprised if his non-therapeutic workshop subjects had a much higher incidence of remembering an interlife. Woolger himself suggests that only those subjects who had lived and, crucially, properly *assimilated* a number of painful lives tended to experience the interlife proper.

Although Hans TenDam does not record the interlife experiences of his own patients in any detail in either of his books, he too acknowledges that they differ from subject to subject – especially in respect of the extent of next-life planning. In fact he is the only pioneer who goes as far as to formalize this into a model involving three separate 'reincarnation populations' of souls with different characteristics that depend upon their level of advancement. This is exactly what I had myself decided was required, and I was delighted to come across such confirmation. So I am obviously in general agreement with this approach, but as far as his specific framework is concerned I would argue that it suffers from a number of drawbacks. First, he oversimplifies the categories somewhat, and they require further distinction by introducing an extra one. Second, there are a number of additional characteristics that need to be brought into each category. So my own version of this framework suggests that all souls go through what I refer to as the 'four stages of karmic evolution'.

The Novice Stage: During this stage, our lives are relatively undirected, to such an extent that we probably do not go through the typical interlife in the ethereal realms at all, and instead attempt to gain as much experience of incarnate life as we can in a short time. For this reason the intervals between our incarnations will probably be short, and our process of choosing a new life will be somewhat haphazard.

The Repetitive Karma Stage: After a while our experience and awareness builds up sufficiently for us to move on to the stage where we are at least *able* to enter the ethereal realms between incarnations. However, we are not yet experienced enough to fully digest the complex karmic lessons that we all have to undergo in earthly life so, although more review and planning guidance is now available to us during the interlife, we may not always properly seek it out or make effective use of it. I would suggest that this is the stage during which we might perceive more compulsion to incarnate again rather than free choice, and continue to be given less choices of potential lives – precisely because they need to have the same characteristics as many of our previous ones in order that we face the same repetitive tests to see if, this time, we will pass them. It is also the stage in which we might have a lengthy but blank interlife experience.

In addition it is likely that a combination of these two stages accounts for the following types of experience reported by a number of our pioneering therapists. First, those souls who appear to hurry back into incarnation without proper thought. And second, those who are so confused or traumatized that they fail to enter the ethereal realms proper at all between lives, and instead wander on the astral plane only before choosing another body to reincarnate into with no planning at all. It is also clear that most of Stevenson's child cases are in one of these stages, although this should not be taken to imply that the population of the less developed world, from which most of his subjects come, is likely to be far more oriented towards less advanced souls; there is no widespread data to support such a potentially divisive assertion, and I will return to this issue in the final chapter.

The Progressive Karma Stage: At some point we make a significant breakthrough, usually by at last waking up to and taking proper notice of our guides' and elders' advice during the interlife. However the patients of past-life therapists, for example, may well achieve this breakthrough by receiving assistance on the physical plane; and there are other more general lessons we can learn while in incarnate life that will help us to move towards this stage, as we will shortly see. From this point on we are far more likely to have the full interlife experience of life review and planning, including more choices of lives and circumstances. However, in this stage we are still very much bound to the earthly karmic round.

The Transcendent Stage: Finally, when we have learned all our earthly karmic lessons by experiencing both sides of every coin, we move on to that stage in which we transcend the need to incarnate on the physical plane, and can commence the process of reuniting properly with the Source in the ethereal realms. I will say more about this in the final chapter, but for now I want to emphasize that this is unlikely to be a swift one-off process, as many esoteric teachings might seem to suggest – indeed in many ways it merely marks the stage when our real work in the ethereal realms is just beginning. But souls that have reached this stage may still choose to come back to assist humanity in one way or another, in which case their goals will be far more group oriented than individual. Of course, they should have no more personal karmic issues that require resolution in the physical plane; but they might still make mistakes while returning and set up new karmic processes for themselves. This might sound ridiculous because this stage tends to be associated with great teachers such as, for example, Krishna, Buddha, Moses, Jesus and Mohammed. But in reality pioneers like Newton and Cannon indicate that there may be many more souls in this stage who still incarnate on earth, even though we may not hear much about them, and even though they are still clearly a very small minority.

This four-stage karmic model represents a massive generalization. I am aware that, although I am attempting to make clear distinctions between them, there will undoubtedly be significant overlap especially between the middle two stages. But the general framework that I have described is, I believe, extremely useful as an analytical tool that helps us to better understand the incredibly complex dynamics of karma. As to how many incarnations we might need in each stage, almost certainly this is highly variable based on the individual soul's experiences and attitudes – although we will examine some estimates from our pioneers in the final chapter.

Let us now turn to our pioneering therapists' case studies in order to attempt to understand more about how repetitive karma works in practice. How can we attempt to break out of repetitive karmic cycles? And, in particular, do their case studies actually support their suggestion that such karma involves paying off debts, either by compensation or even by direct retribution?

The first thing we notice is that the current lives of their patients – even when beset by a variety of phobias, obsessions and other psychological or psychosomatic problems – are in most cases nowhere near as fraught as many of their previous ones; perhaps the main exceptions are those cases in which the patient has suffered terrible abuse of one form or another as a child. There are some obvious reasons for this. For a start, they are all still alive – or were at the time of their therapy – so they have not suffered the sort of violent and traumatic deaths they often have in past lives, which are frequently a major source of their problems. Allied to this, for all that our modern society is clearly far from perfect, in the developed world at least life is in general far less harsh than it has usually been in the past. At various times and in various cultures, the law of the gun, savage wars fought one-on-one with crude weapons, human sacrifice, slavery, contemptible attitudes towards the female of the species, and various other factors – not to mention a multitude of untreatable diseases – meant that appalling violence and trauma was commonplace. So we must not ignore the fact that the dynamics of changing cultural conditions are having a major impact on the mechanisms through which karma operates.

If we commence by looking at what appear to be some relatively simple cases, in her first book Fiore documents a number in which apparently a single major trauma in a past life lies at the heart of the patient's current problem. As a result she derives the following list of general linkages, which are confirmed fully by Modi and at least partially by most other pioneers. Patients who are chronically overweight or, by complete contrast, have anorexic tendencies, have often been close to starvation in a past life. Fear of the dark and insomnia often relate to previous lives in which the patient was either molested or killed while asleep. Assorted phobias of fire, water, guns, knives, snakes, flying, crowds, enclosed spaces, heights and so on can often be traced to related past-life traumas. And chronic pains in various parts of the body often stem from injuries, usually fatal, received in previous lives – which appears to be consistent with some aspects of Stevenson's research into birthmarks and defects.

Of course, it is important to emphasize that not everyone who suffers from one of these obsessions, fears, phobias or even psychosomatic physical pains will be carrying it over from a past life. But, even when they are, the current symptom is rarely anywhere near as bad as the past-life experience that brought it on, as debilitating as it might still sometimes be. In fact, in many cases it appears that the symptom is carried over not primarily to inconvenience the subject but instead to act as a major reminder – the idea of triggers once again springs to mind – that they have a past-life problem that must still be karmically resolved. In these apparently relatively simple cases it is almost impossible to judge whether the subject is primarily in the repetitive or progressive karmic stage without further investigation of other past lives – although clearly a degree of repetition does seem to be involved.

By contrast, most of Whitton's, Woolger's and Netherton's case studies reveal a number of interwoven past lives in which their patients appear to be placing themselves in related traumatic situations repeatedly in successive lives, and in at least some of these cases the patients' current lives are again pretty traumatic. This is clearly indicative of repetitive karma, so they should be able to tell us far more about the nature of the beast.

Woolger provides one example in which a patient that he refers to simply as Chris had definitely had one of the more traumatic current lives. Abused as a child in a drunken and harsh environment on a farm, he repeatedly attempted to run away, and had been in and out of prison in a dismal spiral of depression, alcohol and suicide attempts. Even his efforts to start a family had been thwarted by the cot death of his infant son. His opening statement to Woolger said it all: 'I'm all alone. I'm a piece of shit. I want to die.'

When regressed back to his birth, Chris discovered that his mother had not wanted him and had attempted her own abortion by falling down the stairs; as a result he was born three months premature, and was placed in an incubator for an equivalent period. Alone and isolated, he already knew he was not wanted, and just wanted to die. We might note at this point that many of Fiore's, Netherton's, Woolger's and Modi's patients find that past-life traumas are often mirrored in utero and at birth. This might be by the negative emotions of the parents or obstetrics staff, or by physical complications: for example, the umbilical cord being wrapped around the neck is often mirroring a prior hanging or strangling; the use of forceps, prior blows to the head; and caesarian sections, prior stabbing or cutting. Again it seems that these may be acting as deliberate triggers to remind us of something that requires karmic resolution – although it must be said that very few people would be likely to remember these triggers in adult life, let alone understand their significance, unless they were to be regressed to their time as a fetus by a professional.

A number of Chris's past lives revealed a depressingly similar pattern. As a prisoner in a dungeon in Scotland he had been beaten and was sick with dysentery when he was left alone in chains to die a slow and lonely death – full of hatred for his callous English captors. He had been a sickly adolescent in a besieged native tribe in the American Northwest where, unable to fight and with the medicine man proclaiming his sickness as a sign of evil, his father left him to die – again without food and alone – in the tribal burial grounds; this time his dying thoughts were that he was no good, and deserved to die. In a much earlier tribal life he recalled having been an old man abandoned to die alone in a cave, where he was eaten by a bear while still half-alive.

But further investigation of Chris's case revealed at least two lives that might be thought to justify so much suffering. In one in China his intense anger at his prostitute mother for whom he acted as lookout – and whose only affection lay in attempts to seduce him – boiled over into a life of violent crime and a hatred of all women; and one pregnant woman whose house he was robbing tragically bore the full brunt of his frustrations when he stabbed her and cut out both her heart and her unborn baby. This time his feeling was one of intense remorse. But in another life as an uncontrollably psychopathic Eskimo he took out his hatred of women in general by forcing himself sexually upon as many female members of the tribe as he could, and of his shrewish wife in particular by murdering her. The tribe staked him out in the cold to die – but this time a polar bear provided the finishing touches and he apparently remained unrepentant.

We do not know in exactly what order Chris's lives took place, but this is clearly a case in which the subject alternates between being predominantly perpetrator and victim. Woolger and Netherton describe a number of similar cases, and on the face of it these seem to be reasonably understandable within a classical karmic framework of supposed action and reaction, or more particularly of paying off debts. But what about cases in which the subject is the consistent perpetrator of misdemeanors from life to life, with their only element of victimization being that they were often provoked?

Such was the case with one of Whitton's subjects, Ben Garonzi, who relived a succession of male and female lives in which he killed those who treated him badly. In his current life he had been so brutalized by his father that, at the age of eighteen, he took a knife from a kitchen drawer with every intention of murdering his alcoholically comatose tormentor. But an inner voice told him to resist the temptation, which he did. When regressed into the interlife, Ben found out that he had chosen this incarnation as yet another test to see if he could resist the temptation to react to extreme provocation with equally extreme violence – a test that he finally passed. He retrospectively reported that as a result of his therapy his characteristic aimlessness up to that point had been replaced by ambition, and he had gone on to pursue a successful career. These are all sure signs that he had finally broken free of the cycle of repetitive karma and moved on. It seems he had learned a *lesson* – which was not to repeat the mistakes of the past. There is no obvious paying off of debts here.

Even less readily understandable are those cases reported by both Woolger and Netherton in which the subjects are consistently the victims – and where regression uncovers no lives in which they were the perpetrators of significant misdemeanors that might account for their apparent punishment. For example, one of Netherton's patients came to him suffering from impotence, and abdominal pains that signaled a potential ulcer brought on by the stress of running the business he owned. Under hypnosis he revealed that he had had an early tribal life in which his lover's husband caught them together, cut his penis off and ran him through the stomach with his spear. A later life was that of an aristocrat in which this former guilt resurfaced when he was about to have sex with a mistress; it was sufficient to cause a perforated stomach from which he eventually died – even though such behavior was generally regarded as perfectly acceptable at the time. And a later one still was that of a businessman whose wife conspired with her brother to obtain the money from his business by setting him up to be caught with a prostitute – his recurring guilt this time unhinging him mentally so that he was committed to an asylum in which he died from the plague. On the face of it this man had repeatedly been the victim, and had done nothing of real note to deserve his succession of unpleasant lives.

So what can we say about the repetitive karma involved in all these cases – be they predominantly perpetrator-based, victim-based or alternating? They have far more psychological complexities than I have been able to describe here, but they all have one thing in common: intense emotions of loss, guilt, failure, shame, remorse, sorrow, humiliation, jealousy, anger, hatred or revenge are always attached to the past-life experiences. And, as I hinted in chapters 3 and 5, it would appear that it is our failure to deal with such intense unresolved emotions from past lives, and to assimilate them properly, which leads to us carrying them forward into new lives.

Let us look at the resolution of the three complex cases I have just described. Despite his general views about karma, Woolger himself emphasizes that the key for his patient Chris had nothing to do with looking at his situation as one involving paying off karmic debts, and everything to do with *learning* to adopt the appropriate emotional response to his various experiences. Whitton's patient Ben needed to *learn* not to resort to the ultimate in violent responses, however much he was angry and provoked. He had already passed this test in respect of his father, but it was only when he appreciated the repetitive pattern over many past lives that he was properly able to move on with his life. And although Netherton suggests that his impotent patient's problems improved after therapy, his explanation of why is not exactly clear; my own view is that he needed to get rid of his guilt about sex, and of his intense desire to hold onto a business that had been taken away from him in related circumstances in a past life. This he was able to do by understanding that they involved past-life patterns, and *learning* that he no longer needed to repeat them. In all these cases I would argue that the underlying key was also for patients to learn to *forgive others* that had wronged them, and to *forgive themselves* for misdemeanors they had perpetrated, in order to move on properly. So it seems we can conclude that when we fail to deal appropriately with a situation, and especially our emotional reaction to it, we are faced with the same or a similar situation to see if we handle it better next time. And unfortunately if we do not, we face it again, and again, and again.

This clearly provides us with one of the most important lessons in this book: that fundamentally *all* karma is about *learning*, and not about paying off any sort of debts. Even in the repetitive stage we keep facing the same circumstances because we repeatedly fail to learn the appropriate lesson. In fact, this is blindingly obvious, and something I had always intuitively known. But when I read constant descriptions especially from our therapy-oriented pioneers that most karma involves paying off debts, as the negative form of a classical process of action and reaction, it clouded my judgment for some time. In fact, Stevenson's birthmark and defect cases provide the most obvious clue to the truth, because it simply makes no sense that someone who had been murdered or accidentally killed in a past life, often through no fault of their own, would then carry a physical reminder of this as some sort of debt repayment. Instead, I would argue that these exceptional souls' physical characteristics were karmically imprinted because they were insufficiently experienced to properly assimilate their intense emotions during what was almost certainly a blank or even nonexistent interlife – and arguably to serve as reminder triggers that they had emotional work to complete. But if this seems to imply that all physical disability is related to unassimilated past-life experiences – even if not paying off karmic debts as such – we will shortly see that nothing could be further from the truth.

One issue that might still be thought to prove that repetitive karma can involve paying off debts is that of murder. A number of our pioneering therapists report cases in which their patients go through successive incarnations – particularly with one other soul to whom they are closely linked in various family or partner relationships – killing and being killed by each other in a vicious cycle, which clearly means they are stuck in a repetitive rut. Modi's subjects report that murder does incur a karmic debt that will have to be repaid to the specific victim if the two souls are closely linked – either by looking after them in a subsequent life, perhaps under trying circumstances, or perhaps by having to save their life; or, if the souls are not closely linked, the debt will have to be repaid to humanity in general. But is this an appropriate way to interpret the situation? We have already seen that Whitton's patient Ben consistently murdered those who tormented him in various lives; but he was not forced to pay off the supposed debt to his victims as far as we can tell. All he had to do was to learn not to do it again. And, as one of Cannon's subjects reports, if the fixed retribution of an eye for an eye was in operation he should have been murdered either by that same person or by someone else in a future life. Yet this would in turn place a new karmic burden on them – so, unless we expect everyone to go around murdering each other in an endless orgy of violence, such a view makes no sense at all.

Fortunately, when I was able to pull all this evidence together and stand back from it, everything became clear again. But this clearly shows just how much the received wisdom of the past can continue to mislead us. If our pioneers had never heard of the concept of karma involving paying off debts as a reaction to supposedly negative past behavior, they would probably never have got themselves into the perfectly understandable muddle of trying to incorporate it into their explanations of their cases – and would have realized the simple truth that all karma involves learning much earlier. Admittedly Newton is alone in seeming to suggest this, without mentioning supposed debts. But, in completely avoiding the conclusion we must inevitably draw from other pioneers' evidence, he does not really acknowledge that repetitive karma or blank interlife experiences exist at all; so arguably, and without wishing to be disrespectful, his emphasis on learning owes more to luck than judgment. By contrast, TenDam clearly realizes that there are different stages and types of karma, but his analysis is at least partially based on more advanced Hindu concepts that distinguish between a 'karmic stage' dominated by a system of 'reward and punishment', and a 'dharmic stage' that he interprets as being more dominated by 'moral laws'. This is similar to my ideas of repetitive and progressive karma, but yet again we can see the misleading and unhelpful idea of punishment creeps into the former to confuse the picture.

The extent to which escape from repetitive non-assimilation karma might require us to forgive especially ourselves is vividly demonstrated by the heart-rending case of another of Whitton's subjects called Jenny Saunders. She came to his attention because of a disturbing event in which blood had appeared on a wall in her flat, and further investigation revealed that she had a history of similar psychokinetic manifestations. He knew from prior research that these must be masking some strong repressed emotions, and over a prolonged and difficult period of hypnotic regression he managed to establish that she had been cruelly abused by her mother as a child. She therefore avoided sex because any feelings of pleasure brought on by sexual stimulation were immediately replaced by emotional pain and intense anger. This discovery should have been the end of the matter, but Jenny's symptoms persisted.

Whitton had also discovered that she was terrified of having a child of her own, and not long before becoming his patient had had an abortion after a rare sexual encounter. In fact, the child would have been due on the exact date that the blood first appeared on her wall, which Whitton realized was almost certainly a past-life trigger or karmic reminder of some sort. So he decided to regress her back beyond her childhood, at which point the following series of lives unfolded. As Lucy Bowden she had been the poverty-stricken single mother of a mentally retarded child in London in the late seventeenth century. In those days everyone regarded such children as a mere burden to be disposed of, but Lucy cherished and protected her child with all her might, and they rarely left their rented attic room because of her fear that someone – well-meaning or not – might try to rid her of her supposed burden. But one day she went to fetch some provisions, and stopped to have a drink with some friends at an inn. Not used to alcohol, time slipped by quickly until she realized she had been gone for some hours, and rushed home. When she turned the corner into her street, her blazing house was surrounded by curious onlookers. Pushing through the crowd, she realized there was nothing she could do to save her child. Her unbearable inner torment was to set up a recurring pattern.

In her next life in the mid-nineteenth century Jenny was Angela, a young girl abandoned by her parents and brought up in a Chicago orphanage. At sixteen she left the harsh institution behind to seek a new life in the midwest, ending up as a barmaid and part-time prostitute in a small town in Colorado. The local doctor fell in love with her, and she fell pregnant by him. But, unbeknown to her, the local parson began berating the doctor that his child would be borne out of wedlock to a woman of ill repute, and blackmailed him into agreeing that it should be committed to an institution to preserve its moral sanctity. As soon as it was born the parson, doctor and two assistants came to collect the baby, wrestling it from the convalescing Angela's startled grasp. Instinctively she reached for a shotgun she always kept under her bed for protection, and in the ensuing struggle the weapon discharged right at the baby and the assistant who was carrying it, killing both instantly. Again, Angela's shock and remorse was unbearable, but worse was to come. Their curiosity piqued by the sound of a gunshot, and with the parson egging them on to punish the murderer, six cowboys entered the room and dragged Angela off to a cattle shed. I will try to be brief about what happened next. They gang-raped her, strung her up from a beam, flayed her with whips and finally skinned her alive with their knives. After reliving this nauseating brutality, Jenny wept uncontrollably in Whitton's office – probably for the first time in her life.

On the face of it here we have a girl who has repeatedly been born into cruel circumstances, and has twice tried to rear a child only to have it cruelly snatched away from her pretty much by accident. Was this a punishment meted out by her council of elders? If it were, they would be a harsh bunch indeed, which goes against everything we have learned about them. But no. When Whitton regressed Jenny into her most recent interlife, she perceived herself appearing before them in chains, and it became abundantly obvious that she was meting out her *own* ethereal punishment because of her failure to *forgive herself* for letting her children down in these two previous lives. Her insistence on her guilt was so intense that it seems her elders had little option but to present her with a life in which she would face harsh circumstances again in her current life, although they provided a karmic script that would ensure she would be given the opportunity to forgive herself provided she took the right path. With Whitton's help, this is what she did indeed do – and hopefully all of this indicates that she was finally breaking free from the bonds of repetitive karma.

Woolger discusses two other important cases in which patients spontaneously, and for him rarely, made at least a tentative exploration of the interlife; and both provide important elements of corroboration. In the first, Madeleine had been in a state of almost suicidal depression for a considerable time, her dominant emotion being that she was wicked and deserved to suffer. It appears that she may have had a number of past lives as victim, but certainly two in which she was perpetrator. As a pirate she had taken great pleasure in the torture and execution of her captives, but after his death her former personality had entered into a hellish interlife exile, clearly of his own making, in which he saw all the people he had made to suffer:

> I'm punishing myself. In this dimension a part of me knows that this is what I have to do to atone for what I have done to others, and in order to be human again I have to feel what my victims must have felt before they died, desolate, alone, and without hope.

We could not ask for finer corroboration of Newton's subjects' reports from chapter 5 of severely traumatized souls spending a period of time in reflective seclusion. Nevertheless, after a period of time Madeleine's soul was told in no uncertain terms that enough was enough:

> There's a light ahead of me; it's starting to get warm. I'm stepping onto the grass. There are people and voices ahead of me and I hear an authoritative voice which says: 'Enough, enough. You have done enough.' I know now that my punishment is over.

After this experience she found herself in the womb, and going on to lead the more recent past life of a carpenter who married the woman he loved and experienced great happiness. Moving once more into the interlife she questioned why she had deserved such a good life, but what appears to have been her own higher self insisted that she had to learn through love and not just through suffering. It is unclear whether Madeleine had other experiences during these interlife intervals, particularly relating to the proper planning of her next lives, which Woolger did not elicit from her. But what we can safely say is that, despite her period of depression in her current life, because she was learning progressively more in the interlife she was most likely well on the way to making the transition from the repetitive to the progressive karmic stage. Above all we see that, just as with Jenny Saunders, to the extent any punishment was involved it was entirely *self-inflicted* – and this time restricted to the ethereal realms only.

The second case involves Milton, who came to Woolger after separating from his wife feeling that abandonment and betrayal by partners were his lot in life. Again a series of past lives revealed him as both victim and perpetrator in situations of power and passion. After most of these he did not progress into the interlife at all but, after his regression to what appears to be his most recent past life as the bloodthirsty leader of a band of Moroccan bandits, he spontaneously described how he was met by a spirit guide after his death, who spoke to him as follows:

> You must meditate long on this life, to look at what you have done. You must see the people you have killed, examine the deeds you have done, see if what you have done is good. You will have much time to examine these things – things you have not thought of much in that life, thoughts you had put aside. This task will take as long as you need to perform it.

Milton went on to describe how he derived a state of great peace from his subsequent interlife meditation, in recognizing where he had gone wrong in that life but also seeing why he had to experience it. Again we do not know if Milton went through any other experiences in this interlife, especially relating to next-life planning, which were not properly elicited from him. But it is clear that he had reached a definable point in his succession of lives whereby he was at least starting to have some sort of proper interlife experience involving a review. His current-life problems notwithstanding, I would argue that this means he was probably in the process of making the transition to the progressive karmic stage. And this case seems to provide evidence that this transition is related to starting to take proper advice from our guides and elders during the interlife.

To sum up, I propose that even repetitive karma does not involve paying off debts, but instead derives from us having failed to assimilate intense past-life emotions properly. There are therefore a number of keys to breaking out of such a cycle, which is almost certainly one that we all have to go through as souls, albeit that some appear to remain stuck there for longer than others. One major reason for this will not be that we are being punished by our elders for past misdemeanors, but that we are punishing ourselves through our failure to forgive ourselves. So we might wait until, perhaps even by a process of inevitable attrition, we finally start to wake up in the interlife and properly take the advice of our guides and elders. This in itself will almost certainly be enough to more or less break the chain – as we saw in the case of Woolger's patient Madeleine.

But as long as we fail to do this we will continue to be faced by similar circumstances in our next lives. So is there anything we can do in incarnate life to break the chain? Clearly, we must *learn* to react differently to the problems placed in our path, for example either by not acting as an aggressor as a response to provocation, or by not allowing ourselves to be a victim of someone else acting as an aggressor. Moreover, even if we do to some extent allow these modes of reaction to continue, or are placed in a situation in which we seem to have very little alternative, then the least we can do is to make sure that our emotional response to them is tempered. In this way they no longer hold their karmic charge, and our soul can break out of the repetitive stranglehold and move forwards to more progressive incarnations.

There is a major implication of this view that even repetitive karma primarily involves learning, and it is perhaps an unexpected one. It is that when we appreciate karmic dynamics in this light we can drop the assumption that they always relate to past lives. Under a classical view, we must endure our current tests because we are paying off debts from the past. Now, as we will shortly see, once we are in the progressive stage we should view adverse circumstances as learning opportunities that we have deliberately chosen anyway, and not as being necessarily related to past lives. But under this new view we can also appreciate that even if we are faced by repetitive karma the trick is to react to it properly *in this life* – and this is true even if we have no conscious awareness of the related past-life patterns. So, in fact, we really do not need to know what stage we are in, because our best course of action will be the same. We are *not* condemned to stick in a repetitive cycle, even for the duration of our current life. And, whatever our stage of development, the trick is to maintain balanced emotions and reactions to all circumstances. I will talk about this much more in the final chapter. But for now I want to emphasize that, although past-life and interlife therapy has clearly helped a great many people to overcome psychological and psychosomatic problems, and although I would quite happily continue to recommend it, in fact this concentration on the past may be to some extent unnecessary.

The Sanskrit word *karma* literally means 'action'. But when we think of it in terms of action and reaction, this has two effects. First, in the context of repetitive karma, it tends to place the emphasis on the past – as in past actions leading to the current reaction of having to pay off debts. Second, even in the context of progressive karma and looking towards the future, it tends to suggest that current actions create predetermined future reactions. But clearly my proposed view of karma as primarily involving learning in both the repetitive and the progressive context does require that the emphasis be shifted irrevocably away from the past and towards the future. And it is also essential that we appreciate that karma involves choice and not predetermination. For both these reasons, I propose that we should stop thinking of karma in terms of *action and reaction*, and instead adopt a concept found primarily in Taoist teachings – that of *right action*, pure and simple. This keeps the original meaning of the word, but subtly shifts the emphasis onto the present and future instead of the past, as well as removing the connotation of predetermined linkages that follow some sort of inviolate law. In addition, rather than thinking of our present circumstances as being reactively determined by our past, we should concentrate instead on how our present choices are proactively shaping our future. This ties in well with the oft-touted idea that if we concentrate on right action in the present, the future will take care of itself.

If we now turn to an examination of progressive karma, the first issue we might like to investigate is what proportion of the population has reached the progressive karma stage. Despite my view that whatever stage we are in our approach to life should be the same, the therapeutic case studies show that to be in the repetitive stage is less than ideal. So if the bulk of us were in this stage it would undoubtedly be a rather depressing scenario. Clearly we have few formal statistics to go by, but I did suggest that one facet of the repetitive stage is likely to be that such souls do not plan their incarnations properly with their guides and elders, and also feel more coerced into returning. In the last chapter we saw that over eighty per cent of Wambach's survey subjects felt they were *not* coerced and had some assistance with their decision; and we also saw that Newton, Cannon, Whitton, Modi and Fiore emphasize the extent to which the majority of their subjects were in control of their life choices and planned them in detail. This suggests that the vast majority of us are most likely in the progressive karma stage.

I must emphasize that, in drawing the distinction between progressive and repetitive karma, the last thing I want to do is create an impression of elitism. I have already indicated that the distinction may not be at all clear-cut for many of us as individual souls, and that people who have psychological or psychosomatic problems may not necessarily have derived them from a past life as part of a repetitive karmic rut. As I suggested earlier, I use these terms primarily in an attempt to provide some guidelines for us to examine how karma operates in general. And, although we cannot escape the fact that evidence points towards us all being at different levels of karmic advancement, this is not a competition, and anyone who sees it as such is missing the point – and probably not doing their karma much good into the bargain. We all have to go through the same stages. Some of us started earlier than others. Some might get through some parts faster, and others slower. But I would argue that we are all destined to reach the ultimate transcendent stage eventually.

In attempting to gain an appreciation of how the dynamics of progressive and repetitive karma differ, we need to rely rather more on those pioneers who were not concentrating so much on therapy. And, rather than use this as an exercise in self-congratulation, in fact the best way to understand the distinction is to continue to examine adverse life circumstances. A fine example is provided by Newton, when one of his subjects reports that another soul from his group had 'hurt a girl terribly' in one incarnation, and that after a period of secluded reorientation away from his soul mates he reincarnated in the form of a woman who would herself be abused in similar fashion. On the face of it this is the repetitive karma of direct retribution at its finest. But the subject emphasizes that this was entirely *his choice*, because he himself felt that this would be the best way for him to 'appreciate the damage he had done to the girl'. There is a fine distinction here, but the emphasis – from the subject, not from Newton himself – is clearly on planning the next life on the basis of learning by experiencing the other side of the coin, and not on self-punishment. The best way to describe this would perhaps be karmic *balancing* rather than compensation.

It is highly unlikely that this clarity of interlife understanding would be attained by someone still stuck in the repetitive karma stage, so we can see that we can still be the perpetrator or victim of quite dreadful circumstances even when we have reached the progressive stage. But in most such cases it appears that the emotional reaction to the situation is more balanced and properly assimilated during the interlife, so that the emphasis afterwards is on learning and not on self-punishment. One of Cannon's subjects corroborates this view, indicating that in certain circumstances even a relatively advanced soul might agree to go through the complementary bad experience that they had inflicted on another, but only because they themselves feel this would be the best way to learn the harm they caused by the original act, and not because it is a punishment per se.

It would be easy to attempt to suggest that a key distinction between progressive and repetitive karma is that the latter does relate to past-life behavior, even if it still involves learning, and the former does not. That is exactly what my use of the term 'repetitive' implies. But examples such as these make it clear that we can choose to experience adverse circumstances that are related to past-life errors even when we are in the progressive stage. Perhaps the best way to think of this is that elements of repetitive karma can creep in even when we are in the progressive stage – but the fact that we have nevertheless reached that stage is clear from our interlife experience and the attitude we adopt to planning our next life. That having been said, it is highly likely that such cases are not the norm once we have reached the progressive stage. It is far more likely that when we face difficult or traumatic circumstances they are not related to past-life experiences at all, but rather that we choose them to accelerate our own or even others' learning.

To see how this might be the case, let us return to the issue of murder, and look at it from the victim's karmic perspective. Admittedly they might just be someone who has been the perpetrator of some sort of similar misdemeanor before, and has agreed to come back and have their life cut short to experience the other side of the coin. But this may well be a relatively rare occurrence. It is just as likely that they simply have their own lessons to learn from having their life cut short that are not related to past events. And, as strange as it may at first sound, it may even be that they agreed to be murdered not just to further their own learning but, more altruistically, to also further that of their murderer and of their own family and friends. This is probably also true of untimely death in a more general sense. The test of losing a loved one is one of the most severe we ever have to face, but it is far more severe if they are taken from us suddenly and before time – whether this be by murder, accident or illness. To face it with dignity and without anger, bitterness and regrets is a major test we all have to face at some point. What better service could a loved one perform for us than to force us to face this test, as part of our appreciation that their soul has survived and we will be reunited with them after our own death?

In case anyone thinks that it is all very well for me to talk about such things hypothetically without ever experiencing said circumstances, I might point out that one of my older sisters was taken from our family in a car accident for which she was completely blameless many years ago. She was in her thirties and she and I were very close, even though we lived in different parts of the country. It was a major test for us all to accept what had happened – especially when, for example, several of us had deliberately risked our lives for many years, weekend in, weekend out, while racing motorcycles. Above all we faced the major test of not blaming the other driver – a young man who made the mistake of overtaking before the brow of a hill, the sort of mistake we have all made as inexperienced drivers. I accept that if, for example, he had been drunk, our test would have been more severe; but he was not. I cannot begin to fathom the detailed karmic dynamics that saw her taken early from her two young children and her husband, but I am pretty certain that they will all understand them when they are reunited. Moreover, even with rose-tinted glasses cast aside, she was definitely one of the most beautifully unspoilt examples of a child of nature I have ever had the pleasure to meet; so, although of course I cannot be sure and am unashamedly biased, I would bet good money that her death was not linked to some past-life event. And on a more selfish note, although of course her loss was painful, I am thankful for the time I spent with her – and for the fact that her death was one of the major triggers in my own life that prompted me to start thinking far more philosophically, especially about what might happen after death.

To reinforce this theme of adverse circumstances being deliberately chosen for their fresh learning potential rather than being related to unlearned past-life lessons, another of Newton's subjects reports that he planned a life as an American Indian boy who knew in advance he would die at the age of seven – because 'he was looking for a short-burst lesson in humility and this life as a mistreated starving half-breed was enough'. To take it a stage further with respect to helping others, another reported that she and three other members of her soul group volunteered to incarnate as Jewish girls in Munich, knowing that they would all be taken to the same barracks in the death camp at Dachau in 1941, where they would die together. There was no suggestion that this was a punishment for them. And although it may have involved some personal lessons concerning, for example, courage or humility, they – and presumably many others like them – would almost certainly have known that they were helping humanity as a whole with a much greater lesson.

Nowhere is the principle of souls volunteering to help others with important lessons more at work than in the most untimely of deaths, those of very young children. They might be murdered, die of cot death or other natural causes, or even miscarry or be deliberately aborted in the womb. What can we say to alleviate the suffering of parents who have experienced such loss? Both Newton's and Cannon's subjects confirm that in most of these cases the soul of the child or fetus will have deliberately and unselfishly chosen to have a 'filler life' that involves no karma or learning for them at all, but instead provides fresh learning – or more rarely karmic balancing – opportunities for those closest to them. They are certainly not being punished themselves, and nor are their parents except in those most likely even rarer circumstances that it is self-inflicted as part of a repetitive karmic cycle.

The thorny issue of suicide represents something of a contrast. We saw in chapter 5 that one of Newton's subjects who took her own past-life immediately realized that in bailing out early she had failed to take on her allotted problems properly that time around, and so would have to do it all over again; and another was shown a number of alternative paths she could have taken with her unborn and fatherless child rather than kill herself. Newton, Cannon and Modi all agree that suicide is just about the worst act we can possibly commit, because their subjects universally report that breaking our 'contract of life' is a severe abrogation of responsibility. Unfortunately, they also report that in being forced to face the same tests again, suicides run a high risk of entering a repetitive karmic rut. Newton indicates that the harshest criticism he has ever encountered from a council of elders was reserved for a subject who had repeatedly committed suicide:

> Once again you are here early and we are disappointed. Have you not learned the same test grows more difficult with each new life you terminate? Your behavior is selfish for many reasons, not the least of which is the sorrow you caused to those left behind who loved you. How much longer will you continue to just throw away the perfectly good bodies we give you? Tell us when you are ready to stop engaging in self-pity and underestimating your capabilities.

Moreover, one of Cannon's subjects emphasizes the seriousness of suicide by indicating that it is the one thing that can *never* be planned in advance, even to help others learn. So we are forced to conclude that, although suicide does not lead to direct punishment as such, it is the one act that almost certainly involves little or no learning other than that one must go through the relevant experiences all over again, which is clearly a form of repetitive karma. The only exception to this rule is when Newton's subjects report that committing suicide to escape chronic pain or bodily incapacity is regarded as somewhat more acceptable in the ethereal realms. This seems logical, and also suggests that euthanasia should be perfectly acceptable were it not for the potential of deviousness on the part of grasping family members.

Perhaps the most contentious area of karmic debate is that of physical disability or disfigurement. People in Britain will probably remember that in the nineties the England football manager, Glenn Hoddle, was sacked at least partly for suggesting that people with disabilities were paying for misdemeanors in past lives. I have to say that I felt this was an overreaction, not least because he was only voicing a view that has been held by the majority of people in the East for millennia. It also indicated just how intolerant we can be of views that do not coincide with our own, and was hardly consistent with our supposed right of free speech – primarily because he dared to contravene our often exaggerated subservience to political correctness. But, all that aside, was he right? Of course not. Such a view is far too formulaic and simplistic.

If we are to look at this issue realistically, there is some evidence that physical disability *can* have its roots in the *self-inflicted* punishment of repetitive non-assimilation karma. We have already seen that this might be true of many of Stevenson's birth defect cases, even when the subject was the *victim* of murder in a previous life. And, by contrast, in one exceptional case it seems that a child knew perfectly well that his birth defect – a malformed right arm – arose as a self-inflicted punishment for him having *perpetrated* the murder of his fiancée in his last life. However, one of Newton's subjects reports that in a past life in the nineteenth century she chose to incarnate in the body of a girl that she knew would have a high probability of losing the use of her legs in a carriage accident at the age of six. She chose this deliberately, having had various other lives with a fully functioning and strong body, because she wanted to be fully bedridden and physically inactive to develop her intellectual capabilities – while for their own karmic reasons her parents wanted to care unconditionally for a daughter that would not marry and leave them. So we can clearly see that in this case there was absolutely no connection to past-life events at all, and this subject chose her past life to learn entirely fresh lessons.

Both Newton's and Cannon's subjects repeatedly confirm that, generally speaking, we deliberately choose to be physically disabled because it gives us the opportunity to learn important lessons far faster than we otherwise might. Different disabilities or disfigurements of course provide different opportunities, and the lessons may well be different for someone disabled or disfigured at birth or very young than for someone to whom it occurs later in life. But these lessons are likely to include learning humility without being crushed by ridicule; learning to overcome discrimination; learning who we really are as a person, and not just who people think we are based on how we look; learning to be less judgmental, or how to better identify with disabled or other disadvantaged people in a future life; learning to overcome physical pain by endurance; developing other physical senses if we have lost one or more; learning trust especially if we are blind; teaching others about their responses to disability, or perhaps even more disfigurement, without letting frustration turn to anger; and teaching others what can be achieved even with a severe handicap, thus spurring their own belief that anything is possible.

To sum up, it is likely that most of us primarily choose adverse circumstances such as untimely death or disability because we want to learn entirely new lessons ourselves, or to help others to learn them. On rarer occasions we may choose them as part of a karmic balancing related to past-life experiences, but this will still not be any sort of debt-repayment, compensation or even self-punishment. Only when we remain firmly stuck in the repetitive karma stage will any form of compensation or punishment related to past-life events come into play – and even then this is entirely self-inflicted rather than imposed, and derives from us gaining less perspective and balance from our time in the ethereal realms.

I am acutely aware some of these ideas may be extremely sensitive for a number of people, even if less so than the conventional eastern stance. But I can only hope that on proper reflection the notion that we deliberately choose the circumstances of our lives both good and bad – and that no circumstances, however dire, are brought about by arbitrary chance, as an imposed punishment or by divine whim – can be seen as immensely empowering and liberating. And remember, this is not only true of progressive karma, under which we face predominantly new challenges to learn new lessons. It is also generally true of repetitive karma, except that here we are facing the same challenges as in the past in the hope that we will learn lessons we failed to grasp before.

To continue in this more positive vein, just as we sometimes carry forward unresolved emotions from past lives, it seems we may also carry forward our talents and abilities. I would argue that zenoglossy is an obvious example, and even where such abilities are only displayed under hypnosis I would take a bet that – if the person involved chose to try and learn the language they spoke so fluently while in trance – they would pick it up with ease and far quicker than most. Indeed, why do some of us learn some subjects far faster than others, or show greater aptitude for some activities than others? Where do child prodigies who go on to become geniuses in their field obtain their precocious talent? I do not discount nature or nurture. But nor can we discount the significant role that past-life learning might play.

While we are on the subject of nature versus nurture, there is another vexing issue on which past-life and interlife therapy can, in my opinion and that of most of our pioneers, shed considerable light – and that is gender identity. It is increasingly common for people in modern society to identify with the opposite sex from that of their birth to such an extent that they opt for surgery to change their gender. And I strongly suspect that in many cases the reason for gender identity problems has nothing to do with either nature or nurture, and everything to do with the underlying gender identity of the reincarnating soul.

Newton's subjects report that although all souls are essentially androgynous, and can and do take either gender in incarnation in order to gain a balance of experience, especially less advanced souls tend to favor one sex over the other. They will also tend to express themselves in that gender even when in the ethereal realms, irrespective of whether they are projecting themselves in pseudo-physical form or just as soul energy. Only more advanced souls will be more androgynous, and arguably only similarly advanced souls will perceive this properly.

That being the case, both Newton and TenDam report that it is easy to see how a soul who was having an incarnation in their less-favored sex could become disoriented, especially if this followed a series of lives in their favored sex. This might apply particularly to souls who are moving into the progressive karma stage, because it seems that souls in the repetitive stage are far more likely to stick with one gender again and again, as demonstrated by the examples earlier in this chapter. The key point for me is that they would almost certainly have deliberately chosen their sex for this life in order to further their experience, and this idea is certainly confirmed by Wambach's second group regression survey in which seventy-six per cent of her subjects confirmed that they deliberately chose their sex for one reason or another.

Given that medical progress has led to gender change being a widely available surgical procedure, I accept that in some cases a soul might actually have planned such life-changing surgery during the interlife. But I would argue strongly that many other people might well be avoiding the lessons they specifically came here to learn if they go ahead with a sex change, and that could only be a less than ideal outcome for them as an individual. In these cases, regression therapy might well relieve the person of their inner tensions, and allow them to have a more balanced self-image without resorting to surgery. We might also note that, although we will not be discussing possession properly until chapter 9, Fiore and Modi suggest that possession by a spirit of the opposite sex can also be the cause of gender identity problems.

If we turn now to the issue of homosexuality, a number of our pioneers report on subjects who planned a homosexual life in order to learn something. Clearly more enlightened attitudes are hopefully reducing this learning potential – indeed many homosexuals would probably now argue that they do not see their preferred sexual orientation as an adverse circumstance at all. Nevertheless, it is clear that even quite recently intolerance of homosexuality might have led to the subject being something of an outcast or suffering persecution – and in some cultures around the world that would still happen. Newton's subject from the last chapter who had previously been a pampered Chinese empress is clearly a case in point, and his choice was similar to that of souls who, for example, deliberately choose physical disability for learning reasons. That having been said, as TenDam points out it is not impossible that unassimilated past-life emotions might lead to homosexuality as part of a repetitive karmic cycle; for example, in a man who had not overcome being rejected by a woman in a former life, or in a woman who had vowed never to repeat a painful childbirth in one of hers. Nevertheless, we should remember that such karmic linkages are always variable, so that these past-life experiences might produce completely different reactions in other people.

At this point I would like to say a few words about the American psychic Edgar Cayce, the so-called 'sleeping prophet' who gave over fourteen thousand trance readings to subjects in the first half of the twentieth century – almost all of which were recorded in shorthand by witnesses. He is regarded as one of the forefathers of the holistic healing movement because the majority of his readings dealt with the underlying emotional causes of medical problems, and the reason I make an exception and include such channeled material here is that Cayce took the view that virtually all medical problems had not only an emotional but also a *karmic* content. For him this specifically meant that they derived from a past life.

So do Cayce's readings, which are particularly unusual in the extent to which they attempt to relate primarily physical and medical problems to underlying karma, shed any important light on the dynamics of what appears to be predominantly repetitive karma? A useful summary of his holistic healing is Mary Anne Woodward's 1985 book *Scars of the Soul*, in which she provides extracts from a number of his medical readings dealing with diseases such as cancer, stroke, paralysis, diabetes, tuberculosis, arthritis, asthma, epilepsy, multiple sclerosis and Parkinson's, as well as with congenital abnormalities and with more psychological and physiological problems.

If we start with the negatives, unfortunately I cannot help but report that Cayce's readings are somewhat tiresome to read. The language is stilted, ungrammatical, sometimes repetitive and often includes overtly religious exhortations – which is no real surprise because he was a devout Christian, who for a long time remained surprised if not perturbed by the extent to which his readings involved reincarnation. As for the karma behind the physical problems, many of his medical readings were not accompanied by his somewhat different 'life' readings, in which he provided details of past lives. So in many cases the details of what supposedly brought about current conditions are sparse or nonexistent – although when details are given they are quite specific, usually including the former name. But it has to be said that in many cases Cayce merely states that the problem is karmic, indicates that the subject must learn to be more spiritual through concentrated prayer and meditation, and pretty much leaves it at that. He does also make suggestions for physical therapy in most cases – which include the ingestion of various substances, electrotherapy or hydrotherapy, or the use of various radioactive or 'wet cell' appliances – but Woodward deliberately does not concentrate on these aspects of his work, and neither will I here.

But there are some positives, and they stem from those cases in which he does provide a degree of explanation of the karmic dynamics involved. He told a seventeen-year-old girl with incipient bone cancer in her hip that she was suffering because, as a Roman spectator of Christian persecution during Nero's reign, she had laughed at an injury to one of the girls in the arena – and then felt extremely guilty about it. This might certainly be regarded as consistent with the self-punishment of repetitive karma due to the non-assimilation of intense emotions – although in a later session Cayce reported that she had had two intermediate lives in which she had not suffered unduly because she was not ready, while the link between a general guilt and cancer of the hip is far more tenuous than we normally encounter in our pioneers' therapy. Nevertheless, he also identified the girl she had laughed at as her sister-in-law in her current life, and in a number of cases he confirms the idea that we reincarnate regularly with other members of our soul group to work through mutual karma. Moreover, Cayce regularly indicates that children's problems are as much about their parents' karma as their own, and here learning tends to be stressed rather than punishment. It might even be argued that in avoiding the details of past-life dynamics in many cases he was anticipating my own advice that to some extent these do not matter, and that all that does matter is our emotional reaction to our current circumstances – even if his advice concerning meditation and adopting a more spiritual approach is rather more generalized than that which I have already provided, and will do more in the final chapter.

That having been said, Cayce's emphasis in the vast majority of his readings is that current medical and psychological problems are indeed punishments for past-life misdemeanors, and that in 'meeting self' we are reaping what we sow. So, again, I am forced to disagree with his underlying rationale, because his emphasis is far more on apparently imposed punishments than on self-punishment or learning. It is also true to say that our pioneering therapists would undoubtedly be far more reticent about suggesting that even diseases such as cancer and stroke stem from past-life causes rather than current lifestyle choices concerning diet, tobacco, alcohol, drugs, exercise and levels of stress – except perhaps when they struck young people or those who had led an apparently healthy life.

So much for Cayce's views on karma. But I would also like to examine his work from a broader perspective, to see what we can determine about the success and reliability of his channeling. If we commence with the results of his healing advice, again it is only fair to report that because his was not a formal practice the follow-up of cases was somewhat haphazard. But it would appear that even a number of the subjects selected by Woodward returned for repeat visits with their symptoms little relieved – which, perhaps understandably as a Cayce aficionado, she puts down to the fact that they did not properly follow his advice. Most subjects were certainly told that their cures would be slow, and would require immense patience and fortitude. So what I think we can say safely without bias is that his success rate, and the speed of remission if achieved, was nothing like that of our pioneering hypnotherapists.

If we turn now to his nonmedical life readings, I already knew from my research for *Giza: The Truth* – for which I used a compilation of readings prepared by his son Edgar Evans Cayce entitled *Edgar Cayce on Atlantis* – that in a number of these he had proclaimed that a 'Hall of Records' would be discovered underneath the Great Sphinx of Giza in 1998, and had made various other predictions, most of which have not come to fruition as we will see in the next chapter. I also knew that he regularly indicated his subjects had had lives within the highly technological civilization of Atlantis – indeed that he himself was supposed to be the reincarnation of a high priest by the name of Ra-Ta who lived at the time of the evacuation of survivors from Atlantis to Egypt in 10,500 BC. These too are ideas about which I am extremely dubious, and to which we will return in the final chapter.

An earlier compilation prepared by Woodward in 1971 entitled *Edgar Cayce's Story of Karma* provides more medical readings dealing with supposedly physical karma, and also life readings dealing with family and group karma that echo the point about soul groups made above. But perhaps most revealing are those life readings requested by people wanting to understand their true vocation in life. Here we find that almost every subject has had past lives in which they appear to have been highly influential and powerful people, many again in Atlantis, although Egyptian and biblical lives also abound. And famous personages are not missing from these readings either. The parents of a baby boy who was less than a year old were promised great things because he had supposedly been the composer Franz Liszt in a previous life, while his brother had been the playwright

Molière. Those of another boy of four really had something special on their hands – he had supposedly been both the biblical prophet Elisha, successor to Elijah, and also before that the flood survivor and savior of humanity Noah himself. Unfortunately, follow-up revealed that this latter subject might not have been completely fulfilling his supreme potential as the manager of a supermarket in a small southern town. By contrast, we have repeatedly seen that one of the strongest features of past-life regression is the extent to which subjects recalling their own lives – rather than having a channeler such as Cayce do it for them – do *not* tend to remember being famous or powerful people, but instead recall lives that were often squalid and full of trauma or drudgery, or at least unremarkable.

To step back for a moment, Cayce did as much as anyone in the twentieth century to bring a spiritual worldview based on karma and reincarnation to the fore in the western world; and the Association for Research and Enlightenment in Virginia Beach that was founded to perpetuate his work has done much good since his death. But clearly I have serious doubts about his life readings. And because we can only assume that the same ethereal source was responsible for his medical readings as well, this must place a question mark over both.

This must necessarily lead us into a discussion of channeled material in general. How can I argue that information derived from hypnotic regression is broadly speaking reliable, and at the same time that channeled material is often not? It would definitely appear that when we act as our *own* channels, albeit with the aid of hypnosis, the results seem to go through far less distortion than when someone else purports to do it for us using an apparently external spiritual source. In a completely general sense, and without making any judgment about Cayce himself, one explanation could be that the channeler is something of a charlatan, so that although they have a gift they may sometimes augment their material with complete fantasy. Or it could be that they are completely trustworthy as individuals, but sometimes unwittingly distort their genuine source material with additional subjective material from their own subconscious. For example, as K Paul Johnson shows in his 1998 book *Edgar Cayce in Context*, contrary to the impression given for a long time we now know that in his normal life Cayce had a number of acquaintances who had read extensively about Atlantis, Egypt and similar esoteric subjects, and that his Atlantean readings only commenced after he had been introduced to them.

But what if the ethereal source itself is unreliable? The leading Qabalist Dion Fortune makes this comment in her introduction to her excellent 1949 book *The Cosmic Doctrine*, which was also channeled:

Do not think that because a piece of information is obtained in an abnormal way it is bound to be true, any more than a thing is bound to be true because it is printed in a book.... A spirit communication may come from a perfectly genuine spirit, and yet be valueless. Even if a man survives bodily death, dying is not going to cure him of being a fool; if he had no sense on the physical plane, he will not have any more on the astral.

I am inclined to agree with this sentiment. We should remember that, although the insights that our pioneers' subjects seem to achieve when regressed into their past lives and the interlife are often extremely valuable, and although they are incapable of lying as such, they can still make mistakes – especially when questioned about general and non-personalized spiritual or historical issues. By the same token, there may be some discarnate souls who are attracted to channelers but whose access to akashic information and other insights is less than perfect; nor can we totally discount the possibility that some of them may be deliberately mischievous, pure and simple. Another possibility is that the channeled source may not be an external one at all, but rather the channeler's own higher self. If this is the case, then as I have already suggested it would appear their ability to discern akashic information about other people, rather than just themselves, is far less impressive than they and their supporters might think. This might certainly be true of Cayce, in that his first and arguably most successful medical diagnosis, which set him on the path to notoriety, was on himself. Having been unable to speak for ten months, he traced the cause of his own loss of speech to a psychological problem affecting the muscles in his vocal cords; and it is worth noting that in this particular trance session he not only concentrated on his own ailment, but was also being hypnotized by someone else – rather than being in one of the self-induced trances that he used for his subsequent readings on other people.

We can hardly consider the issue of karmic punishment without saying a few words about the concept of hell. We saw in chapter 5 that Newton's subjects universally report that there is no such thing other than the self-imposed exile and seclusion that some souls put themselves through in the interlife, and we have discussed two examples of this above – Woolger's case of Madeleine and Newton's subject who had abused a girl. Ramster confirms this view when he reports that some of his subjects seem to go to places 'of great trouble and discontent' in the interlife, but indicates that they only stay there for a period of time before going on to somewhere better. Also in chapter 5 we saw that Whitton's subjects regard the interlife review as the closest thing to hell, albeit that again this will only be the case if the soul makes it that way with their own perceptions of their lack of worth – as happened with his subject Jenny above. Again in chapter 5 one of Cannon's subjects reported that the closest thing to a hell is failure to progress, which is certainly true to the extent that not making proper use of the interlife and sleeping instead leads to repetitive karmic cycles that are like a 'groundhog day' of recurring traumatic experiences. Meanwhile, Fiore explicitly reports that she has never encountered anything approximating to the popular concept of hell, although she feels the closest one can get is to fail to make the proper transition to the ethereal realms and to remain trapped in earth's astral plane.

Do the subjects of near-death experiences ever experience a hell? Raymond Moody and Kenneth Ring found absolutely no genuinely hellish experiences in their studies, although Moody does suggest that attempted suicides are more likely to have unpleasant experiences. Michael Sabom found none in his first study, but came across a very small number of unpleasant experiences in his subsequent Atlanta study. So did Peter Fenwick in his study, although interestingly he reports that his suicide cases were not among them. However, both indicate that even their unpleasant cases either tended to represent an interlude that was followed by the normal pleasant experience, or could be put down to subjects seeing what they expected to see – both of which are entirely consistent with our existing interlife findings. Ring and Sabom both discuss the somewhat exceptional findings of cardiologist Maurice Rawlings, a fervent Christian who has unashamedly attempted to use various pieces of anecdotal evidence to indicate that hellish experiences are far more common during near-death experiences, perhaps occurring in as many as half of them. However, they both agree that his findings are hardly reliable, with Sabom in particular indicating the extent to which Rawlings was prepared to doctor the evidence of one case to suit his argument that all true Christians go to heaven and all others to hell. There are some other sources of similarly questionable reliability that attempt to confirm Rawlings' views, but we will come back to them in chapter 9.

Another of Cannon's subjects confirms the extent to which any interlife exile is self-imposed and temporary, and to which reports of hell derive from some people's negative expectations actually helping to create a 'virtual reality' hell:

What about the area the Catholic Church refers to as purgatory? Is there any such place in the levels?
The nearest thing I can see that would possibly equate with purgatory

would be the place of resting for the damaged souls. But it is not a place of punishment, not like the Catholics imply with their term of purgatory. There's really no such specific place as purgatory or hell. Any experience like that is created by your own mind as a result of things that have happened in past incarnations.

I was going to ask about hell. Some people have described places that seemed 'bad' to them when they've had near-death experiences. Do you know anything about that?

They were expecting this. It's the result of someone believing they have lived a life sufficient to make them 'go to hell'. Due to the type of life they have lived they have attracted negative energies and influences unto themselves. When they cross over to the spiritual side of things, the negative influences are still clustered about them. But now they are conscious of these influences and they can perceive them because they are on the spiritual plane themselves. These things surround them totally and it affects their minds and makes them think that they are at a place that is very unpleasant, when in reality it's a state of mind due to the negative energies that have been attracted to them in their past incarnations.

But it's not a place where you would have to stay?

No. The condition of hell is all a matter of what state your mind is in during the period of transition. The idea of heaven or hell has become somewhat of a fable or a legend from your perspective. Those who choose to believe this create their own reality to such an extent that when they do pass over they find that elemental reality that they themselves helped to create, and therefore it is indeed real. The descriptions of heaven and hell in your holy writings are a result of people who have had near-death experiences. They come back and describe what they saw. And what they saw was how they perceived the spiritual energies around them during the period of transition. But they did not cross over far enough to be able to realize what was actually going on. If they reported something that was good and very pleasant, that was reported as being heaven. Those who reported something that was very horrible and terrible, that was reported as being hell.

They always talk about fire and things like that.

The negative energies can torture the mind in a way that would make you feel like you are burning. This is not a physical burning because the mortal body had been left behind.

I cannot fail at this point to say a few words about the Christian Church's rejection of the concept of reincarnation, and its replacement with either eternal salvation in heaven or damnation in hell – although under some Christian theology all souls go into a limbo awaiting the Day of Judgment. This is not intended to be a complex treatise on the history of western religions, and plenty of other researchers have concentrated on the issue of how and when this rejection happened, and how some early and influential

Church fathers such as Origen supposedly still held firm to a belief in reincarnation but were overruled in various council meetings. It is also not entirely clear how the original Judaism from which Christianity emerged viewed the issue, especially when we find that the Qabalistic teachings that also sprang from it are entirely based on reincarnation and karma. What we do know is that this rejection occurred some time in the first half of the first millennium AD, and that when Islam developed based on the teachings of Mohammed in the early seventh century, it too rejected reincarnation. I have always felt that at the very least the *original* rejection almost certainly had nothing whatsoever to do with theology or philosophy, and everything to do with the fundamental human vice of political power; and this view is confirmed by Cannon's subject in a continuation of the above session:

> It's a matter of power for them. Religion was corrupted into a political or power play, such that what was spiritual became a tool for the sublimation of the masses in order to control their behavior. There are in their embellishments some aspects which would perhaps be true in a very elementary sense. However, the overall picture is grossly misunderstood at this time by most on the physical plane.

To clarify exactly why this was a political move, ask yourself this. What would you do if an external, all-powerful God could sentence you to eternal hellfire, and you only had this one life to get it right? And if, as has been the case for the majority of the world's population for most of the last two millennia, you were part of the masses of the underclass with little education or access to information other than what was fed to you by your political and religious masters? Unless you were exceptionally brave and insightful, you would tow the line. You would do exactly as you were told. You would live your *one* life in permanent fear of damnation, and according to whatever supposedly moral code they dictated at the behest of their one and only true God. What a terrible distortion this is of the true spiritual worldview that we each as individuals build our own moral and spiritual code, and are therefore the masters of our own fate over many incarnations as we strive for enough learning and perfection to be reunited with the Source.

This is how another of Cannon's subjects reinforces the point:

> *On earth we have the Bible and it says that many things are sins.*
> Many of those that you have been told are sins – like you hear of the 'seven deadly sins' that the Catholics thought up – were later additions that they added at their own wish. It was a control.
> *Then the people on the other side do not consider these to be so bad?*

Some of them are [the subject has pointed out previously that this is especially when we intentionally do something we *know* to be wrong], but each person has to work out their own. There's no such punishment as saying this person is going to be thrown into the pit of fire for everlasting. There's no such thing as that, unless that person is punishing themself in that manner. 'They' don't do it.
People say everything is black and white and goes by the Bible.
But the Bible itself has been changed throughout the centuries to what they feel is right or what they feel the truth to be. For centuries that was the control they had over the people, the masses. By saying, if you don't do what we say, then you will burn in – as they called it – hell.

Picking up on this issue of the true provenance of much supposedly original scripture, let us take as an example the fact that an increasing number of fundamentalist Christians are returning to a literal interpretation of the creation account in Genesis, and even to the date originally placed on it by biblical scholars of 4004 BC. But what of the brief accounts of the pre-flood patriarchs, and of Noah and the flood itself, which come only a few chapters later? Are these part of scripture? And, if they are, what would these people make of the similar but lengthier accounts of the patriarchs and flood that come from Mesopotamian literature, with all its accompanying *multitude* of gods? It is beyond doubt that these Akkadian and even older Sumerian texts are the prototypes on which the Genesis account is based, but the oldest examples predate it by *over 1500 years*. Indeed, the original oral traditions most probably predate the biblical date for the creation. Admittedly this earliest part of the Old Testament is not necessarily fundamental to Christian or even Judaist ethics, but similar doubts exist as to the extent to which even the New Testament gospels reflect the genuine teachings of Jesus. Can such scripture ever have any real objective authority in providing a moral code by which we should all be judged? And is it not far more empowering and rational for us to concentrate instead on our own control over our own karmic advancement, which – rather than requiring that our supposedly single life be judged by an inherently subjective moral code – is based on accumulating a vast store of experiences of all different kinds over many, many lives?

It will not be difficult to detect that I have what I regard as an entirely justifiable anger about the travesties perpetrated for millennia in the name of various religions. But my anger is not directed at the millions of people who have followed these religions in good faith throughout this period, and continue to so do. Many of them have performed heroic deeds in their name, and shown great selflessness, fortitude and bravery – and although clearly a great many have also committed grave travesties, most probably did so out of pure ignorance. Nor is my anger even directed at the hierarchies that keep these religions going, most of whom are acting in similarly good faith. It is directed at the people – whoever they were – who hatched the original plot to fool and control the masses, and to deprive them of their spiritual birthright. And, because they are long gone, even anger is a wasted emotion that is no longer appropriate. What I really feel is a great sorrow. But perhaps even that is inappropriate, because it achieves nothing. All I really care about is that people are at last given sufficient information to reclaim their birthright, and to stop the travesties being perpetrated further.

Of course, I accept that the followers of all major religions at least believe in the separate existence of the soul, even if not always in reincarnation. To that extent, if our respectable religious institutions have allowed ordinary people – who might otherwise be put off by what they regard as alternative new age nonsense – to develop and maintain a spiritual worldview of some sort, then that is arguably better than nothing. But in recent decades people have been leaving at least the Christian Church in droves. And, as I indicated in the opening chapter, I believe it is finally possible to offer the spiritual worldview I am promoting in this book as an entirely rational and logical alternative to the orthodox religions of old – one that hopefully will not deter people who are suspicious of the new age movement.

In any case, one of the finest ways to diffuse anger is to use humor. So perhaps it will be appropriate for me to close this section with one of my favorite regression cases that involves another of Newton's subjects. In his last life in the early twentieth century this man had been an evangelical preacher in America, and had taken every opportunity to petrify his congregation that their sinful transgressions would lead them directly to hell. Here he is at the gateway to the ethereal realms having just died in that life – and exhibiting such real distress that Newton is struggling to keep him calm:

Oh, god. No!
What's going on?
Oh… oh… lord almighty! It's the devil. I knew it. I've gone to hell!
Now, take a deep breath and try to relax as we go through this together. You are not in hell.
Oh yeah – then why do I see the devil right in front of me?
Try to calm yourself. There is some misinterpretation here and we will find it soon.
Ohooo… it's over for me… I'm in hell.
Tell me exactly what you see.
A… being… demonic… reddish-green face… horns… wild-eyed…

fangs... the facial skin is like charred wood. O sweet Jesus, why me of all people, who spoke so much in your name?
What else do you see?
What else is there to see? Can't you understand? I'm in front of the devil!
I meant the rest of the body. Look below the head and tell me what you see.
Nothing... just a wispy ghostlike body.
Stay with me. Doesn't this seem unusual to you – that the devil would appear with no body? Move forward in time rapidly now and tell me what this figure does.
[Big sigh of relief] Oh... that bastard... I might have known. It's Scanlon. He is taking his mask off and smiling wickedly at me.
Who is Scanlon?
My guide. This is his crude idea of a joke.
What does Scanlon really look like now?
Tall, aquiline features, gray hair... full of mischief-making, as usual. I should have known. He caught me unawares this time.
Does Scanlon have a habit of this sort of thing? Why frighten you just as you were coming into the spirit world a little disoriented?
Listen, he is a great teacher. That's his way. He has got our whole group using masks but he knows I don't like them much.
Tell me why Scanlon used a devil's mask to scare you right after this life? Talk to him now.
[Period of silence] I had it coming. Oh, I know it! I spent a lifetime preaching about the devil, scaring good people... telling them they were going to hell if they didn't pay attention to me. Scanlon gave me a dose of my own medicine.
And how do you feel about his methods?
He made his point.

That he did, rather brilliantly in my opinion. This subject went on to emphasize that both he and his guide realized that he had meant well in that life, that he had believed in what he was saying, and that he had certainly not been trying to deliberately mislead people. But he had got carried away, and had masked his basic insecurity with a fiery temperament that had made him look and feel like he was in control.

So, according to the vast majority of our interlife and near-death-experience pioneers, there is no such thing as the fiery hell into which aberrant souls are cast perhaps even for eternity, as suggested by most strains of Christianity, Judaism and Islam. There may be a period of seclusion that might be perceived by the soul involved as a hellish exile, especially if they are unable to forgive themselves or have attracted negative energies to themselves by their preconditioned expectations; but even such an exile will be temporary and entirely self-imposed. But what of the ideas of hell and punishment postulated by the major eastern religions?

It is not always easy to get to grips with Hindu and Buddhist teachings. On the one hand, modern commentaries are either full of complex attempts at translating certain key words and concepts in original sacred texts, or they simplify and generalize based on particular strands of belief that have developed over time. On the other, the original texts themselves are manifold, and often lengthy and difficult to understand even in English translation, which process itself may lose or distort much of the original meaning.

In no way could I suggest that I am a scholar of these multiple texts, but I have consulted translated extracts from a number of them and their accompanying modern commentaries, and can make a few general observations that may prove useful to those who have not done so. In chronological terms the oldest are the Indian *Vedas*, which are commonly thought to date from between 1500 and 800 BC – although some commentators stress that the ideas contained in them would have been developed far earlier by the civilization that flourished in the Indus valley from the middle of the third millennium BC. In these lengthy texts elements of extremely broad-reaching philosophy combine with what appear to be relatively prosaic mythological passages, which is arguably indicative of their diverse origins. In particular they are not specific about the ideas of karma and reincarnation at all, although that is not proof that such ideas were not in place at the time, and a number of commentators have sought to indicate that they are hinted at in the *Vedas*. However, these concepts are only given proper expression in the later *Upanishads* composed between 800 and 200 BC, the two major 'epics' entitled the *Mahabharata* and the *Ramayana* of between 500 BC and 500 AD, and the *Puranas* which emerged around the latter date.

Many elements of all of these texts can be complex and difficult to comprehend, as well as apparently contradictory of each other. This may well be one of the reasons why Gautama Buddha felt compelled to extract himself from the ever more complex tenets of Brahmanism and the emerging Hinduism in the middle of the first millennium BC, with the result that by the middle of the first millennium AD Buddhism had migrated from northern India to become the dominant religion in the Orient. But even then a number of different strands developed.

It is precisely because the teachings of the various sects of Hinduism and Buddhism each rely upon their own versions of revealed wisdom that

I am not inclined to go into detail about their various beliefs concerning reincarnation, karma and the afterlife. But what I will say, again without wishing to be deliberately offensive to the many millions of people who follow their teachings, is that – just as with the Christian Bible – any originally revealed wisdom has almost certainly been massively distorted by the passage of time to suit the interpretations of a succession of scholars and gurus.

I will examine Buddhist tenets a little more closely in chapter 9, but perhaps the finest and most quoted Hindu text – which combines great spiritual focus and philosophical depth with refreshing simplicity – is the *Bhagavad Gita*, which forms part of the *Mahabharata* epic. This is a relatively short text full of love, which beautifully illustrates Krishna's fundamental advice that anyone who wishes to break free of the compulsion to reincarnate must learn to divest themselves of undue emotional and physical attachments:

5.20 The man who sees Brahman abides in Brahman: his reason is steady, gone is his delusion. When pleasure comes he is not shaken, and when pain comes he trembles not.

5.21 He is not bound by things without, and within he finds inner gladness. His soul is one in Brahman and he attains everlasting joy.

5.22 For the pleasures that come from the world bear in them sorrows to come. They come and they go, they are transient: not in them do the wise find joy.

5.23 But he who on this earth, before his departure, can endure the storms of desire and wrath, this man is a Yogi, this man has joy....

12.15 He whose peace is not shaken by others, and before whom other people find peace, beyond excitement and anger and fear – he is dear to me.

12.16 He who is free from vain expectations, who is pure, who is wise and knows what to do, who in inner peace watches both sides, who shakes not, who works for God and not for himself – this man loves me, and he is dear to me.

12.17 He who feels neither excitement nor repulsion, who complains not and lusts not for things; who is beyond good and evil, and who has love – he is dear to me.

12.18–19 The man whose love is the same for his enemies or his friends, whose soul is the same in honor or disgrace, who is beyond heat or cold or pleasure or pain, who is free from the chains of attachments, who is balanced in blame and in praise, whose soul is silent, who is happy with whatever he has, whose home is not in this world, and who has love – this man is dear to me.

This idea of total harmony with oneself and one's surroundings is entirely in accord with the idea that we need to balance our emotions and moderate our reactions to both favorable and adverse circumstances if we are to maintain a progressive rather than repetitive karmic impetus. But although we are encouraged to make space and time for silent contemplation and meditation, in no sense does Krishna suggest that we should completely withdraw from physical life, and in this he is echoing the flavor of the original *Vedas*. Rather, he encourages us to maintain a certain sense of balanced impassivity or detachment while still actively engaging:

3.4 Not by refraining from action does man attain freedom from action [that is, from the earthly karmic round]. Not by mere renunciation does he attain supreme perfection.
3.5 For not even for a moment can a man be without action. Helplessly are all driven to action by the forces of nature.
3.6 He who withdraws himself from actions, but ponders on their pleasures in his heart, he is under a delusion and is a false follower of the path.
3.7 But great is the man who, free from attachments, and with a mind ruling its powers in harmony, works on the path of karma yoga, the path of consecrated action.
3.8 Action is greater than inaction: perform therefore thy task in life. Even the life of the body could not be if there were no action.

Krishna, who 'remembers his past lives' even though ordinary mortals do not, is adamant that those who *strive* for such progressive karmic balance – even if they 'fail in yoga' on many occasions – will live again in good circumstances until they attain perfection:

6.40 Neither in this world nor in the world to come does ever this man pass away; for the man who does the good, my son, never treads the path of death.
6.41 He dwells for innumerable years in the heaven of those who did good; and then this man who failed in yoga is born again in the house of the good and the great.
6.42 He may even be born again into a family of Yogis, where the wisdom of yoga shines; but to be born in such a family is a rare event in this world.
6.43 And he begins his new life with the wisdom of a former life; and he begins to strive again, ever onwards towards perfection.

Whether we really learn all our lessons by only reincarnating in the 'houses of the good and the great' is debatable, but the essential elements of our modern views on maintaining progressive karma are nevertheless more or less confirmed.

So much for the positives we can take from Hindu scripture. But let us turn now to a perfect illustration of my point about how ideas can become distorted. In considering the issue of family life, in the *Gita* 13.9 Krishna encourages 'freedom from the chains of attachments, even from a selfish attachment to one's children, wife, or home'. He deliberately uses the adjective *selfish*, which I take to mean that we should strive for the same evenness of temperament in our family life as in all other things, but – taken with his recommendation to lead an active life – not that we should avoid family life altogether. But in the later and far lengthier *Bhagavata Purana*, or *Srimad Bhagavatam*, we find the following dreadful – and loathsomely misogynistic – analysis of family life, provided by another incarnation of Krishna's called Kapiladeva:

3.30.6 Such satisfaction with one's standard of living is due to deep-rooted attraction for body, wife, home, children, animals, wealth, and friends. In such association, the conditioned soul thinks himself quite perfect.

3.30.7 Although he is always burning with anxiety, such a fool always performs all kinds of mischievous activities with the unfulfillable hope of maintaining his so-called family and society.

3.30.8 He gives heart and senses to a woman, who falsely charms him with *maya*. He enjoys solitary embraces and talking with her, and he is enchanted by the sweet words of the small children.

3.30.9 The attached householder remains in his family life, which is full of diplomacy and politics. Always spreading miseries and controlled by acts of sense gratification, he acts just to counteract the reactions of all his miseries, and if he can successfully counteract such miseries, he thinks he is happy.

3.30.10 He secures money by committing violence here and there, and although he employs it in the service of his family, he himself eats only a little portion of the food thus purchased, and he goes to [through] hell for those for whom he has earned the money in such an irregular way.

3.30.11–13 When he suffers reverses in his occupation, he tries again and again to improve himself, but when he is baffled in all attempts and is ruined, he accepts money from others because of excessive greed. Thus the unfortunate man, unsuccessful in maintaining his family members, is bereft of all beauty. He always thinks of his failure, grieving very deeply. Seeing him unable to support them, his wife and others do not treat him with the same respect as before, even as miserly farmers do not accord the same treatment to their old and worn-out oxen.

3.30.14 The foolish family man does not become averse to family life although he is maintained by those whom he once maintained. Deformed by the influence of old age, he prepares himself to meet ultimate death.

3.30.15 Thus he remains at home just like a pet dog and eats whatever is so negligently given to him. Afflicted with many illnesses, such as dyspepsia and loss of appetite, he eats only very small morsels of food, and he becomes an invalid, who cannot work any more.

3.30.16–17 In that diseased condition, a man's eyes bulge out due to the pressure of the air from within, and his glands become congested with mucus. He has difficulty breathing, and upon exhaling and inhaling he produces a sound like *ghura-ghura*, a rattling within the throat. In this way he comes under the clutches of death and lies down, surrounded by lamenting friends and relatives, and although he wants to speak to them, he no longer can because he is under the control of time.

3.30.18 Thus the man who engaged with uncontrolled senses in maintaining his family dies in great grief, seeing his relatives crying. He dies most pathetically, in great pain and without consciousness.

This translation is by His Divine Grace AC Bhaktivedanta Swami Prabhupada – who founded the International Society for Krishna Consciousness, or Hare Krishna movement for short, in New York in the mid-sixties – and he chooses this passage particularly to illustrate 'bad' karma. In his commentaries on the text, His Divine Grace goes further: 'Womanly love exists just to agitate the mind of man. Actually, in the material world there is no love. Both the woman and man are interested in their sense gratification.' He adds the somewhat confusing suggestion that 'the Vedic scriptures enjoin that as soon as one passes fifty years of age, he must give up family life and live alone in the forest'. I can only suggest that, even though I agree with the fundamental message that anyone who engages in the material world entirely at the expense of the spiritual is sadly mistaken, this harsh interpretation of all family life is complete anathema to me.

But, unfortunately, the torment of the subject of this passage is only just beginning. Because we now find that the idea of a fiery hell, although not contained in, for example, the *Gita*, is not completely absent from at least later Sanskrit scripture – and may or may not have had an influence on the formulation of the Christian concept:

3.30.19 At death, he sees the messengers of the lord of death come before him, their eyes full of wrath, and in great fear he passes stool and urine.

3.30.20 As a criminal is arrested for punishment by the constables of the state, a person engaged in criminal sense gratification is similarly arrested by the Yamadutas, who bind him by the neck with strong rope and cover his subtle body so that he may undergo severe punishment.

3.30.21 While carried by the constables of Yamaraja, he is overwhelmed and trembles in their hands. While passing on the road he is bitten by dogs, and he can remember the sinful activities of his life. He is thus terribly distressed.

3.30.22–4 Under the scorching sun, the criminal has to pass through roads of hot sand with forest fires on both sides. He is whipped on the back by the constables because of his inability to walk, and he is afflicted by hunger and thirst. But unfortunately there is no drinking water, no shelter, and no place for rest on the road. While passing on that road to the abode of Yamaraja, he falls down in fatigue, and sometimes he becomes unconscious, but he is forced to rise again. In this way he is very quickly brought to the presence of Yamaraja. Thus he has to pass ninety-nine thousand *yojanas* [apparently 792,000 miles] within two or three moments, and then he is at once engaged in the tortuous punishment he is destined to suffer.

3.30.25 He is placed in the midst of burning pieces of wood, and his limbs are set on fire. In some cases he is made to eat his own flesh or have it eaten by others.

3.30.26–8 His entrails are pulled out by the hounds and vultures of hell, even though he is still alive to see it, and he is subjected to torment by serpents, scorpions, gnats, and other creatures that bite him. Next his limbs are lopped off and torn asunder by elephants. He is hurled down from hilltops, and he is also held captive either in water or in a cave.

I suspect that even the worst of us would struggle to come up with a psychologically self-imposed hell of quite this degree of ferocity and unpleasantness. But what of the other great punishment proffered by the eastern religions – that of returning as a lower form of life? Such a fate indeed awaits our unfortunate subject above:

3.30.34 Having gone through all the miserable, hellish conditions and having passed in a regular order through the lowest forms of animal life prior to human birth, and having thus been purged of one's sins, one is reborn again as a human being on this earth.

Although without the literal hellish intermission, this idea is in fact confirmed by Krishna in the *Gita*:

16.19 In the vast cycles of life and death I inexorably hurl them down to destruction: these the lowest of men, cruel and evil, whose soul is hate.
16.20 Reborn in a lower life, in darkness birth after birth, they come not to me, Arjuna; but they go down the path of hell.

What do our pioneers make of this suggestion – which is, of course, related to but separate from the idea that we *evolve* up the plant and animal ranks before achieving human status, which we will consider in the final chapter. Although many of them do not comment on it specifically, it is clear just from reading their case studies that even the most tormented souls do not return as anything other than human beings. Indeed, Newton's subjects report explicitly that human souls do *not* regress into animal forms, while Netherton is equally adamant that he has never come across such a case of *de*volution – that is, not after human status has been attained.

One of Cannon's subjects is even more enlightening, suggesting that while devolution might at one time have been a possibility, it is no longer:

> *Well, do people ever go backwards? I was thinking about the theory that humans incarnate as animals.*
> No. Unless you are extremely beastly. In other words, if you acted like an animal, you could, yes, but that is very rare. This is not usually allowed. It was at one time possible. However, it is no longer. It was done during the early days of the experimentation, but no longer. It is not that it is not possible, but that it is not allowed. If a person had dropped that low they would probably stay upon this side until they had raised, rather than going any farther down the scale. It is possible for a person to drop to an animalistic level mentally, but they would be unlikely to enter an animal's body. Once you have attained the human consciousness, it is very rare that you go back to an animal existence because you have evolved out of that.

Stevenson indicates that in his experience with children's spontaneous memories such cases are extremely rare, although very occasionally 'intermediate' animal lives are supposedly remembered but obviously cannot be verified. And Wambach has had a few subjects who have hinted at a past life as an animal, but it is unclear whether these were between human lives or before them. Even supposedly intermediate animal lives can perhaps be explained by TenDam's suggestion that souls who do not properly pass into the ethereal realms might allow themselves to become pathologically identified with a particular incarnate animal for a period of time; or by Newton's subjects' reports of the space of transformation in which, as we saw in chapter 5, they can experience any animal form without genuine incarnation. There is also the possibility of people remembering incarnations as an intelligent life form on another planet, something we will again consider in the final chapter.

So, it seems we can conclude that none of the punishments threatened by the major religions of the world – whether permanent or temporary banishment to the torments of hell, or returning as a lower form of life – have any fundamental reality. Worse than this, however, the very introduction of the idea of hell on the physical plane may have conditioned some souls to perceive and experience such an interlife state while in self-imposed exile.

If there is one thing more than any other that I hope comes out of this chapter, it is that it is time for us to seriously reappraise our historic reliance upon the revealed wisdom of all our worldwide religions. I trust I have done enough to show that they all contain serious flaws, although some more than others. Of course, this is not a new sentiment. Atheists have been saying as much for centuries, but clearly I am not in their camp. And in the West there has been a growing trend towards a 'mix-and-match' approach to developing more personalized religious and philosophical approaches, which originated with the theosophical movement of the late nineteenth century. Its founder, Helena Blavatsky, certainly mixed and matched a variety of eastern philosophies with western esotericism – although arguably she failed to produce a spiritual framework with any real coherence and, as we will see in the final chapter, much of her work is riddled with obvious errors and distortions. This trend moved on apace in the mid-sixties with the great Harvard psychologist and psychedelic researcher Timothy Leary encouraging everyone to 'turn on, tune in and drop out', and to start their own religion. But we still seem to remain stubbornly reliant on mostly self-proclaimed gurus, many of whom merely reinterpret the revealed wisdom of old – and usually not very well. Perhaps this reflects a natural human need to have someone to follow, and who acts as a leader, rather than relying on ourselves.

Nevertheless, at the start of the twenty-first century we have an incredible source of insight that no longer relies upon the revelations of old, even if it too inevitably requires a degree of subjective interpretation. Nor does it rely on gurus, self-proclaimed or otherwise. And that source is the wisdom of the thousands of everyday people who have been hypnotically regressed by our pioneers. People whose profound insights into the interlife and into karmic dynamics can allow us to retain the universal elements of our various religions, but properly amended by their modern testimonies in which they cannot help but tell the truth as they see it. People who come from across the full spectrum of religious belief and nonbelief, and from all walks of life – but who, when regressed, consistently deliver the same messages. Above all, people who have no political axe to grind, and no ambitions to dominate their fellow man with their dogma.

If the flaws in our existing worldwide religions were restricted to their various views on hell and other imposed punishments, and the failure of some of them to accept the fundamental concept of reincarnation, this might not be so bad. Many people have already woken up to these distortions, and refuse to let them condition their lives any more. Arguably, the far more serious issue is the way in which the workings of karma have been consistently misrepresented. For all that original Hindu teachings did distinguish, for example, between karma and dharma, the former concept has always, as far as I can discern, been associated with action and reaction. This idea has become so ingrained, and the dynamics of karma are so complex, that even most of our pioneers have allowed this prior conditioning to muddle their thinking.

What I hope I have proved – via a comprehensive analysis of their case studies, and by formulating a detailed model that distinguishes properly between the different stages of karmic evolution – is not only that adverse circumstances such as untimely death and physical disability will normally constitute progressive learning opportunities rather than any form of karmic punishment, but also that even repetitive karma is primarily about learning rather than paying off karmic debts. As a result, those of us who are stuck in a repetitive karmic cycle are not condemned to remain in it. We can break free by adopting the proper emotional responses to the various circumstances we are faced with in this life. By forgetting about reactions to the past, and concentrating on current choices and responses and how they will feed through into the future. Fortunately, inasmuch as it would be arrogant for us to *assume* we are in the progressive stage – even if most of us probably are – this is the appropriate course of action for all of us, irrespective of our level of advancement. I would also suggest that, even though our pioneers' case studies seem to show that our religious beliefs or otherwise have little influence on our interlife experience, it can do us no harm to adopt a general spiritual worldview – and preferably one based on reincarnation and karma – that will hopefully prepare and condition us to take a more active role in the interlife after we die.

8

HYPNOTIC PROGRESSION
Can We See Into The Future?

The earth will be broken up in the western portion of America. The greater portion of Japan must go into the sea. The upper portion of Europe will be changed as in the twinkling of an eye. Land will appear off the east coast of America. There will be the upheavals in the Arctic and in the Antarctic that will make for the eruption of volcanoes in the torrid areas, and there will be the shifting then of the poles – so that where there have been those of a frigid or semitropical will become the more tropical, and moss and fern will grow. And these will begin in those periods in '58 to '98 when these will be proclaimed as the periods when His Light will be seen again in the clouds.

This is a prophecy – difficult grammar and all – made by Edgar Cayce, who we met in the last chapter. In fact he had predicted that there would be great 'earth changes' during the thirties, but when these did not come to pass his attention switched to the period from 1958 to 1998. We can see that he associated these physical changes to the earth with a profound spiritual change that he said would be ushered in by the dawning of the age of Aquarius – which in turn was associated with the reemergence of Atlantis and the 'second coming' of Christ. Cayce passed away in 1945, far too early to know that his predictions at least as regards physical earth changes had not come to fruition by 1998, and nor have they at the time of writing over five years later. Of course, this has not deterred some of his followers from falling back on the failsafe position that the content was right, it was merely his timing that was inaccurate.

In 1980 Helen Wambach decided to experiment with progressing subjects forward into the future, rather than regressing them into the past. As her collaborator Chet Snow reports in his 1989 book *Mass Dreams of the Future*, she was clearly interested to see how her subjects' reports might compare with those of seers like Cayce, with whose predictions she was entirely familiar. Of course, both at the time she was experimenting, and even when Snow subsequently published his book, there was still plenty of time for Cayce's predictions to be proved correct. Using exactly the same hypnotic techniques she used for regression, she worked with both groups and a number of individual subjects, but there were problems with the latter. Some early results from group progressions to the year 2100 – which we will examine shortly – indicated that life had become pretty bleak by then. Her curiosity was piqued as to what might have caused this, but when she took her first eight individual subjects forward into the twenty-first century they all reported they were just 'floating' – their current personalities had clearly died, and they had not reincarnated. So she decided to instruct one of her relatively young subjects to progress to a specific date in the late-nineties – Snow does not say exactly what year, but given her interest in the Cayce readings I would not be surprised to find it was 1998. Although this was less than two decades away and the young woman might reasonably have been expected to still be alive, Wambach was shocked to find her choking to death from a 'big black cloud' of some sort.

This is clearly the most difficult type of hypnotic journey. Being regressed into a traumatic death in a past life is bad enough, but because it is in the past and cannot be changed most subjects can accept the experience from an emotional perspective. Being progressed far ahead into future lives does not seem to represent a major psychological problem for some individuals either. But being progressed in the current lifetime, and especially to the point of death, is understandably a frightening experience – indeed one that most of us would probably prefer to avoid altogether, even if we do have an awareness that death is merely a transition.

Nevertheless, Wambach persevered. After some delay because of health problems and other commitments, in 1983 she selected two relatively young and stable subjects and took them forwards carefully a year at a time, concentrating on normally happy occasions like birthdays and Christmas. To make them focus on general issues that she hoped would hold the least emotional charge, she asked them to see themselves buying provisions and to describe the nature of the foodstuffs available and their prices. She also suggested they report on any television or radio broadcasts of which they became aware. But when they progressed to about fifteen years ahead, again they were both just floating. Despite her curiosity, Wambach did not force them to relive the events that precipitated their deaths.

The most prominent of her progression subjects was Snow himself. He was a civilian employee of the US Air Force who had come to her in 1983 for regression therapy related to recurrent back pain and a writer's block that was affecting his work as an archivist and military historian. He was impressed by the results, Wambach was impressed by his abilities as a regression subject, and they formed an increasingly close working relationship. It is worth looking at their progression work together in some detail because it will help us to understand the nature of the phenomenon and its associated pitfalls. But clearly we must temporarily suspend our knowledge of the fact that, just as with Cayce, none of Snow's own predictions for the world have come to fruition at the time of writing.

In July of that year they undertook their first progression session in which she took him forwards directly to his birthday in July 1998. He found himself on a ranch somewhere north of Phoenix in Arizona. But the noonday clouds were dark, and it was cold – totally unlike the normal summer climate. It appeared to them both that the earth changes Cayce had prophesied had come true. He realized he was part of a commune that had been set up some years before in an area that was expected to escape the worst of the dramatic climate changes to come – which their unofficial leader, who he identified as a woman called Patsy, had foreseen. But their purpose was not just to survive the catastrophe, and to avoid being overcome by lawless marauders fighting for their own survival afterwards, but also to develop their spiritual abilities – especially by learning to make telepathic contact with similar groups that had been set up in a variety of other locations. It would be their job to help to rebuild the shattered world.

In October 1983 she took him forward again, this time to Christmas 1996. He was again at the ranch, but this time making preparations to stock foodstuffs and so on, and the climate was much hotter so the main catastrophe had clearly not occurred yet. But in watching a television bulletin he could see that the process had begun, with freak storms and new records of hot and cold weather, excessive droughts and rainfalls in various parts of the globe, and widespread flooding already occurring in coastal areas as sea levels rose. Global inflation was rife, food prices especially had rocketed, and the world's economy was already going into a tailspin. In the same session she then took him forward to Christmas 1997, when everything was much the same except they had all their provisions in place at the ranch. But when she took him forward another year to Christmas 1998, a very different picture emerged, similar to the one he had seen in his first progression. The climate in Arizona was cold and wet, and black clouds of ash and debris hung permanently in the sky. Aftershock tremors still occurred frequently. There was no television now, but local radio stations were still keeping people in touch with the outside world. They reported that much of the west coast of America had sunk into the sea, along with parts of the east coast although other parts of this had risen right up. The sea had also rushed into the low-lying parts of middle America from the Gulf of Mexico in the south and up through Texas, almost cutting the country vertically in two. Millions of people had died right across the planet.

It was not until April 1984 that Snow and Wambach were able to conduct their third progression, but in this session they established more details. The major problems had been triggered in March 1998 by the massive volcanic eruption of Mount Fuji in Japan. In America this had caused widespread problems of flooding especially in southern California, and major panic, but many people had been evacuated to higher ground and the government – which was still in control – was insisting that the worst was over. They were wrong. In May of that year the real event took place, a huge quake in southern California, as well as massive disruption in other parts of the world. Even the survivors could no longer trust the government, which lost all control. The sun did not return for months, and all the crops at the ranch withered and died.

When asked in this same session to move forward to a time when things were getting better, Snow progressed to late 2002. He was making the journey to somewhere in Alberta in western Canada to work with another spiritual survivor group, who had retained more technology because their part of the world had been less affected. In fact, possibly as a result of Cayce's predicted pole shift, the climate there had become more temperate, and there were several thousand survivors in this group, although they still lived in lightweight and temporary structures for fear of further tremors causing collapse. They wanted him to make radio broadcasts encouraging people to develop and use their spiritual talents, on account of his voice having special qualities that helped people to open up psychically.

Wambach worked with five other subjects individually to see whether they would confirm Snow's predictions. His reports of their progressions are insufficiently detailed for us to gain any real insight into the extent of their corroboration, but in general it seems they too saw increasingly severe climate problems leading to a major catastrophe some time in the late nineties. It also seems that most of them had died by the time of the new millennium.

What are we to make of all this? Admittedly some people are becoming more and more preoccupied with climate change and increasingly erratic weather patterns – with great debate surrounding whether these changes derive from man-made global warming or, for example, solar flares and sunspot radiation whose fluctuations have always affected our planet. But, for example, no major financial collapse has begun yet, over five years after 1998, despite many other commentators continually warning of impending doom. Nevertheless, in his prologue Snow uses the failsafe gambit that 'I would be the first to agree that the exact timing of individual future events is by far the least reliable aspect of precognition, prediction and prophecy'. So might he still be proved right at some point?

Another aspect we cannot escape is the similarity of Snow's predictions to those made by Cayce. Not only is the date of 1998 'confirmed' but also – despite his details of events in other parts of the world being sketchy – he specifically mentions, for example, the bulk of Japan falling into the sea. He devotes considerable time to discussing Cayce's predictions in his book, and openly indicates Wambach's prior knowledge of them – for example, one of her group progression workshops was actually conducted at the Association for Research and Enlightenment in early 1983, and over two hundred Cayce followers attended. So, although he is somewhat reticent on this point, it is only reasonable to suggest that he too probably knew about them, and that in large part his imagination was creating a future fiction based on them. Unfortunately this conclusion is bolstered to the extent that his ego may have been at play in giving him a future role of some importance.

We do not know about the extent to which prior knowledge may have influenced the other five subjects. Indeed we are not provided with detailed transcripts from any of Snow's or the other subjects' sessions, but we cannot discount the additional possibility – normally rare with regressions – that Wambach to some extent subjectively led them on with her questioning. We will discuss to what extent they may have been seeing any sort of 'real' future later, but for now I must make a vital distinction so that I am not accused of adopting double standards. If these are not real lives as such then, unlike past lives, the subjects would be far more susceptible to subjective and leading questioning. It might even be possible that Wambach projected her own preconceptions about the events of the late nineties to her subjects without saying anything at all, just by telepathy.

Despite these various objections, to dismiss all this lightly would still be a mistake. And although it is not directly relevant to the issue of hypnotic progression, I would now like to consider the extent to which our expectations might influence the future. We have seen in previous chapters that our thoughts and intentions as individuals have great power to influence our lives in either a repetitive or a progressive way. Positive thinking does work, but so does its negative counterpart, and we will pick up on this issue again in the final chapter. We even saw in the last chapter that the introduction on the physical plane of the idea of hell might have created sufficient mass expectations to bring it into some degree of virtual reality on the ethereal plane. And Snow himself hints that if a significant proportion of the human population is expecting something to happen then they might just make it happen via the mechanism of the collective unconscious – or, as I would prefer to call it, group karma. So are there definite trends in new age consciousness that might have an impact on our collective future?

Galvanized as Wambach clearly was by the Cayce readings, many other people do associate worldwide catastrophes with a new spiritual dawn. In fact, rather like the Hindu concept of 'world cycles' of degeneration, destruction and reemergence, she regarded them as regular cyclic events – although tying them into precessional cycles of a little less than 26,000 years that are then subdivided into twelve astrological ages of approximately 2160 years each, all of which are far shorter than those in the Hindu view. Snow himself devotes a whole chapter to this idea, tying the great flood that supposedly occurred some 12,500 years ago during the age of Leo into a prediction of a similar event around about now during the transition to the age of Aquarius – at the halfway point of the precessional cycle. However his attempts to prove this is a genuine cycle of more than two events fall somewhat short, relying on various native traditions of multiple ages of man that arguably have little archaeological, geological or other scientific evidence to back them up. Moreover, with greater or lesser degrees of relevance he uncritically quotes material from researchers such as Zecharia Sitchin in respect of supposed twelfth planets and cosmic collisions, and Peter Lemesurier in respect of the Great Pyramid's internal geometry supposedly acting as a predictive timeline of the future of the human race. Because I have spent considerable time demonstrating the poor scholarship behind these ideas in my previous books, I have no intention of repeating the arguments here.

Despite these additional reservations, and although my reasoning is somewhat different, I too tend towards the view that catastrophes and spiritual awakening are closely linked, except not in a regular cyclic way. As I mentioned briefly in the introduction, one of the main themes of my last book, *Genesis Unveiled*, was that the ancient texts and traditions all around the world suggest that there was a huge catastrophe around 11,500 years ago, brought on by humanity's increasing focus on materialism at the expense of their true spiritual roots. I argued that although in a natural sense this catastrophe was precipitated by an asteroid or comet impact of some sort, from an underlying spiritual perspective it was a karmic event working off the universal karma of humanity as a whole – and that the destruction effectively gave us a fresh start to try and get it right. I also argued that the esoteric wisdom displayed in these same ancient texts – concerning, for example, cosmology and the formation of the universe – precluded the materialistic explanation that they were written by philosophically primitive people who, having experienced a major catastrophe, automatically assumed that the gods were blaming them for some misdemeanor. I then concluded that in treading a path we have been down before we have failed again, and so may well face the same karmic consequences. I was not specific about dates or possible natural causes, or even that such an event would definitely occur – after all, karma is all about choice whether applied to the individual or on a more universal scale, which is another reason why I reject any predictable cyclic element to catastrophes. But I did argue that it was a definite possibility that was worth considering.

I should emphasize that I do not long for a return to the past, or at least I am not against technological progress per se inasmuch as I strongly suspect that it is an unavoidable and ethereally anticipated part of humanity's evolution. What I am extremely concerned about, as are so many others, is our obvious failure to integrate technological progress with our spiritual birthright, so that the two are maintained in balance. On top of this, in my private discussions I repeatedly agonize about whether the reinstatement of a universal spiritual worldview that I so wish for can ever be brought about without some major collapse to break the stranglehold of self-interested and ruthless global power brokers – who may stop at nothing to protect the status quo.

So we must still ask whether a major catastrophe may not indeed be precipitated if a sufficient proportion of the world's population merely *expect* it to happen – whether or not they agree with me that we might *deserve* or even *need* it as well. These expectations were running mighty high in the run up to 1998, with the fast-approaching new millennium of the Christian calendar also playing its psychological part. Those key points have now passed without the predictions of catastrophe coming to fruition. But, showing admirable fluidity, plenty of people have now switched their allegiance to a slightly later date for the coming of the age of Aquarius – this being feasible because it is virtually impossible to pinpoint the transition from one age to another with any accuracy due to the poorly defined boundaries between the zodiacal constellations. Many also couple this with, for example, Mayan calendrical predictions focused on the year 2012 – although in their original form these seem to be at least as much about spiritual awakening as they are about any form of catastrophe.

Perhaps the increasingly erratic weather and climate changes we have seen developing over recent decades, whether man-made or not, are indeed a sign of things to come. Perhaps we are ready for a major spiritual awakening, which does need a major catastrophe to precipitate it and to strip out all the deadwood of materialism. Or perhaps by choosing a more spiritual path of our own volition humanity can avoid the need for such a catastrophe. Or, then again, maybe this is all so much new age hype, and the struggle between materialism and spirituality will continue on for centuries with no major resolution one way or the other. Perhaps, even, I am completely mistaken about group karma, and a natural catastrophe may occur that has nothing to do with spiritual reawakening. There are numerous possibilities, and I do not even begin to have any definitive answer as to which is most likely. But I will have more to say about the bigger picture that encompasses such discussions at the end of this chapter.

Let us now consider progressions into the more distant future. As I indicated earlier, from the outset in 1980 Wambach also worked on progression with groups of subjects, just as she had in her regression research. She offered them a hypnotic journey to a choice of any one of five time periods: three past ones before 1900, and two future ones of 2100 or 2300 – which, being beyond any subject's current lifespan, would hopefully minimize any potential psychological blockages. With two of the five options involving progression then, all other things being equal, the assumption at the outset was that at least forty per cent would experience the future rather than the past. In fact, given that on average over sixty per cent of group subjects indicated a biased interest in progressing rather than regressing when questioned before the sessions, and given that one might expect current population expansion to continue, she hoped that the figure would be more like fifty per cent. But that was not what happened. She consistently found that only between five and seven per cent of the subjects in each group progressed to 2100, and another eleven to fifteen per cent to 2300.

Although Wambach did evaluate other possible explanations, she could not avoid the conclusion that this unexpectedly small percentage of progressions was caused by the catastrophes before the new millennium that both Cayce and her individual subjects had predicted. Far fewer humans would be on the planet and so far fewer souls would be incarnate at these points. This would also explain why nearly twice as many were going to the more distant time period, at which point the population would presumably be recovering somewhat. From this perspective her group data might seem to support the fact that a significant catastrophe is indeed on the way, although we must allow for the probable existence of a considerable number of other mostly unforeseen variables that might have an impact on her data.

Wambach conducted several dozen of these group workshops right across America from 1980–4, while a number of identical sessions were held by an associate, psychologist Leo Sprinkle from the University of

Wyoming. Wambach unfortunately passed away quite suddenly in 1985, so Snow himself was left with the job of collating the results. More than this, however, because he had by now left his former job and qualified as a hypnotherapist himself, he performed a number of similar group sessions from 1985–7 in both America and France – although in these his subjects were primarily offered the chance to go to 2100 rather than 2300. In his analysis he differentiates between his own findings and those obtained earlier by Wambach and Sprinkle, but for our purposes they display sufficient similarities that we can concentrate on the combined results.

Despite the small percentages that progressed rather than regressed, and the fact that a small proportion of the progression data sheets were too incomplete to form part of a proper analysis, Snow was left with a total of nearly four hundred progressions to study. As Wambach had previously in her regression studies, he commenced with an analysis of future life sex, which more or less showed a fifty-fifty split between male and female in both future periods, despite their being as usual a far greater proportion of currently female subjects in the groups. He is right to argue that this is again indicative of the validity of the experiences – remember that the group subjects were not in therapy, so that if we can infer they were more likely in the progressive stage then they would be less likely to favor one sex over another for their incarnations. Interestingly, about five per cent of subjects reported they were androgynous in 2100, with this figure rising to six per cent in 2300 – a factor that is clearly absent from past-life regressions. By asking how old subjects were when they died in their future lives he also established that, although there were some significant individual and collective extensions, average life spans in both periods seemed to be more or less consistent with today.

But by far the most interesting aspect of Snow's analysis was the emergence of different types of life experience that were broadly speaking common to both future periods. He categorized these into Type I, which involved living in a traveling spaceship, a space station or a colony on another planet; Type II, which involved living in spiritually evolved, new age communities in predominantly mountain or coastal environments on earth; Type III, which involved living in usually enclosed, high-technology, city environments on earth; and Type IV, which involved living a relatively backward life usually in small rustic communities on earth.

	2100 AD		2300 AD	
	No.	%	No.	%
Type I: Space	35	26	109	43
Type II: New Age	24	18	52	21
Type III: High Tech	41	31	56	22
Type IV: Rustic	33	25	34	14
Total	133		251	

The totals for each type in each period are shown in the table above, and I will summarize a few of Snow's more pertinent findings about each. If we start with the progressions to 2100 or thereabouts, as we might expect the Type II experiences seemed to be by far the most pleasant and fulfilling. Part of their spiritual development was to coordinate their limited use of technology with their natural environment – there being a suggestion that they were able to maintain their pleasant habitats by their spiritual approach, while many other parts of the planet remained virtually uninhabitable. Their diet consisted of natural fruits and vegetables, and their average life spans had increased to over ninety years of age. A few reported that they used telepathy to communicate, and that they could 'vacate' their bodies if they chose once their life tasks were completed. The Type IV's also experienced largely pleasant and uncomplicated lives, but their distinguishing factor was the absence of any spiritual emphasis, an almost complete lack of technology, and a reversion to relatively backward nineteenth-century style living in small communities – usually in a rural or small town environment, but occasionally in ruined cities.

The Type I and III experiences were linked inasmuch as high-technology cities on earth still acted as the home base for many of the space travelers. Both types indicated that contact and cooperation with extraterrestrials was commonplace. And although a degree of continuation of a family-style life was reported by both, and the Type I's tended to be slightly more fulfilled by their scientific work, many of these subjects also reported boredom, isolation and loneliness, brought on it seems by the dominance of technology in their environments. Type III's especially emphasized the extent to which mere survival seemed to be the name of the game in their cold and mechanical society, in which art, literature and other humanistic aspects seemed almost completely absent. Most reported that if they left their enclosed cities there was no greenery or vegetation, and that they had to wear full breathing apparatus because the atmosphere was poisonous – as well as suits that protected them from the sun's radiation – and that if these failed they died. Their purely functional domed cities were often built partially underground, or even underwater.

The progressions to 2300 and beyond were in many ways similar. The proportion of Type I's had increased, especially as a result of human colonization of planets outside our solar system. Although domed structures were often mentioned in these reports, in many cases it seems the planets had a similar atmosphere to earth and vegetation was commonplace. While the lives of the Type 1's in spaceships, space stations and enclosed colonies on planets within our solar system continued to be somewhat lonely in many cases, those on planets in other parts of the galaxy were more family-oriented and fulfilling, and also in many cases spiritual. The lives of the Type II's had continued much as before except in some cases the relatively small community settlements had expanded into major population centers with more modern technology, but without losing their fundamental spirituality. There were hints from some that their higher vibrational state had made them less densely physical, and extraterrestrial contacts for these people often had a strong spiritual dimension.

Although considerably more than half of the Type III's continued to live in enclosed cities because of the still-polluted atmosphere, a change was detectable in that a significant minority reported the atmosphere in their part of the globe was safe. These latter also reported that their lives were more fulfilling, and it seems that they were living in a far less harsh, more humane and even spiritual environment. Snow suggests that a process of convergence between the Type II's and III's was at least partially under way by this point, and in fact I am not at all sure why he did not categorize these more spiritual Type III's living in unpolluted environments as Type II's in the first place. Meanwhile, apart from an apparent increase in the size of their communities, the rustic Type IV's lives seemed pretty much unchanged. From a general perspective it seems that by this time attitudes to death had changed completely, with most people fully realizing it was just a transition to another state. As a result reports of choosing to leave a body that was worn out, or because all tasks for that life had been accomplished, were commonplace among all types.

What are we to make of these group progressions? Many of the Type II's, III's and IV's from both time periods reported living in various still-identifiable parts of the globe that overlap considerably. Is it possible that the members of two of these groups could be quite happily living in pollution-free environments while, at the same time and perhaps only a few hundred miles away, those in the other did not dare to emerge from their domes without protective suits and helmets? Somehow I doubt it, which must at the very least cast some doubt on the extent to which these can *all* be regarded as genuine glimpses of the future. The only solution would be if the Type III's were mistaken and were actually, like the Type I's, living in colonies on other planets and not earth. But this is pure conjecture on my part.

Snow himself seems to be quite ambivalent about the extent to which we should regard these as genuine lives. On the one hand, he emphasizes that the equal distribution of the sexes supports the view that they are genuine and not just based on fantasy projection. And he backs this up with the argument that only a relatively small percentage of group subjects progressed into new age lives, even though we might reasonably expect that the sort of people who would attend such workshops would have a far greater than average desire to see humanity evolving in a spiritual direction. But on the other hand he seems to go along with a plethora of supposedly extraterrestrial channelings of recent decades that suggest that humanity is facing a critical time in its history and must make a *choice* between spiritual evolution and apocalypse – which stands in direct contrast to the idea that the two might go hand in hand that we discussed earlier. This suggests that he does not regard *all* these progressions as genuine, at least in any fixed, deterministic sense, and that the apparent mutual exclusivity of the two types of atmospheric environment encountered on earth represent at least two alternative futures: one apocalyptic, the other spiritual. So, despite a certain lack of coherence in his arguments, it seems that he does favor the idea that these are 'mass dreams' of the future that are not fixed and unchangeable. As to my own view, that will have to wait until the end of the chapter.

Apart from Wambach, most of our pioneers hardly mention hypnotic progression. But in *Journey of Souls* Michael Newton emphasizes the vagueness of any impressions his subjects have received from the future:

> The opposite of past-life regression is post-life progression, which enables some subjects to see snatches of the future as incomplete scenes. For instance, some have told me earth's population will be greatly reduced by the end of the twenty-second century, partially due to adverse soil and atmospheric changes. They also see people living in odd-looking domed buildings. Details about the future are always rather limited, due, I suspect, to built-in amnesia from karmic constraints.

He adds a few more details in *Destiny of Souls*:

> While in the ring people are not able to view events into the future beyond the next immediate life span of the bodies presented to them. Evidently, this might cloud the way souls see the lives they are viewing. Taking my cue from this spirit world practice, I prefer not to work with progression in hypnosis except in spiritual screening rooms [that is, the ring]. Once in a while, in conjunction with something else under discussion out of the ring, a subject will get brief flashes of scenes where they are participating in a future event, such as being on a starship. I usually don't push for more information here. Moreover, these flashes of future existences are mercurial since people may only see a single possibility that could change when the time actually arrives, owing to a whole host of new circumstances and decisions based upon the timelines of history leading up to these events.

Clearly Newton has actively avoided progressing his subjects, precisely because he regards any results as far too open to change to be of any value, and this seems to be the general consensus among pioneering regressors. So as far as I am aware the only other researcher to have consistently experimented with progression is Bruce Goldberg. His scientific background meant he had no particular interest in reincarnation until he began to read about past-life regression while at dental school. After graduation he took a course in clinical hypnosis, with the idea of using it to reduce anxiety or as an alternative to anesthetic, but when subsequently asked to regress an acquaintance into her past lives he immediately became convinced of the reality of reincarnation. So in 1976 he set up a joint dental and hypnotherapy practice in Baltimore, while some time later in 1984 he also gained a qualification in counseling psychology, before moving his practice to Los Angeles in 1989.

In his 1982 book *Past Lives, Future Lives* Goldberg discusses a number of the important themes that we have covered in previous chapters: the transition to the interlife assisted by guides and other soul mates, with us at least initially seeing what we expect to see; the life review with guides and elders involving the akashic records; choosing and planning the next life with guides, elders and other linked souls; the ideas of group and progressive karma, and of free will to ignore interlife advice and plans; and the absence of punishment in hell or by reversion to animal form. However, only the ideas of group and progressive karma and of non-reversion to animal lives are definitively placed in the context of his own regression research. The rest are only introduced under the heading 'popular explanations of karma and their basic principles'. It is because of this doubt about the extent to which he was merely summarizing the interlife findings of other pioneering researchers rather than his own that I have not previously included his work alongside theirs.

He also provides a number of detailed case studies of regression, the most extraordinary of which involved two patients who, he reports, came to him quite separately and were completely unknown to each other. The first, Arnold, recalled the life of Thayer, an apprentice to a master guildsman called Gustave in Bavaria in the twelfth century. Thayer was brutalized by his master, who completely denigrated him at work, kept him chained up like a slave at home, and took his frustrations out on him not only violently but sexually as well. He also thwarted Thayer's potential romance with a well-bred local girl called Clotilde. Eventually Thayer snapped, and in trying to murder his master was stabbed and killed himself. The second patient, Brian, came to see Goldberg about eighteen months later. Incredibly he regressed into the life of Gustave, and confirmed all the main names, dates and events – albeit that, as one would expect in any such account, his perspective on certain aspects was slightly different. Arnold reported that he knew Clotilde as his current sister-in-law, but did not know Gustave in this life, while Brian was not asked the same question. Despite this apparently incredible synchronicity, Goldberg decided that it was not his karmic role to introduce the two.

If we turn now to Goldberg's experience with what he describes as 'hundreds' of progressions, he accepts that many people are fearful of them and that this in itself acts as a block, making them much less easy to initiate than regressions. He also indicates that even when subjects are progressed, their experiences are far less stable than in regressions, and tend to swap from one scene to another without warning or continuity. As to why he experiments with them at all, he argues that the past, present and future are all happening now, so that in some cases progressions can have as much therapeutic effect as regressions. He accepts that karma involves choice, and that to some extent this might act as a further intrinsic block, but also insists that 'if we weren't supposed to know the future, progressions simply wouldn't work'. We will return to these issues later, but for now we might note that he summarizes the future of life on earth over the next five centuries based on these cases, and his summary does not seem to correlate with the Cayce predictions of catastrophe – and remember that at the time Goldberg was writing, 1998 was still some years away. Instead, Goldberg's patients predict that a major nuclear war will decimate the population, but not until the twenty-fifth century, after three hundred years of world peace.

As part of his desire to see hypnotic regression demonstrated on television, Goldberg worked with a presenter from his local network in 1980. But when the following year this subject indicated a willingness to explore progression into the future as well, he decided that the best way to try to prove its validity would be to take him forward one week and look at the news he would be presenting. In two sessions he came up with six news items that on subsequent checking proved to have some validity, although any skeptic would point out that at least some of the items might have been expected to happen anyway – such as house fires, road accidents and political developments. But while in most of these cases few details were provided, in some they were sufficient to seem impressive. A balanced view would be that the information was by no means foolproof, but may have been more accurate than pure guesswork or chance. Of course, one thing that everyone wants to know is, if it is possible to look into the near future, why do people not do it to predict lottery numbers and so forth? The standard response to this is that karmic dynamics do not allow for such greed-motivated activity, so such details would be blocked.

One case in which Goldberg felt that progression had a therapeutic effect was that of Janet, a dietician who came to him suffering from low self-esteem after the break-up of a relationship – one in a long line of bad experiences with partners, apparently caused by her choosing the wrong sort of men who regularly cheated on her. Two past-life regressions revealed some repetitive group karma between Janet, her most recent ex-partner, and his ex-wife to whom he had returned. But Goldberg wanted to go further, and to take her into the future. So he progressed her to an apparent life in the year 3015 – considerably further ahead than any of the other cases we have studied so far – where she described her life as a confident, assertive and successful scientist on another planet, who ended up having a highly successful relationship with one of her senior colleagues who was unknown to her in her current life.

Goldberg reports that Janet subsequently became more self-confident and gained a far more suitable partner. But he also asserts that it was her progression more than her regressions that led to this improvement, because it assured her that by that time in the future she had worked out her karma with her ex-partner in that he was no longer present. However, he provides no details of how many sessions he had with her, and he certainly does not indicate that, for example, he only took her into the future because she had failed to respond to past-life therapy alone. Indeed, I suspect that the karmic ties revealed by her regressions would probably have satisfied most of our pioneers in terms of their therapeutic benefits. Nor does he allow for the fact that her ex-partner might simply have been absent from that particular future life. So, all in all, his suggestion that the progression itself had significant therapeutic effect is somewhat unproven. Having said that, if it were clear to any of us that our current problems were definitely going to be resolved by the time of a future life, it would almost certainly make us feel better. But can such guarantees really be given? Would they not act as a short cut to violate the basic concept of ongoing choices dictating future events? We will return to this issue shortly.

The case that I want to examine in some detail is that of another patient called Pete. He came to Goldberg with a hand-washing obsession, something he readily recognized as a clinical psychologist himself, and which he said was related to an intense but apparently illogical fear of contamination. He was regressed into three past lives that again threw up details pertinent to his compulsion, and this time Goldberg indicates that his symptoms were starting to be alleviated after these sessions. Nevertheless, in the next session Pete progressed into his next life, and it appears this was spontaneous rather than as a result of a deliberate instruction by Goldberg.

He found himself as a young man called Ben Kingsley attending a high-school physics class in Tulsa, Oklahoma in the year 2074. He reported that his father was a psychiatrist, his mother an architect, and that he had a loving and stable family background. The only problem was that he had a tendency to lose his temper, and was being treated for it by one of his father's colleagues. This was an especially sensitive issue because he wanted to work as a technician at the local nuclear power plant, and if his problem was revealed his hopes would be dashed. So his father ensured that it stayed off the record.

Ben's life progressed well. He went to work at the plant, fell in love, married, had children and gained increasing responsibility in his job. He was something of a workaholic, but even this did not seem to be a problem for him or his family. His temper tantrums had not surfaced for some years, and his psychiatric treatment had been discontinued. Goldberg kept progressing him forwards in that life, probing for further causes of his current problems, and it must be said that his commentary is illuminating. He was clearly adamant that Ben's temper problems would resurface at some point, even though the patient himself was equally adamant that they were under control – and understandably expressed some irritation that Goldberg should keep coming back to them. From the transcripts one could certainly argue that Goldberg was leading his patient far more than most of our pioneers would, based on his own subjective judgment of the situation and his desire to find an incident related to the current compulsion. One might even use the term 'bullying' to describe the tone of his questioning, and as we will see there are other examples of this in his work.

In any case, his relentless pursuit appeared to pay off when eventually Ben found himself alone one night at the nuclear research facility that he by now headed. His calculations contained a mistake that produced an emergency he could not control. Apparently unable to accept his failure, instead of requesting assistance he went into meltdown himself. He knocked a security guard unconscious, sealed off the unit, and let it blow up. Not only did he kill himself and the rest of the skeleton crew, but the surrounding area was heavily contaminated by the blast. After death, he realized his stupidity. But, more tellingly, Goldberg had apparently uncovered the major cause of his current compulsion.

But that is not the end of the story. Clearly this was a highly negative scenario that hardly inspired Pete to look forward to his next life as Ben. Nevertheless Goldberg had an answer for this as well, and it was based on certain assumptions he makes about the way in which different spiritual planes operate. He separately describes five lower vibrational planes – the physical, astral, causal, mental and etheric – and seven higher ones, and states that we cannot progress from one to another until we have raised our vibrational rate sufficiently. As we will see in the final chapter this bears some resemblance to Qabalistic ideas, although his descriptions fall well short of providing a coherent practical framework in my view. In any case, with even less discernable logic he then suggests that any future life has five alternative frequencies that apparently correspond to the lower planes: these are then labeled very bad, below average, neutral, above average and excellent. Nevertheless, they all share the same basic patterns in terms of family circumstances, key people and so on. So all he had to do was progress Pete through his four alternative-frequency lives and let him choose the one he liked best – in this case, not surprisingly, one in which he did not go into meltdown along with the research facility, and lived on happily. According to Goldberg, merely 'programming' Pete to this 'ideal frequency' was sufficient to finally alleviate all his problems.

It will perhaps be obvious by now that I have certain doubts about the reliability of Goldberg's work. These stem from other issues as well, which I must mention before we can draw any proper conclusions. For example, if I have understood him correctly he reports that he had performed of the order of 25,000 regressions and progressions by the time he published this first book in 1982. This seems a great many in only about six, or at the most seven, years. Even if he worked seven days a week and took no holidays, it would require him to encounter of the order of ten different past or future lives with his subjects every single day throughout that period – and even if this were possible, one wonders where he got the time to simultaneously carry on with his dental practice. The only pioneer who comes even close to this degree of activity is Edith Fiore, but her report of 20,000 regressions was achieved in some twelve years of full-time dedication. It is therefore only reasonable to suggest that Goldberg might be somewhat prone to exaggeration.

It is also clear that he is something of a self-publicist who consistently sought television and other media exposure at the earliest opportunity. I do not automatically denigrate such an approach – indeed I applaud his efforts to gain further public exposure for the benefits of hypnotic regression – but I cannot help but report that his whole demeanor appears somewhat different from that of most of our pioneers. A further example of this is related to my earlier suggestion of his occasional bullying tone, when we find that in another case he had apparently regressed a patient to his time as a 'light being' with a higher than normal vibrational rate, and the patient had questioned Goldberg's authority to interrogate him about what he was doing while in some sort of apparent interlife state. As a result Goldberg issued this threat: 'It is your function to report your progress to me at this time. Your vibrational rate will be altered downward if you don't cooperate.' This is hardly the sort of respectful approach to sensitive issues adopted by most of our pioneers.

Worse, though, was my personal experience with him. Despite these other reservations, I was deeply troubled by his work. Although most other commentators summarily reject hypnotic progression as far less reliable than regression, it was clear to me that the level of detail emerging in many of his progression case studies was just as impressive as that contained in the best past-life regressions – Pete being an obvious example. He identified key dates, the names of all key people in his life, and even the detailed names of the different units at his research facility. So how could I reject them like other commentators without being guilty of double standards?

Yet if I were to accept them I would have even greater problems, because I do not find Goldberg's suggestion that karmic free choice is maintained by having the choice of five alternative frequencies for future lives at all persuasive. For him these alternatives still share the same basic circumstances in terms of parents, environment and other key people and interactions. But, according to our interlife pioneers, these are exactly the things we choose as probabilities only for the life we are about to enter – that is, effectively, the current one. To fix them for all future lives as well would drastically reduce, indeed completely minimize, the extent to which ongoing events, actions and decisions would have an impact on our choices of future lives – in fact, it would border on predetermination. Even Pete, discussing his life in the late twenty-first century, was progressing at least one life in advance. And even though we are given no details of her other future lives we can only assume that Janet, in progressing over a thousand years ahead, was going far farther than this.

It is precisely because this issue is so important that I have spent some time discussing my general reservations about Goldberg's work. It is also why I wrote to him expressing these concerns, and asked him in the politest possible terms whether he felt he could shed any further light on this important conundrum that his research had raised. His somewhat curt response was as follows:

> I suggest you read my later books *Custom Design Your Own Destiny* and *Time Travelers from Our Future* for answers. Check my homepage for fees and procedures for consults. I charge for my time.

I was somewhat taken aback at this insistence that he charges for his time, when I was clearly asking a research question related to my own book rather than requesting therapeutic assistance. Moreover, subsequent investigation of his own summaries on his website and various less than positive reviews gave me no confidence that these two further books would be at all relevant to my enquiry. So again I responded politely but pressed him on the important point. His reply was again a curt one – that being so 'cheap' as to not buy his other books would not 'win me any friends in this or any other field'. At this point I must admit that I sent him a rather stronger-worded reply, not to continue a pointless disagreement but as a last attempt to elicit some sort of meaningful response to my question. And, given that being polite had not worked twice, I changed tack and goaded him that if he did not attempt to answer my question I would have to assume that it was because he could not. This did indeed elicit a reply, but not one that I expected even from someone who had been as unhelpful as he already had. I will not reproduce it in full, but suffice to say that he called me some rather rude names, accused me rather strangely of trying to 'weasel free consults from him' and, above all, resolutely refused to make any attempt to answer my question. Arguably this reveals more than anything else about the strength and validity of his arguments about how progressions operate.

I would not normally raise such issues, but as I have already suggested Goldberg's findings would clearly have serious implications for karmic choice – which is, after all, the primary theme of this book – if they were completely reliable. The fact that they are so at odds with those of our pioneers, and that they may be somewhat less than reliable, are therefore of the utmost importance. That having been said, I still believe there is enough in Goldberg's progression research to leave us with questions that deserve some sort of answer, even if I regard his own explanations as completely unsatisfactory. So I will now try to pull all this material together and offer some tentative conclusions.

Snow discusses Einstein's theory of relativity in some detail in what appears to be an attempt to suggest that time does not operate in a flowing linear fashion – that is *from* the past, *through* the present and *into* the future. Goldberg does likewise, although by mere passing reference that suggests little real understanding. But I would argue that both are somewhat misrepresenting this theory. It is true that Einstein proved that space and time are not independent of each other and that, because light takes time to travel over long distances, events can only be described with complete accuracy by knowing the combined space-time coordinates of the observer. This is best illustrated over the massive distances encountered in outer space. To take the most extreme example, galaxies in the furthest reaches of our universe can now be detected by modern space telescopes. Because of their distance from us and the time it takes for the visible light they emit to get to us, what our astronomers are observing is the state of these systems as they were many billions of 'light years' ago – that is, much closer to the point when the physical universe came into being. But this does not imply that time does not flow as a linear phenomenon – it merely indicates that it can only be measured *relative* to the position of the observer.

Nevertheless, on the face of it this theory suggests that we cannot objectively define anything called 'now' because that moment is indeed relative to the observer. But this is a red herring for the type of analysis that is relevant here, especially because modern science – via the EPR experiment and Bell's theorem for the technically-minded – has also proved beyond doubt that other forms of non-light-based communication occur not only faster than the speed of light but in fact instantaneously. So, for example, if I were sufficiently advanced to be able to develop a telepathic rapport with an extraterrestrial on a planet 10,000 light years away, and I asked them what they were up to *now*, they would not translate this into the context of visible light delays and try to tell me what they were doing all that time ago. Indeed, such an experiment would test their past-life memory to the full. Instead, they would understand that in the instantaneous world of telepathic communication their now is exactly the same as mine. So it is perfectly acceptable to use the concept of a universal 'now' when we are operating in areas that are clearly beyond the normal constraints of the visible, physical world.

On that basis I would propose that we think of time operating something like this. The past, present and future do exist as separate linear concepts, so that cause and effect do occur. However, there is a sense in which the future has already happened. Or perhaps it is better to say that a virtually infinite number of futures have already been *envisaged*, but not *happened* in any physical sense.

To understand what I mean by this, let us remind ourselves of Newton's place of life selection. Let us imagine that we can freeze time at a particular now, when one particular soul is seeing the next life they might lead, and a number of major probabilities in that life, as if it was already happening. This represents the most likely outcome if they follow their life plan and recognize their various triggers, and so on. But we know that their life plan interacts closely with those of a number of other souls, to a greater or lesser extent. And the life plans of particularly more removed souls will interact with a completely different group of souls that must then be considered in this version of the future. In fact, especially now that we live in times of extensive global travel and communication, it is almost certain that we could extrapolate the connections in our original soul's life plan to every other soul on earth. As we saw in chapter 5, this is exactly what one of Dolores Cannon's subjects emphasizes when discussing the tapestry room. But these connections would not just stop when our original soul dies in that life. They would carry on into the future ad infinitum. And this future of life on earth would almost certainly at some point allow for space travel and colonization as a major probability, thereby connecting it to the future of every other inhabited planet in the universe.

In other words, the sum total of all the karmic actions and decisions of all souls both incarnate and discarnate that have accumulated up to this particular point in time must by definition produce a 'most probable' future at that point. And we can see just how complex and all encompassing this version of the so-called future envisaged by the time masters that control the tapestry would have to be. I would suggest that this means there is a sense in which this future does already exist – in the exact detail that is seen by the time masters at the particular point in question. At this point, as Cannon's subject confirms, the tapestry is there with all its threads interwoven, both from the past and into the *future*. We as individual souls are not experiencing that particular version of the future, and we never will. It will never *happen* exactly like this, but at our fixed point in time it nonetheless *exists* as a conception of the time masters.

The real complexity occurs, however, as soon as we move away from this particular now and onto a new one. It is obvious that, even in the split second it has taken you to read the last few words, millions of decisions that were not part of people's original life plans have just been made around the world. These effectively infinite and continuous adjustments to the tapestry are totally overwhelming to our mortal minds, but from all the evidence we have been given by our pioneers we must assume that they are well within the compass of the time masters that control it. This process of what we might call 'tapestry management' is arguably the closest we might get to understanding the real meaning of the common suggestion that all possible futures occur in parallel universes.

So what are the implications of this analysis? The past is indeed fixed, and cannot be altered. But the future is not. At any one now point there is only one version of the future that is most probable, but it changes almost instantaneously based on decisions taken by individual souls from moment to moment. I would argue that this means that at any now point a subject can be hypnotically progressed so that, with varying degrees of clarity, they see the most probable version of the future as it is conceived by the time masters at that point in time. But are they seeing their own *individual* future, or just being allowed a more general snapshot? I would argue that the level of detail provided in the progressions we have reviewed suggests that they must be seeing their own individual future lives as they stand at that point. And why should this not be the case? We have already seen that for the tapestry to work in providing a completely coherent future at any now point, each individual thread must be represented and must extend throughout that future – and Cannon's subject confirms this.

However, this leaves us with no definitive explanation as to how subjects in the same group progression sessions could see apparently mutually exclusive atmospheric environments on earth in more or less the same place at more or less the same future time. On this issue I can only conclude that some other subjective factors come into play, perhaps related to the individual subjects' own expectations and imaginations – which might be able to exercise more influence on some subjects' visions of the future than on others, especially in a group rather than a one-on-one hypnosis environment. On this basis, for example, we might turn Snow's previous conjecture right around, and argue that the albeit-significant minority of subjects who foresaw an unpolluted future in a new age or even rustic environment were the very ones who allowed their individual hopes to conquer the underlying realism of the connection that the other group subjects made with the tapestry at that point in time. But this is purely conjecture on my part, and nor do I want it to suggest that I am unduly skeptical – because I was as heartened as anyone by their hopeful visions of the future.

By contrast, what about Snow progressing to a consistent future in his current life over a number of sessions spanning nearly a year? We know that his vision of the future was inaccurate, at the very least as regards his timings. But where did his consistency come from? In this case I would argue either that his preconceptions from the Cayce readings subjectively dominated and distorted his visions, or that after he had 'genuinely' progressed once his experience formed a blueprint or imprint that dominated his future sessions – and acted as a block to viewing any alternative future. Or, perhaps, he was seeing his own thread in the tapestry all the way through, and it simply did not change much for the duration of his progression sessions. But, again, all of this is purely conjecture on my part.

So, in a more general sense, what does all this actually mean for us as individuals? I would suggest that it means virtually nothing. If as we have seen progressions only a few decades into the future are arguably rendered valueless by the changes to the tapestry in the interim, how much more valueless is any progression into our next life – let alone into lives several centuries or even millennia in the future? These future lives may have been envisaged by the time masters in the tapestry at the time the progressions took place, but they have not been, nor will they ever be, individually experienced by the relevant subjects in genuine incarnation. These subjects have not loved, suffered, made mistakes and learned in them as they do in the lives they genuinely experience when the proper time comes. This is exactly why I believe that the evidence of life progressions does not contradict the fundamental assumption that underlies this book – that karma does indeed involve choice and not predestiny.

In fact Goldberg unwittingly supports this interpretation when he makes an important general observation:

> It is interesting to note patients' lack of emotions during future progressions. With rare exceptions, the scenes, no matter how horrible, are described with little reaction. Earthquakes, nuclear wars, accidental deaths, and so on, do not seem to bring out the same emotional response during progression as they do during past-life regressions. The reason for this is unclear.

I would argue that the reason for this is actually completely clear – and it is because the lives they are progressing into are only conceptions, and *not* genuine in any physical sense. Of course, this would tend to suggest that using progression as a therapeutic tool should have no value. Is this a feasible argument in the light of Goldberg's experience? On the one hand, most patients like Janet go to a positive future life – although why she ended up so far in the future is entirely unclear. So the experience appears to have a positive impact, but this is arguably only a placebo and has no underlying karmic validity. On the other, on those rare occasions when patients like Pete progress to an unpleasant future life, the therapy involves programming them onto a different vibrational frequency. Not only do I regard Goldberg's suggestions concerning these highly similar alternative lives entirely unconvincing and contrary to the findings of all our pioneers, but I also regard his suggestion that merely reprogramming a patient to a more positive frequency – without them having to do any karmic striving for themselves – as a complete travesty. It seems there are very good reasons why our pioneers do not get involved in progression, particularly for supposed therapeutic purposes, and I would argue that any therapist like Goldberg who refuses to properly consider the real implications of what they are doing is treading on dangerous karmic ground.

To Snow's credit, although as I previously suggested his arguments tend to meander back and forth and do not leave us with any real sense of coherence, he does make the following statement that I regard as highly perceptive:

What we see in such cases need not be considered a rigidly fixed and predetermined future but the most probable outcome of all the untold multitudes of already expressed choices of all the self-aware components of the Ultimate Reality.

This is undoubtedly consistent with the ideas I have put forward. And Joan Grant provides further support in her first autobiographical account of a past life, *Winged Pharaoh*, published in 1937 – with a poetic beauty far superior to anything I could achieve:

The past is fixed, that which has happened cannot be changed. But every action changes a future that is fluid and can be modified in a past that is lasting. Your next day or the next life you will be born in is like your mirrored image in a pool. At any moment you can check what the pool of your future looks like, but through your own free will you can make storms rage over it or make waves on its peaceful surface. That is why so few forecasts bear out.

All of that having been said, we must also consider the possibility that all progressions into the future – whether individual or in groups – are entirely based on imagination, and do not involve genuine access to the tapestry at all. This view would still mean that the tapestry does exist as I have described above, but it would satisfy those who feel that access to it must surely be karmically denied – except to a limited extent in the place of life selection. Indeed, Cannon's subject indicates that incarnate souls do quite regularly come to view the tapestry when meditating or asleep, but that looking at the future portion is not encouraged. Nevertheless, my own view is that Wambach's and Snow's finding concerning equal sex distribution in future lives does seem to reflect more than just imagination. Moreover, the impressive level of detail encountered in many individual progressions might also be thought to preclude complete fabrication.

Finally, it is fitting that we should return to the issue of what all this means for humanity as a whole. If we imagine our collective future as represented by the branches of the ubiquitous tree of life, one route through it may take us more or less directly towards the more spiritual existence that many think is our ultimate destiny. Another route may be much more tortuous and winding, but it may still, eventually, emerge into the light of the sun. But I do not think we can be foolish enough to ignore the fact that some branches will wither and die, trapped in dense foliage before they get to the sunlight. Because of karmic choice and free will, these *are* all possible courses for the future of humanity. If we were to end up taking a dead end and destroying our magnificent planet it would be a terrible indictment on our ability to treasure our physical birthright. But, even then, most earth-connected souls would in all probability transfer over to other inhabited planets – to continue with the ultimate quest of the transcendent evolution of all souls, wherever their temporary physical home might be.

9

SPIRIT POSSESSION
Are We Really Who We Think We Are?

Our pioneers are broadly in agreement on most of the issues we have discussed so far, with the possible exception that some concentrate more on progressive karma and others more on its repetitive counterpart, mainly due to differences in the nature of their subjects. I hope that I have been able to show that these two elements can be placed into a single consistent framework that validates all of their findings without contradictions. But we must now turn to certain complexities related to the nature of the soul and its behavior that I have so far ignored, and here we find that there is sufficient disagreement among our pioneers that their views cannot be reconciled. So we need to pick our way carefully through the evidence to see what conclusions we might draw.

As a preliminary, we have already seen in chapter 5 that Michael Newton's subjects report they divide their soul energy, leaving some of it behind in the ethereal realms even when they are in incarnation. In *Destiny of Souls* he goes into some detail on this issue, and his subjects report that if we were to bring all of our soul energy into incarnation we would 'blow the circuits of the human brain'. Nevertheless, they also indicate that the word 'divide' is somewhat misleading because the soul acts like a hologram, so that if a part splits off it still retains its essential 'wholeness'. The amount of soul energy taken into incarnation varies, with more advanced souls typically using only about a quarter, while less advanced souls can take as much as half or even three quarters. It is for this reason that especially more advanced souls can choose to lead parallel or multiple lives at the same time, and this is one way of speeding up our development – although they report that it is far less commonplace than many researchers assume, and that it is so draining that souls do not often try this experiment more than once.

Newton's subjects also insist that although we are advised about the amount of energy likely to be required for any life we are about to choose, the decision of how much of our soul energy to use rests with us, although possibly with some outer limits, and we can sometimes take less than we need – for example, because of our desire to continue concurrently and as much as possible with other learning activities in our real home in the ethereal realms. Such misjudgments of soul energy requirements can lead to difficult and draining lives. Even so, when we return to the ethereal realms we must reunite with the remainder of our soul energy, and this process takes place with or without assistance and at the time of our choosing. Most souls reunify their energy when they return to their soul group, but some may do it earlier to allow swifter reorientation, while others may delay it somewhat so that the experiences of their last life remain dominant during the initial life review. Whenever they do it, they all report that as soon as the process is complete they feel a huge surge in their awareness, accompanied by an intense feeling of wellbeing.

We should not assume, however, that everything in the Newtonian garden is rosy. We saw in chapter 6 how his subjects report that if the characteristics of the ethereal soul and physical brain are not well-matched this can have a huge bearing on the subsequent life, and he regards this as a prime source of mental illness. And when we refer to mental illness now, we are not just talking about the more commonplace psychological problems treated by hypnotherapists that may or may not have a karmic origin and relate to past lives, but to serious disorders. This is not intended to be a treatise on mental illness, for which I would be totally unqualified. But the subjects we are about to discuss by definition take us into these realms. So, for example, Newton suggests that a soul struggling to retain some degree of control over an aberrant brain may give up at some point, leading at least to a dissociated personality. On the other hand, we all know that many brilliant and exceptionally gifted people often teeter on the brink of insanity. Have they perhaps brought too much of their soul energy with them into incarnation, so that their brain struggles to handle the incredible insights they possess?

In this context Helen Wambach provides a fascinating case study of a young child brought to her who would not speak and shunned any sort of physical contact. She was clearly autistic. But at the same time she could read and showed a high degree of mathematical ability, even though she had not been taught either of these skills. Although Wambach was unable to hypnotize her as such, based on intuition and a great deal of patience she developed a telepathic rapport with the girl, at which point it became clear that she felt like an adult trapped in a child's body, and was rejecting the experience. In any case, once she had been able to make someone else understand her predicament she seemed to get better. Intriguingly, when she started school she seemed to forget her previous skills and returned to being a normal child. Wambach implies that she was remembering too much of her adult experiences from past lives, and in Newtonian terms we might argue that her reduced amnesia resulted from bringing too much of her soul energy into incarnation.

Other therapists such as Roger Woolger discuss the extent to which we are made up of multiple secondary or sub-personalities, this being a cornerstone of Jungian psychotherapy. At their most severe these can manifest in multiple-personality disorders, in which each personality dominates the subject one at a time and claims no knowledge of any of the others; or in the contrasting condition of schizophrenia, in which the subject remains terrifyingly aware of the multiple voices or selves within them that they cannot control. Our pioneering hypnotherapists offer two explanations for such sub-personalities, and although they are not mutually exclusive most tend to favor one over the other. On the one hand they may be aspects of the one self that derive either from the current life only, or from various past lives as well. But on the other, more worryingly, they may represent other earthbound spirits that have to some degree possessed the patient.

Edith Fiore was the first of our pioneers to take possession seriously. As she reports in *The Unquiet Dead*, from her earliest use of hypnotherapy she had sometimes found her patients slipping into other apparently 'external' personalities, but she assumed these were all aspects of their own selves deriving either from the current life or from past lives. However, she started to rethink when she came across historical accounts of possession – which exist in most religious and shamanic writings in one form or another, although sometimes alluding to demons rather than human spirits. She then studied more modern sources as well, such as spiritual psychiatrist Carl Wickland's seminal 1924 book *Thirty Years Among the Dead*, and Arthur Guirdham's 1982 study *The Psychic Dimensions of Mental Health*.

Fiore did not give up on other methods of therapy after this discovery. As a number of her detailed case studies show, she went through all the normal therapeutic channels, and past-life therapy as well, with most patients. But as she became more experienced she recognized that in certain cases possession was the most likely explanation for a patient's problems. Signals might be verbal, with patients saying things like 'that's just not me' or 'I feel like two different people', or reporting having conversations inside their own head that felt like someone else was talking – especially if these dialogues involved confrontation. Other signals include sudden mood swings, especially under the influence of alcohol or drugs; significant loss of energy, because a possessing spirit always saps energy from its host; a marked reduction in the ability to concentrate; and loss of memory, perhaps forgetting why they were doing something because the possessing entity temporarily took over and instigated the activity, or worse still suffering from complete memory blanks over whole segments of time. And although she reports that some cases of possession stem from childhood – so that the two or more personalities have been merged for a long time and the patient is less aware of the distinction – one of the most distinguishing features of possession is when an adult patient reports a sudden and complete change in their personality that they simply cannot explain. This is markedly different from the symptoms normally reported by patients for whom past-life regression, or other more conventional therapies, would be more appropriate.

We have already seen in chapter 5 that there are a number of reasons why souls might fail to enter the ethereal realms proper after death, and remain trapped in earth's denser astral plane instead. Fiore expands these to include not realizing they are dead, or at least nonacceptance of the situation, after a sudden death; a sense of injustice, or of unfinished business, and other strong unresolved emotions such as love, fear, revenge, hate and jealousy; intense attachment to particular people or places; an assumption that there is no life after death so they must still be alive, or a belief in hell that prevents them from trying to move towards the light; and cravings for earthly pleasures like food, sex or alcohol, tobacco and other drugs.

Such trapped spirits may just wander around for many years before finally listening to their guides and moving into the light. Or, as we have seen, some might eventually resolve to enter a new unoccupied fetus without any proper interlife experience, probably condemning themselves to a further bout of repetitive karma. But, according to Fiore, some may be sufficiently confused or even destructive that they take an alternative route and, either soon after death or even after many years of lonely wandering, decide to enter another body that already has its own soul in occupation. She suggests that sometimes the possessing spirit's intentions are benign, thinking they are helping their host – and this is especially true of parents or other spirits that possess children from an early age. But more often their motives are entirely selfish, and may even be positively aggressive – for example, when revenge is involved. Whatever the background, Fiore emphasizes that the situation is always a negative one – for both intruder and host – even when it might appear otherwise. As we might expect, she also indicates that possessing entities always seem to be somewhat spiritually immature.

Apart from the distinguishing signs of possession already mentioned, she also emphasizes that because the intruders remain in their astral bodies they retain all the physical problems they had when they died. These are usually transmitted to their host to a greater or lesser extent, so that a variety of physical symptoms whose cause is apparently unknown may arise. Their emotional attitudes and general mental state are also retained, again crossing over into their host – so if, for example, the intruder was intensely depressed and suicidal, these symptoms will come out in their host. From this perspective possession can be confusing because it can cause many of the same symptoms as patients' own past lives – for example, problems of a sexual and relationship nature, with weight, or with alcohol, tobacco and drug cravings. She even insists, perhaps with a little too much zeal, that anyone who indulges in these cravings is almost certainly possessed.

From the host's point of view, the reasons they were vulnerable are varied. Fiore reports that some people's auras, which are effectively designed to protect us from possession and other negative energies, have an inherent weakness that makes them more easily penetrable than other – in exactly the same way that some people's physical immune system is generally weaker than others. But auras can also be weakened by particular activities or events, including traumas such as the death of a loved one, accidents or operations that require hospitalization, any other periods of intense emotional turmoil or depression, and excessive drinking or drug-taking – which then represents a cause rather than an effect. Moreover, as soon as one spirit has successfully entered the aura is further weakened so that the subject is even more vulnerable to attack – which is why so many people are multiply possessed. She also points out that people who experiment with séances, Oiuja boards and automatic writing without the proper spiritual protection are explicitly, even if unintentionally, opening themselves up to possession – as to some extent are mediums and clairvoyants, even though they are sometimes attempting to help the very spirits that might end up possessing them. On top of this she suggests children's imaginary playmates are often confused spirits that can end up possessing them, while sometimes people can effectively invite themselves to be possessed by a loved one that has just died through their extreme grief and refusal to let go.

Fiore applied the finger-raising technique often used in hypnosis to get her patients' subconscious minds to disclose whether or not a possessing spirit was present – although often these signals could be manipulated by the intruder so that she had to persevere. Her approach was to point out the real condition of the intruder by addressing them directly, and to emphasize that they had loved ones of their own waiting to take them into the light. By being extremely sensitive to the intruder's confusion and fear – rather than aggressively asking them to leave, which would probably only result in them possessing someone else – in many cases she found that one or two sessions would achieve release and the cessation of all negative symptoms. But especially because multiple possessions were common – in one case more than fifty spirits were present – she found that some intruders were more persistent than others, the most stubborn sometimes taking many sessions just to emerge, as if some sort of delayering was required. In fact she found that the spirits of former family members or other close associates of the patient were the hardest to release, and that these cases usually appeared to involve past-life ties as well. She even suggests that such cases may involve the repayment of a karmic debt, although it will come as no surprise that I have my doubts that something as destructive as possession would ever be karmically planned, so that at best they would involve repetitive karma between relatively immature souls only.

Fiore concludes that most cases of multiple personality and schizophrenia, and many cases involving other psychiatric or psychosomatic disorders, can be attributed to possession. Indeed, she found that once she started using spirit-releasement therapy more than seventy per cent of her patients appeared to have at least one possessing spirit, and most more than one. She indicates that the extent of possession can vary widely, the implication being that ordinary people might not even know they have a problem because most of the time they are strong enough to keep the possessing spirit under control. On the other hand, although she reports that she tried as hard as possible not to subjectively influence her patients, she does not rule out the possibility that at least in some cases the apparent possession may have been a complete fantasy – which might even have been brought on by her mere suggestion that the patient should try spirit-releasement therapy.

In an attempt to keep all this reasonably in perspective Fiore also emphasizes that the common symptoms of possession, such as lowered energy and memory loss, are by no means exclusive to this phenomenon and can easily arise from other more prosaic causes. Moreover, when we meditate we often talk to our own higher self, or perhaps our guides, as if we are having a genuine conversation with someone else; and we also know that the souls of loved ones who have passed on can attempt to make some sort of telepathic contact with us on occasions. Fiore is clear that none of this should be mistaken for any sort of possession. However, her insistence that these conversations and contacts will be overwhelmingly positive in nature, or at least identifiable as benign, is no great help – inasmuch as it is clear that some possessing spirits would tend to hold themselves out as benign, and if we are at all confused in ourselves it may not be easy to be objective about what is really going on in our heads. More reassuring, perhaps, would be to take general comfort from the fact that possession may be nowhere near as common as Fiore suggests, and I will return to this issue shortly.

The only other one of our pioneers who has really concentrated on possession is Shakuntala Modi – albeit that, like Fiore, she does not rely exclusively on spirit-releasement therapy and only regards it as another option in her therapeutic toolkit. In *Remarkable Healings* she does not indicate why or how she became involved in such therapy, and she does not explicitly mention Fiore's work, but she nevertheless confirms pretty much every aspect of it.

Having said that, Modi also goes considerably further in a number of areas about which I have some major concerns. She suggests first that spirits reside in different parts of the body, and that literally hundreds can reside in variously shaped layers. Second, that they can enter even when their host is still in the womb, or by contrast that the spirits of aborted or miscarried fetuses can themselves act as possessors. Third, that animal spirits and those from another planet can sometimes act as possessors. Fourth, that in cases of a close relationship from past lives, especially one involving intense usually negative emotions, the spirit might possess their victim over many lives. Fifth, that even rock music and video games can weaken our auras. Sixth, that people with too much compassion, and especially those who are spiritually advanced themselves, are some of the most vulnerable potential hosts – a pretty depressing conclusion that if true would act as a serious disincentive to two of the most honorable motivations we can have. Seventh, that actively refusing to believe in the phenomenon of possession itself can act as a trigger to make it happen – even though karmically one might expect the exact opposite, inasmuch as it is normally an explicit fear of something that attracts it and turns it into physical reality. And eighth, that many possessing spirits could not even find the light to go into, even though they wanted to – although apparently they could easily find it as soon as she asked them to simply 'look up'.

On top of this, Modi's statistics make even grimmer reading than Fiore's – indicating that, from a sample of one hundred patients, ninety-two were possessed, eighty-two of them by more than one spirit. These statistics are made worse by the following observation:

> Even when I work with so-called normal people, almost all of them find one or more human spirits inside them, even though they did not have any obvious physical or emotional problems.

I can only suggest that if possession were a virtual certainty for most of us it would be a devastating indictment of incarnate life on earth, suggesting a massive restriction of personal responsibility and free will. But there is even worse to come from Modi concerning the extent to which possessing spirits have usually been demonically influenced by Satan himself, an issue to which we will return shortly.

In *Deep Healing* Hans TenDam makes it clear that he too believes possession is a genuine phenomenon. He refers to it in terms of attachments and obsessions, which are effectively the same except that obsessions are the more aggressive but less prevalent of the two. He appears to confirm many of Fiore's main findings, although he does not discuss how commonplace the phenomenon might be.

As she reports in *Between Death and Life*, Dolores Cannon's subjects have a completely different take on the matter. They agree that possession can only occur if there is an imbalance in the host's energy field or aura. But one insists that the possessing energy is that of elementals or nature spirits – which we will discuss in more detail in the final chapter – rather than of human spirits:

> These cases of so-called 'possession' are generally caused by someone who has allowed their karma to become seriously imbalanced, leaving a vacuum in part of their karmic energies where other energies can enter in. These are usually disorganized energies, for the energy that constitutes your souls and your body are not the only energies there are. Some of the superstitious terms that used to be common in your language – earth sprites, water sprites, elementals, and various things like that – referred to collections of loosely organized energy that usually are connected to certain physical characteristics on the earth. Because of the type of energy they are, they're attracted to certain physical situations....
>
> They don't do it on purpose; it is just an accident. And the violence that ensues is because they are not as organized, in energy terms, as the human soul is.... There are things that they do out of mischief, but things like this generally happen because of an imbalance in the energies.... Possession is a reality; however, elementals are drawn and not invaders as such.

The solution to the problem, according to this subject, is to meditate to restore an energy balance that will automatically expel such disorganized energies. Moreover, when questioned about the influence of alcohol and drugs in opening people up to possession, this subject reported that in fact they do not tend to lower our protection, and that such cases were rare. Meanwhile, another of Cannon's subjects describes possession as involving rather more general negative energies:

> People who are presumably 'possessed' are actually examples of those

spirits who have a particularly bad dose of negative energies attracted to them. It had gotten strong enough to start influencing them on the physical plane. These spirits when they cross over will have to spend quite some time in the resting place to rid themselves of this.

The only other one of our pioneers that makes anything more than a passing reference to possession is Newton. In *Destiny of Souls* he tends to go along with Cannon's last subject, indicating that to the extent the phenomenon exists at all it involves nothing more than the attraction of negative energy in general – with neither human nor elemental spirits playing any part:

> My subjects do not see the devil or demonic spirits floating around earth. What they do feel when they are spirits is an abundance of negative human energy exuding the intense emotions of anger, hate and fear. These disruptive thought patterns are attracted to the consciousness of other negative thinkers who collect and disseminate even more disharmony. All this dark energy in the air works to the detriment of positive wisdom on earth....
>
> In all my years of working with souls, never once have I had a subject who was possessed by another spirit, unfriendly or otherwise.... Even those who came to me with conscious beliefs in demonic forces reject the existence of such beings when they see themselves as spirits.

To be clear, while we have seen previously that Newton accepts there are such things as earthbound spirits, he does not accept that they can possess other people. To back this up, he emphasizes that when patients have come to him believing they were possessed, in most cases their fears proved completely groundless – while in a few they had misinterpreted an attempt to contact them made either by a loved one that had passed on, or occasionally by some other disturbed spirit that had some sort of unresolved karmic issues.

What are we to make of these clearly differing views on possession? I do not automatically reject Cannon's first subject's suggestion regarding elementals and nature spirits, but I do not believe it can be used to explain away the apparently human spirit possessions discussed in detail by Fiore and Modi. So we are really left with the evidence of these two, and to a lesser extent TenDam, against that of Newton – although the silence of our other pioneers on this issue might be taken as implicit support for his position. Newton clarifies his skepticism further with this important observation:

Our physical world may have unhappy or mischievous spirits floating round, but they do not lock in and inhabit the minds of people. The spirit world is much too ordered to allow for such muddled soul activity. Being possessed by another being would not only abrogate our life contract but destroy free will.

I have already indicated that I find this an extremely persuasive argument. After all, personal responsibility and free will are the main themes of this entire book. By contrast, in her afterthoughts Modi tends to blame many of societies ills on an ever-increasing spiral of often-demonic possession, and personally I do not find this attitude at all helpful. Nevertheless, I cannot in all conscience completely reject the huge volume of evidence for possession that Fiore and Modi have collated. Their spirit-releasement sessions produce levels of detail that are just as impressive as those from past-life regressions – often including the possessing spirit's name, how they died, why they failed to move into the light and why they were able to enter the body of their host. Moreover, in many cases it appears that their spirit-releasement therapy has been just as successful as its past-life counterpart – which this time I am not prepared to dismiss as a mere placebo, as I was with supposed progression therapy.

The real issue that bothers me is their conclusion that possession is relatively commonplace. This I think must be an exaggeration, caused partly again by the fact that therapists' patients, troubled as they are by varying degrees of psychological and psychosomatic problems, are not representative of the general population as a whole – however much Modi might argue that even apparently normal people are usually possessed. Added to this, I have little doubt that in concentrating on spirit-releasement therapy, or at least providing it as an alternative in their toolkit, they may have subjectively influenced at least some of their patients – a possibility that Fiore readily accepts.

Above all, if possession was as common as Fiore and Modi make out, surely our other pioneers would have inadvertently been faced by at least some cases that were so definitive they would not have been able to ignore them. If so, surely they would have included such an important phenomenon in their reports of their work; or, at the very least, their therapies should have been generally less successful than they often proved to be. One might argue that in fact they were sometimes facing cases of possession without realizing it, and that in getting the possessing spirits to talk about their unassimilated traumas – which they then mistook for their patients' own past-life experiences – they allowed them to escape into the light anyway. This could be true in a few cases. But such an argument would ignore the karmic patterns and lessons over many past lives and interlives that patients so regularly uncover – patterns that are far too individualized and consistent to represent a mish-mash of the experiences of various external spirits. This is especially proven by the fact that past-life memories repeatedly involve karmic connections with other key souls known to the patient in both their past *and* current lives – which, at the very least in cases of supposed possession by an unconnected spirit, could not relate to an intruder.

On that basis I am inclined to conclude that possession by earthbound spirits may well exist as a phenomenon, but that if it does it is nowhere near as commonplace as its main proponents suggest. This means that most of us are still in complete control of our lives, and should not worry about the 'conversations' we all have in our own heads from time to time. These might be with our higher self or guides, or indeed with elements of sub-personality at least from our current lives – but provided they do not cause intense feelings of disruption or lack of integration they are all part of life's rich tapestry.

I would also suggest that even those unfortunate people who might be possessed, and who might fail to repatriate their possessing spirits by therapy, would be automatically rid of any intruders when they died – so that they could not influence any future lives. This would certainly be the case if they entered the ethereal realms proper, because I cannot conceive that an intruder would be allowed to remain attached to them there. But I would also expect it to be the case even if they were themselves sufficiently immature and disoriented that their own soul remained trapped in the astral plane alone before reincarnating – because, after all, a possessing spirit's main desire is normally to have a physical body to inhabit. The only exception I would make would be if, in the latter case, the two souls were karmically linked – so that when the former host's soul reincarnated without any sort of planning the intruder, rather than choosing a body of its own, might decide to keep a clearly repetitive karmic cycle going via possession. But I would expect such possession across multiple lives to be far rarer than even the normal phenomenon.

As for protection against possession, it can do no harm to indicate that all of its proponents recommend the 'white light' approach. This is a simple exercise to repeat daily that strengthens the aura by imagining the light energy of the ethereal realms flowing into the solar plexus, and pulsing throughout the body to form a protective shield that cannot be invaded by unwanted guests – be they earthbound or elemental spirits, or simply negative energies. We will return to this exercise in the final chapter.

Let us now return to Modi's insistence that demonic possession is rife. She reports that at its least harmful this involves Satan's demonic followers tricking earthbound spirits into following them to hell after death – although in some cases they go willingly because they want to share Satan's power, or because they are angry with God. Here they receive intensive and specific training in the arts of aura entry, general disruption and incitement to commit acts of evil – needless to say under threat that if they fail they will be punished severely. But in many cases demonic entities supposedly envelop these unfortunate spirits and enter possessed hosts along with them, where they can then be perceived as black blobs of energy. Even these can still, however, be repatriated into the light – albeit sometimes after much cursing and blaspheming.

Modi provides endless details and case studies to emphasize how common demonic influence is on the phenomenon of possession. She even goes into great detail about the mechanisms of various astral 'devices' that are used to penetrate hosts' auras and keep them in demonic bondage. In fact she reports that seventy-seven out of her sample of one hundred patients were demonically infested – seventy-one of them by more than one demon – and boldly states that 'the facts lead to the conclusion that demons are the single leading cause for psychiatric problems in general'.

I will readily admit that, whatever I might have felt about possession in general, I found all this demonic material completely nauseating. Doubtless there are those who might suggest that such an intense reaction was caused by me being demonically possessed myself, and this material is so insidious that even I considered that possibility. But to place all this in perspective I had to bring myself back to the findings of the vast majority of our other pioneers, whose subjects have stated repeatedly and categorically that any concepts of Satan, hell and demons are entirely the products of human imagination – a conclusion that is to some extent supported by Modi's own admission that her patients perceive their demonic possessors in whatever form their preconceptions dictate. As we have seen, that is not to say that in concentrating on such matters we might not, at least to some extent, bring them into nonphysical reality. But if that is the case then the last thing I want to do is assist this process, and I would argue that the more people reject such notions the less nourishment we provide to them.

One of Cannon's subjects sums this danger up succinctly:

These evil creatures, as you call them, are indeed real to those who would create them in their mind. There are those who do not *believe* in such and therefore they do not exist. However, it would be wrong to say that they are

234

not *real* to the individuals who believe in them, for indeed they *are* real. It is that ability of yours to create what you wish that is even more important now than it was previously. It is essential that you be aware of this power, this ability to create what you will. For in so doing you have the very real choice of creating that which would be good or that which would be evil. It is entirely up to the individual as to the reality they create.

But even this ability to create demonic influences by thought projection may not stretch as far as genuine possession. It is no surprise that Newton categorically states that he has never come across a case of demonic possession, because he does not even accept the validity of human spirit possession. But Fiore makes exactly the same statement, which is pretty strong stuff given that she, like Modi, to some extent specialized in spirit-releasement therapy for a number of years.

I have little doubt that Modi's motives are entirely beyond reproach. But I cannot escape the conclusion that, at the very least as far as the issue of demonic possession is concerned, her work is subjectively influenced by her Christian beliefs – and that it may have similarly influenced her patients via telepathy or some other mechanism. She insists that all the terminology she uses belongs specifically to them, that she tried not to influence them, and that they came from a variety of religious backgrounds. But when we find that at least in the case studies she reproduces they consistently name the beings of light that come to help them as Jesus, or the archangels Michael, Gabriel, Uriel or Raphael, we must wonder about the degree of objectivity involved.

Of course, in coming to this conclusion I am again laying myself open to accusations of double standards. I accepted Modi's findings about past-life and interlife regression, and to some extent about human spirit possession, but I am rejecting them in relation to demonic possession. This is despite the fact that I accept it may be possible for hellish interlife experiences and other negative – even demonic – influences to be effectively created by the power of individual or collective thought and expectations. And despite the fact that her evidence for demonic possession arises from exactly the same sessions as for normal possession, often with the same patients and using the same regression methods, and is provided in abundance. She emphasizes that if we deny the reality of the all-pervasive demonic influences in our world we are only serving their purpose by aiding them in their subterfuge. On that basis, if I am wrong I am actively helping such influences to proliferate. But in that case the majority of our other pioneers would be wrong as well. That is, of course, a possibility. But I can only call it as I see it – in this case with a heavy dose of personal intuition.

We are all, of course, a mixture of many sub-personalities. Any one of us will have had periods when, for example, the rebellious or indignant child, the misunderstood adolescent, or the successful or failed businessperson or lover resurfaces as the dominant personality in our adult life. And clearly the number of our potential sub-personalities is significantly increased by our different past-life experiences. These only represent a problem if for some reason they become sufficiently separated from the main body of our personality, or indeed soul, that they are not properly integrated.

Modi's research has led her to the conclusion that the soul can actually fragment into many pieces, which means that we can effectively be self-possessed. Her reasoning is that severe traumas can cause the personality at that point to split off from the main body of the soul, ready to rear its head again as an effectively externalized sub-personality in either the current or a future life. TenDam seems to support this analysis, adding that in more extreme cases the sub-personality actually portrays itself as someone else entirely, making it a 'pseudo-obsessor'.

But Modi goes further and – apart from her suggestion that Satan and his demons can possess soul fragments as well, which I will ignore – she insists that they can become lodged with other people. She argues that the predominant causes of such fragmentation are, as usual, intense emotional, sexual and physical traumas, but that it can also arise from intense love or compassion. In most cases the fragmentation involves an exchange of soul parts between the two participants, and even when the situation that caused it was benign the loss of soul integrity is not a positive outcome. Accordingly, she regularly attempts to retrieve and reunite all the fragmented soul parts of her patients during therapy, while at the same time repatriating those fragments belonging to other people with their rightful owners – obviously at a distance, and without them being consciously aware of the process. And she reports that fragments can be located by following the 'silver cord' that still connects them to the main soul – an idea similar to that of the cord reported by near-death experiencers that attaches their soul, or at least their astral body, to their physical body, and which if broken would precipitate physical death and prevent them from returning to it.

Is this idea of soul fragmentation a sound one? The basic idea of energy interchanges is there in much spiritual literature, including James Redfield's *The Celestine Prophecy* as I mentioned in chapter 6. We all know that some people are so selfish and self-obsessed that they tend to be energy takers, draining the energy from others around them, while others are liberal energy givers – sometimes too much for their own good unless they have perfected the art of replenishing it from ethereal or other sources. Most of us are somewhere in-between, sometimes giving our energy to others and sometimes taking it from them. Newton echoes this point:

> We can lose shards of positive energy to people whom we give it to voluntarily, or by others who drain it out of us with their negativity. It takes energy to erect and maintain defense mechanisms to protect ourselves. A subject once said to me, 'When I share my light with those I think worthy of receiving it, I can recharge it faster because it was given freely.' One of the best ways we revitalize our energy is through sleep.

As an avid taker of siestas, I totally agree with Newton's view. But can these energy interchanges ever become so intense that we leave a small part of our soul with someone else, to such an extent that it actually fragments? Most of our pioneers, even including Cannon and Fiore, do not mention this idea. But somehow – and this time I will not even bother to attempt to defend my apparent double standards, given that the idea comes primarily from Modi's research – my intuition tells me that such fragmentation should not be summarily dismissed. It seems from her case studies that although the exchanged soul fragments cause some ongoing disruption for their hosts, they do not act as possessing spirits, so personal responsibility and free will are usually maintained. Their influence appears to be more subtle, causing us to retain links with the other person that make it harder to let the memory of them or their activities go than it perhaps should be. To this extent they are perhaps not unlike TenDam's concept of attachments, as opposed to his more aggressive obsessors. I am less sure about the idea of soul fragments remaining attached to but at the same time somewhat detached from their own soul, although again I do not dismiss the idea completely.

So I do not necessarily reject the idea of fragmentation as it applies to our current lives. But, just as with possession, I would argue that our own soul fragments would not remain separated after death – whether they were attached to others or not – provided we enter the ethereal realms proper. After all, if we reintegrate with that portion of our soul energy that we left behind, we – or at least our guides – would hardly be likely to allow other fragments to be scattered all over the place. On this basis I would not expect us to retain fragments belonging to someone else either; and, for the same reason, I would expect these to be automatically repatriated if they died before us. Again, the only exception whereby I could conceive of fragments remaining separate, and ready to interfere again in a future life, would be if a confused or immature soul remained trapped in the astral plane, or perhaps entered the ethereal realms but simply slept all the way through, before reincarnating without any sort of planning. But I would expect even this to be a relatively rare occurrence, if it happens at all.

When Modi and to a more limited extent TenDam discuss soul fragments, they are made out to be something far more concrete and supposedly integral to our soul than mere energy interchanges. If they are right, and they may be, I have argued that at least in most cases these fragments will be reunited with their originating soul after death. On the other hand, it may be that their assumption that these fragments are effectively irreplaceable is incorrect. It certainly seems to me that we can lose genuine fragments of soul energy to other people, but still replenish them from other sources so that our soul's essential integrity and strength is not violated. In this context, we know that intense negative emotions – which at heart derive from negative energy interchanges – can, if they remain unassimilated or unresolved, do immense damage, whether in this life or future ones. From this perspective, instead of concentrating on pulling lost fragments back in, I would suggest that we might be better off visualizing 'cutting off the ties that bind us' to past situations, so that these essentially regressive energies no longer hold any charge for us. Accompanying this, the white light visualization that I mentioned earlier can then be used to fill any gaps in our energy field that might have been created by others selfishly taking our energy from us, or by us giving it freely and then to some extent regretting it because of subsequent events.

Another concept related to possession is the 'walk-in'. The idea is that an incarnate soul can actively decide that they no longer want to remain in their physical body, and therefore relinquish it to another. The clear difference from possession is that this process involves a complete exchange, so there is no multiple occupation of one body.

It appears that Cannon is the only one of our pioneers to support this idea, which she first encountered when one of her subjects claimed under hypnosis to be a recent walk-in. The subject reports that this phenomenon is becoming increasingly common because, in not going through the normal memory-blocking process of childhood and adolescence, the replacement souls bring far more spiritual wisdom from the ethereal realms into incarnation – which is apparently important at the current time. She also indicates first that the exchange can take place either during an experience that brings the subject close to death, or even when they are merely asleep. Second, that the subject will not be consciously aware of the agreement, but all the planning will have been done previously during sleep periods, and their subconscious self will be an entirely willing partner in the exchange. And third, that the replacement soul will be aware of the departing soul's current life memories and life plan, but not of their past-life memories – and although it will not work out their karma per se, it will fulfill their important obligations.

Another subject confirms that walk-ins do take place, but stresses that the replacement soul does in fact take on the departing soul's immediate karma – which it must then work through before it can begin working on its own karma – and that for this reason the two souls will be closely connected. They also stress that the replacement soul must be sufficiently advanced that they do not need the lessons of childhood and adolescence, and can handle the relative lack of spiritual amnesia.

The only other pioneer to even mention this concept is again Newton, but he is absolutely adamant that it is a complete falsehood:

> If this theory is true, then I must turn in my great-guru white robe and gold medallion. Not once, in all my years of working with subjects in regression, have I ever had a walk-in soul. Also, these people have never heard of any other soul in the spirit world associated with such practices. In fact, they deny the existence of this act because it would abrogate a soul's life contract. To give another soul permission to come in and take over your karmic life plan defeats the whole purpose of your coming to earth in the first place! It is deluded reasoning to assume that the walk-in would wish to complete their own karmic cycle in a body originally selected and assigned to someone else.

As we have already seen, he is also adamant that the process of attuning our soul energy to our human brain is a lengthy and complex one, and not something that would go consciously unnoticed by an adult who suddenly found themselves playing host to a completely new soul. Indeed he argues that it would drive them insane.

What are we to make of this disagreement? Cannon's subjects both report that, inasmuch as the soul being replaced has had enough of that life, a walk-in is far preferable to suicide because the physical body remains as a useful vehicle for another soul. This seems to imply that there is a shortage of appropriate bodies for advanced souls, which is an issue we will return to in the final chapter. But I find this argument somewhat unconvincing in that, as we saw in chapter 7, other subjects of hers, and indeed those of most of our other pioneers, report that it is the breaking of the life contract that makes suicide so frowned upon – not the killing of the physical body per se. And, as Newton insists, a walk-in would clearly involve exactly the same breaking of the contract even if the physical body did not die. I have previously accepted most of Cannon's subjects' reports, so again the accusation of double standards can be laid at my door. But, again, I can only call it as I see it.

On a slightly different topic, several of Cannon's subjects also report that exchanges can occur even with young babies, although in these cases clearly the main advantages of walk-ins are lost. The idea is that the newly incarnated soul may realize it has made a bad decision – perhaps because it cannot adapt to that particular human brain, or because another key player in its life plan has suddenly and unexpectedly died – and agree to an exchange. However, they also accept that in some cases no replacement is found – which seems to contradict their previous suggestion about a general lack of appropriate bodies – so that cot death supposedly ensues. Newton provides somewhat more support for this type of exchange arrangement, indicating that in just two cases he has come across a soul who reported they came in after another soul had pulled out – but he stresses that both exchanges occurred before birth, and indeed before the eighth month of pregnancy. Moreover, while discussing overlapping lives TenDam gives details of a few cases of what appear to be walk-ins with young children who were ill almost to the point of death, although in these cases the replacement souls were, by contrast to Cannon's supposed adult walk-ins, relatively immature and had had no interlife proper – indeed their previous personalities had only died after the child they had taken over had already been born. Personally I am generally more open to the idea of these much earlier exchanges.

Some people argue that any idea that the soul exists as an individuality in its own right, with its own choices and control, is mere illusion in itself – and an illusion founded on excessive ego at that. It would appear that this was a major concern for the Buddha, who went to great lengths to avoid the question of what actually reincarnates so as to lessen his pupils' attachments to ego. Buddhist teachings often seem to involve paradoxes involving flames, such as whether the flame from one lamp remains the same flame all night long, or whether if the flame from one lamp lights another that is the same flame or not. The solution appears to be that these are both the same flames and different ones all at the same time. His successors' ongoing confusion ultimately resulted in the Buddhist doctrine of 'no-soul', whereby there is supposedly no such thing as an individual soul that reincarnates, nor any notion of individual karma that is carried forward, although it does contribute to a more generalized group karma. Such reasoning may have been useful to people who were trying to escape from the bondage of a strict Hindu caste system, under which only the souls from the highest class could attain release from the earthly karmic round, but personally I find it totally misleading in a modern context.

The corollary to this view, that belief in the continuity of an individual soul is based on ego, is that it goes against the idea of the fundamental unity of everything in the universe. Yet virtually all worldviews that involve reincarnation agree that, despite the fact that we have split off from the Ultimate Source, our purpose is ultimately to reunite with it. So surely this essential and underlying unity is not denied. Indeed, there is a dualistic element to any intelligent spiritual worldview that accepts we are individual souls, but also merely parts of the ultimate oversoul, all at the same time. Nowhere is this perhaps better illustrated, at least as far as humanity is concerned, than in the idea of the individual yet interwoven threads of the tapestry; as Cannon's subject reported in chapter 5, 'the absolute oneness of humanity' is represented within it.

It seems to me that to suggest that belief in an individual soul is an ego-based illusion is actually a gross oversimplification made by people who do not understand the dynamics of karma at all. On the one hand, in being unduly self-deprecating about the power of individual souls it panders to the notion that we have no control over our lives, and that everything is either in the hands of fate or divine whim. And, on the other, it completely ignores the extent to which karmic progress across many lives is a severe struggle – although hopefully enriched by some moments of joy and satisfaction – and is hardly full of continual experiences that are likely to feed material vanity and ego.

In addition, of course, all the research we have considered so far has led us to the conclusion that, as individual souls, we retain an individual identity and individual memories – of past lives and interlives. Even though possession may sometimes occur, these memories can be seen to be our own by the consistency of their karmic patterns and connections as they relate to us as individual souls. Why would some of Ian Stevenson's subjects have birthmarks and defects that corresponded so well to injuries received by *someone else* in a past life? Above all, without this concept of genuine individuality, our whole idea of karmic progression and learning would have to be thrown out of the window.

However, again one of Cannon's subjects has something to add that is relevant to our discussion of soul individuality, and that is the idea of 'imprinting'. He had already recalled several past lives in sessions with Cannon when she asked him if he had had many lives on earth. His response took her by surprise:

This is my first physical life, my first true incarnation on this planet. I have had imprints from many others and been assistant to others. However, this is my first true physical incarnation on earth.

When questioned further, this subject went on to suggest that any soul can experience any of the lives that have been lived by any person on earth, fully and completely, by accessing the relevant akashic records. This is, of course, a substantiation of the idea that I mentioned in chapter 4 of tapping into universal memory. He explains that the primary purpose of this is to provide a soul that has never incarnated on earth before, or at least not for a long time, with a reference point and cultural background; this then prevents them from being overwhelmed by the experience to such an extent that it hampers their learning processes. He seems initially to imply that this is a method used by souls that have incarnated on other planets, rather than completely new souls. But later on in the session he also seems to imply that this method is used quite regularly by many souls to accelerate their learning by using other people's experiences; for example, if they are going to be a leader, they might experience the lives of certain leaders from the past to assist them. But he qualifies this by adding that not everyone makes use of imprints, and it is entirely a matter of choice.

This subject indicates that the experience is so 'real' that there is no way to distinguish it from a genuine incarnation, which is presumably why he recalled various imprints as his own past lives in his initial regression sessions with Cannon – although this does not explain why he subsequently developed an awareness that this was his first non-imprint incarnation on earth. But there is one serious distinction, which is that the imprint is used for experience only and has absolutely no karmic 'charge' – which is exactly what we would expect. So imprinting is no substitute for genuinely experiencing the life itself – in just the same way that, as I suggested in the last chapter, future-life progressions are not genuinely experienced. He also suggests that imprinting explains both parallel lives, and the idea that many people can experience the same 'famous' life when regressed.

So what are we to make of this added complexity? The first thing we can say is that none of our other pioneers mention the idea of imprinting at all. We might argue that, if imprints have no karmic charge, they should not and would not be revealed in regression therapy anyway. But what of our other pioneers who, like Cannon, were not concentrating exclusively on therapy? Should we not expect someone like Newton to have at least come across the idea if it is as common as Cannon's subject suggests?

My overall feeling on this issue is that imprinting would certainly be possible, inasmuch as many of our pioneers' subjects report accessing their *own* akashic records as a virtual reality experience during the interlife; so if souls were sometimes given permission to access *other* soul's lives, I can see why it could be useful in certain situations. What I would expect, however, is that the soul involved would have to be relatively advanced, and would definitely be able to distinguish between the imprint and their own genuine incarnations. I would not expect them to recall an imprint under regression exactly as if it were one of their own past lives, because this would make it impossible for them to separately identify their own genuine incarnations, and the exclusive karmic patterns and progress that arose from them. Nor would I expect imprinted lives to be included in the interlife review, otherwise it would be a mockery from a karmic perspective. Cannon's subject might, of course, be talking nonsense. But if he is not I would only accept his testimony with these clear reservations. And, arguably, the fact that imprints do not figure in the case studies of most of our pioneers bears these assumptions out.

Just to further confuse the picture, Modi reports that sometimes her patients have appeared to recall past lives that they subsequently realized were not their own, and resulted from what she calls 'cross-talk'. They have explained to her that there are seven godheads, masters or oversouls beneath the Ultimate Godhead or Source, and that souls are connected to their own godhead by the ubiquitous silver cord – although this time it is performing a somewhat different function. On that basis they can tap into the memories of other souls within that godhead, and because important or interesting lives resonate more within the godhead they tend to be picked up more often.

Again, I do not completely reject this idea. But I also have serious reservations. Apart from the fact that I suspect there must be many more sub-groupings into different godheads than Modi's patients suggest in order for all the souls in the universe to be properly organized, cross-talk does not seem to have the educational value ascribed to imprints. Moreover, she emphasizes that lives recalled via cross-talk have no therapeutic value either, which is again exactly what we would expect given that they have not actually been experienced personally. But the only example she then provides is that of a female patient suffering from guilt and depression, who initially recalled Eve's life with Adam as the source of her symptoms. These were then apparently relieved when she was regressed into the interlife and realized that Eve was one of the counselors helping her to plan her current life, and that she had merely tapped into her feelings. This not only contradicts her own statement, and goes against the obvious view that cross-talk should have no emotional or karmic impact on the subject; it also, as usual, brings in a famous biblical figure that makes it, for me, rather unconvincing to say the least. Indeed, even if both of them were historical rather than just mythical figures, the idea that someone of Eve's status would be still sitting on planning councils, still suffering from guilt about her failing of Adam, and then allowing that guilt to be felt by another soul in her charge, seems somewhat preposterous.

There is one final contribution to the debate about the individuality and integrity of the soul that I would like to consider, and it is provided by Peter Novak in his 2003 book *The Lost Secret of Death*. He is a former psychological counselor who, after the tragic suicide of his wife, decided to turn full-time researcher into death and the afterlife in his quest for some answers. Like myself in *Genesis Unveiled*, he was motivated to discover the commonalities in all religions and philosophies around the world from all eras, but could not help but be confronted by the glaring differentiation between those that have reincarnation at their core and those that do not. In his attempts to tie them all into modern research into near-death experiences and past-life regression he came to support the 'binary soul doctrine'. This rests on the idea that we have a logical left brain and an intuitive right brain, which components of consciousness separate after death. According to Novak, this doctrine solves all the inconsistencies between the world's religions, showing that to some extent they are all correct – because the left brain component is the part that carries on in the earthly round of reincarnation, while its right brain counterpart remains in a state of dream-like suspended animation in the ethereal realms, which is characterized as either heavenly or hellish.

To be more specific, his argument runs as follows. The left brain represents the conscious, active, intellectual mind that makes all the decisions. The right brain, by contrast, represents the unconscious, reactive, emotional mind, and also contains all memories. After death, if they split, our conscious mind would possess free will and intellect, but no emotion or memory, so it would be able to choose to reembark into incarnation but without any memories of its previous lives. Meanwhile, our unconscious mind would possess emotion and memory, but have no free will or intellect, and so would replay all the emotions from that life again and again in an endless loop. If these emotions were fundamentally positive they would generate a heavenly state of being, but if they were fundamentally repressed and negative they would generate a hellish state. His conclusion from all this is that we as human beings must work far harder to integrate our conscious and unconscious minds in our incarnate lives if we are to escape from this depressing cycle of endless division, with meditation and other such practices as the key.

Novak's work is for the most part well-written and reasoned, even if a little repetitive at times. Indeed, anyone who did not have the requisite understanding might well find it highly persuasive, not least because the arguments against it are sometimes complex. It is for precisely this reason that I will devote no little space to analyzing it, allied to the fact that I fundamentally disagree with his arguments – which would, if correct, totally contradict my own in this book – because I believe they are based on a serious misinterpretation of modern research evidence.

His primary reasons for being convinced of this duality of soul experience are twofold: on the one hand, the idea that the 'dark', or tunnel, and 'light' elements of the near-death experience represent the two separate paths that the two elements of consciousness follow; and, on the other, that the full and effectively blank types of interlife experience represent the same two paths. Let us examine the near-death experience aspect first.

Novak accurately characterizes the first or dark stage of the near-death experience as one of complete emotional detachment but increased analytical perception, and the second or light stage as one of intense emotions and feelings of connectedness. From this he argues quite convincingly that the dark experience is what we would expect if the conscious mind were suddenly divorced from the unconscious, and vice versa for the light experience. This is perhaps his strongest suit. But there are weaknesses. For example, he argues somewhat unconvincingly that although almost all near-death experiencers, and for that matter interlife regression subjects, see these two stages as consecutive, with the dark always preceding the light, in fact they are simultaneous because time does not really exist in the ethereal realms.

He also suggests that the light stage is characterized by a complete lack of analytical judgment, whereas the life review element of many near-death experiences – in which both positive *and* negative aspects of the subject's past lives are instantaneously laid bare *by themselves* – is about as analytical a process as it is possible to achieve. He attempts to get round this by suggesting that the actual judgment took place at the time the emotion or action occurred in life, but was often suppressed, and that all the unconscious mind is doing after death is releasing all those prior judgments; but this completely ignores the subtleness and complexity of the life review, which is established even better by interlife research. And another paradox that he readily admits to is that near-death experiencers nearly always return in a far more balanced and spiritually healthy frame of mind, even though according to him they have experienced what should have been a frightening episode of fragmentation in which neither part of their consciousness could operate properly as an independent unit. His suggestion that neither part would actually be aware of the separation, and that a 'rubber-band effect' might cause them to snap back into far greater harmony when back in the body after separation, is unconvincing and does nothing to fundamentally resolve this apparent paradox.

Perhaps rather more damning is Novak's overemphasis of the extent to which near-death-experience researchers are divided about the existence or otherwise of a hellish state. And remember, in his framework this hellish state is not to be confused with the dark stage that the conscious mind enters; it is instead – perhaps somewhat confusingly – the light stage experienced by the unconscious mind that is overcome by negative rather than positive emotions. He readily admits that most of us regularly repress negative emotions and judgments during our lives, lacking the self-knowledge and courage to see ourselves as we truly are. If all these negative emotions were released on death within the divided soul framework that he champions, there would undoubtedly be massively more reports of *permanent* hellish near-death experiences than there are. Permanence is important here because, according to his reasoning, the unconscious element of the soul does not have the ability to make a decision to forsake its self-imposed hell and repatriate into the light, even though most near-death experiencers insist that they *do* have that choice.

Nevertheless, Novak suggests that a veritable war broke out over this and other related issues in the summer of 2000 in the *Journal of Near-Death Studies*. But in fact this disagreement between Kenneth Ring and Michael Sabom was primarily about the extent to which the latter placed his research into a clearly Christian framework in his second book, something we have already noted in chapter 2. And we saw in chapter 7 that both of these leading figures have come across minimal evidence of hellish experiences – indeed that *both* place little credibility on Maurice Rawling's attempts to bolster the extent of the phenomenon. In fact we saw that all the leading professional researchers seem to suggest that reports of hellish near-death experiences are self-imposed, usually only temporary in that they are followed by entry into the light, and above all incredibly rare.

Moreover, in his attempts to boost the number of hellish reports Novak uses a number of sources that can arguably be described as less scientifically objective and reliable than professional researchers such as Moody, Ring, Sabom and Fenwick. These include Angie Fenimore and Howard Storm, whose personal experiences are recorded in their respective autobiographical accounts *Beyond the Darkness* and *My Descent into Death*; Phyllis Atwater, whose *Beyond the Light* details her own experiences and those of a number of others; and Maurice Rawlings himself. Most of these sources stress that the hellish experience is more common than the aforementioned professional researchers suggest. But, even if we were to accept that these additional sources could be considered objectively reliable, they still do not point to it being as common or indeed permanent as Novak's theory would require.

Let us now turn to his handling of interlife research. This time he attempts to equate the blank and full interlife experiences with the dark and light aspects of the near-death experience respectively. He again suggests there is serious disagreement in the professional community about whether the dark or blank interlife experience predominates over the light or full one, and in fact he suggests that in the work of many of our pioneers – and he specifically mentions Whitton, Fiore, Weiss and Woolger – the blank rather than full interlife experience is emphasized. As we have seen in previous chapters this is quite simply not accurate, either in respect of Whitton and Fiore as individuals, or of our pioneers as a whole.

But even if these two types of interlife experience more or less balance out, the real flaw in his normally coherent arguments is that – unlike with the dark and light aspects of the near-death experience – quite clearly any one soul only has one or the other interlife experience after any one death, and not both. So they cannot represent the simultaneous paths taken by the two different components of consciousness. In fact, he would have been on far safer ground if he had stuck with the clear evidence that near-death and interlife experiences are in fact identical – because under both any one soul experiences both the tunnel and the light. Indeed, he completely fails to appreciate that even most souls who have the blank interlife experience will almost certainly have gone through the tunnel and into the light, even if once there they only sleep rather than actively engage. The only exception to this would be, of course, those souls who do not enter the ethereal realms proper at all between incarnations, and instead remain trapped in the astral plane before choosing another body. But, in resolving this conundrum for him, am I now validating his theory? The answer is no. Because we still have all the objections that I have raised previously regarding his analysis of near-death experiences themselves, which are in my view insurmountable.

In fact it is when we come to Novak's discussion of Newton's work that his arguments are perhaps at their weakest. He uses Newton's arguments about soul energy division that we covered at the beginning of this chapter as if they implicitly support his idea of the binary soul. But they clearly do nothing of the sort, precisely because under Newton's hypothesis our soul energy is divided while we are incarnate, and then *reunited* in the interlife – this being the exact *opposite* of the binary soul doctrine; while in any case Newton's soul division is holographic, and has nothing whatsoever to do with separate functions of the brain, or with differentiating between the conscious and unconscious mind.

Nevertheless, in accepting that interlife learning can take place in the light, and because only an undivided soul could learn *and then remember* any lessons, Novak turns to the somewhat contradictory idea that our souls may not divide immediately after death, but instead just before reincarnation. We might suggest that this completely contradicts the bulk of his previous arguments concerning the evidence of near-death experiences, and the immediacy with which subjects encounter both the dark and the light elements, but let us allow him this assumption on the basis that time does not really exist in the ethereal realms. But he then uses the suggestions of some interlife researchers, to the effect that we do not always take heed of the lessons we learn in the interlife, to argue that this is because *all* souls forget their interlife lessons when they reincarnate. In reality, as we have seen, we may have deliberate amnesia when we reincarnate, but this *does not* mean that our life plans go out of the window. And what sort of ridiculous system would allow us to go to all the trouble of learning important lessons in the interlife that could not then be applied for future benefit?

Perhaps above all Novak's theories fall down on one basic element more than any other. If, as he suggests, the soul divides after death so that the conscious reincarnating part can have no possible access to its past-life memories, how could past-life regression ever work? This is a question he refuses to even acknowledge, let alone answer. Of course, using his framework we might speculate that particularly advanced souls who were sufficiently balanced to be able to maintain their integrity after death might be able to accomplish this feat; but in reality we know that virtually *anyone* can access their past-life memories under hypnosis. This in itself is surely all the proof we need that the constituent elements of our consciousness are not divided by death at all, either temporarily or permanently.

We have covered a variety of contentious subjects in this chapter, and I readily accept that my conclusions on each are colored by my overall spiritual worldview, which more than anything insists on the supremacy of the individual soul and its control over its own actions and destiny. But in most cases I also attempt to take into account the context of the majority view of our pioneers, as well as that of the framework of karmic evolution that I developed in chapter 7 where appropriate. Nevertheless, I have had to apply considerably more personal speculation in this chapter than in most others, and for that I do not apologize because it is unavoidable if I am to express any definitive opinion on these arguably unresolved but important issues. At least I hope I have been successful in my attempts to differentiate between the underlying facts and my personal interpretation of them – so that people can make up their own minds about what are sometimes rather disturbing phenomena.

10

ENDGAME
Why Are We Here, What Should We Do?

In this chapter I hope to pull together various loose strands, and also to investigate a number of more complex issues that I have so far avoided. This before I attempt to finally place everything we have learned into context by looking at the big questions of why are we here, and how should we conduct ourselves, in the light of the spiritual framework we have developed.

One additional element of a spiritual worldview that is often raised is that of logistics. In particular, what is the source of souls when we have such a rapidly expanding human population on the planet? One solution might be that less advanced souls that have incarnated previously as various types of animal could be promoted up the ranks, and this idea is found in most eastern philosophies. However, Michael Newton's subjects seem unanimous that this is not how the logistics of soul progression work. They strongly assert that there are different types of soul, which are created as required for the various broad categories of life such as plants, animals and humans.

One of Newton's relatively advanced subjects specifically reports on how new human souls are born as individual identities from a swirling mass of pure soul energy, and how in the interlife she, as a specialist 'incubator mother' in training, nurses and protects them. Shakuntala Modi seems to have confirmed this idea by regressing certain of her subjects right back to the birth of their soul, finding that there were only human incarnations thereafter. Indeed, it has been implicitly supported by a number of esoteric commentators for some decades, inasmuch as they insist that other animal species do not have individual souls as such, but rather a 'group soul'. Newton's subjects partly confirm this idea but seem to suggest that there is both a group and an individual aspect to animal souls – the main difference from their human counterparts being that their soul energy has a different, somewhat simpler constitution, with a far lesser sense of ego or identity.

By contrast, Morris Netherton appears to have regressed a number of patients into animal lives that preceded their human ones, and Dolores

250

Cannon also supports this idea. One of her subjects argues that although animals do have group souls, which is where much of their herd instinct and group telepathy comes from, some of them can break free and become more consciously individualized via human love or other human interactions, which then allows them to evolve into a human soul. In fact this same subject supports the idea that all souls have to go through the mineral, plant and animal stages before reaching human status; and in this soul evolution model the subject also includes the basic collective energy forms of elemental spirits that relate to particular places, and of nature spirits that protect particular species of plant or animal, even though these are clearly not physical forms as such.

Hans TenDam straddles these two positions by splitting souls into different 'evolutionary families' according to the experiences they had before they began incarnating on earth, something which he argues has great significance for the therapist because of its bearing on the types of psychological problems they might develop. One family is what he refers to as 'starter souls' who had no other incarnatory experiences before, whether in physical or nonphysical form, and who were clearly created from scratch to incarnate as humans on earth. But another family evolved from animals, and he echoes Cannon's sentiment regarding human interaction making subsequent human incarnation more likely – while at the same time providing fascinating evidence of the group nature of animal souls from research conducted in the late nineteenth century by AF Knudsen into hypnosis with horses. And another family primarily involves souls that evolved from a whole plethora of different elementals or nature spirits, some of which seem to incarnate as humans as a result of inadvertently possessing one originally – which ties in with Cannon's subject's take on possession from the last chapter, even though he does not mention her as a source.

I accept the conceptual validity of the idea that animal or elemental soul energies might split off from their group soul to become more individualized – after all, I accept that the Ultimate Source is the ultimate collective soul from which every form in the universe sprang, whether physical or nonphysical. However, we saw in chapter 7 that even those very few of all our pioneers' subjects that appear to remember an animal incarnation may have been mistaken – perhaps remembering experiences in the space of transformation, or on other planets, for example. Moreover, as far as I can tell Cannon's information comes from one subject only, while the extent to which TenDam is quoting from other sources that are sometimes relatively old and not necessarily reliable, rather than from his own practical experience, is not entirely clear. And I do not necessarily accept his claim that the vast bulk of human souls were originally nonhuman spirits that incarnated in nonphysical form, with only a very few being freshly created human starter or for that matter animal souls – again because the source of these statistics is unclear. By contrast, Newton's and Modi's detailed findings seem to derive consistently from a significant number of their own regression subjects – and while the same appears to be true of Netherton, he provides scant details and no case studies to support his claims.

On that basis, I do not discount the possibility that in rare cases the soul energy of an animal, or of an elemental or nature spirit, might become sufficiently individualized to evolve into human form. Nor do I discount the possibility that in a more general sense these collective soul energies might be allowed the opportunity to evolve by somehow being recycled into human soul energy sources as part of a grand plan, although even if this were the case I cannot conceive that there could be any continuity of individual identity. However, I am inclined to side more with Newton's and Modi's testimony that, as a general rule, human souls do not progress through the animal or any other ranks, but are instead created afresh. It is also worth noting that, if animal souls are predominantly collectivized, my rejection in chapter 7 of the idea that human souls can be punished by devolution or reversion to animal form is arguably strengthened.

From a logistics perspective I would therefore argue that we can assume there is a sufficient stock of human souls that can be created afresh if need be to match any increase in population on earth. But this is only part of the story because, even if we ignore the rare occurrence of advanced souls choosing to lead parallel lives, another factor that influences soul availability is the speed with which souls return into incarnation. A number of our pioneers have attempted to produce statistics on intervals between incarnations. For example, the shortest duration Joel Whitton had come across was ten months, while the longest was over eight hundred years, with an average of about forty years – although he suggests that this average has been coming down in the last few centuries, coincident with the increase in world population. Peter Ramster is even more insistent about this steady decrease in interval duration, suggesting that in the distant past lives might be separated by anything from one hundred to a thousand years, while more recently the gaps reduce to between one and thirty years. Bruce Goldberg agrees with this, suggesting that his patients had centuries between incarnations in the middle ages, about seventy-five years in the eighteenth and nineteenth centuries, and as little as between one and twenty-five years in the twentieth century. Meanwhile Ian Stevenson reports that most of his child cases reincarnated within less than three years, with an average of fifteen months – but we must remember that these are special cases that we have strong reason to suspect have no interlife proper, so they are not representative of the population as a whole.

But even these attempts at averages are to some extent invalidated because they fail to take account of further complicating factors. For example, a number of our pioneers explicitly state that more advanced souls tend to incarnate less frequently – because they are taking on increasing responsibilities in the ethereal realms. So it might easily be that average intervals between incarnations have reduced recently precisely because more immature souls are incarnating to satisfy population demands, rather than because the same stock of souls is coming back more regularly. On the other hand, Whitton argues that the world is now changing so fast that souls can come back more frequently and still have different experiences, on which basis he argues that it may be existing souls who are driving the population explosion, and not vice versa. And one of Cannon's subjects even goes as far as to suggest that there is a huge surplus of souls that have already been created, creating general competition for bodies to incarnate into – although, as we will see shortly, this suggestion is complicated by the fact that earth is not the only possible destination.

The only way to have a degree more certainty about this issue would be to collate statistics about intervals between incarnations for *individual* subjects stretching right back to their earliest incarnations, to see if they showed a marked decrease for each individual – despite the fact that they should, on the face of it and all other things being equal, be increasing as that soul becomes more advanced. It is difficult to establish the extent to which Whitton, Ramster and Goldberg have attempted to do this. From Newton's description of studying the 'incarnation *chronology* of *a* client' it appears he may have paid more attention to this issue, and he still reports the same trends. He indicates that individual subjects regressing as far back as the nomadic cultures of the Paleolithic had intervals between incarnations of hundreds or even thousands of years, which reduced to about five hundred years on average by the time that regular settled agriculture had been introduced in the Neolithic. By the middle ages the same subjects were experiencing one life every two centuries, by the eighteenth and nineteenth centuries about one life per century, and by the twentieth century more than one life per century was common.

But even then, as Newton and Ramster admit, it might be that some less interesting past lives from more distant ages are simply not recalled, or that our general past-life recall abilities fade over time – either of which would mean that these statistics would not contain all the base data in the first place. Nevertheless, it seems to me that they are sufficiently consistent that they do strongly suggest that average intervals between incarnations are reducing significantly for all of us as individual souls, century by century. This does seem to go against the grain of everything we have learned about soul advancement, and none of our pioneers really comments on this rather disturbing discrepancy. There is one rather morbid interpretation, which is that our increasing hunger for the experiences of the material world is blinding us to the spiritual truths we once knew, and causing many souls who were on an upward path to regress somewhat. This would coincide with my general view about humanity becoming increasingly divorced from its spiritual roots. And this argument is not invalidated by suggestions that the physical population explosion is forcing us to return more regularly, precisely because there is supposedly an unlimited supply of new human souls.

On the other hand, as has been repeatedly stressed by our pioneers' subjects, it may be that it is completely wrong to think of the interlife in terms of earth-time duration, and that the quality of the experience is far more important than the apparent quantity. But, if that is the case, we must still ask why already reasonably advanced souls appear to be accelerating their experiences of the physical world, rather than letting new souls take the population strain. Perhaps Whitton is right, and the pace of cultural change does now allow us to pack far more rewarding lives into a more condensed time frame, thus accelerating our group learning curve – at least in the developed world, which is by definition what all of our pioneers' subjects tend to inhabit at least in their current incarnation. But this argument fails to take account of the unavoidable fact that most of the population explosion is occurring in parts of the world where, arguably, conditions of deprivation make these lives far less tolerable, let alone varied, than they have ever been. Regression therapy is, of course, rarely used in places where people are just struggling to survive. So we have no idea whether these souls are experienced and have deliberately chosen such lives, or are predominantly new souls faced by some of the severest of tests. But, in any case, Newton's subjects also report that the population explosion risks severe damage to our planet, a viewpoint that common sense alone tends to support. So, ultimately, the question of the underlying reason for the general pattern of accelerating incarnations is one to which I feel unable to provide a definitive answer.

It is now appropriate for us to consider the issue of soul advancement in a little more depth. Newton has developed a set of classifications using his subjects' perceptions of the color and depth of energy that their own and other souls radiate in the ethereal realms, and has been able to match these more or less consistently to the context of their interlife activities. Although there are a number of complicating factors, in basic terms he reports that 'beginner' souls have a bright white radiance, which becomes increasingly off-white and then yellow before reaching bright gold as they progress through the 'intermediate' stages, while 'advanced' souls display a light-blue radiance that gradually deepens in color to a dark bluish-purple for the most advanced. These colors do not appear to correspond to those radiated by our earthly aura, because by contrast this tends to be a projection of our physical and mental condition at that time in our incarnate life. Both Cannon and Ramster confirm the importance of soul energy color as a mechanism of recognition in the ethereal realms, although neither goes into any detail.

Of course, as soon as we start talking about these different stages of karmic advancement, the temptation to allow our egos to ponder what level we are at as an individual soul is a strong one. Arguably this is exactly the practice that, as we saw in the last chapter, the Buddha was trying to discourage. But perhaps we can find more practical methods of achieving this aim without resorting to the doctrine of no-soul. In the absence of being regressed into the interlife to obtain direct verification of their energy color and therefore level of karmic progress, there are a number of assumptions that people might attempt to fall back on to establish their supposed degree of spiritual advancement. But, in fact, none of these is reliable.

The first port of call would be to claim to have had many, many past lives. But this assumes that quantity is more important than quality, which is rarely the case in any aspect of life. It also assumes that every soul's rate of learning is identical, which is just as ridiculous as suggesting that all schoolchildren learn every subject at exactly the same rate, and with the same proficiency. Newton deliberately highlights this point when discussing his subjects' progress from beginner to intermediate status – which in our terms is relatively advanced, as we will shortly see. Although a number of his subjects have required hundreds of lives stretching back as much as fifty thousand years to make this transition, in more exceptional cases subjects have achieved it in only a few thousand years with presumably far less lives. This variability gains support from one of Cannon's subjects, who reports that the number of lives required to advance sufficiently to break free from the earthly karmic round entirely is on average one hundred and twenty, but can be as little as ten or as many as several hundred. However, it has to be said this view generally suggests a somewhat faster rate of progress than Newton's.

Some people might turn to their apparent psychic abilities to press home their claim to karmic advancement. But, again, Newton emphasizes that he has found no obvious correlation between the two. Failing this, then, what about current incarnate circumstances? In fact Newton argues that this may be a more reliable indicator, but in exactly the opposite direction to that which many people might anticipate:

> My classification of soul development is intended to be neither socially nor intellectually elitist. Souls in a high state of advancement are often found in humble circumstances on earth. By the same token, people in the upper strata of influence in human society are by no means in a blissful state of soul maturity. Often, just the reverse is true.

The other factor that I feel duty bound to comment upon is those people who are sufficiently ego-driven to proudly proclaim themselves as an 'old soul' to anyone who will listen – often having had their vanity stimulated by mediums or other psychics who cannot exactly be expected to provide consistently independent confirmation, given their financial relationship with their client. All I can say is that, although I make no great claims for my own spiritual progress, it is sufficient to tell me that no truly advanced soul would be sufficiently ego-conscious to make this type of claim. The same is true of those who make such claims on behalf of their newborn offspring – after all, we have already seen that most babies retain a great deal of spiritual wisdom, which can perhaps be detected deep in their eyes as the window to the soul, because their amnesia has not fully kicked in. This does not make them especially advanced, just normal. And we would also do well to remember that the vast majority of spiritually advanced souls who still incarnate out of choice, to assist humanity in one way or another, may tend to operate in relative obscurity and show no obvious signs of their spiritual maturity. They may not even be fully, or even partially, aware of it themselves.

Newton estimates from the totality of his case files that approximately three-quarters of the current human population are only in the earliest stages of soul development – that is beginners or 'lower intermediates' – while a mere one per cent can be categorized as advanced. We have already seen that it is too simplistic to argue that this is purely because of rapid population increase, so that many of these are completely new souls. But how does this finding relate to my previous assertions about stages of karmic evolution in chapter 7? According to Newton, advancement to the intermediate stage proper is characterized by starting to train in other specialisms in the interlife – for example as spirit guides and so on – and moving increasingly away from the focus of the primary soul group, even if our bonds with these original soul mates remain strong and are never fully broken. So we can see that even in his beginner stage souls will still have a full interlife experience with their guides, elders and other members of their soul group.

This is consistent with my argument in chapter 7 that, because most of our pioneers' subjects appear to report at least a degree of review and planning activities in the interlife, they have reached, or are at least close to reaching, the progressive karmic stage. Although in Newton's terms many of these might still be categorized as beginner souls, this is because his emphasis is on the information that can be gleaned from what are in our terms really quite experienced intermediate and even advanced souls, and his categories are therefore qualitatively skewed in their favor. In quantitative terms, there is no discrepancy.

Nevertheless, Newton is the one pioneer whose research might initially appear to contradict the suggestion that souls in the novice and to some extent repetitive karmic stages do not have a full interlife experience. He is not explicit on this matter, and his statistics lump completely 'novice' souls in with beginners, but it is only these novices that might be argued to have no interlife experience proper under his schema. He reports that they tend to experience the interlife in relative isolation because they have not yet been assigned to soul groups – albeit that once they are they often recognize friends and family members from their past lives, so that the principle of soul mates must be there in the background from the outset – while their incarnate lives are characterized by 'confusion and ineffectiveness'. He does not specifically state that they engage in minimal review and planning activities, if at all, but we can perhaps assume this is the case.

But Newton also suggests that on average novice souls only require about five incarnations to graduate to beginner status, and it would appear that very few of his subjects are still in the novice category in their current incarnation. This still leaves us with a potential discrepancy between his findings and those of certain other pioneers who have a significant minority – or, in the case of Netherton and Woolger, majority – of subjects reporting a blank interlife experience. Although other factors may be playing a part, I can only fall back on the explanation I have repeatedly used, which is that Newton's case studies derive from his concentrating on interlife research rather than on therapy.

One of Cannon's subjects describes seven 'planes of existence', and compares them to an inverted pyramid with the physical plane at the pointed base. This is consistent with most esoteric models, in which the world of physical form does indeed lie at the base, while the astral plane, as the gateway to the ethereal realms, is the next level up. The higher levels relate to the ethereal realms proper.

On the other hand, either this same subject or another – it is not clear from Cannon's description – goes on to describe ten 'levels of existence'. Cannon herself does not comment upon this apparent discrepancy, but it seems clear that her subject is now referring to different levels of spiritual advancement, in an entirely ethereal context. The first three levels are associated with elementals, and nature and animal spirits; the fourth with immature or damaged human souls; the fifth with the bulk of reincarnating human souls; the sixth through ninth with increasingly evolved spiritual 'master souls' who only reincarnate in physical form out of choice; and the tenth with the Ultimate Source itself. Similarly, in chapter 5 we saw that both Ramster and Weiss suggest that there are different planes in the ethereal realms proper, with Weiss's patient Catherine specifically reporting that there are seven of these.

This idea of different levels or planes is often a source of confusion, precisely because commentators do not make it clear in which of these contexts they are discussing them. Certainly anyone reading these two contrasting descriptions in Cannon's work might find themselves thoroughly confused, and I already noted in chapter 8 that Goldberg's suggestion that there are five lower and seven higher planes comes across as a somewhat complex and confusing framework. So I will now attempt to make the proper distinctions.

Earth's astral plane might easily be thought of in semi-physical terms as a translucent sphere that surrounds the physical earth, occupied by a variety of energy forms. However, this does not necessarily make these energies in any way spiritually superior to those that inhabit earth's physical plane. We only have to look at the confusion of ghostly spirits who have not properly entered the ethereal realms to justify this view. Meanwhile, elementals and nature spirits can also be thought of as occupying the astral plane, and Cannon's subject reports that they do operate primarily as a force for good in their protection of the environment and so on, although they can be mischievous with humans if they feel they are threatening the environment. And one of Newton's subjects confirms the existence of elementals and nature spirits, emphasizing that they operate at a higher vibrational frequency than that of the physical world. Both indicate that these spirits – variously termed little people, leprechauns, fairies and elves – can be powerful, have been around since long before the advent of human civilization, and were more commonly 'seen' by our more agriculturally oriented predecessors because their energy vibrations were somewhat denser then. Nevertheless, both also report that they are primarily a form of collectivized consciousness that is not as advanced as that of the individualized human soul – however much that might seem to be contradicted by the destruction that we as the human race are wreaking on our planet.

If we now turn to the ethereal realms proper, to the extent that there may be any levels within it, these clearly do relate to different stages of karmic advancement. But Newton is adamant that the basic idea of a hierarchy of ethereal *planes* is misleading because it implies some sort of physical, and perhaps even elitist, separation. He argues that instead we should think of different *zones* or *areas* that souls can visit in the ethereal realms proper depending on their vibration level and desire. And another of Cannon's subjects emphasizes that it is entirely inappropriate to think of the ethereal realms proper in physical or locational terms – for example, as further layered spheres around the earth. So I would argue that we should refer to the physical plane, the astral plane and the ethereal plane *singular*, accepting that the latter may include various nonphysicalized zones.

Nevertheless, if we do drop the elitist and physical connotations, the historic idea that different levels of spiritual advancement and awareness can be portrayed in a hierarchical fashion are still, to some extent, both useful and consistent with modern research findings. It is perhaps best depicted by the Qabalistic 'tree of life', which can be used to consistently represent both the macrocosmic view of the evolution of the universe as a whole, and the microcosmic view of the evolution of individual souls. I discuss these ideas at some length in *Genesis Unveiled*, referencing both Dion Fortune's *The Cosmic Doctrine* and her protégé Gareth Knight's excellent two-volume *Practical Guide to Qabalistic Symbolism*, first published in 1949 and 1965 respectively. Indeed, despite my view that we should rely far more upon modern research findings than the revealed wisdom of old, and despite some reservations, I find this particular material has much to offer those who seek a greater depth of esoteric understanding – and it is interesting to note that Qabalism in general has gained much exposure in recent years via a number of celebrities who have been attracted to its teachings.

In addition to all this, many esoteric systems attempt to match the different planes of existence to different types of body. So, for example, we sometimes see references to the physical, astral, emotional, mental and etheric bodies of any given individual. I have yet to find a convincing explanation of why all these distinctions should be so important, and I normally find that the more complicated frameworks are vague, confusing and contradictory, sometimes even within themselves. I indicated in the opening chapter that for the most part I would treat the spirit and soul as synonymous for simplicity, but in line with my separation of the planes or realms of existence into three – that is the physical, astral and ethereal – I also believe that there is only a trinity of components of the individual being with which we need to primarily concern ourselves. These are, perhaps unsurprisingly, the physical body, the astral spirit or body, and the ethereal soul.

The astral body is the intermediary between the physical body and the ethereal soul. Normally it shadows our physical body on the astral plane, although it is of course the component that can sometimes be astrally projected beyond the confines of the physical body when we sleep or meditate, or even when we are unconscious or in coma – albeit remaining connected by the silver cord. It is also the component that best registers our emotional and mental wellbeing or otherwise while we are incarnate, although physical problems will also be mirrored in the astral body. To this extent it might be regarded as comparable to our aura, even if the latter's role as a protective shield is somewhat different again.

The astral body's other main feature is that it survives the death of the physical body, and is not shed until some time later. In fact, at least one of Newton's subjects reports that it is when we engage in the process of reuniting with the soul energy we left in the ethereal realms that we shed our astral body. This is why, as Kenneth Ring points out, some near-death experiencers refer to having retained a nonphysical body very similar to the one they had while alive. However, this should not be confused with the tendency of less advanced souls to continue to project and receive simulations of physical appearance right through the interlife experience, and even after they have shed their astral body.

In this context it will be interesting to return to the issue of what death really means. Michael Sabom emphasizes that certain reflex functions in the brain can carry on for some days after it is supposedly clinically dead, and therefore concludes that death is a *process*, not an identifiable event. This is certainly true in physical terms, so perhaps it would in some ways be more appropriate for us to think in terms of death occurring when the soul leaves the physical body, carried within the astral body. But as we have seen even the astral body can come and go as it pleases, not only when we sleep or meditate, but also if we are unconscious or in coma. So the real event of death is not the departure of the astral body per se, but the moment when the silver cord that connects it to the physical body is broken.

It seems that this can happen some time before the process of physical death is complete, especially if death is foreseen, as in progressive illness or old age. As I indicated in chapter 2, this may well have been the case with my own father. And what about my mother, who was in a coma?

Admittedly we agreed to let the hospital staff take her off her drip, but arguably her body could have continued to function for some days on its own stored reserves. I would suggest that the fact it did not is because its death was accelerated by her own conscious decision to sever the cord. I would therefore argue that it is the soul that effectively *decides* when death will take place under normal circumstances – although not if the person, through fear or other motivation, holds on to physical life at all costs, or in the case of sudden murders or accidents. But even then Newton suggests that the soul is able to leave the physical body immediately before a sudden and painful death, if it foresees that the trauma might disrupt its energy.

How does the process of birth compare with that of death? We saw in chapter 6 that our pioneers' subjects report variable timings for the entry of the soul into the fetus, but it seems that this must be the point at which the silver cord is attached. And we also saw that the astral body can regularly absent itself after this, so there are similarities to the process of death except in reverse.

Of course, any individual who does not move on to the ethereal realms proper after death will retain their astral body, which is why it is perfectly reasonable to refer to ghosts as spirits. By the same token those souls that incarnate in nonphysical form, for example as elementals or nature spirits, only operate on the astral rather than the physical plane, which is why it is again appropriate to refer to them as spirits. So I would suggest that the key thing to remember is that body is synonymous with physical, spirit is synonymous with astral, and soul is synonymous with ethereal. This is exactly why I do not, for example, use the phrase etheric body instead of astral body, or spirit realms instead of ethereal realms, because unless we use consistent terminology our message can become confused. The only exceptions to this are twofold. The first is that I always use the term spirit guide because of its general acceptance – and because I do not particularly like the alternative of guardian angel – even though such guides clearly operate in the ethereal realms; and, even then, perhaps there are advantages to this in that it conveys the idea that our spirit guides are active in assisting us while we are incarnate on the earth's plane. The other is my general use of the phrase spiritual worldview – which is clearly based on my views about the interaction of all three realms – but which again has a certain degree of general acceptance.

There are two potential complications to this basic trinity of body, spirit and soul components that we should briefly consider. First, some commentators suggest that the logical mind, and less logical emotions, must be separately identified. Clearly these are considered to be the two main aspects of the physical brain, as we saw in the last chapter. However,

I would argue strongly that they are fundamental and intrinsic aspects of all components of the individual being, and that they continue to play a dualistic role in the ethereal soul. After all, it seems perfectly clear that subjects regressed into the interlife are perfectly capable both of using logic and of displaying emotion. Accordingly I do not believe that recognition of these two aspects requires us to amend our basic trinity of components, each of which contains both of them. Second, TenDam reports on the work of Robert Crookall, who collated a great deal of empirical material about the process of death from a variety of spiritualist and psychic sources, and presented it in a number of books – perhaps the most complete being his 1978 publication *What Happens When You Die*. He argues that we should distinguish between the psychic – or in our terms astral – body and what he refers to as the 'vehicle of vitality'. Although he suggests that this vehicle is a distinct and separate body that acts as an intermediary this time between the physical and astral bodies, and can remain more with one than the other during out-of-body experiences, he accepts that it has no real purpose after physical death. On that basis, and although I may be oversimplifying somewhat, I would argue that his vehicle of vitality is not much more than the silver cord itself.

I have already made a number of brief references to intelligent life on other planets. In chapter 5 I briefly mentioned Newton's subjects' reports of how souls undergoing interlife training as specialist explorers, designers, harmonizers and ethicists visit the astral realms of other planets without incarnating on them, and it is clear that some of these are very much like earth. And in the hypnotic progressions we discussed in chapter 8 we regularly encountered the assumption that we will not only be colonizing other planets in the future – some being outside of our own solar system with atmospheres similar to that of earth – but will also be in touch with intelligent extraterrestrials that come from such planets.

I would like to think that most open-minded people realize that the statistical likelihood of us occupying the only planet in the entire universe able to sustain complex life forms is about as close to zero as you can get. Increasingly sophisticated space telescopes now allow astronomers to study other solar systems that appear to show signs of orbiting planets, and the only issue of contention that remains is whether or not more advanced extraterrestrials have actually visited earth and made contact. This is not an issue on which I am prepared to make a definitive statement, mainly because I have not conducted anywhere near enough research into an area that is a veritable minefield of claim and counterclaim, and which is so beset with the politics of conspiracy theory. All I will say is that I support those researchers who increasingly recognize that supposedly physical extraterrestrial experiences may often be better analyzed in a nonphysical, and perhaps even spiritual, context. In addition, in *Genesis Unveiled* I discuss at some length the fact that, although I have no conceptual problem with the idea that we may have been visited by extraterrestrials throughout our history, I do not find the evidence currently put forward to support this notion at all persuasive.

In any case, what I am convinced about is that in general terms we cannot afford to take a parochial view of the universe as if we were its only intelligent inhabitants, and this has a major impact on our understanding of a spiritual worldview. Because it would be philosophically inconceivable that advanced life forms on other planets would not have souls too, no longer can we assume that the ethereal realms revolve around humanity and earthly matters alone. That is one reason why I find Fortune's *The Cosmic Doctrine* persuasive, because at least in part it discusses the universal perspective. And in suggesting that each solar system or 'logos' has its own population of various soul-types or 'life swarms' in varying stages of evolution, and that each logos has its own godhead, it forces us to realize that, if we thought the organization of the ethereal realms must be complex when viewing it from a primarily human and geocentric perspective, the schema for the universe as a whole must be incredibly much more complex again. This is why I indicated in the last chapter that Modi's suggestion of a mere seven godheads underneath the Ultimate Source was likely to be a massive underestimate. It is also why I repeatedly insist that any esoteric model that purports to show the way in which we can reunite with the Ultimate Source that does not show successive stages of reunification – first with the godhead of our solar logos, then perhaps that of our galactic logos, before finally we reach the Ultimate – is only demonstrating its geocentric limitations of context. This is perhaps to be expected of historical models, but modern ones have no excuses.

Fortune suggests that souls are primarily attached to their own solar system, and given that complex physical life forms such as human beings can only evolve and survive on planets that are the appropriate distance from their sun – so that they are neither so close as to be raging gaseous infernos, nor so far as to be frozen wastelands – there would normally only be one planet per system on which they might evolve, if at all. Nevertheless, in assuming in *Genesis Unveiled* that certain highly advanced souls must have incarnated in human form as much as 100,000 years ago in order to bring a spiritual worldview into the physical plane of earth for the first time, I was always intrigued as to how such souls might have gained their own karmic experience. In fact in an unpublished accompanying novel called *Autobiography of an Angel* I postulated that one option would have been to gain this experience by incarnating on other planets in intelligent life forms that were further along the evolutionary path at that time.

This supposition was subsequently confirmed when I came across Newton's work, because his subjects specifically confirm that souls can and do incarnate on other planets. They even report that normal human souls sometimes incarnate in other perhaps slightly more primitive life forms on other planets before incarnating as humans, and it seems such 'introductory' lives will always be relatively easy and less demanding than those on earth. Alternatively human souls may sometimes request an intermediate incarnation on another planet to gain a different type of experience – and this is a genuine incarnation, rather than an interlife visit to the planet's astral plane. The life form they incarnate into is always the most dominant intelligence on that planet, and in the latter case these lives on other worlds are in no sense seen as a temporary demotion or punishment. As I indicated in chapter 7, this new context might well explain apparent animal incarnations on earth. And some of his subjects are able to recall, for example, genuine incarnate lives as intelligent flying creatures or marine animals, where the details indicate that the planet is not earth.

But Newton suggests that there also exist relatively old souls whose former planet was destroyed or rendered inhabitable so they could not return, or who come to earth to face a more difficult challenge, and that these 'hybrid souls' sometimes have great trouble in adapting. He indicates that, although many go on to live a series of productive and fulfilling lives on earth, those who fail to adapt can often become inflicted with severe psychological problems. One of his subjects even suggests that the most maladjusted humans on earth, those that tend to repeatedly commit heinous crimes, are almost certainly hybrid souls – and these are the ones who, if they persist in their destructive behavior over repeated incarnations, are most likely to be 'remodeled' in the ethereal realms.

Most of our other pioneers make no real mention of incarnations on other planets. This is not necessarily surprising, from a number of perspectives. First, they may not have been open to the possibility, and so did not deliberately investigate it, even perhaps ignoring any potential leads from their subjects. Second, they may not have taken their subjects back to any incarnations before they first came to earth. And third, they may have confused such incarnations with interlife experiences in the ethereal realms, or with incarnations on earth itself. Nevertheless, Ramster records one subject making a brief reference to coming from 'another universe' before her first incarnation on earth, although she was supposedly not allowed to remember much about it. And Modi makes a brief reference to the possibility of possession by extraterrestrial spirits.

The one other pioneer that does discuss this issue in any detail is TenDam, and he does so once again within his context of souls having different experiences before commencing their incarnations on earth. His final evolutionary family, which I did not mention at the beginning of this chapter, are those of extraterrestrial origin. He makes the distinction between fully physical incarnations, and nonphysical but still genuine incarnations, on other planets – although he actually places the latter in with his 'originally spirit' family. It is also interesting that he categorizes some of these extraterrestrials with animal-like bodies as genuinely 'alien', although accepting the limitations of this word, while he categorizes others as human, on the basis that the physical bodies they remember are clearly similar to our own:

> Sometimes they sense themselves in stranger bodies: heavier, lighter, bigger or smaller, or with other proportions. Probably they are all related to us; we could mate with them. They resemble us; perhaps they lack ears or teeth, perhaps they have fewer toes, perhaps their proportions are different, but they have a similar body structure. With all these differences, they are clearly human.

His sources for this are again not entirely clear, but it does raise the fascinating question of what we really mean by the word *human*. In older science-fiction series such as *Star Trek* the people from other planets usually resembled humans with 'stick-on bits', and we know that these portrayals were governed by the limitations of attempting to use human actors. Now that computer animation has evolved, films like *Men in Black* have a far greater range of alien types. But what if there is an essentially human-type body that is not restricted to earth alone, but has a far greater universality?

If we stuck to materialistic evolutionary theory alone, this possibility would be so remote as to be a nonsense. But do our pioneers have anything to add to this picture? I have briefly referred to Newton's specialist designer souls already, and now is the time to look at their work more closely. His subjects report that these designers visit the astral realms of life-supporting planets to manipulate energy patterns by 'thought-form', and those who are in training create first inanimate objects such as rocks, and then animate forms such as plants, trees and eventually various animal life forms of increasing complexity. This is how one relatively advanced soul reported on her interlife assignment as a trainee designer, in which she was part of a team that had to redress an imbalance in the ecosystem of a distant planet that was not being resolved by evolutionary adaptation alone:

So, basically the problem on Jaspear involves the ecosystem?
Yes, the thick vines... a voracious vinelike bush. It grows so fast it kills those plants needed for the food supply. There is little space left for the land creatures of Jaspear to graze....
What is the assignment?
To create an animal which will eat the vines – to control the spreading of this bush which chokes off so much other vegetation.
What animal?
It is the Rinucula.
How are you going to do that with an animal that is not indigenous to Jaspear?
By creating a mutation from an existing small four-footed animal and accelerating its growth.
Kala, you can change the DNA genetic codes of one animal to create another?
I could not do this by myself. We have the combined energy of my training class, plus the skillful manipulation of the two seniors who have accompanied us on this field trip.
You use your energy to alter the molecular chemistry of an organism in order to circumvent natural selection?
Yes, to radiate the cells of a group of the small animals. We mutate the existing species and make it much larger so it will survive. Since we don't have the time to wait for natural selection, we will also accelerate growth of the four-legged animal.
Do you accelerate the growth of the mutation so that the Rinucula appears right away, or do you accelerate the size of the creature itself?
Both – we want the Rinucula to be big and we want his evolutionary change to take place in one generation.
How many earth years will this take?
Oh... fifty years or so... to us it seems like a day.

This and other accounts lend a completely new meaning to the idea that the 'Hand of God' lies behind all of creation, and arguably provide significant support for the 'intelligent design' view of evolution. It seems that highly advanced 'masters of design' would have been involved in the creation of entire solar systems and their physical planets, and presumably also in the initial blueprint designs for the various life forms available to inhabit different types of planet. But the example above shows that subsequent implementation of these designs on evolving planets is delegated to less highly trained designers whose work can sometimes prove slightly fallible. It also shows that evolutionary patterns on any planet are not totally predetermined, precisely because natural selection and other evolutionary mechanisms still have a vital role to play.

If we apply this to the idea of a human-type body, I would suggest that this might well be one of the initial blueprints created by the design masters for planets with atmospheres similar to our own. The notion that many of these might exist is not beyond the bounds of scientific possibility, and in fact Newton's subjects specifically confirm it. So on those planets where it was appropriate – which would not be all of them because of atmospheric and other variations – I would suggest that the evolutionary process might well follow a general earthlike blueprint. For example, designer souls might nudge the processes of evolution to ensure that mammalian life forms developed on the given planet at some point, then nudge them a little more to ensure the development of a particular mammalian species towards an apelike creature, and then nudge one strain of this a little further so that it eventually evolved into a human form. Such a process would also produce natural evolutionary variations in the human form from planet to planet, dictated by local environment and circumstances. Impossible? Far-fetched? Perhaps, but personally I do not think so.

What proportion of souls incarnating on earth originally come from other planets? TenDam suggests that the figure is about ten per cent, although this omits the nonphysically incarnating extraterrestrial souls that he lumps in with his 'originally spirit' family. However, again, I am not inclined to place undue reliance on his statistics. Unfortunately Newton makes no attempt to provide a comparison figure for the proportion of souls of extraterrestrial origin. But, on the one hand we know that very few of our pioneers report subjects having had extraterrestrial lives. And, on the other, I tend to favor Fortune's suggestion that in the main our souls are attached to their planet of choice. Based on these two factors, I would suggest that the number of souls currently incarnating on earth who are of extraterrestrial origin is not likely to be particularly high.

I indicated in chapter 7 that I am extremely doubtful about suggestions of a supposedly high-technology civilization in earth's distant past, often under the guise of Atlantis or Lemuria. But what if such supposed memories can be explained by incarnations on other more evolved planets? I originally suggested this in *Genesis Unveiled*, before reading Newton's second book in which he confirms the possibility.

Most of our main pioneers do not regress their subjects back as far as this. Goldberg makes a passing reference to having regressed many patients back to lives in Atlantis and Lemuria, but he provides no details and seems to place this very much in a Caycean context. Again TenDam has more to say, although as usual it is unclear whether he is referencing other people's material or his own when he discusses past lives on these continents. However, he does admit that such regressions are often influenced by theosophical and Caycean material, and warns against assuming that they are either lives on earth or, for that matter, physical incarnations at all.

From a broader perspective, in *Genesis Unveiled* I discuss Helena Blavatsky's celebrated idea of various 'root races' that have colonized earth for millions of years; and I indicate that I can only conceive of the Atlantean and Lemurian elements of these as having any validity in relation to earth itself if they are placed in an entirely nonphysical context. Even Blavatsky herself accepts that the earliest root races were purely nonphysical forms and, if my point is accepted, there is some similarity between Blavatsky's root races and Fortune's idea of life swarms attached to our solar logos. But to what extent do these root races or life swarms, which may have been visiting earth's astral plane for millions of years, represent relatively advanced human-type souls?

I postulated in *Genesis Unveiled* that the traditions of the creation of man, and especially of unsuccessful first attempts in which the creations could not 'speak' or 'sing the praises of the creator', might represent references to attempts by relatively advanced human-type souls to incarnate on earth before the physical vehicles available – for example, earlier hominid forms – were sufficiently advanced to properly accommodate their soul energy. I also indicated that Newton's subjects specifically bear this explanation out, even though I only came across his material after I had made my own interpretation. But Newton's subjects only date such experiments to a million years ago at most.

Intriguingly, I now find that TenDam reports on the findings of another past-life researcher, Pieter Barten, whose subjects consistently regressed to a time when they were able to enter large primates for short periods only – but during which time the primates temporarily walked upright instead of on all fours. Even more astounding is TenDam's report of how one subject – not his own – recalled attempting to enter the body of a dinosaur but being unable to sustain the experiment because of her human consciousness. This new evidence – new to me, that is – suggests that such experiments go back far farther, to at least sixty-five million years ago. It also suggests that rather than involving full incarnation as I had assumed, these experimenting souls were able to merely visit earth's astral plane and enter certain physical forms on a temporary basis to 'try them out' – presumably dominating any lower form of collectivized soul energy already in occupation. Above all, these experiments seem to involve individualized and arguably human-type souls.

All of this tends to imply that for millions of years there may have been a significant stock of relatively advanced human-type souls either genuinely incarnating in some sort of nonphysical form on earth's astral plane – or for that matter the astral planes of any of the other planets in our solar system – or at least visiting earth's astral plane regularly and performing temporary experiments to determine when a suitable physical vehicle had become available. It seems such souls were not of the collective energy type associated with elementals or nature and animal spirits, but nor were they extraterrestrial inasmuch as they were clearly associated with earth – or at least with our solar system. And if I am right that these were then groundbreaking experiments whose outcome was unknown, rather than merely attempts by particular curious souls to briefly experience early physical forms on earth, arguably we would then have to assume that earth may have been the first planet in the universe to harbor the types of life form suitable for our atmosphere – and possibly the first to harbor the human-type life form. But this would not necessarily imply that other planets in the universe would not have evolved far more advanced but different life forms before earth did. As to where and how complex physical life forms evolved for the very first time, it seems logical that certain planets in various solar systems in various galaxies would have been chosen for initial experiments in creation by thought-form for which there would have been no previous physical blueprints.

Nevertheless, does this mean that the bulk of human souls have been around for millions of years? I would still argue not, and that most of us who are incarnating on earth now do not form part of these pioneering and perhaps rather less populated human-type life swarms. On that basis, Newton's and Modi's evidence as regards recent, continuous and ongoing human soul birthing still stands. I would also still argue that distant memories of Atlantis and Lemuria, or at least those that involve high levels of technology, are likely to relate to experiences of other planets – whether physical or not.

Newton's subjects consistently express the view that incarnation on earth in human form is in fact one of the most testing of experiences, partly due to the complexity of the human condition especially in the modern world, and partly due to its general combination of both physical and mental challenges. By comparison they report that some other planets play host to essentially nonphysical though still incarnatory life forms – which backs up what they said in chapter 5 about explorers visiting purely mental worlds, as well as TenDam's comments about nonphysical incarnations on other planets above – and that these provide a less challenging existence. They also report that incarnation on earth is made more difficult because our amnesia about our true spiritual nature is greater than that of most life forms on other planets, and I would conjecture that this may be related to their separate reports that souls can take more of their energy into incarnation on other planets without blowing their brain circuits. Indeed, they report that our amnesia has actually increased in the last few millennia, but that there may be some ethereal pressure for this trend to be reversed:

> A number of my more advanced subjects have stated there is a growing movement in the spirit world to 'change the game rules on earth'. These people say their souls had less amnesia about Self and the interlife when they lived in earlier cultures. It seems in the last few thousand years there has been tighter blocking, on a conscious level, of our immortal memories. This has been a contributing factor in the loss of faith in our capacity for self-transcendence. Earth is filled with people who feel an empty hopelessness toward the meaning of life. The lack of connection with our immortality combined with the availability of mind-altering chemicals and over-population has created rumbles upstairs. I am told large numbers of souls who have had more frequent incarnations in recent centuries on earth are opting, when they get the chance, for less stressful worlds. There are enlightened places where amnesia is greatly reduced without causing homesickness for the spirit world. As we approach the next millennium, the masters who direct earth's destiny appear to be making changes to permit more information and understanding of who we are and why we are here to come into our lives.

To the extent that this increased amnesiac blocking is the same as our general separation from our true spiritual wisdom and roots, I argue in *Genesis Unveiled* that it occurred for the first time tens of thousands of years ago. I also suggest that this led to the karmic catastrophe and rebuilding of 11,500 years ago, when a spiritual worldview was once again reintroduced, but that a second separation has since occurred progressively in the last five thousand years or so. My argument has always been that both of these separations, or falls from grace, resulted purely from humanity making its own karmic choice to become totally immersed in the material world at the expense of the spiritual – and not from any deliberate policy in the ethereal realms over which we had no control. It is not entirely clear from Newton's description which of these two possibilities he supports, but one of Cannon's subjects makes some interesting observations about what appears to be the original fall from grace:

> We enjoy these times when we can commune. This was the way it was at one time before on your planet when all could converse freely as we do now. However, there was the time of the fall.... This was the time when the knowledge was lost, and the consciousness turned down, so to say, towards the earth and this higher energy plane was disregarded and discarded. So you can see from a strictly analogical standpoint there was a definite fall of consciousness from the higher plane to the more base earth plane. There was not, as has previously been felt, a surge of evil present when this fall occurred. It was simply that the attention of those inhabitants was shifted from the higher to the lower planes, so to say. This is what is meant by the fall. This is not a right or wrong judgment. It is simply a fact which is in the realm of truth. So you can see that when you lose your sight of who and what you are, then you would tend to wander, as humanity has done on this planet for many millennia now. It was simply a forgetting of the true identity. A lowering of the consciousness, so to say, and forgetting that all are truly part of the whole.

Although this subject also briefly mentions the fallen angel Lucifer – 'who was one with God at the time of formation, but who, through his own want for power, lost all' – we can see that he is not explicitly mentioned as being associated with the fall of humanity. Nor, for what it is worth, is there any support for the separate but related Christian idea that humanity was divorced from God right at the outset when Adam and Eve partook of the forbidden fruit. And the general tenor of this report still suggests that for the most part we were and are the masters of our own fate, and the architects of our own downfall or salvation.

By contrast, as we might expect Modi has a few words to say about Lucifer in *Remarkable Healings*, and even more in a follow-up book called *Memories of God and Creation*, which was first published in 2000. In fact in this book she provides considerably more transcripted details from her sessions with patients about interlife reviews and planning, which broadly speaking is entirely consistent with our other pioneers' findings – and even adds some previously missing elements that would fill in some of her gaps in the grids in chapters 5 and 6. But because it is so recent its independence from their work is even more questionable than that of her first book, so I have not included these new details in my previous analysis.

Her main focus in this second book, as the title suggests, is on the information she was able to glean from her subjects about the nature of God and the original creation of the universe. In fact I find her descriptions of the original state of the Ultimate Source, and of how it split apart to create all the ethereal, astral and eventually physical forms in the universe during what I normally refer to as the 'dawn of Brahma', highly compelling – and consistent with both my own reinterpretations of ancient cosmological traditions in *Genesis Unveiled* and with Fortune's channelings. However, much of Modi's remaining material again shows a high degree of Christian bias. She devotes a whole chapter to her subjects' reports of how Lucifer rebelled against the Ultimate Source right at the outset, and how he took a significant number of other angels with him – although this is admittedly consistent with Cannon's subject's report above. Her subjects then go on to describe how God created plants, animals and humans all in physical form and all seemingly at the outset, which would totally bypass the processes of physical evolution. And one even reports that a number of souls entered the bodies of apelike creatures that had been specially created for them on earth – so far so good in some senses – but also that some of these then entered a garden, which is clearly Eden even though the name is not used, where their eating of fruit belonging to Lucifer resulted in their own separation from God. Accordingly, I am unable to take much of this material seriously.

In any case, even if our spiritual separation cannot be blamed on the influence of Lucifer, is it possible that it was instigated by a deliberate ethereal policy to increase humanity's level of amnesiac blocking at some point in our past, as Newton is perhaps suggesting? I have to say that the possible motives for this remain entirely unclear. After all, we can no longer fall back on the normal explanation that if we did not have our current levels of amnesia we would be too homesick for the ethereal realms, or would blow our brain circuits, because the suggestion is clearly that in our original state as humans on earth we did suffer from far less amnesia and were not adversely affected. The only other explanation I can think of is that the ethereal powers might have decided to make earth the toughest test of all, and experimented by deliberately increasing our amnesia from its original level. But this implies a degree of premeditated harshness, even cruelty, that I find hard to credit.

It seems much more likely that our levels of amnesia were set at the outset to be just enough that it would require dedicated effort on our part to maintain a spiritual worldview. This would then ensure that our progress would be entirely in our hands. A severe test, admittedly, but not an impossible one. Now, I suggest in *Genesis Unveiled* that we have been assisted in this process by the incarnation of certain angelic-type souls, who were specifically assigned to the task precisely because they suffered from far less incarnate amnesia about the ethereal realms than the majority of human-type souls. I argue that they can incarnate at any time, but that they did so in particular at two key points in humanity's history. First, around 100,000 years ago – a date based on the often-overlooked but crucially important first appearance of deliberate human burial in the archaeological record – to introduce a spiritual worldview into the physical plane for the first time, thereby ushering in the 'golden age' of spirituality that all ancient traditions describe. And second, after the catastrophe of 11,500 years ago in order to reintroduce it. I also argue that on both occasions we have failed the test by gradually slipping back into materialism. If I am right it just may be that, as Newton reports, the ethereal powers have decided that earth is too tough a test as currently configured, and are considering deliberately reducing the levels of amnesia for all humans incarnating on earth in the future to help us to reestablish our spiritual roots en masse – without the need for a catastrophe or a new influx of angelic-type souls – and this time to maintain them more successfully as well. And if they do not regard this as cheating, then I am all for it.

So, finally, what does everything we have learned in this book tell us about why we are here? We have seen that the ultimate aim of all spiritual worldviews that base themselves on the dual principles of karma and reincarnation is escape from the earthly karmic round. That is, by continual refinement and karmic progression, to reach a stage where we no longer have to reincarnate in physical form unless we choose to, in order to serve a higher purpose than our own advancement. Most esoteric commentators in the past were unable to say much more than this, and were forced to assume this was more or less the end of the story – and that, in escaping the earthly karmic round, we would automatically reunite with the Ultimate Source. As we have already seen, others went somewhat further and speculated – based on their visions and attempts to connect with the higher realms by meditation and contemplation – that there might be further ethereal levels that we would have to progress through.

These esoteric thinkers were clearly on the right lines, because we now have a mass of evidence from interlife regression subjects that once we have reached the transcendent stage of sufficient enlightenment and balance that we no longer have to incarnate on earth, and are therefore free to continue our progress in the ethereal realms, there are still a whole range of assignments that require our attention. More advanced souls are continually involved in helping new souls to develop, in assisting other souls with their life reviews and plans, and with other more universal activities such as exploring a multitude of other planets throughout the universe, and assisting and monitoring the evolution of life on them. In fact, there will undoubtedly be a huge range of ethereal activities of which even the most advanced of our pioneers' regression subjects remain completely unaware.

So escape from the earthly karmic round is just the start, even if it may take us hundreds of incarnations and tens of thousands of elapsed earth-years to achieve. And it will most likely take us far, far longer before we develop sufficiently to get anywhere near reuniting with our own logos, let alone the Ultimate Source. Indeed, full reunification may well only take place on the dissolution of the entire universe, when the Source once again enters the sleeping or inactive phase of its great cycle, referred to in Hindu terminology as the 'night of Brahma'. Be that as it may, escape from the earthly karmic round is clearly a good start, and it is the objective on which we as still-incarnating humans should be concentrating. Earthly incarnation may bring its share of pain and pleasure, hopefully in more or less equal measure over many lifetimes, but one thing that virtually all of our near-death experiencers and regression subjects seem to agree on is that life in the ethereal realms is infinitely better.

So what does all this imply for how we should attempt to live our lives? As invidious as it is to take on the role of 'moralizing preacher', I promised previously that I would attempt to provide some practical advice, and I would be failing in my duty if I did not attempt to derive some lessons from the wealth of material we have now studied. These are lessons that I attempt to put into practice in my own life, and if they help others too then so much the better. We are, of course, all individuals. We all have our own circumstances, our own hopes and ambitions, our own preoccupations and concerns. Nevertheless, I believe there are a number of general attitudes we can all adopt that will help us to progress as individual souls. And these derive particularly from the conclusions I drew in chapter 7 concerning the dynamics of karma.

As a prelude, it is worth noting that some religious approaches stress that our specific attitude at the time of death is of paramount importance, and this is how the teachings about the *bardo* in the *Tibetan Book of the Dead* are normally interpreted. Both Woolger and Netherton, perhaps because of their overexposure to repetitive karma, tend to follow this line. Indeed, in many of their therapeutic case studies it appears on the face of it that it was the intense emotion generated by a sudden and unexpected death that led to the subject returning immediately into incarnation in a repetitive karmic cycle, and the same might be said of many of Stevenson's child subjects. But, of course, I would actually argue the reverse: that it is the very fact that the subject was still in the repetitive stage – through general soul immaturity or for other reasons – that prevented them from having a full interlife experience, rather than their attitude at death. Many of our interlife pioneers' subjects have died in similar circumstances, and arguably experienced the same sudden and intense emotions, but still moved on to the interlife proper. We can only assume that they were already in the progressive stage.

Nevertheless, more enlightened commentators suggest that in fact the *bardo* teachings represent a manual for readying ourselves for death that should be practiced *during life*, and this is certainly the view expressed by Chögyam Trungpa in his commentary on a modern translation. That is not to say that I think these teachings are the panacea that many commentators suggest. They suffer from many of the shortcomings of most ancient religious teachings. But one thing that this more enlightened approach to them does stress is that it is not only our emotional attitude *at* death that matters, but the whole attitude *to* death that we develop throughout our life. On that basis the general fostering of a broad spiritual approach during life, and of an understanding that death is only a new beginning and a return to our real spiritual home, should help to ensure that our transition into the ethereal realms is as seamless as possible.

But if we return now to my own main conclusions, we saw that souls in the progressive karma stage are more likely to adopt a balanced view towards the circumstances of their lives – and indeed deaths – and to see ostensibly adverse situations for what they really are; that is, learning opportunities rather than punishments. They may not always understand the specific lesson relevant to any particular situation at the time – often it only becomes clear much later, and maybe not even until we gain proper clarity in the interlife after death; but that does not prevent them from looking at the situation in this way, and from attempting to both adopt a balanced reaction at the time and to subsequently work out what the lesson was. We also saw that the reason souls get stuck in repetitive karmic cycles is that they fail to adopt the appropriate emotional responses to situations, and have to face them repeatedly until they too learn the relevant lesson. So in either situation adopting the appropriate response is paramount while we are in incarnate life, because it should ensure that we either enhance our progressive karma or break the chain of any repetitive karma – and we do not even have to know which stage we are in.

As I suggested previously, souls in the repetitive stage could wait until, perhaps even by a process of inevitable attrition, they finally start to wake up in the interlife and properly take the advice of their guides and elders. But it is surely more appropriate to work on these issues while in incarnate life, and at the same time to adopt a broad spiritual worldview, in order to enhance the prospects of moving towards the progressive stage and having a full interlife experience; future lives will then be properly planned and become far more productive. As for souls already in the progressive stage, consistently adopting inappropriate responses could lead to a reversion to more repetitive karma – and in any case, if my suppositions are correct, adopting appropriate responses is what they will have planned to do, and is indeed what is expected of them. So, for all these reasons, the following advice should be relevant to anyone.

1. Foster A Sense Of Balanced Detachment

Some religious approaches suggest that asceticism is the answer to everything, and that the trick is to be so detached from physical life that we do not generate any more karma at all. Their supporters argue that all actions create future reactions. So while 'bad' actions mean we have to come back for our punishment, even 'good' actions mean we have to come back to gain our reward. But clearly this relies far too much on a cause and effect model of karma. We saw that Krishna emphasizes that it is important to be fully involved in physical life in the *Gita*, and most of our pioneers' more enlightened subjects confirm this view. Indeed the greatest rewards, whether in love or work, require us to take the greatest risks – because fortune does favor the bold. But the greatest courage is that required to pick ourselves up after failure, and to be prepared to risk all again.

So if we are going to be fully involved in life, it appears that the most balanced approach of the truly wise is to stare our inevitable victories and defeats straight in the face, and to treat both with equal disdain. Perhaps disdain is too harsh a word. We should certainly take pride in our work, in our hobbies, in our families and so on. What a drab and unrewarding world it would be if we could not. But at the same time we should be humble about our achievements, in the certain knowledge that excessive pride, of the kind that borders on arrogance, comes before a fall. As for our setbacks and defeats, our rejections and humiliations, the same balanced attitude of keeping our emotional reactions to them in check, of trying to learn the lesson and move on without being dragged into the depths of depression and self-pity or loathing, will undoubtedly maintain a progressive rather than repetitive karmic impetus. In this context, although it does us no harm to concentrate on the plights of those who are clearly less fortunate than ourselves, this does not always work and can leave us feeling even more ashamed. But remembering that we almost certainly volunteered for these lessons – or at least that they are definitely the ones we need to learn in order to move on – can be a great help, however hard they seem to be. As is appreciating that when the going gets really tough – for example when *every* area of our life, including love, work and friendships – seem to be in trouble *simultaneously*, it is almost certainly a karmic wake-up call that we need to make significant changes.

I do not pretend that any of this is easy. If it were, we would all escape the earthly karmic round in no time. As I have already suggested, often the lessons to be learned from adverse circumstances do not become clear until long after the event. But the general advice stands. The trick is to prune our emotions, even if only retrospectively, so that adverse reactions are robbed of their potential charge; and, on an ongoing basis, to foster a balanced sense of detachment to all circumstances, whether pleasant or unpleasant.

The one area where this advice may seem somewhat contrary is that of love. Love, especially of one's partner or children, is probably the most intense emotion we can ever experience. It is matched only by the corresponding negative emotions if such people are taken away from us – whether by accident or design, by death or by other mode of separation during life. I have no wish to denigrate the emotion of love; indeed, it is vitally important in an even more general sense, as we will shortly see. Nor am I suggesting that we should not fully immerse ourselves in it when it comes along, and nurture and treasure it as much as possible. But we all know that undue intensity that borders on obsession is clearly unhealthy. So when I advise balanced detachment in love for a partner, for example, what I am really suggesting is that we should enjoy it while it lasts, but be ever mindful that it may not last forever, for one reason or another. One of the hardest lessons to learn in life, and this has certainly been one I have personally faced on more than one occasion, is to let go of love when it is no longer reciprocated. Ultimately we do not have, nor should we have, any real hold over any other human being, and everyone must be allowed to follow their own path. And if we are rejected, we really must take it on the chin and keep our anger or sorrow in check. We do ourselves, and our former partner, no favors by holding on to intense thoughts of revenge or reconciliation. By the same token – and although I have no desire to exacerbate what is already a serious cultural problem in the modern world – we must ourselves be free to leave a partner if, over a lengthy period, it becomes overwhelmingly clear to us that it would be the right thing to do, and even if it is disruptive and painful for all parties at the time.

As for love for one's children, this is unconditional and survives all challenges – although this may well represent a cultural phenomenon deriving at least partly from evolutionary survival instincts, rather than a karmic bargain per se. Nevertheless, clearly it is sensible to remain aware that, again, they are their own person, with their own lessons to learn, and that only a balanced rather than a smothering or oppressive love for them will help them to grow.

2. Have Faith And Patience, And Do Not Be Afraid

Everything we have learned points towards the idea that to a large extent we create our own reality. We make a life plan during the interlife. But on top of this our thoughts and intentions in incarnate life have great power to influence what happens to us. So if we are constantly afraid of how life is going to turn out – for example, worrying that we will never get the job we want, or have enough money, or meet our true soul mate, or even fulfill our real destiny, and so on – then the negative energy of these constantly transmitted thought-forms will undoubtedly carry the potential to become self-fulfilling prophecy. Many of our pioneers' more enlightened subjects report that fear is one of the most destructive of human emotions.

By contrast, if we have faith that we are on the right path, and that all these things will happen as they should, if they should, then we stand a much greater chance of bringing them to fruition. Again, of course, there are problems with this. For example, we might assume that we are supposed to pair off with our soul mate at some point in our life. We might think we have found them, and then when the going gets tough change our minds and look elsewhere. We might spend our whole life constantly searching for them, trying to maintain a positive outlook but becoming increasingly frustrated. How do we balance having a positive attitude with being realistic, and not creating expectations that cannot be fulfilled? Unfortunately there are no easy answers to this question – not least because, for example, it is always possible that in this life we planned not to pair off with a soul mate at all.

Nevertheless, this general approach of tempering a positive outlook with a degree of realism should be applied to all areas of our lives; and, as always, balance is the key to such 'positive realism'. We should be open to possibilities, but not burden ourselves with expectations. We should accept our circumstances, but be ready to change them if our intuition strongly urges us that we should. We should develop ourselves via appropriate ambitions, but not become so obsessed that we lose sight of what is important in life. We should welcome change, but only when it is constructive and not just for its own sake. Above all, we need to be *patient*. Many people have spent lifetimes trying to push a stubborn door open, only to discover when the time is right that they can easily pull it open instead. All of that having been said, this balance between proactively trying to develop positive outcomes, and passively waiting for things to happen as they should when the time is right, is extremely hard to achieve in practice. The only way forward is to be vigilant in paying proper attention to important synchronicities, and to listen closely to our intuition – which, as we will shortly see, requires us to be properly in touch with our higher selves.

3. Forgive Everyone, Especially Yourself

All of my other pieces of advice tend to be forward rather than backward looking, precisely because of the emphasis that I placed on this in chapter 7. But we saw there that one of the most influential perpetrators of repetitive karma is lack of acceptance, and whatever surface emotions are generated by this – of loss, guilt, failure, shame, remorse, sorrow, humiliation, jealously, anger, hatred or revenge, and so on – in fact the overriding emotional cure for all these is *forgiveness*. So it is absolutely clear that to maintain progressive karma we need to be able to forgive those who have wronged us, or who we perceive have wronged us, and also to forgive ourselves for our own mistakes.

This is clearly an ongoing task as it relates to the continuous unfolding of events in our current lives. But it is also an area where past lives can most come into play. Some of the worst aspects of repetitive karma will be maintained between souls who are closely linked, and all our pioneers emphasize that we must work out our karma with such people in order to move on more progressively. Again, we do not *need* to have any prior knowledge of relationships in past lives in order to adopt the appropriate responses to our relationships in this one. And this is one of the best areas where retrospective work can pay dividends. We can all harbor intense emotions against others, or against ourselves in how we have handled others, for a period of time – but it is never too late to forgive them or ourselves while still incarnate, even if this is only in our own head rather than face to face. Of course, it is all the better if other people subsequently forgive us for things we have done to them, but that is their own decision, and does not alter the fact that it is our forgiveness of ourselves that we can control and that matters most. Moreover, it is far preferable to sort this out while still incarnate, however late on, rather than to trust to luck that it will all be sorted out in the interlife.

But, yet again, this can be extremely difficult in practice. And it is for this reason more than any other that I am still perfectly comfortable about recommending past-life regression to anyone, because the one thing that it does seem to consistently uncover is important past-life relationships, and whether they are absent or maintained in our current life. This has clearly given thousands of regression subjects far greater clarity and understanding about current relationships and patterns, and allowed many of them to break repetitive links. Of course, the services of regression experts are not always widely available, and can sometimes be relatively expensive.

But many of them have written self-help books in which they describe how the techniques they use can be applied by ordinary people to regress themselves into their past lives – and I regard this as a useful development, even though I have not tried it myself as yet and so cannot make any specific recommendations. It is also worth noting that in 2004 Newton published a third book, *Life Between Lives: Hypnotherapy for Spiritual Regression*, which is probably the first real attempt to put details of the specific techniques used in interlife regression into the public domain. If this leads to the even more far-ranging insights obtainable in the interlife becoming more widely available, then so much the better.

4. Practice Selflessness And Unconditional Love

Clearly we can attempt to develop our spiritual understanding on an intellectual level. But how often do we meet people who talk about spirituality and then, in their actions, reveal how far removed they are from putting their understanding into practice? How often do we meet individuals who wear their spirituality somewhat on their sleeve, and who can at times come across as sanctimonious, patronizing, self-satisfied or even arrogant? Getting rid of our egos, and fostering humility deep in our souls, is not easy. Coming originally from a competitive background where the biggest ego stood the best chance of winning, it is something I have personally tried to work on for a long time, and I am sure I still have a long way to go yet. But we do need to work on these things if we are to be unselfish in our attempts to help others, and in learning to love our fellow man, our planet, and everything on it unconditionally – precisely because we are all one. The people that do this best may not talk about spirituality at all, but they are the ones who possess true spiritual integrity.

Of course, dispensing love and charity to others that we love or like anyway is easy enough. Dispensing them to others that we do not know, or actively dislike, is far harder. But even when we do this it is sometimes motivated by ego. Even if we are not actively seeking a reward as such, it makes us feel good in ourselves. There is nothing much wrong with this. But the real key, according to all of our pioneers' most enlightened subjects, is to give totally unconditional and selfless love, freely and without any thought for ourselves. This is incredibly hard to achieve. But, as always, the harder the task, the greater the reward.

5. Foster And Maintain Proper Contact With Your Higher Self

One of the major reasons I wrote this book was to pull together all the evidence that suggests just how much control we have over our lives. As I suggested above, in order to realize this control we need to be sufficiently in touch with our intuition, or more formally with our higher self, to spot the triggers or synchronicities that point towards the path we agreed on in our life plan. And almost all spiritual teachings, along with many of our pioneers' subjects, suggest that we should make time to meditate to improve our intuition and spiritual balance – because when we are 'in touch' or 'connected' in this way our path becomes clearer and, hopefully, somewhat easier.

In this context I am somewhat reluctant to discuss my own meditation practices in any detail, because I have grave reservations about my suitability to dispense advice in this area. However, meditation is indisputably of the utmost importance. Moreover, as the pieces of advice I have just discussed began to crystallize in the course of writing this book, I began to use them regularly as affirmations in my meditations. Indeed, my intuition or higher self seemed to come into play considerably during this process, so that over the course of several months I refined and honed them to the point that, albeit with some hesitation and reluctance, I felt they might be worthy of inclusion here. Nevertheless, I emphasize that there are really no hard and fast rules, and that everyone should practice meditation in whatever way they feel most comfortable.

Most advice suggests that initially you should attempt to meditate for at least five to fifteen minutes every day, increasing this to at least half an hour as you become more proficient. But, above all, do what feels right for you. Only in that way will you persevere and keep the practice up, which is by far the most important goal. The specific time of day is unimportant, but ideally it should be the same time each day to establish a rhythm. One factor if you have a noisy family is that you will need to select a time and place of quiet where you will not be disturbed, because the ability to ignore distractions takes considerable time to develop. Again, your posture should be whatever you feel most comfortable with – for example, I have not yet developed the ability to sit in a proper yoga position with my legs crossed and tucked up, so trying to use that posture because it is 'the right one' may only make you uncomfortable and distracted. In fact, I simply lie flat on my bed. The key is to adopt a comfortable position and then focus on relaxing your whole body, concentrating on each part in turn. Do not be afraid to move, even after your meditation has begun, if a part of your body becomes uncomfortable. And all the way through keep a background lookout for any tension in the body – and if you find it, move or relax your muscles to get rid of it.

At the same time as relaxing your body, you need to establish a rhythmic pattern of breathing – indeed, to some extent the two go hand in hand. Think of your breathing as part of an endless cycle. In order to establish a steady pattern, I tend to repeat the following affirmation during the inhalation stroke – only in my head, although you could say it aloud if you preferred:

my *breathing* is in *harmony* with the *pulse* of the *universe*

This affirmation has four main words, shown in italics. As with all subsequent affirmations, I tend to emphasize these in order to keep a four-four timing to my breathing; that is, four beats for the inhalation or affirmation stroke, and another four for the exhalation or silent stroke.

Some practitioners will now tell you, for example, to imagine yourself in a lift going down several floors until you reach the basement, counting each one as you go. All variations on this theme are intended to get you to progressively enter an altered state of consciousness by slowing your brain waves down, and they are not dissimilar to the approaches used in hypnosis. For my own part I prefer to think in terms of 'up' rather than 'down', and I tend to gradually raise my forearms from the prone position as a sign to my subconscious that I am attempting to shift levels. Again, this is similar to the finger-raising method practiced by many regressors, although this time I am asking my movement to act as a sign *to* my subconscious, rather than vice versa. While I am doing this I am still repeating my breathing mantra, and it probably takes a few minutes for my forearms to reach the vertical, by which time I should have entered a higher state of consciousness. After this point, I maintain the same breathing pattern for the rest of the session, but without the mantra.

All practitioners will advise you to provide yourself with some sort of psychic protection when meditating – precisely because of the possibility, whether remote or not, that you might open yourself up to negative energies or even possession. Some will suggest you do this at the beginning, for example by envisaging the creation of a protective ring around yourself. My own approach is to wait until I have reached the altered state, and then concentrate on the white light protection that I mentioned in the last chapter. For me this involves envisaging the powerful source of pure energy that pervades the universe as the bright light of the sun, acting as a vortex that shoots straight into my body via my solar plexus, and from there down my legs, up through my chest and shoulders, along my arms and up into my head, and then out into my surrounding aura until it is full to the brim. I feel this replenishment occurring especially during the inhalation stroke, and I take at least seven breathing cycles to complete this exercise. I then imagine any repairs that my aura requires being carried out, along with any energy gaps in any part of my astral body being similarly repaired and filled. During this process I am focusing on the operation in hand, and so not using any affirmations, but once it is complete I repeat the following affirmation a few times:

my *aura* is *strong*, and *keeps* me *protected*

From this point on, I repeat the following affirmations, again on the inhalation stroke only. They correspond to the five pieces of advice given above, albeit that the last comes first, and the fourth contains an element to affirm the energy replenishment from the white light exercise, as well as an affirmation of hope that relates to maintaining a positive outlook in general. I do not repeat them a set number of times, just however much each one seems to deserve on any given day:

I am *properly connected* to my *higher self*

I *balance* and *moderate* my *emotions* and *reactions*

I have *patient faith*, and *fear nothing*

I *forgive everyone, especially myself*

I am *full* of *hope, energy* and *love*

Sometimes I will let my mind extend into particular issues of current concern related to any one of these affirmations; and if that means that I stop repeating it for a time, and give my intuitive mind free rein to contemplate that particular issue for a while, then that is not a problem. Of course, anyone might want to change these affirmations to suit themselves, especially if they did not agree with some of my advice and reasoning in the first place. Your intuition will tell you if they feel right or not. You may even find that sometimes, especially as you progress, you would prefer to stay silent and just empty your head, which is the classic form of meditation. However this is far more difficult, and affirmations tend to provide a focus, which is especially helpful when you are inexperienced. Having said that, verbal affirmations clearly rely on words and thoughts, which happen to suit my brain pattern. Other people might find it easier to focus on visual images, for example of a Tibetan mandala or other esoteric symbol. But, whatever your preference, do not forget that verbal affirmations can carry great power if you are properly focused.

At the end of my meditation I always give general thanks using the following affirmation, again repeated as many times as feels appropriate:

I give *respectful thanks* for all the *help* I *receive*

I do not direct this to any particular set of ethereal beings, it is merely intended to convey my general respect for the higher powers that help us all. If you feel more comfortable naming the beings you think are helping you, such as 'spirits of light' or whatever, then that is fine. After this, I might utter a few special requests for help, either for myself or for friends facing difficult circumstances and so on, or a few special thankyous for requests that have been answered. Of course, these might easily be regarded as 'prayers', but it should be obvious by now that they are requests made not to 'God' as such but to my own higher self and guides. There is nothing wrong with this, and often when we ask for help we will receive it. But we must also be mindful of what we wish for, because integrity of intention is crucial. And if a request appears to go unanswered, we must be patient until either it is granted, or a clearer perspective allows us to realize how lucky we are that it was ignored – or, if we continue to find no understandable lesson in the karmic dynamics of a particular situation, exercise the ultimate patience of waiting to obtain proper clarity in the interlife.

To close my meditation, I continue with my breathing patterns, but I am now silent inside my head as I allow my forearms to gradually lower back to the horizontal. During this process I am gently returning to a normal state of consciousness.

I sincerely hope this advice is useful, especially to those who are unfamiliar with meditation. Those who are more advanced will undoubtedly find much of it somewhat trite, perhaps even more a system of advanced prayer than meditation per se. It is certainly true that advanced, perhaps even proper, meditation involves completely emptying our minds – that is, avoiding affirmations or any sort of conscious thought – and it is probably only then that really profound insights become available to us. But I sincerely hope they will forgive me for my simplistic approach, and appreciate that I am directing this advice primarily at beginners – which is what most of us, including myself, are.

Stevenson suggests that many people are reluctant to believe in the concept of reincarnation and karma precisely because it places the emphasis on their personal responsibility for their lives and circumstances. If that is the case, then my attempts to place this degree of responsibility beyond doubt – by concentrating specifically on the evidence of interlife experiences such as review and planning – will put them off even more. But I have to say that in my own experience nothing could be further from the truth, because people do not seem to be put off by the idea of personal responsibility. Some might initially struggle with the idea that in many cases we deliberately choose to experience adverse circumstances in our lives. But they soon seem to appreciate how superior such an idea is to falling back on the notions of divine whim or random chance.

People increasingly talk about stress in the modern world. Many seem to think that it results from us taking on too many responsibilities, or working too hard. But working hard is not at all stressful per se. The real cause of stress is *lack of control*. Think about it. When, many years ago, I used to sell computer software, people used to say to me, 'Oh, that must be a very stressful job.' It was not. And the reason was that, although I worked hard to learn my trade and build up my patch, once I had done this and become reasonably successful my bosses left me alone to get on with the job. Now, if I had been struggling, they would undoubtedly have been on my back all day long. *That* would have been stressful, because I would no longer have felt that I was in full control of the situation. But, as it was, the job was hard work but relatively stress-free. And people in general are not stressed because they are working too hard, or trying to balance too many plates in the air in our action-packed modern world – albeit that I do not regard this way of living as a healthy progression for humanity as a whole. Instead, they are stressed because often they do not feel in control of various aspects of their lives.

To translate this into the more general realm of the spiritual approach I have described in this book, any worldview that emphasizes personal control is bound, in my opinion, to lead to reduced stress in general. To a greater acceptance of, and improved perspective on, the ups and downs of life. To less immediate concern for personal ambition and material success, and more general concern for humanity as a whole and our planet. To less desire to pack everything into one life and hang onto it at all costs, and greater acceptance of death. To reduced seduction by the material world, and increased anticipation of a return to our real ethereal home.

What we do as individuals does determine what happens to our society and culture as a whole. Despite what I said earlier about adopting an unselfish approach, if we concentrate on getting our own house in order before worrying about everyone else's, the rest will surely follow. We cannot be effective in helping others until we have helped ourselves, and achieved personal balance, first. I have repeatedly suggested that I am not unduly optimistic about the future of humanity, at least not in the short term. Nevertheless, there is no doubt that the more individuals wake up to a true spiritual path based on personal integrity and unconditional love, the greater our chance of redeeming ourselves and pulling back from the brink. I will not go as far as to suggest the future is bright, but I do emphasize that as individuals we have a choice. And if enough of us make the right choice, then collectively we might just pull off a miracle.

In 1902 the philosopher William James made the following plea in *The Varieties of Religious Experience*:

> If philosophy will abandon metaphysics and deduction for criticism and induction, and frankly transform herself from theology into a science of religions, she can make herself enormously useful. The spontaneous intellect of man always defines the divine which it feels in ways that harmonize with its temporary intellectual prepossessions. Philosophy can by comparison eliminate the local and the accidental from these definitions. Both from dogma and from worship she can remove historic incrustations. By confronting the spontaneous religious constructions with the results of natural science, philosophy can also eliminate doctrines that are now known to be scientifically absurd or incongruous.... I do not see why a critical science of religions of this sort might not eventually command as general a public adhesion as is commanded by a physical science.

I suspect James would be shocked at the extent to which his plea has been ignored. As an isolated area of specialist study philosophy has disappeared completely up its own fundament in the century since James wrote these words, primarily because of the materialist preoccupation that has overtaken most academic disciplines. Philosophy needs to get back to its roots. The Classical Greeks understood that a philosopher, as literally a 'lover of knowledge', was someone who immersed themselves in all areas of study. Philosophy should be a discipline that brings science and theology together. As I indicated in the opening chapter, new developments in theoretical physics are forcing scientists to abandon their isolation and confront the metaphysical as well – and I believe trailblazing scientists themselves will be, indeed already are, at the forefront of a new, more holistic, philosophy.

Nevertheless, we have seen that the sciences of psychology and psychiatry have a vital contribution to make to this new synthesis. What I hope I have proved is that the insights of our pioneers' regression subjects make a massive contribution to the 'natural scientific' evidence that James hoped would emerge to confront the 'spontaneous religious constructions' of old. And that, when brought together and applied logically as I have tried to do, they do indeed 'eliminate doctrines that are now known to be absurd or incongruous'. Whether or not this emerging synthesis will 'command as general a public adhesion as is commanded by a physical science', only time will tell. But even if this does not happen in the immediate future, we can at least retain one fervent hope: that we will find, when we come back again in our next lives, that good progress has been made towards this end.

I have written this book in the hope it will help individuals to make greater sense of their lives, and to see them from a broader perspective. But it is up to each and every one of us to consider how general spiritual messages should be applied to ourselves. Nobody else can do this for us, and there is no substitute for personal effort and learning, even if books like this can hopefully assist the process. Ultimately we are all in charge of our own karma, and cannot ask someone else to resolve, improve or even understand it for us. It is true that cheating never pays, and nothing comes for free. The reward of release from the bonds of earthly karma is only attained by integrity and perseverance.

That having been said, and despite all its pitfalls and imperfections, never forget to enjoy earthly life as much as possible. Take time out to be fully aware of the beauty in your surroundings and in nature, by looking through the eyes of a child. Live in the here and now, and if you must think about the future concentrate most on the next step you need to take, trusting that after that things will take care of themselves – because the ultimate destination in your life matters far less than how you handle the journey itself. If you can laugh in the face of adversity, pick yourself up, learn the lesson and move on in the hope of better things to come, you are a true spiritual warrior. And your enjoyment of life will be infectious, spreading its warm glow of energy and love to everyone around you.

Due to what I think may be fairly described as a certain shortsightedness on the part of various publishers, I have been forced to publish this book myself. If you have found it useful and would like to recommend it to friends and acquaintances, as I sincerely hope you will, please bear in mind that it is primarily only available via my website at *www.ianlawton.com* – where I am able to discount the price significantly because no intermediary suppliers or distributors are involved – or via *www.amazon.co.uk*.

Key Conclusions

Chapter 1: There is indisputable scientific evidence that the physical world is made up of pure energy and not physical matter, and that multiple nonphysical dimensions exist that scientists cannot as yet analyze.

Chapter 2: The evidence of near-death experiences suggests strongly that there is an element of individual consciousness that exists entirely independent of the physical body and brain. Skeptics' attempts to dismiss this evidence are simplistic and reductionist.

Chapter 3: The evidence of children who spontaneously remember past lives is strongly suggestive of reincarnation, especially when birthmark and defect cases are brought into play. Again, skeptics' attempts at more materialistic explanations are simplistic and reductionist.

Chapter 4: A huge number of case studies now suggest that hypnotic regression can produce verifiable evidence of past lives, which in the vast majority of cases can only be explained by the reincarnation of the individual. In addition, a number of pioneering psychologists and psychiatrists who were initially skeptics became convinced of reincarnation by the unprecedented therapeutic results they achieved with regression. Some of these went on to discover the interlife experience, mostly by accident and almost certainly independent of each other.

Chapter 5: Regression subjects consistently report on their transition to the ethereal realms in similar ways to near-death experiencers. Once in the interlife proper, they engage in life reviews in a variety of settings. Some of these are emphasized more by one pioneer than another, but there is considerable consistency in respect of the general principle.

Chapter 6: Regression subjects consistently report on a variety of life-planning activities. Again, certain aspects are emphasized more by one pioneer than another, but there is considerable consistency in respect of the general principle. This is also true of their subjects' reports of their return into incarnation, and of their experiences in the womb.

Chapter 7: We can identify four stages of karmic evolution through which individual souls progress. In particular, souls still in the repetitive stage may not have the full interlife experience, and these are encountered more often by regressors who are concentrating exclusively on therapy. Their repetitive karma is characterized by facing similar adverse circumstances in successive lives, and results from intense emotions being carried forward that they need to assimilate, as well as learning to react to adverse circumstances in a more balanced way. They are not paying off karmic debts, and any punishment is entirely self-inflicted. Souls in the progressive stage may choose ostensibly disadvantageous life circumstances, but again these are opportunities for learning and advancement rather than any form of karmic punishment. So all karma is primarily about learning, and not about 'action and reaction' but rather 'right action'. The concept of hell has no underlying reality, and is only ever created by our own expectations and perceptions; and nor are we punished for supposed misdemeanors by reversion to animal form. Above all, modern regression insights provide a massively important alternative source of spiritual information to the revealed wisdom of old.

Chapter 8: Hypnotic progressions into the future are not reliable indicators of what will happen. They may derive from tapping into a complete version of the future that is envisaged in the ethereal realms at that time, but this version will never be realized in actuality because karmic choices and free will constantly change its dynamics. Nevertheless, mass perceptions of the future may have the power to influence the course of events.

Chapter 9: Possession by earthbound spirits is a possibility, but if it does occur it is relatively rare. Given that there is no such thing as hell, demonic possession is likely to be a construct with no underlying reality. A variety of phenomena related to possession have greater or lesser degrees of plausibility, but there is no convincing evidence that detracts from the individualized nature of the human soul and its personal responsibility for its own karma.

Chapter 10: Our objective is to escape the earthly karmic round, but after this there is a great deal of further learning to do in the ethereal realms before we get anywhere near our logos, let alone the Ultimate Source itself. There are a number of general pieces of advice that we can all follow in our attempts to progress our karma while in incarnate life, and these can be usefully combined into meditation practice. Above all, although the immediate future of humanity may not look promising, the more we as individuals take responsibility for our spiritual growth and lead a practically spiritual life, the more chance we have of getting back on course as a collective.

Source References

Excerpts from *Between Death and Life* by Dolores Cannon reproduced by kind permission of Gateway, an imprint of Gill & Macmillan, and of Ozark Mountain Publishers. Excerpts from *Remarkable Healings* by Shakuntala Modi reproduced by kind permission of Hampton Roads Publishing Company. Excerpts from *Journey of Souls* and *Destiny of Souls* by Michael Newton reproduced by kind permission of Llewellyn Publications. Excerpts from *The Search for Lives Past* by Peter Ramster reproduced by kind permission of Somerset Film & Publishing. Excerpts from *Light and Death* by Michael Sabom reproduced by kind permission of Zondervan Publishing House, a division of HarperCollins Publishers. Excerpts from *Life Between Life* by Joel Whitton and Joe Fisher reproduced by kind permission of Doubleday & Company, an imprint of Random House. All other excerpts fall within the guidelines on 'fair dealing for the purposes of criticism and review' provided by the UK Society of Authors.

Short ellipses (…) in extracts from regression transcripts only represent pauses by the subject. Longer ellipses (….) indicate that I have omitted elements that are inconsequential, irrelevant or repetitive. All italics in quotes are original, except where I have amended regression transcripts so that the regressors' questions are always italicized for consistency. Rounded brackets in quotes are original, whereas any comments of my own are inserted in square brackets.

Although most of the professionals I quote in this book have doctorates in psychology or psychiatry, I do not use the title 'Dr' except when quoting from the work of others. This is not intended to be disrespectful, it is merely to avoid laborious repetition.

See the bibliography for further book details.

Chapter 1: A Personal Journey

Lawton, *Genesis Unveiled*: esoteric science, chapter 19.

Chapter 2: Near-Death Experiences

Sabom, *Light and Death*: Pam Reynolds case, chapter 3 and chapter 10, pp. 184–9; realness of other self and realms, chapter 3, p. 26 and chapter 9, p. 135; analysis of scientific explanations, chapter 10.

Fenwick, *The Truth in the Light*: general details of study, introduction, pp. 2–3; ignorance and fear of ridicule of respondents, introduction, p. 3 and chapter 1, p. 14; children's near-death experiences, chapter 12; comparison of international studies, chapter 11, pp. 159–66; widening of spiritual horizons, chapter 4, p. 62 and chapter 9, pp. 133–4; analysis of scientific explanations, chapters 14 and 15; no fear of death, chapter 9, p. 130; Vicki Umipeg (aka Emily) case, chapter 6, pp. 85–7; boy as empty shell, chapter 3, p. 37.

Ring, *Life at Death*: analysis of scientific explanations, chapter 11.

van Lommel et al, 'Near-death experience in survivors of cardiac arrest: a prospective study in the Netherlands', *The Lancet*, 15 Dec 2001: anonymous 'teeth' case.

Morse and Perry, *Transformed by the Light*: George (aka Yuri) Rodonaia case, chapter 4, pp. 95–7 (see also www.near-death.com/experiences/evidence10.html).

www.horizon-research.co.uk: Parnia and Fenwick's Horizon Research project.

Weiss, *Many Lives, Many Masters*: consciousness while under anesthetic, chapter 10, pp. 146–7.

CHAPTER 3: CHILDREN WHO REMEMBER PAST LIVES

Stevenson, *Twenty Cases Suggestive of Reincarnation*: Swarnlata Mishra case, chapter 2, pp. 67–91.

Stevenson, *Children Who Remember Previous Lives*: research methods, chapter 6; typical case characteristics, chapter 5; analysis of alternative explanations, chapter 7; conclusion, chapter 7, p. 158.

Stevenson, *Where Reincarnation and Biology Intersect*: introduction and methodology, chapter 1; Chanai Choomalaiwong case, chapter 5, pp. 38–41; Cemil Fahrici case, chapter 10, pp. 74–5; Sunita Singh case, chapter 6, pp. 45–6; Necip Ünlütaskiran case, chapter 6, pp. 48–9; Tong In Songcham case, chapter 12, pp. 89–90; introduction to birth defect cases, chapter 16; Ma Khin Mar Htoo case, chapter 17, pp. 122–3; Semih Tutusmus case, chapter 18, pp. 129–31; Ma Htwe Win case, chapter 19, pp. 137–9; stigmata and hypnosis, chapter 2, pp. 14–17; maternal impressions, chapter 3, pp. 24–7; analysis of other possible explanations, chapters 15 and 26; conclusion, chapter 15, p. 112.

www.healthsystem.virginia.edu/internet/personalitystudies: University of Virginia Division of Personality Studies.

www.hi.is/~erlendur/english/index.html: Erlendur Haraldsson.

CHAPTER 4: HYPNOTIC REGRESSION

Gardner, *Fads and Fallacies in the Name of Science*: view of hypnotic regression, chapter 26.

Bernstein, *The Search for Bridey Murphy*: all original case details.

Ducasse, 'How the case of *The Search for Bridey Murphy* stands today', *Journal of the American Society for Psychical Research* 54, pp. 3–22: refutation of exposé.

Stevenson, *Children Who Remember Previous Lives*: suggestibility, source amnesia, historical anomalies and imagination in hypnotic regression, chapter 3, pp. 40–6 and notes 2–11, pp. 280–2.

Ramster, *The Search for Lives Past*: initial skepticism, foreword, p. 16 and chapter 4, p. 129; Gwen MacDonald case, chapters 2 and 3; bruising and birthmarks related to past-life recall, chapter 4, p. 158, chapter 6, p. 219 and chapter 7, p. 260;

improved eyesight under hypnosis, chapter 5, p. 186; Cynthia Henderson case, chapter 1, pp 29–30 and chapter 6.

Ramster, *The Truth about Reincarnation*: more on initial skepticism, chapter 1, p. 13; Spanish heretic case, chapter 4, p. 95; Alexander Cochrane case, chapter 3, pp. 90–1; Jenny Green case, chapter 2, pp. 21–5 and 37.

Stevenson, *Unlearned Language*: Dolores Jay case, pp. 7–71 and 169–203.

de Rochas, *Les Vies Successives*.

Cannon, *The Power Within*: changing attitude to past-life regression, chapter 16, p. 170; number of patients regressed, chapter 16, p. 183.

Grant and Kelsey, *Many Lifetimes*: background to past-life regression, including female identification case, chapter 2.

Keeton, *Encounters With the Past*: background, inside back cover (Ray Bryant case, see www.mysteries.pwp.blueyonder.co.uk/1%2C6.htm).

Netherton, *Past Lives Therapy*: background to past-life regression, introduction (see also Fisher, *Coming Back Alive*, chapter 5, pp. 58–60).

Fiore, *You Have Been Here Before*: early experiences with past-life regression, introduction, pp. 4–6; brief reference to interlife experiences, chapter 11, pp. 216–17.

Fiore, *The Unquiet Dead*: later attitude towards past-life regression, chapter 2, p. 11.

Wambach, *Reliving Past Lives*: background to past-life research, chapters 1–6; results of statistical survey, chapters 7–11; Hammurabi case, chapter 8, p. 113.

Woolger, *Other Lives, Other Selves*: extracts from Jung's memoirs concerning Freud, chapter 3, p. 47; introduction to past-life regression, chapter 1, pp. 3–15.

Weiss, *Many Lives, Many Masters*: background to Catherine case, preface and chapters 1–4; other cases, epilogue, p. 217.

Wambach, *Life Before Life*: background to interlife research, introduction and chapters 1–2.

Whitton, *Life Between Life*: Harold Jaworski case, chapter 11, pp. 167–9; early experiences with past-life regression, introduction and chapter 1; background to interlife research, chapter 3.

Cannon, *Between Death and Life*: background to interlife research, chapter 1, pp. 3–4.

Modi, *Remarkable Healings*: early experiences with past-life regression, chapter 1, pp. 21–2; overview of interlife experiences, chapter 3, p. 186; exposure to other research, chapter 1, pp. 22–3 and chapter 3, pp. 107–10.

Newton, *Journey of Souls*: early experiences with past-life and interlife regression, introduction, pp. 2–3.

Chapter 5: Past-life Reviews

Kramer, *Two Elegies*: judgment in Sumerian netherworld reference, 'An Elegy on the Death of Nannaya', lines 88–90 (see also www-etcsl.orient.ox.ac.uk/section5/tr552.htm).

Budge, *The Egyptian Heaven and Hell*: weighing of the heart ceremony, volume 3, chapter 11, pp. 158–60.

Prasad, *The Fountainhead of Religion*: similarity of judgment after death in Zoroastrian and Judaic systems, chapter 4, p. 68.

Newton, *Journey of Souls*: the death experience and reacquaintance with the ethereal realms, chapters 1–4; orientation, chapter 5; transition to soul group and formal life review, chapter 6; soul groups and guides, chapters 7–8.

Newton, *Destiny of Souls*: comforting loved ones after death, chapter 2; ghosts and souls in seclusion, chapter 3; severely damaged souls, chapter 4, pp. 93–104; more details of soul groups, chapter 7, pp. 259–90; more details of formal life review, chapter 6; the library of life books, chapter 5, pp. 150–69; role-playing in soul groups, chapter 5, pp. 190–4; rest and recreation, chapter 7, pp. 290–315; training specializations, chapter 8, pp. 323–54.

Moody, *Life After Life*: life reviews during the near-death experience, chapter 2, pp. 64–8.

Ring, *Life at Death*: life reviews during the near-death experience, chapter 4, p. 67 and chapter 10, pp.197–8 (he also references a 1977 paper by Noyes, R and Kletti, R, 'Panoramic Memory: A Response to the Threat of Death', *Omega* 8, pp. 181–93).

Fenwick, *The Truth in the Light*: life reviews during the near-death experience, chapter 8, pp. 114–15.

Ramster, *The Truth about Reincarnation*: Jenny Green's interlife experiences, chapter 2, pp. 49–56; transition to interlife and rest periods, chapter 6, pp. 133–4; accuracy of memories of early childhood, chapter 2, p. 57.

Ramster, *The Search for Lives Past*: levels in ethereal realms, chapter 7, p. 252; Gwen McDonald life review, chapter 2, pp. 59–60; life reviews in general, chapter 7, p. 269.

Lawton, *Giza: The Truth*: the Hall of Records, chapter 5.

Lawton, *Genesis Unveiled*: more on the Hall of Records, chapter 4, pp. 85–6.

Whitton, *Life Between Life*: early stages of interlife experience including life review and classroom learning, chapter 4, pp. 29–43 and 48.

Cannon, *Between Death and Life*: the death experience, chapter 1; transition to interlife, chapter 2; spirit guides, chapter 8; ghosts, chapter 11; Temple of Healing, chapter 5, pp. 62–7; the general council, chapter 13; review council during a near-death experience, chapter 3, p. 32; interlife schools, chapter 4, pp. 36–9; library, chapter 5, pp. 74–7; Tapestry Room, chapter 5, pp. 68–71; unconditional love, chapter 16, pp. 235–6.

Modi, *Remarkable Healings*: early stages of interlife experience including council review and ongoing learning, chapter 3, pp. 114–21.

Fiore, *You Have Been Here Before*: transition to interlife and life review, chapter 11, pp. 216 and 222–3 and chapter 12, p, 240.

Fiore, *The Unquiet Dead*: more on life reviews, chapter 4, p. 22.

Weiss, *Many Lives, Many Masters*: renewal, recollection and astral planes, chapter 10, p. 140, chapter 12, pp. 171–2 and chapter 13, p. 185.

Wambach, *Life Before Life*: karmic ties between soul group members, chapter 5, pp. 91–7.

Netherton, *Past Lives Therapy*: interlife experience, chapter 16.

CHAPTER 6: LIFE PLANS AND CHOICES

Newton, *Journey of Souls*: place of life selection, chapter 12; body selection, chapter 13; place of recognition, chapter 14; returning into incarnation, chapter 15; amnesia, chapter 5, p. 67.

Newton, *Destiny of Souls*: more on life plans, chapter 9, pp. 355–81; case study mapping human relationships to soul groupings, chapter 7, p. 276; more on returning into incarnation, chapter 9, pp. 384–94.

Whitton, *Life Between Life*: life plans, chapter 4, pp. 43–51; returning into incarnation, chapter 4, pp. 51–7.

Cannon, *Between Death and Life*: overview of life plans, chapter 16, p. 228; choice of family, chapter 16, p. 231; group planning sessions, chapter 12, pp. 181–4, and chapter 4, p. 43; council planning, chapter 13, pp. 192–3; coercion to return, chapter 4, pp. 56–8; extent of control, chapter 16, p. 237; learning by incarnation, chapter 4, p. 46; incarnating without a plan, chapter 7, pp. 120–1; returning into incarnation, chapter 15, pp. 225–6 and chapter 16, pp. 233–4; soul leaving child's body, chapter 15, p. 221 and chapter 16, pp. 229–30; amnesia, chapter 4, pp. 43–4 and chapter 15, p. 219.

Wambach, *Life Before Life*: choosing the next life, chapter 2, pp. 28–39 and chapter 3; returning into incarnation, chapter 6 and chapter 7, pp. 122–3; premature births and adoption, chapter 8, pp. 160–7.

Ramster, *The Search for Lives Past*: supposed lack of choice in life plans, chapter 7, p. 265; Gwen McDonald life choices, chapter 2, pp. 60–1.

Ramster, *The Truth about Reincarnation*: one subject on his choice to return, chapter 6, p. 135.

Modi, *Remarkable Healings*: life plans, chapter 3, pp. 121–2 and 186–7; returning into incarnation, chapter 2; amnesia, chapter 3, pp. 183–4.

Fiore, *You Have Been Here Before*: life plans, chapter 12, p, 240–1.

Fiore, *The Unquiet Dead*: more on life plans, chapter 4, p. 22.

Weiss, *Many Lives, Many Masters*: life plans, chapter 10, p. 140 and chapter 12, pp. 172–3.

Grant and Kelsey, *Many Lifetimes*: awareness in womb, chapter 2, p. 53; Grant's childhood memories, chapter 7.

Netherton, *Past Lives Therapy*: awareness in womb, chapter 13, pp. 145–6.

CHAPTER 7: THE DYNAMICS OF KARMA

Stevenson, *Children Who Remember Previous Lives*: views on karma, chapter 11, pp. 257–60; subjects' brief reports of interlife, chapter 5, pp. 109–11; rare cases of intermediate animal lives, chapter 10, p. 210.

Stevenson, *Where Reincarnation and Biology Intersect*: case of murderer with malformed arm, chapter 17, pp. 126–7.

Ramster, *The Search for Lives Past*: views on karma, chapter 7, pp. 253–4; therapeutic case studies, chapter 4; unpleasant places in interlife, chapter 7, pp. 252–3.

Modi, *Remarkable Healings*: views on karma, 'afterthoughts', p. 603; relation of symptoms to past-life traumas, chapter 3, pp. 172–81; symptoms mirroring experiences in utero or at birth, chapter 2, pp. 94–5; murder, chapter 3, pp. 166–8; suicide, chapter 3, pp. 164–5; gender identity problems arising from possession, chapter 4, pp. 269–70.

Wambach, *Life Before Life*: views on karma, chapter 5, pp. 90–1; choice of sex, chapter 4, pp. 75–9.

Fiore, *You Have Been Here Before*: views on karma, chapter 12, p 241; relation of symptoms to past-life traumas, introduction, pp. 6–8; therapeutic case studies, chapters 2–10.

Fiore, *The Unquiet Dead*: symptoms mirroring experiences in utero or at birth, chapter 2, p. 7; gender identity problems arising from possession, chapter 6, pp. 36 and 43; views on hell, chapter 18, p. 160.

Netherton, *Past Lives Therapy*: views on karma, 'questions', p. 219; impotency case, chapter 4; other therapeutic case studies, chapters 3–12; no devolution to nonhuman ranks, 'questions', p. 218.

Woolger, *Other Lives, Other Selves*: views on karma, chapter 6, pp. 147–51; death and past-life reviews, chapter 11, pp. 294–7; case of Chris, chapter 10, pp. 264–71; cases of Madeleine and Milton, chapter 11, pp. 298–303; other therapeutic case studies, chapters 5–9.

Whitton, *Life Between Life*: views on karma, chapter 6, pp. 74–5; different uses of the interlife experience, chapter 4, p. 34; Ben Garonzi case, chapter 6, pp. 75–6; Jenny Saunders case, chapter 12; other therapeutic case studies, chapters 7–11.

Cannon, *Between Death and Life*: views on karma, chapter 7, pp. 110–17 and chapter 12, pp. 188–9; murder, chapter 7, p. 118; choosing complementary experience, chapter 7, p. 113; filler lives, chapter 8, p. 140; suicide, chapter 7, pp. 128–31; disability, chapter 4, pp. 59–61; views on hell, chapter 6, pp. 105–8, chapter 7, p. 115, and chapter 10, pp. 153–8 and 167; rareness of devolution to nonhuman ranks, chapter 6, p. 98.

Weiss, *Many Lives, Many Masters*: views on karma, chapter 5, pp. 68–9, chapter 12, p. 172 and chapter 14, p. 195.

Newton, *Journey of Souls*: views on karma, chapter 4, p. 51; abused woman case, chapter 4, pp. 50–1; American Indian and Jewish learning cases, chapter 12, p. 220; filler lives, chapter 12, p. 220 and chapter 15, pp. 226–7; suicide, chapter 5, pp. 57–8; disability, chapter 10, pp. 152–3 and chapter 13, pp. 222 and 226–9; gender identity, chapter 5, p. 66; no devolution to nonhuman ranks, chapter 11, p. 193.

Newton, *Destiny of Souls*: more views on karma, chapter 4, p. 104 and chapter 6, p. 252; more on filler lives, chapter 9, pp. 381–4; more on suicide, chapter 5, pp. 153–6; more on gender identity, chapter 9, pp, 363–5; case of preacher met by devil, chapter 3, pp. 80–4; more on no devolution to nonhuman ranks, chapter 6, p. 203.

TenDam, *Exploring Reincarnation*: reincarnation populations, chapter 13, pp. 300–1 (cf. his four different 'reasons for reincarnating' on p. 274); karma and dharma, chapter 13, p. 287; choice of gender, chapter 15, pp. 331–2; homosexuality deriving from unassimilated emotions, chapter 13, p. 293; pathological identification with animal forms, chapter 12, pp. 263–6.

Mitchell, *Tao Te Ching*: concept of right action, chapter 15.

Johnson, *Edgar Cayce in Context*: balanced analysis of holistic healing, chapter 1; analysis of Cayce's normal sources for Atlantean material, introduction, pp. 6–7.

Woodward, *Scars of the Soul*: limited extent of accompanying life readings, chapter 3, p. 98; hip cancer case, chapter 3, pp. 47–52; parents' karma as much as child's, chapter 3, p. 80–97; remaining cases of physical karma, chapter 3.

Lawton, *Giza: The Truth*: analysis of Cayce's readings on Atlantis and the Hall of Records, chapter 5, pp. 242–63.

Woodward, *Edgar Cayce's Story of Karma*: more cases of physical karma, chapter 3; family and group karma, chapters 5 and 6; Franz Liszt case, chapter 4, pp. 99–101; Molière case, chapter 5, p. 141; Elisha and Noah case, chapter 4, pp. 106–9; remaining vocational life readings, chapter 4.

Fortune, *The Cosmic Doctrine*: reliability of channeled material, introduction, p. 12.

Moody, *Life After Life*: hell, chapter 2, p. 97; suicide, 'questions', pp. 143–4.

Ring, *Life at Death*: hell, chapter 10 pp. 192–6 and chapter 12, pp. 249–50;

Sabom, *Light and Death*: hell, chapter 9.

Fenwick, *The Truth in the Light*: hell, chapter 13, pp. 187–94; suicide, chapter 13, pp. 194–6.

Mascaro, *The Bhagavad Gita*: chronology of Indian texts, p. ix; harmony from lack of attachment, pp. 29 and 60–1; action not inaction, pp. 17–18; Krishna's memory of his past lives, p. 22; reincarnation in the search for perfection, p. 35; family, p. 63; rebirth in lower life forms, pp. 74–5.

Feuerstein et al, *In Search of the Cradle of Civilization*: seed of concepts of reincarnation and karma in *Vedas*, chapter 5, pp. 96–7 and chapter 10, pp. 173 and 181–2.

O'Flaherty, *The Rig Veda*: hints at concepts of reincarnation and karma, 10.16.5 and commentary thereon, pp. 48–51 and 2.33.1, p. 221; no need to renounce physical world, commentary , p. 229.

Prabhupada, *The Laws of Nature* (extracts from *Bhagavata Purana*): bad karma of family life, chapter 2, pp. 56–65; fiery hell, chapter 2, pp. 66–70; rebirth in lower life forms, chapter 2, p. 76.

CHAPTER 8: HYPNOTIC PROGRESSION

Cayce, *Edgar Cayce on Atlantis*: earth changes reading, chapter 6, pp. 158–9 (for an analysis of Cayce's earth changes prophecies see also Johnson, *Edgar Cayce in Context*, chapter 3, pp. 81–5).

Snow, *Mass Dreams of the Future*: personal progression, chapter 1; background to experiments with progression, chapter 2; inaccurate timings, prologue, p. xviii; cyclic linkage between catastrophes in ages of Leo and Aquarius, chapter 3; details of Cayce predictions, chapter 4; group progressions to 2100, chapters 5 and 6; group progressions to 2300, chapters 7 and 8; extraterrestrial contacts and channeling, chapter 10; discussion of issues in theoretical physics, chapter 9; references to karma, chapter 3, pp. 56–7; progressions as most probable future at that time, chapter 4, p. 94.

Lawton, *Giza: The Truth*: analysis of Sitchin's work, chapter 2, pp. 95–108; analysis of Lemesurier's work, chapter 3, p. 157.

Lawton, *Genesis Unveiled*: more on Sitchin's work, chapter 3, pp. 53–4, chapter 9, pp. 168–9, chapter 14, p. 275 and chapter 16, p. 315.

Newton, *Journey of Souls*: views on progression, chapter 12, p. 204.

Newton, *Destiny of Souls*: more views on progression, chapter 9, pp. 362–3.

Goldberg, *Past Lives, Future Lives*: background, chapter 2, pp. 13–14; the interlife, chapter 3, pp. 36–42; karma, chapter 3, pp. 25–33; Arnold and Brian cases, chapter 12; introduction to progression, chapter 14, pp. 134–5; nonlinear time, chapter 3, p. 44 and chapter 5, pp. 64–6; general predictions for earth, chapter 14, pp. 135–6; news item experiments with local reporter, chapter 15, pp. 137–41; Janet case, chapter 21; Pete case, chapter 22; spiritual planes, chapter 3, pp. 34–5 and 42–3; number of cases, chapter 3, p. 27; bullying example, chapter 7, p. 83; lack of emotion in progressions, chapter 14, p. 136.

Cannon, *Between Death and Life*: visits to, and viewing the future in, the Tapestry Room, chapter 5, pp. 71–4.

Grant, *Winged Pharaoh*: changeability of future, p. 130.

CHAPTER 9: SPIRIT POSSESSION

Newton, *Journey of Souls*: soul energy division, chapter 6, p. 85; multiple/parallel lives, chapter 10, p. 155; conflicts between soul and brain, chapter 13, pp. 230–48;

Newton, *Destiny of Souls*: more on soul energy division, chapter 4, pp. 116–24; more on multiple/parallel lives, chapter 4, p. 119; more on conflicts between soul and brain, chapter 3, p. 77 and chapter 4, p. 93; no cases of spirit or demonic possession, chapter 3, pp. 74–6; energy interchanges, chapter 4, p. 118; no cases of walk-ins, chapter 3, pp. 78–9; souls pulling out from womb, chapter 9, p. 387.

Wambach, *Reliving Past Lives*: autism case study, chapter 1, pp. 3–5.

Woolger, *Other Lives, Other Selves*: sub-personalities, chapter 3, p. 67; multiple personality disorder and schizophrenia, chapter 9, p. 214; Buddhist thought, chapter 3, pp. 75–7 and chapter 12, p. 333.

Fiore, *The Unquiet Dead*: background to possession therapy, chapters 1–2; historical attitudes to possession, chapter 3; why souls do not move on, chapter 5; symptoms of possession, chapter 6; case studies, chapters 7–11; how possessing spirits gain entry, chapter 12; signs of possession, chapter 13; further thoughts, chapters 17–18; white light protection, chapter 15, p. 138; no cases of demonic possession, chapter 1, p. 4.

Modi, *Remarkable Healings*: spirit possession, chapter 4; demonic possession, chapter 5; soul fragmentation, chapter 6; statistics, chapter 10, pp. 570–82; cross-talk, chapter 3, pp. 135–7.

TenDam, *Deep Healing*: attachments and obsessions, chapter 8, pp. 213–22; evil and demonic influences, chapter 8, pp. 222–4; sub-personalities and pseudo-obsessions, chapter 3, pp. 61–71.

TenDam, *Exploring Reincarnation*: more on sub-personalities and pseudo-obsessions, chapter 14, pp. 305–19; overlapping lives and child walk-ins, chapter 14, pp. 320–1; Buddhist thought, chapter 2, pp. 26–7.

Cannon, *Between Death and Life*: possession by elementals, chapter 10, pp. 158–63; white light protection, chapter 10, pp. 164–5; demons as imaginative constructs; chapter 10, p. 166; walk-ins, chapter 15; souls pulling out from baby, chapter 15, p. 227 and chapter 16, p. 229; imprinting, chapter 14.

Novak, *The Lost Secret of Death*: two halves of the brain, chapter 2; near-death experiences, chapter 3; past-life regression , chapter 4, pp. 92–105; division delayed until just before reincarnation, conclusion, p. 292.

CHAPTER 10: ENDGAME

Newton, *Journey of Souls*: human soul as separate category, chapter 10, p. 162; intervals between incarnations, chapter 12, pp. 202–3; soul colors and classifications, chapter 7, pp. 102–5; beginner, intermediate and advanced souls, chapters 9–11; examples of animal-style lives on other planets, chapter 11, pp. 190–3; early incarnations on unknown landmasses, chapter 11, 171–2; incarnation on earth as testing experience, chapter 10, pp. 157–8; ethereal pressure for reduction in amnesia, conclusion, p. 276.

Newton, *Destiny of Souls*: more on human soul as separate category, chapter 5, pp. 125–33; animal souls, chapter 7, pp. 296–302; more on soul colors and classifications, chapter 5, pp. 170–88; more on advancing through soul levels, chapter 8, pp. 320–3; nature spirits, chapter 3, pp. 53–4; ethereal planes, chapter 3, pp. 51–3; shedding of astral body on soul energy reunification, chapter 4, p. 121; soul leaving body immediately before painful death, chapter 7, p. 272; incarnation as dominant life form on other planets, chapter 6, p. 203; psychotic hybrid souls, chapter 4, pp. 100–3; designer souls, chapter 8, pp. 334–44; Atlantean lives as memories of incarnation on another planet, chapter 4, p. 100; incarnation on mental worlds, chapter 8, p. 351.

Modi, *Remarkable Healings*: soul birthing, chapter 2, pp. 89–91; possession by extraterrestrial spirits, chapter 5, p. 356; Lucifer, chapter 5, pp. 314–21.

Modi, *Memories of God and Creation*: more on the transition to the interlife, past-life reviews and life plans, chapters 9 and 15–17; the Ultimate Godhead, chapters 2–4; Lucifer, chapter 5; creation of all life forms, chapter 7; the fall in Eden, chapter 12, pp. 138–46.

Netherton, *Past Lives Therapy*: evolution up nonhuman ranks, 'questions', p. 218.

Cannon, *Between Death and Life*: animal souls, chapter 6, p. 96; elementals and nature spirits, chapter 6, pp. 91–5; excess of souls, chapter 16, pp. 234–5; recognition by soul color, chapter 8, p. 137; number of incarnations required to break free from karmic round, chapter 5, pp. 84–5; levels of existence, chapter 6, pp. 88–9, 91 and 97–105; Lucifer and the fall, chapter 10, pp. 153 and 166–7.

TenDam, *Exploring Reincarnation*: origins of souls, chapter 12, pp. 248–66; Crookall's distinction of etheric from astral body, chapter 11, pp. 226–9; Atlantis and Lemuria, chapter 12, pp. 252–3 and 262; experiments with entering a dinosaur and a primate, chapter 12, pp. 251 and 254–5.

Ten Dam, *Deep Healing*: origins of souls, chapter 8, pp. 224–35 (abbreviated from material in previous book).

Whitton, *Life Between Life*: intervals between incarnations, chapter 4, p. 52.

Ramster, *The Search for Lives Past*: intervals between incarnations, chapter 7, pp. 268–9; recognition by soul color, chapter 7, pp. 251–2; incarnations on other planets, chapter 7, p. 267.

Goldberg, *Past Lives, Future Lives*: intervals between incarnations, chapter 3, p. 37; Atlantis and Lemuria, chapter 3, pp. 36–7.

Stevenson, *Children Who Remember Previous Lives*: intervals between incarnations, chapter 5, p. 117; reluctance to believe in reincarnation because of implications for personal responsibility, chapter 10, pp. 233–5.

Lawton, *Genesis Unveiled*: the Qabalistic tree of life, chapter 17, pp. 342–7; Fortune's *The Cosmic Doctrine*, chapter 18; ancient technology and astronauts, chapter 15; Atlantis and Lemuria, chapter 14; Blavatsky and root races, chapter 13; the creation of man, chapter 8; cosmology traditions, chapter 16; dating of the onset of the golden age, chapter 10, pp. 188–9; dating of the catastrophe, chapter 12, pp. 230–1.

Ring, *Life At Death*: the astral body in near-death experiences, chapter 12, pp. 224–32.

Sabom, *Light and Death*: physical death as process not event, chapter 3, pp. 50–1.

Woolger, *Other Lives, Other Selves*: importance of emotions at death, chapter 11, pp. 288–93.

Netherton, *Past Lives Therapy*: importance of emotions at death, chapter 16, pp. 176–80.

Freemantle and Trungpa, *The Tibetan Book of the Dead*: manual for life not death, commentary, pp. 1–6.

James, *The Varieties of Religious Experience*: plea for a science of religions, 'Philosophy', lecture xviii.

BIBLIOGRAPHY

This bibliography is strictly limited to those books I have specifically referenced in this work. When the distinction is chronologically important, the date for a publication in the text refers to the first publication, whereas the date below may be a later one for the imprint or edition I have personally consulted.

Bernstein, Morey, *The Search for Bridey Murphy*, Doubleday, 1956.

Blackmore, Susan, *Dying to Live*, Grafton, 1993.

Budge, E A Wallis (trans.), *The Egyptian Heaven and Hell*, Dover, 1996.

Cannon, Alexander, *The Power of Karma in Relation to Destiny*, Rider, 1936.

Cannon, Alexander, *The Power Within*, Rider, 1954.

Cannon, Dolores, *Between Death and Life: Conversations With a Spirit*, Gateway, 2003.

Cayce, Edgar Evans, *Edgar Cayce on Atlantis*, Howard Baker, 1969.

Fenwick, Peter and Elizabeth, *The Truth in the Light: An Investigation of Over 300 Near-Death Experiences*, Berkley Books, 1997.

Feuerstein, Georg, Kak, Subhash, and Frawley, David, *In Search of the Cradle of Civilization*, Quest, 1995.

Fiore, Edith, *You Have Been Here Before: A Psychologist Looks at Past Lives*, Ballantine Books, 1979.

Fiore, Edith, *The Unquiet Dead: A Psychologist Treats Spirit Possession*, Ballantine Books, 1988.

Fortune, Dion, *The Cosmic Doctrine*, Samuel Weiser, 2000.

Freemantle, Francesca and Trungpa, Chögyam (trans.), *The Tibetan Book of the Dead: The Great Liberation through Hearing in the Bardo*, Shambhala Publications, 1992.

Gardner, Martin, *Fads and Fallacies in the Name of Science*, Dover Publications, 1957.

Goldberg, Bruce, *Past Lives, Future Lives*, Ballantine, 1993.

Grant, Joan, *Winged Pharaoh*, Harper, 1938.

Grant, Joan and Kelsey, Denys, *Many Lifetimes*, Ariel Press, 1997.

Hall, Manly P, *Death to Rebirth*, Philosophical Research Society, 1979.

Johnson, K Paul, *Edgar Cayce in Context*, State University of New York Press, 1998.

Keeton, Joe and Moss, Peter, *Encounters With the Past*, Sidgwick & Jackson, 1979.

Knight, Gareth, *A Practical Guide to Qabalistic Symbolism*, Kahn and Averill, 1998.

Kramer, Samuel N, *Two Elegies on a Pushkin Museum Tablet: A New Sumerian Literary Genre*, Oriental Literature Publishing House, 1960.

Lawton, Ian, and Ogilvie-Herald, Chris, *Giza: The Truth*, Virgin, 2000.

Lawton, Ian, *Genesis Unveiled: The Lost Wisdom of our Forgotten Ancestors*,

Virgin, 2004.

Mascaro, Juan (trans.), *The Bhagavad Gita*, Penguin Classics, 2003.

Meduna, Ladislas, *Carbon Dioxide Therapy*, University of Illinois Press, 1950.

Mitchell, Stephen (trans.), *Tao Te Ching by Lao-tzu*, Macmillan, 1989.

Modi, Shakuntala, *Remarkable Healings: A Psychiatrist Uncovers Unsuspected Roots of Mental and Physical Illness*, Hampton Roads, 1997.

Modi, Shakuntala, *Memories of God and Creation: Remembering from the Subconscious Mind*, Hampton Roads, 2000.

Moody, Raymond, *Life After Life*, Bantam, 1976.

Morse, Melvin and Perry, Paul, *Transformed by the Light*, BCA, 1993.

Netherton, Morris and Shiffrin, Nancy, *Past Lives Therapy*, Ace Books, 1979.

Newton, Michael, *Journey of Souls: Case Studies of Life Between Lives*, Llewellyn, 2002 (5th edition).

Newton, Michael, *Destiny of Souls: New Case Studies of Life Between Lives*, Llewellyn, 2003.

Newton, Michael, *Life Between Lives: Hypnotherapy for Spiritual Regression*, Llewellyn, 2004.

Novak, Peter, *The Lost Secret of Death: Our Divided Souls and the Afterlife*: Hampton Roads, 2003.

O'Flaherty, Wendy Doniger (trans.), *The Rig Veda*, Penguin Classics, 1981.

Prabhupada, A C Bhaktivedanta Swami, *The Laws of Nature*, Bhaktivedanta Book Trust, 1991.

Prasad, Ganga, *The Fountainhead of Religion*, Book Tree, 2000.

Ramster, Peter, *The Truth about Reincarnation*, Rigby, 1980.

Ramster, Peter, *The Search for Lives Past*, Somerset Film & Publishing, 1992.

de Rochas, Albert, *Les Vies Successives*, Chacornac, 1911.

Ring, Kenneth, *Life At Death: A Scientific Investigation of the Near-Death Experience*, Quill, 1982.

Ring, Kenneth and Cooper, Sharon, *Mindsight: Near-Death and Out-of-Body Experiences in the Blind*, Institute of Transpersonal Psychology, 1999.

Sabom, Michael, *Recollections of Death: A Medical Investigation*, Harper & Row, 1981.

Sabom, Michael, *Light and Death: One Doctor's Fascinating Account of Near-Death Experiences*, Zondervan, 1998.

Snow, Chet, *Mass Dreams of the Future*, McGraw-Hill, 1989.

Stevenson, Ian, *Twenty Cases Suggestive of Reincarnation*, University Press of Virginia, 1974.

Stevenson, Ian, *Unlearned Language: New Studies in Zenoglossy*, University Press of Virginia, 1984.

Stevenson, Ian, *Children Who Remember Previous Lives: A Question of Reincarnation,* University Press of Virginia, 1987.

Stevenson, Ian, *Where Reincarnation and Biology Intersect* (short version of two-volume *Reincarnation and Biology*), Praeger, 1997.

TenDam, Hans, *Deep Healing: A Practical Outline of Past-Life Therapy*, Tasso Publishing, 1996.

TenDam, Hans, *Exploring Reincarnation*, Rider, 2003.

Wambach, Helen, *Reliving Past Lives: The Evidence Under Hypnosis*, Hutchinson, 1979.

Wambach, Helen, *Life Before Life*, Bantam, 1979.

Weiss, Brian, *Many Lives, Many Masters*, Piatkus, 1994.

Whitton, Joel, and Fisher, Joe, *Life Between Life*, Warner Books, 1988.

Woodward, Mary, *Edgar Cayce's Story of Karma*, Berkley Books, 1972.

Woodward, Mary, *Scars of the Soul: Holistic Healing in the Edgar Cayce Readings*, Brindabella Books, 1985.

Woolger, Roger, *Other Lives, Other Selves: A Jungian Psychotherapist Discovers Past Lives*, Bantam, 1988.

INDEX